Encouraging Authenticity and Spirituality in Higher Education

Arthur W. Chickering,
Jon C. Dalton, and Liesa Stamm

Encouraging Authenticity and Spirituality in Higher Education

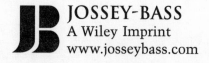

JOSSEY-BASS
A Wiley Imprint
www.josseybass.com

Published by Jossey-Bass
A Wiley Imprint
989 Market Street, San Francisco, CA 94103-1741   www.josseybass.com

Jossey-Bass books and products are available through most bookstores. To contact Jossey-Bass
directly call our Customer Care Department within the U.S. at 800-956-7739, outside the U.S. at
317-572-3986, or fax 317-572-4002.

Jossey-Bass also publishes its books in a variety of electronic formats. Some content that
appears in print may not be available in electronic books.

Library of Congress Cataloging-in-Publication Data

Chickering, Arthur W., 1927-
    Encouraging authenticity and spirituality in higher education / Arthur W. Chickering, Jon C.
Dalton, Liesa Stamm.
        p. cm.
    Includes bibliographical references and index.
        ISBN 0-7879-7443-9 (alk. paper)
    1. Education, Higher—Aims and objectives—United States.   2. Spirituality—Study and
teaching (Higher)—United States.   I. Dalton, Jon C., 1941-   II. Auerbach, Liesa Stamm,
1944-   III. Title.
    LB2324.C49 2005
    378.01—dc22   2005012620

Printed in the United States of America
FIRST EDITION
PB Printing   10 9 8 7 6 5 4 3 2

Contents

Foreword   vii
Alexander W. Astin, Helen S. Astin

Preface   xiii

The Authors   xvii

Part One: Framing Perspectives   1

1 **Our Orientation**   5
   Arthur W. Chickering

2 **The Dynamics of Spirituality and the
   Religious Experience**   37
   Liesa Stamm

3 **The Influence of Religion and Spirituality in
   Shaping American Higher Education**   66
   Liesa Stamm

Part Two: Institutional Amplification   93

4 **Policy Issues: Legislative and Institutional**   97
   Arthur W. Chickering

5 **Curricular Content and Powerful Pedagogy**   113
   Arthur W. Chickering

6 **The Place of Spirituality in the Mission and
   Work of College Student Affairs**   145
   Jon C. Dalton

7 **Integrating Spirit and Community in Higher
   Education**   165
   Jon C. Dalton

Part Three: Getting There from Here   187

8 **Planned Change and Professional Development**   189
Arthur W. Chickering

9 **Assessing Ineffable Outcomes**   220
Arthur W. Chickering, with Marcia Mentkowski

10 **Leadership for Recovering Spirit**   243
Liesa Stamm

11 **Principles and Practices for Strengthening Moral
and Spiritual Growth in College**   272
Jon C. Dalton

**Appendix A: University of Missouri-Columbia
Policy Statement**   283

Appendix B: Illustrative Course Syllabi   294

Appendix C: Rutgers Evaluation and Dissemination Plans   310

Appendix D: Teacher Formation Evaluation Results   316

**Appendix E: Inventory for Assessing the Moral and
Spiritual Growth Initiatives of Colleges and Universities**   318
Jon C. Dalton

References   331

Name Index   345

Subject Index   351

⎯ᴧᴧ⎯ Foreword

Although American higher education can justifiably take pride in its capacity to develop the student's ability to manipulate the material world through its programs in science, medicine, technology, and commerce, it has paid relatively little attention to the student's "inner" development—the sphere of values and beliefs, emotional maturity, moral development, spirituality, and self-understanding.

What is most ironic about this neglect of the student's interior is that many of the great literary and philosophical traditions that constitute the core of a liberal education are grounded in the maxim, "know thyself." This imbalance in emphasis on outer versus inner development has enormous implications for the future not only of our society but also of our world. Self-understanding is fundamental to our capacity to understand others: our spouses, partners, parents, children, friends, coworkers, and neighbors, not to mention people of different races, religions, cultures, and nationalities. If we lack self-understanding—the capacity to see ourselves clearly and honestly and to understand why we feel and act as we do—then we severely limit our capacity to understand others.

In exploring the connection between spirituality and higher education, a good way to start is to take a look at the interior lives of today's students. Thus, if we look at how our students' *values* have been changing during recent decades, the good news is they have become strong supporters of both gender and racial equity and of students' rights in general. The bad news is that they have become much less engaged both academically and politically, much more focused on making a lot of money, and much *less* likely to concern themselves with "developing a meaningful philosophy of life." These contrasting values—the material and the existential—have literally traded places since the early 1970s, a time when developing a meaningful philosophy of life was the number one value for students. Today "being very well off financially" is the top value, whereas developing a meaningful philosophy of life has dropped way down on the list. In short, a focus on the spiritual interior has been replaced by a focus on the material exterior.

It's probably safe to say that this shift in values is a reflection of changes not just in students but also in the larger society. Research suggests that at the societal level, the ascendance of television during the 1950s and 1960s—with its wall-to-wall message of acquisitiveness and its near-total absence of any emphasis on self-reflection—had been a major cause of these value shifts. Today, of course, we have many other kinds of electronic distractions that make it even more difficult for the student to engage in serious self-reflection. In higher education, our colleges and universities have become larger, more acquisitive, and increasingly impersonal, as exemplified by the rapid increase in commuting and part-time attendance, not to mention the current burgeoning market in so-called distance education. In the academy we've also seen the ascendance of business and physical science—with their exclusive focus on material exteriors—and the parallel demise of the humanities, the very fields whose priority is (or at least ought to be) our interiors. Our own field of psychology—in its eagerness to emulate the hard sciences—long ago separated itself from philosophy and, for a period of time—during the heyday of behaviorism—argued vigorously that there was *no such thing* as the interior. Cognitive science and neuroscience have subsequently tried to acknowledge the existence of a human interior reality, but view it primarily as an epiphenomenon of physical processes.

In recent years the two of us have become increasingly interested in educational transformation and reform, and nowhere is the importance of this issue of "the inner versus the outer" more obvious than in the case of attempts to change institutions. When we talk about educational reform in the academy, for example, we usually focus heavily on exterior "structures," such as programs, policies, curricula, requirements, resources, and facilities. As a consequence, we ordinarily give little attention to the "interior" of the institution, by which we mean the *collective* or *shared* beliefs and values of the faculty that constitute the "culture" of the institution. Research, however, suggests strongly that any effort to change structures has little chance of success if it ignores our collective interiors or culture. In other words, changing our institutions and programs necessarily requires us to change the academic culture—our collective interiors—as well.

As a response to this external and materialistic emphasis and to the fragmentation it generates, we see a movement gradually emerging in higher education where many academics find themselves actively searching for meaning and purpose and trying to discover ways to make their lives and their institutions more whole. We think this movement reflects a growing concern with recovering a sense of meaning and authenticity in American society more generally. How do we achieve a greater sense of community and shared purpose in higher education?

Given that "spiritual" issues cover such a wide range of questions, each person will view his or her spirituality in a unique way. For some academics, religious beliefs form the core of their spirituality; for others, such beliefs play little or no part. *How* one defines his or her spirituality or, if you prefer, sense of meaning and purpose in life, is not the issue. The important point is that academia has for far too long encouraged us to lead fragmented and inauthentic lives, in which we act either as if we were not spiritual beings or as if our spiritual side were irrelevant to our vocation or work. Under these conditions, our work becomes divorced from our most deeply felt values, and we hesitate to discuss issues of meaning, purpose, authenticity, and wholeness with our colleagues. At the same time, we likewise discourage our students from engaging these same issues among themselves and with us, even though many of us personally and privately engage in reflection about these concerns.

These observations were confirmed in a recent in-depth study of faculty members from four diverse colleges and universities.[1] Personal interviews with randomly selected faculty from each institution revealed that virtually all these faculty members were willing and able to speak openly about the role of either "spirituality" or "meaning and purpose" in their professional and personal lives. Many respondents expressed their spirituality through their scholarly work. Other avenues of expression included teaching and working with students, community service, social activism, church activities, and child rearing.

When it comes to the issue of authenticity, many faculty members report conflicts between their own values and those of their institutions, the most frequent being the devaluing of work with students in order to fulfill expectations for research and scholarly achievement.

---

[1] A. W. Astin & H. S. Astin, with the assistance of A. L. Antonio, J. Astin, & C. M. Cress. (1999). *Meaning, purpose and spirituality in the lives of college faculty.* Los Angeles: Higher Education Research Institute.

Other areas of inauthenticity involve performing administrative work that they see as a waste of time, sacrificing personal research interests in order to carry out studies that will receive collegial approval, not fulfilling family responsibilities in order to meet institutional expectations, and not giving colleagues honest criticism of their work.

Our clear impression from this study—that college faculty are eager to discuss issues of meaning, purpose, and spirituality—has been strongly reinforced by our experience at several national conferences where sessions have been convened for academics to discuss these same issues.

Under these circumstances, this book could not be more timely. And given the complexity and importance of the topic, it would be difficult to find three authors whose collective backgrounds and experience are more appropriate to the task, considering that in addition to their many scholarly accomplishments, one or more of them has served higher education in the capacity of faculty member, policymaker, administrator, and student affairs professional. They have approached their challenging task in a comprehensive fashion, integrating cultural and historical perspectives with practical advice about how to reshape programs in order to give greater attention to the spiritual dimension of student growth and development.

The authors' first chapter in Part One introduces us to the topic by addressing a number of fundamental and potentially sensitive issues concerning the place of spirituality in higher education: what spirituality means and how it differs from religiousness, education versus indoctrination, and the fundamental importance of self-knowledge. They also provide us with three brief autobiographical essays so that we may understand the personal perspectives each one brings to the task. They conclude with a series of powerful arguments for why higher education needs to begin giving greater priority to issues of spirituality and authenticity.

In the next chapters, the authors discuss the changing roles of religion and spirituality, both in higher education as well as in the larger U.S. society. These discussions help us not only see how and why the twentieth-century process of secularizing American higher education ended up throwing out the student's interior along with the religious bathwater but also understand some of the ethical and legal issues surrounding religion and spirituality in higher education.

Part Two takes us from the conceptual to the very practical issues of how we can begin to enrich our curricula, pedagogy, student affairs programs, and sense of community by giving greater emphasis to cultivating spirituality and authenticity in our colleges and universities.

Part Three addresses the challenges of "institutional amplification" Part Two has suggested. It considers issues concerning planned change and professional development, assessment, and leadership. The book concludes with a very insightful and practical summary of principles and practices that can be followed by any institution that might be interested in "strengthening spiritual growth and the search for meaning and purpose."

We congratulate the authors for a very difficult job well done. At a very critical time in the history of American higher education, they have produced a comprehensive and very accessible treatise that should be widely read by faculty members, student affairs professionals, staff, trustees, and administrators in all types of institutions.

Alexander W. Astin
Helen S. Astin
University of California, Los Angeles

Art Chickering: *To my grandchildren, Lars, Gabriel, Silas, and Luke, hoping for a better world for their grandchildren.*

Jon Dalton: *To my family, Beverly, Stacy, and Jonathan.*

Liesa Stamm: *To my family with whom I continue to engage in the search for the truth and who serve as models for acting out of conviction: my parents, John and Beverly, my brother, Eric, my children Aaron, Peter and Ana, and my granddaughter, Rebecca.*

⟳ Preface

This book aims to help two- and four-year colleges and universities amplify existing programs in ways that encourage increased authenticity and spiritual growth among our students and among us professionals. It argues that our almost exclusive emphasis on rational empiricism needs to be balanced by similar concern for other ways of knowing, being, and doing. We do not suggest neglecting our devotion to scientific research and theory. We do suggest complementing this work with policies, programs, and practices that create a better balance.

We believe that our institutional effectiveness with our students will be enhanced when we help them address these key developmental issues. We also believe that it is important for us to recover our own sense of calling, to recapture our sense of the values and purposes that brought us to our various roles and responsibilities. We believe that by participating in these efforts, we strengthen our motivation to plug away at this work in the face of budget cuts, political neglect, and public challenges. Most important, perhaps, we believe that our work life, day in and day out, year in and year out, will include more joyful, satisfying, and rewarding experiences.

We suggest various areas for what we choose to call "institutional amplification." We are not talking about "transformation." One definition of *amplify* is "to make larger or great, as in amount, importance, or intensity." We want to acknowledge and to build on the good work we all are doing, not discount it. We want to sharpen our sense of our own worth and to build on our professional strengths and purposes. We think our diverse higher education colleagues and other professionals have the talents and perspectives needed for them to undertake and implement a variety of additional alternatives. Indeed many of these efforts are already under way here and there around the country. We want to examine these perspectives and to share working examples.

The book has three major sections. Part One supplies some framing perspectives. Part Two offers specific suggestions for changes to strengthen authenticity and spiritual growth. Part Three discusses how these changes can be pursued.

In Part One, Chapter One addresses our orientation. It discusses our definitions of spirituality and authenticity and shares some of our personal backgrounds. It closes with a discussion of issues that make us believe these amplifications are urgently needed, for ourselves and our students, for our colleges and universities, and for our domestic and global societies. The next two chapters offer theoretical, historical, and social perspectives on religion and higher education and on the current situation. This work is based on Liesa Stamm's extensive literature surveys, face-to-face and telephone interviews, and years of direct experience in higher education.

Part Two considers general implications for practice. Chapter Four discusses public and institutional policy issues. It presents recent court cases dealing with church-state issues and notes that there is no legal bar to undertaking the changes we suggest. It then argues for creating institutional policies that can support and legitimize these efforts. Chapter Five addresses curricular content and powerful pedagogy. Chapters Six and Seven discuss the implications for student affairs policies and practices and for fostering an increased sense of community. We illustrate general propositions with specific policies and programs under way at diverse institutions across the country. Many of these illustrations come from presentations at the annual Institute on College Student Values conducted by Jon Dalton and his colleagues at Florida State University. Jon, through his Center for the Study of Values in College Student Development, has also completed surveys of college and university presidents and student affairs professionals that have generated useful, up-to-date results.

Part Three shares our thinking concerning strategies and processes necessary to achieve the amplifications suggested in Part Two. It opens with a chapter on institutional change and professional development. The next chapter tackles the challenges involved in assessing the "ineffable outcomes" associated with this complex arena. Following that is a chapter on the special leadership characteristics necessary to help us move in this direction. We close with some principles for good practice to strengthen authenticity and spirituality in higher education. Appendixes give examples of policy statements and detailed syllabi that illustrate our discussion of curricular content and powerful pedagogy. Appendixes also share evaluation and dissemination plans of Rutgers University, evaluation results with regard to a "teacher formation" program, and an assessment instrument based on the principles discussed in Chapter Eleven.

Throughout this volume we have tried to combine general propositions, principles, and recommendations with specific working examples. We do not believe that the institutional amplifications we suggest are mysterious or esoteric. They are consistent with what we know from prior research. Concrete, illustrative programs and practices can demystify ways to encourage authenticity and spiritual growth; for this reason, this book includes quite lengthy quotations, reports, case studies and such. You can choose which you wish to learn about in detail.

ACKNOWLEDGMENTS

Needless to say, our work stands on the shoulders of a multitude of theorists and practitioners. There are too many for us to attempt a comprehensive list. There are, however, a few key people we need to recognize. Chickering's initiation into the issues of spirituality in higher education began with a series of workshops stimulated and organized by Tony Chambers when he was a program officer at the Fetzer Institute. A working group that came to call itself the Initiative for Authenticity and Spirituality in Higher Education grew out of and is helping to carry forward that initiative. In addition to Chambers and Chickering, it includes Alexander and Helen Astin, Jon Dalton, Paul Elsner, John Gardner, Stuart Hunter, Cynthia Johnson, James and Cheryl Keen, Laura Rendon, Eugene Rice, and David Scott. The wisdom, activities, and support of these colleagues provided the backbone for Chickering's motivation and substantive contributions.

Dalton would like to acknowledge the John Templeton Foundation for their support of his research and dissemination efforts on character development in college. He also thanks the many colleagues who have, over the past fifteen years at the annual Institute on College Student Values at Florida State University, shared their work and concern for the moral and spiritual development of college students.

Stamm would like to acknowledge the John Templeton Foundation's support of the research that, in part, provided the basis for Chapters Two and Three. Special recognition goes to Arthur Schwartz, the foundation's vice president for programs and services in the human sciences, for his valuable insights and contributions during the development of this research.

We also need to recognize both the editorial and substantive contributions David Brightman made through his penetrating critical suggestions and his leads to important relevant literature. Specific references and a variety of practitioners are mentioned in the text. All of them are quick to recognize their indebtedness to others. We hope that by pulling this wide-ranging work together we provide a basis for legitimizing and expanding conversations about this key arena for human development throughout our two- and four-year colleges and universities. Those conversations in turn may lead to the broad-based incremental changes required to balance our emphasis on rational empiricism with equal talent and energy that helps our students, and us professionals, address the lifelong, recurrent challenges to our authenticity and spiritual growth.

⟶ The Authors

Arthur W. Chickering is special assistant to the president of Goddard College. He began his career in higher education as a psychology teacher and coordinator of evaluation at Goddard College from 1959 to 1965. From 1965 to 1969, he directed the Project on Student Development in Small Colleges. In 1969–70, he was a visiting scholar in the Office of Research at the American Council on Education. From 1970 to 1977, as founding vice president for academic affairs, Chickering played a major role in creating Empire State College. He was Distinguished Professor and director of the Center for the Study of Higher Education at Memphis State University from 1977 to 1986; from 1986 to 1996, he was university professor at George Mason University. From 1996 to 2004, he was Visiting Distinguished Professor at Vermont College.

Chickering is the author of many publications, including *Education and Identity* (Jossey-Bass, 1969, 1993), *Commuting Versus Resident Students: Overcoming Educational Inequities of Living Off Campus* (Jossey-Bass, 1974), *The Modern American College: Responding to the New Realities of Diverse Students and a Changing Society* (Jossey-Bass, 1981), *Improving Higher Education Environments for Adults: Responsive Programs and Services from Entry to Departure* (Jossey-Bass, 1989, with N. K. Schlossberg and A. Q. Lynch), and *Getting the Most Out of College* (Allyn & Bacon, 1995, with Nancy Schlossberg).

Chickering has received the E. F. Lindquist Award from the American Educational Research Association for his studies of college impacts on student development, the Outstanding Service Award from the National Association of Student Personnel Administrators, the Distinguished Contribution to Knowledge Award from the American College Personnel Association, and the Distinguished Service Award from the Council for Independent Colleges.

Chickering has been board member and chair of the American Association for Higher Education, the Association for the Study of Higher Education, the Council for Adult and Experiential Learning, and the National Society for Experiential Education. He has served on the editorial boards of the *Journal of Higher Education,* the *Journal of Higher Education Administration,* and *About Campus.*

Jon C. Dalton is associate professor in the Department of Educational Leadership and Policy Studies at Florida State University in Tallahassee. He serves as the director of the Hardee Center for Leadership and Ethics and for the past fourteen years has directed the annual Institute on College Student Values. He served as vice president for student affairs at Florida State University and Northern Illinois University and is a past president of the National Association of Student Personnel Administrators and a current senior scholar of the American College Personnel Association. He edits the e*Journal of College and Character* and has written widely on topics related to moral and spiritual development, the impact of college on students' values, and student affairs management and administration in higher education.

Liesa Stamm is currently a Senior Associate at Rutgers University Center for Children and Childhood Studies. She has contributed to higher education for many years in a variety of capacities at the institutional, state, and national levels. As a faculty member in the University of Wisconsin-Milwaukee's Department of Anthropology and International Relations program, she participated in initiating the university's women's studies program and in the development of policies to support women faculty, staff, and students. Her anthropological research on women's roles and reproductive health contributed to the emerging women's studies field. As a senior academic affairs administrator with the Connecticut Department of Higher Education, she conducted institutional and program accreditations and participated in the development of state education policies. For many years she has been committed to bringing the expertise of higher education to improving the needs of society. In Connecticut she worked toward initiating policies and programs in public education, health care and social service delivery, and children's welfare. Between 2000 and 2002 she directed the Civic Engagement Cluster with Arthur Chickering to promote university engagement among ten diverse institutions around the country. Her current work at Rutgers University involves designing and evaluating programmatic interventions in early childhood education and healthcare to address racial and ethnic disparities and improve the life opportunities of children in Camden, New Jersey.

Encouraging Authenticity and Spirituality in Higher Education

PART ONE

Framing Perspectives

In Part One we provide some broad theoretical, historical, societal, and educational perspectives that frame our thinking and our orientation. These chapters underlie the suggestions addressed in Parts Two and Three. Over the last century, American colleges and universities have developed a system of higher education that is unparalleled in its ability to produce disciplinary-based knowledge through faculty research and scholarship. By the 1960s the university was accepted as the institutional center for developing the knowledge on which our modern, scientifically based, and technologically driven society depends. Reflecting the societal definition of the university's central function, a major purpose of higher education today has become the dissemination of disciplinary knowledge through the education of hundreds of thousands of undergraduate students each year. American undergraduate education is largely focused on the transmission of theories, empirically derived facts, and the disciplinary frameworks and methods used to create and interpret empirically derived information. Unfortunately, examining the ways in which students can use the information and analytic processes about which they are learning to create meaningful individual lives and positive social structures has largely been excluded. Such characteristics as wisdom, compassion, and integrity, and such concepts as justice, ethics, values, morality, virtue, and character are ones that most undergraduates fail to consider because the curriculum does not encourage them to do so. It is students' grappling with a personal understanding of these concepts, however, that will determine if they will use the knowledge and skills they have acquired through an undergraduate education for the betterment of the individual, their communities, and the larger society.

In recent years, at colleges and universities around the country, an expanding and increasingly vigorous dialogue has begun, centered on examining personal values, meaning, and purpose—including religious and spiritual values—as part of the educational experience. Individually and collectively, the voices of campus leaders, of faculty, of student affairs personnel, and of students themselves have begun calling for an exploration of ways to better integrate students' search for meaning and their spiritual quests with their academic preparation in the classroom and through campus activities. And faculty are increasingly communicating their own need to find a place in the institutional environment to express their deeper values and hopes for societal change as they engage in the enterprise of producing and conveying knowledge.

In Chapter One, we have adopted Teasdale's definition of spirituality and Karen Armstrong's view of religion and spirituality. To emphasize our commitment to authenticity we each include personal statements describing how we came to this work and our current orientation toward it. The last part of the chapter cites global and national conditions that call for the changes we recommend. We then include recent data documenting students' quests for authenticity, purpose, meaning, and spiritual growth. We close with observations concerning the need among many faculty members, administrators, student affairs professionals, and staff to supplement our heavy emphasis on rational empiricism with equal concern for these fundamental dimensions of human development.

Chapter Two examines the complexity of the individual experience of religion and spirituality, and outlines major theories of religious and spiritual development. Understanding the processes of religious and spiritual development is critical if colleges and universities become committed to the moral as well as intellectual development of young people. Sharon Daloz Parks (2000) emphasizes the potentially critical contribution of higher education to enhancing young adults' discovery of their own moral compasses. She proposes that higher education is "distinctively vested with the responsibility of teaching critical and systematic thought and initiating young lives into a responsible apprehension first of the realities and questions of a vast and mysterious universe and second of our participation within it. Higher education is intended to serve as a primary site of inquiry, reflection, and cultivation of knowledge and understanding on behalf of the wider culture" (p. 10). And she enjoins us to assume this mantle as essential to our mission as educators: "Not only the equality of individual young adult lives but also our future as a culture depends in no small measure upon our capacity to recognize the emerging competence of young adults, to initiate them into big questions, and to give them access to worthy dreams" (p. xi).

College and university campuses often act as if they are secluded kingdoms of the mind that observe and perhaps inform but do not necessarily engage with the turmoil and complexities of their region, their state, or our country. But they do in fact generally reflect and perpetuate the values and practices of the larger society in which they are embedded. In asking that institutions of higher education become centers where we address, individually and collectively, the tremendous global, national, and local challenges that have sapped the soul of our society, it is important to understand the historical and societal context in which today's colleges and universities operate. Chapter Three delineates historical trends in Americans' religious attitudes and practices as a framework for understanding the current climate of religion and spirituality on college and university campuses. During the last half century a major transformation has occurred in the American population in the ways in which individuals seek deeper meaning and purpose through religious and spiritual practices and in which they define their moral beliefs and values. The resulting movement away from established religious institutions and their associated theologies, doctrines, and prescribed practices, toward a focus on the self and the personal spirituality of seeking is reflected in the emerging data on the spiritual beliefs and practices of today's students.

The historical and social changes in Americans' attitudes toward and practices of religion and spirituality described in Chapters Two and Three signal the need for explicit changes in institutional policies and practices. It has become critically important to recognize the significant diversity of religious orientations among our citizens and to learn about these in our colleges and universities. Parts Two and Three explore a wide variety of institutional amplifications to address the challenges of our global and national condition. They address our institutions' need to provide a climate of openness for examining these issues so as to foster the development of authenticity and spirituality among our students and among us professionals. By creating such a climate, we may recapture the spirit that underlies our commitment to the academy.

CHAPTER ONE

Our Orientation

Arthur W. Chickering

"The physicist Leo Szilard once announced to his friend Hans Bethe that he was thinking of keeping a diary: "I don't intend to publish. I am merely going to record the facts for the information of God.' 'Don't you think God knows the facts?' Bethe asked. 'Yes,' said Szilard. 'He knows the facts, but he does not know this version of the facts'" (Baeyer, 1992, p. 9). Szilard's orientation is similar to ours in writing this book. There are many perspectives on authenticity and spirituality. Moral development and character development were key purposes for our early colleges. There is substantial research and theory concerning the development of identity and integrity, of purpose and meaning. Authenticity and spiritual growth interact with and in many ways encompass these other conceptual orientations. And there are many perspectives concerning whether higher education should help students address such issues and, if so, how. We don't pretend to have the "truth" about this complex area, but we do have our own "version" concerning these issues and what needs to be done.

This work grows out of our shared concern about the limits of the heavy emphasis higher education places on rational empiricism and its increasingly narrow focus on professional and occupational training.

This combination has led to growing neglect of larger human and societal issues concerning authenticity, spiritual growth, identity and integrity, purpose and meaning. We aim to help create a better balance by proposing a wide range of policies and practices that address these aspects of human development, that will strengthen authenticity and spiritual growth—for our students, for us as professionals, for our institutions, and for the larger society we want to serve.

This chapter opens with our definitions of spirituality and authenticity and then turns to issues of values and indoctrination, our "bedrock orientation," and personal statements. We close with why we think that higher education must move in this direction. We believe the needs are great and that getting started expeditiously is critical.

THE LANGUAGE CHALLENGE

When we gather with colleagues to discuss "spirituality in higher education"—a problematic, many-faceted arena—we find ourselves using diverse terms that vary depending on our personal and professional backgrounds. Persons anchored in various religious traditions and from faith-based institutions are typically accustomed to, and comfortable with, the language of spirituality. But for others, that language carries baggage from the worlds of established religions and churches with which they do not identify. They do not want be understood to endorse anything that hints at proselytizing or indoctrination. Atheists, agnostics, and persons with strong humanistic orientations find that words like *authenticity, purpose, meaning, integrity, wisdom,* and *values* express their concerns. For these persons character development and moral development are legitimate concerns for higher education, but "spiritual growth" raises red flags. Nevertheless, when we have been in half-day and weekend workshops with 40 to 150 persons whose backgrounds span the world religions and every shade of humanist, and whose institutional affiliations are similarly diverse, we rapidly move beyond the language challenge. We quickly find that we share very similar hearts and desires, disaffections and dismay, at the social and institutional conditions that characterize most of our communities and institutions. We find that we yearn for safe spaces and for colleagues with whom we can discuss these concerns. In creating these safe spaces we need to recognize and respect the different conceptual orientations and linguistic differences among our colleagues. We believe that two- and four-year colleges and universities need to legitimize and value such conversations and to create changes that do the same for our students.

For the purposes of this book, we need a shared definition of spirituality. The one we have adopted (Teasdale, 1999) opens with what for us is an important distinction and goes on to language with which we three identify:

> Being religious connotes belonging to and practicing a religious tradition. Being spiritual suggests a personal commitment to a process of inner development that engages us in our totality. Religion, of course, is one way many people are spiritual. Often, when authentic faith embodies an individual's spirituality the religious and the spiritual will coincide. Still, not every religious person is spiritual (although they ought to be) and not every spiritual person is religious. Spirituality is a way of life that affects and includes every moment of existence. It is at once a contemplative attitude, a disposition to a life of depth, and the search for ultimate meaning, direction, and belonging. The spiritual person is committed to growth as an essential ongoing life goal. To be spiritual requires us to stand on our own two feet while being nurtured and supported by our tradition, if we are fortunate enough to have one [pp. 17–18].

Karen Armstrong's way of thinking about religion and spirituality also resonates with us:

> Religion is not about accepting twenty impossible propositions before breakfast, but about doing things that change you. It is a moral aesthetic, an ethical alchemy. If you behave in a certain way you will be transformed. The myths and laws of religion are not true because they conform to some metaphysical, scientific, or historical reality but because they are life enhancing. They tell you how human nature functions, but you will not discover their truth unless you apply these myths and doctrines to your own life and put them into practice. The myths of the hero, for example, are not meant to give us historical information about Prometheus or Achilles—or for that matter, about Jesus or the Buddha. Their purpose is to compel us to act in such a way that we bring out our own heroic potential.
>
> In the course of my studies, I have discovered that the religious quest is not about discovering "the truth" or "the meaning of life" but about living as intensely as possible in the here and now. The idea is

not to latch on to some superhuman personality or to "get to heaven" but to discover how to be fully human—hence the images of the perfect or enlightened man, or the deified human being. Archetypal figures such as Muhammad, the Buddha, and Jesus become icons of fulfilled human-ity. God or Nirvana is not an optional extra, tacked on to our human nature. Men and women have a potential for the divine, and are not complete unless they realize it within themselves [2004, pp. 270, 271].

Those are the ways we define and think about spirituality and reli-gion. Please note that this definition includes atheists. Many atheists, though not religious, share "a contemplative attitude, a disposition to a life of depth, and the search for ultimate meaning, direction, and belonging" and are committed to growth. Many atheists are trying to discover how to be fully human. Estimated at about 5–10 percent of the population, they need to be respected by, and included in, our var-ied efforts.

Authenticity seems to be a more straightforward and less loaded term. Being authentic means that what you see is what you get. What I believe, what I say, and what I do are consistent. Of course creating that consistency is a lifelong challenge as we encounter new experi-ences, new persons and new information. As we mature and move to new levels of cognitive and affective complexity, deconstruction and reconstruction must occur.

We must recognize that we usually assume that authenticity car-ries a positive value, that authentic persons are good, honest, trust-worthy, and so forth. But that need not always be the case. History tells us of individuals who were authentically evil. Their words and deeds had a high degree of internal consistency used for selfish and ma-levolent ends. Also there are historical precedents for authenticity—strong consistency among words and deeds—driven by religious beliefs. Today's suicide bombers are a case in point. But we strive for an authenticity that is kind, caring, and socially responsible.

We can put flesh and blood on these abstract definitions and il-lustrate the kind of authenticity we espouse by recalling some exem-plars. Some who come to mind for me are Mahatma Ghandi, George Fox, Barbara Jordan, Martin Luther King, Nelson Mandela, Eleanor Roosevelt, Mother Teresa, Sojourner Truth, and Desmond Tutu. Each of us has his or her list. These internationally recognized exemplars set a high standard. But there are many others, closer to home and not widely known, who in less dramatic ways live up to the values we espouse. In totally unbiased fashion, I would include my mother, my wife, my son and three daughters, and my two colleagues who are the coauthors of this book. There are local friends and good neighbors, community leaders, and socially responsible citizens who display the qualities of those well-recognized exemplars in their daily lives. Each reader probably knows similar individuals, so this kind of personal development is not beyond our reach.

These definitions of spirituality and authenticity imply that these domains intimately interact with other major vectors of human development: integrity, identity, autonomy and interdependence, meaning and purpose. Striving for integrity—for a life where word and deed, word and word, deed and deed are consistent with a personally owned value structure, over time and across varied contexts—is critical for spiritual integrity and growth. "Stand[ing] on our own two feet while being nurtured and supported by our tradition" calls for a significant level of autonomy even as we recognize our necessary dependence on family and friends as well as on our local, national, and global communities. And it requires that we recognize the importance of our own support and contributions to those personal, institutional, and political entities that depend on us. Our character and our purposes configure our lives. Our interdependencies depend on our capacity to identify with something larger than our own self-interest. Ultimately, it is our character, our purposes, and the values inherent in the way we live these out in our daily lives that express our spirituality as "a way of life that affects and includes every moment of existence." Therefore, when we talk about encouraging authenticity and spirituality in higher education and the changes called for in our institutions and in ourselves, we are talking about all these major dimensions of human development.

VALUES AND INDOCTRINATION

Higher education is not value free. Each policy and practice we adopt, each resource allocation judgment or staffing and personnel decision we make expresses a value priority. The gap between our espoused values and the values actually in use is often large, unrecognized, and unarticulated. Stephen Glazer (1999) addresses one of these gaps:

> A great irony is that while spiritual indoctrination, in particular, has been banned from our classroom, indoctrination and imposition continue

unimpeded. Students aren't indoctrinated into religious liturgy but instead into dualism, scientism, and most especially consumerism. We have been indoctrinated into a severely limited, materialistically biased world view.

Rather than learning to nurture and preserve spirit, we learn to manipulate the world: to earn, store, and protect wealth. Rather than learning to be sensitive—understand and attend to the needs of others—we learn to want, rationalize, and do for ourselves. With the rise of a kind of "economic individualism" as our basic sense of identity has come the centralization of wealth and power, the loss of the commons, and the ravishing of the planet. The fact is, within our schools and culture, identity is being imposed: not spiritual identity but material identity [pp. 79, 80].

Like most of our colleagues in higher education, we certainly do not approve of indoctrination of any kind. Yet wittingly and unwittingly, we and our institutions do indeed indoctrinate. We believe we must become aware of the subtle, and not so subtle, kinds of indoctrination expressed through our daily practices, and address those institutionally and in our own professional lives.

OUR BEDROCK ORIENTATION

Our approach to strengthening authenticity and spirituality in higher education is rooted neither in a church nor religious orientation, nor in the state nor in politics. We believe we need to move from the inside to the outside, to work out from the core of our experiences. Kant said that logical concepts are abstracted from empirical experiences. The language of science is our most precise way of communicating meaningfully about facts. But because it is based on observing external facts, the language of science and logic does not cope well with our inner experiences. It follows that the most central tenet of our orientation toward strengthening authenticity and spirituality in higher education is that each and every one of us must be as candid and open as we can about our own orientations, motives, prides, and prejudices. We also recognize that we are all possessed by our own "mental models." We recognize that our biases compromise our "objectivity." Our beliefs and behaviors are rooted in our prior experiences and preconceptions. And of all the areas for potential sharing, self-descriptions and self-attributions are most subject to bias. We all—the "good" and the "bad," the "evil" and the "righteous," of whatever political or religious persuasion—create personal systems of self-concepts and beliefs we live by, stories that explain ourselves to ourselves and make sense, to us at least, of our checkered existence. The secret to a satisfying existence—remaining open to new experiences, saying *yes* to life—is to recognize and accept those formulations and live them as best we can. Unfortunately, it is also true, as we have learned recently to our sorrow, that people defend nothing more violently and fanatically than the preconceptions they live by. But given all this, we believe that the path to hope and reconciliation, to strengthened authenticity and spirituality, lies in sharing those preconceptions, exposing our assumptions and preconceptions, and risking the vulnerability entailed.

That is what is required for significant amplification of higher education.

We higher education professionals need to be knowledgeable about—and to appreciate—our religious and spiritual historical antecedents and social perspectives. We need to create new curricular content and to become competent with a wide range of pedagogical strategies. We need to introduce new experiences for students through creative student affairs programming accompanied by powerful partnerships, all of which are well integrated with courses and classes. We need to be aware of various strategies for intervention. Leadership, not only "at the top" but throughout the organization, is critical. But these leaders will need courageous followers who ask tough questions, who address gaps between "espoused values" and "values in use," who challenge policies and practices that run counter to realizing a shared vision. Finally, of course, hard-nosed evaluation, formative more than summative, is necessary, as we try to create an integrated complex of college and university policies, practices, and cultures that helps us balance our considerable talents for rational analysis and scientific research with similar competence and effectiveness concerning authenticity and spiritual growth.

But all the structural changes, all the creative, adventurous innovations, will only scratch the surface unless each of us professionals can be authentic ourselves. Each of us needs to be as forthcoming as possible about our own passions and prejudices. We need to declare why we believe being authentic is critical not only for higher education but for the United States, where we are struggling to sustain, if not to create, a multicultural, civil democracy in the face of terrorist threats and growing gaps between the haves and have-nots, at home and abroad.

THE AUTHORS

To be consistent with this fundamental tenet, we each, in alphabetical order, make our own declarations. And, as you will note in the Table of Contents and in the chapter openers, we have each written chapters individually. Some readers may find our personal statements and changes in style from chapter to chapter distracting or off-putting. If so, we simply ask you to bear with us. We are trying to act with the professional authenticity we believe is critical. This orientation does not imply differences among us in the positions taken. We have all reacted to each other's work, made suggestions, and profited from those reactions. We all agree on the strength of the underlying research and the soundness of the views expressed. So by agreeing that each of us will write from his or her own foundations, we do not dodge accountability for the whole.

Please recognize one final point. In all our chapters we address large ballparks where there is wide-ranging research, theory, and practice. We do not aim to be comprehensive, to provide exhaustive reviews of all relevant literature. We are selective, relying on research, theory, and practices that are directly pertinent to our concerns and that seem sound given our own knowledge and prior experiences. Of course all scholarly work is selective and seldom encompasses or recognizes all the relevant perspectives. We simply want to be forthright and up front here about our own orientations.

Art Chickering

Until I reached about age fifty, I was strongly anchored in rational empiricism. I thought of myself, and in many ways I was, the stereotypical "rational man." One fundamental reason for that posture, that orientation, was that—for a variety of reasons I won't belabor here—I had very limited access to my emotions. Of course that does not mean they were not there. But I had been quite successful in sealing them off. So I was not very sensitive to, or behaviorally affected by, hostility from others, anger, anxiety, fear, or sadness. I was strong and tough. I went toward conflict and a good fight rather than away from them. I had a solid history of keeping my cool in the face of personal attack, whether verbal or physical.

My professional work built on those strengths. It was firmly anchored in my own empirical research and in comprehensive knowledge of pertinent prior and ongoing work by others. I had a good capacity to stand back and synthesize my own findings and relevant literature to create useful books and journal articles. I was very productive because I was much more "task oriented" than "relationship oriented." I certainly appreciated and felt honored by public recognition of that work, beginning with the annual book award from the American Council on Education for the 1969 edition of *Education and Identity,* which took me from the woods of Vermont into the national scene. Subsequent awards—one from the American College Personnel Association for contribution to knowledge, the E. F. Lindquist award from the American Educational Research Association, the Howard R. Bowen Distinguished Career Award from the Association for the Study of Higher Education for "outstanding scholarship, leadership, and service"—bolstered my sense that I had been, and was, making useful contributions.

In short, I was a good product of, and exemplar of, the Age of Reason. I clearly remember assuming that as reason and research liberated our minds, cultural transformation toward peace, equality, and prosperity would surely follow. And the decade of the 1960s, when I was in my thirties and early forties, seemed to validate powerfully all those assumptions.

Since the Industrial Revolution our technological evolution has been on an accelerating upward curve. New machines and medical practices, anchored in scientific research, have brought marvelous new capacities and cures. Our social and psychological research has brought increased understanding of individual and group behavior and dynamics. In the 1960s, Gardner Murphy—an elder statesman in the same generation as such groundbreaking scholars as Ted Newcomb, Gordon Allport, Nevitt Sanford, Erik Erikson, Abraham Maslow, and Robert White—wrote a wonderful book called *Human Potentials.* His thorough review of the literature documented our growing capacity to understand and guide human behavior to speed the realization of human potentials and aspirations. "Self-actualization" and the human potential movement, together with the so-called greening of America, were gathering momentum. Surely equal justice, truth speaking, environmental awareness and self-discipline, and global peace were just around the corner.

But for me, and for many others, that faith, hope, and promise has waned during the past thirty years. Our cultural transformation, at least in terms of things I value, seems to be on an accelerating downward curve. "Rational man" continues to kill, and to exploit the poor, the "underdeveloped," the less powerful and well organized. (Pardon the apparent sexism, but despite progress during the last thirty years, it has been and continues to be a male-dominated world.) We now wage wars for economic and political purposes. Terrorists respond to economic oppression and Western cultural imperialism by murdering children, women, and men who are simply going about their daily lives. Our capacity for atrocity seems limited only by our imagination. It turns out that rational man can be as greedy, power hungry, dominating, and cruel as the hordes of Genghis Khan; the Vandals and Vikings; the seventeenth- and eighteenth-century western conquerors who went throughout the world killing and exploiting indigenous populations; and our own forebears, who systematically dislocated and demolished native populations.

Rational man seems bent on using the explosion of new technologies for managing machines and for manipulating information and communication as means to diminish our democracy, deplete and desecrate our environments, and exploit any globally available sources of cheap labor.

Colleges and universities are supposed to be bastions of rationality, dispensing knowledge and encouraging its application. But, ironically, despite our almost exclusive emphasis on rational empiricism in research, teaching, and service, we do not typically apply the substantial body of research concerning college impacts on student learning and a variety of developmental outcomes to our own policies and practices.

During 1963–64, Tim Pitkin (then president of Goddard College), Ernie Boyer (on his way to SUNY with Sam Gould), and I conceived the Project on Student Development in Small Colleges and got funding for it from the National Institutes of Mental Health. The basis for the project was simple, growing out of my work as coordinator of evaluation at Goddard. We identified thirteen very diverse institutions that were part of the then Council for the Advancement of Small Colleges, now the Council for Independent Colleges. All the institutions administered a comprehensive set of surveys and tests to entering students and repeated the process at the end of the second and fourth years. We also collected extensive information about students' experiences, using an Educational Testing Service instrument, a self-designed survey, and extensive site visits. We then carried out three-day workshops at each campus, sharing our findings, many of which were very persuasive concerning effective and ineffective policies and practices across the institutions, and discussing their implications.

We were operating on what turned out to be a misguided assumption that the institutions would then undertake appropriate changes based on evidence from their own students and from those at peer institutions. Deeply etched into my mind is the first summer workshop that brought together the presidents and academic vice presidents of the participating institutions. My first question was, "Let's hear from you about the changes you are undertaking based on the research findings from your students and the other institutions." Now, as a Quaker and an experienced psychotherapist and counselor, I had become comfortable with silence. It was literally three or four minutes before anyone spoke—a psychological infinity for our academic cultures. Not one of these small colleges had taken any action on those results.

The classic change theory during the 1960s was "RD&D": research, development, and diffusion. This theory was primarily based on agricultural extension efforts to improve farming. We were acting on that. The idea was that the change process started with research to document effective practices; some practitioners then tried out the ideas; finally, their experiences were "diffused" through various media, consultation, and so forth. Agricultural extension workers soon learned that changing farming behaviors was much more complicated than that simple model suggested. Thirty-five years later we are still struggling to understand and manage institutional change in higher education. So rational man seems no more adept at creating humane cultures and conditions on our own campuses than when at large in the world.

Thus for me "rational empiricism," though necessary, is no longer sufficient as a way of knowing, a way of thinking, or a way of being. My soul, the animating force that gives me purpose and meaning, needs to be rooted in something more than simple rationality. I certainly cannot articulate what that "more" is or may be. I do know when I experience it.

I experience it being with my wife, whose life I have shared for more than half a century, through serious challenges to our psychological and physical health and well-being. I experience it sitting quietly watching the wildlife around the beaver ponds in front of our house. I experience it working with chain saw, ax, and tractor when getting my winter wood supply under cover. I experience it when I am in the presence of classical and contemporary visual and performing arts, music, novels, poems, plays, and apt metaphors. I experience it when I am with others, in a context where there is authentic sharing. I experience it through energetic collaboration trying to address mutual concerns about societal problems. Thus the collaborative work with friends and colleagues who share my concerns continually nourishes my soul, as does working on this book with good friends and colleagues.

Jon Dalton

I began student affairs work in higher education in the 1960s with a deep personal sense of calling, a sense that I was meant for this work. My undergraduate years in a small liberal arts college had been life changing. I entered college with a vague notion of preparing for a good job. By graduation I had developed an overriding commitment to make a difference in the great social and moral problems of the day. Something about college touched my spirit.

It could all have been very different. In high school I was in a vocational training program with no plans for college. Nobody in my immediate family had attended college; few of my high school peers planned to go. A benefactor I barely knew opened the door by providing my college tuition and pocket money. Those four undergraduate years transformed and liberated me intellectually, socially, and spiritually. In a way I could not anticipate or comprehend at the time, I found my "soul" in college. Nothing else I had experienced brought together my head and heart in such a personal and powerful way. My experiences convinced me that colleges and universities can be among the most transforming institutions in our society.

The challenge of working with young people at a pivotal time in their lives in the powerful environment of higher education led me to become a college teacher and administrator. Over four decades I have worked with college students as a student affairs vice president, dean of students, counselor, and professor in four large public research universities. For the past fifteen years I have conducted the annual Institute on College Student Values at Florida State University. I join with colleagues from around the country to examine how colleges and universities can better influence moral and spiritual development. My observations about the connections of spirituality to college student learning and development draw on this professional history. So forty years later, that calling I first felt in college remains strong.

Something is wrong with higher education that greatly diminishes its effectiveness as a transforming societal institution. What is wrong can best be seen in what so often fails to happen to students during their college years. In so many students today we see unfulfilled hope and idealism, unrealized commitments, and private ambitions disconnected from social and moral purposes. Students come hoping that learning and growing will not only enhance their knowledge and skills but clarify their deepest commitments and calling. They expect college to transform both intellect and spirit. But too often these two domains are severed in their daily lives. The possibilities of what they can become and what our nation needs for them to become at this time are lost. Disturbing trends in higher education's priorities and practices work against educational and developmental transformation. I believe that a renewed commitment to recognizing and honoring spirituality in the academy is essential if we are to succeed in providing higher education that integrates intellect and spirit.

I am persuaded that my own experience of transformation in college was not unique. I believe that most students share a sense of calling or purpose, a sense that their lives are destined for something special, something unique. Some express this sense in a religious context, others as a spiritual quest, and still others as a vague notion of personal destiny. However they conceive of it, most students feel that they are meant for some special role or task and that college is their time, their best time, to discover this destiny.

There are, sadly, too few occasions during their college years when students are intentionally helped in connecting their learning and development with their sense of spiritual calling. As a result, students often remain silent about one of the most important, most deeply felt aspects of their lives. They are eager to explore and share the deep meaning and purpose they associate with their sense of spiritual identity and calling, yet find few opportunities to do so.

What I have learned about students' needs and circumstances has been shaped in part by a perspective on college student life that is largely unobserved by most faculty and staff. The work of student affairs is largely invisible in the academy. Much of students' lives take place in a shadow land, when most in the university have closed up shop. Anne Matthews (2001) describes this zone of college student life as the "night campus" and accurately observes that it is the most dangerous and unsupervised domain in higher education. The night campus is the turf of student affairs staff in residence halls, crisis centers, student clubs and organizations, recreation programs, and fraternities and sororities. The night campus is where students are most active and open, most intensely engaged, and where their passions are most visible. The night campus is the place for social bonding, experimentation, spiritual search, and emotional expression.

In contrast, the day campus is cool, dispassionate, and intellectual. Students learn quickly that success in the day world of the academy depends on demonstrating intellectual skills and objectivity divorced as much as possible from emotion and spirit. Students perceive that intellectual life, the life of the mind, does not accommodate matters of deep personal meaning and emotion. The day campus treats many of the things students believe in and feel most deeply about as matters of private emotion or irrelevant subjectivism. Separating intellect from personal meaning and purpose makes many students feel alienated almost immediately. They routinely describe their experiences in the day campus as "impersonal" or "uncaring," saying that they feel "like a number" among so many faces. This makes the night campus even more important to students. There, many of them find some sense of wholeness and belonging. The night campus provides escape from the day world, a world that students prize and compete in intensely but that does not allow them to feel authentically themselves. To work in the night campus is to see a part of students' lives that desperately needs connecting to the day campus.

Things have gotten worse as higher education has moved increasingly toward a market-oriented enterprise model. Individual self-interest is the chief value communicated by the popular culture. Most colleges and universities reinforce this value in the curriculum and extracurriculum. Colleges market good jobs, good times, and the good life as their primary benefits. They promote their institutions as essential gateways to these high prizes of private self-interest and materialism.

The shift from a student or learner orientation to a customer or consumer orientation reflects this fundamental change. Although the consumer orientation strengthens some aspects of student welfare, it focuses almost exclusively on responding to students' self-interest. Purdy (1999) compares this self-interest orientation to "free agency" status. Students expect colleges and universities to compete for them and to do everything possible to meet their needs and interests. At the same time, students know that they are ultimately on their own in college and graduate school competition, so they learn to take safe paths early (p. 84). The "free agency" mind-set is reflected in the student attitude, "You can't change the world, so you might as well get ahead in it" (p. 96).

Students' privatism of values and beliefs and their disillusionment with much of what they see in society's leaders and institutions help explain their increasing interest in spirituality and religion. Youth is an idealistic and introspective time of life. The inward journey is heightened even more when young people feel cut off or disillusioned by their perceptions of the world outside. The scandals, deception, and greed they see so evident in business, politics, and in institutions of higher education make them outwardly cynical and inwardly guarded. They seem willing to deal with the world outside on its own terms, but, as Purdy (1999) suggests, they want to keep a sacred, internal place that is their own and unspoiled by the world they must live in. Students' increasing interest in spirituality may reflect a refusal to accept the sacrifice of soul that is demanded by the standards of success they confront in college and in the world outside.

Denny Reuel (1965) once described his perspective for studying young people as that of a "spy in the country of the young (p. 156)." I like his analogy because it suggests that the country of the young is very different from the place I inhabit as a college administrator and faculty member. I need to make a special effort to know that youthful country. It also suggests the importance of quietly listening and observing in order to understand the inner terrain of students' lives. When we do such "spying" well we can create powerful educational environments that help students to integrate the rich context of meaning and purpose in their lives with what they are called upon to learn in college.

Liesa Stamm

For more than twenty-five years I have contributed to higher education in a variety of capacities. I have often characterized my professional endeavors as involving the extreme ends of the higher education spectrum—from teaching in the college classroom to state-level academic affairs administration involving oversight of the state's colleges and universities, particularly the development of new degree programs, institutional accreditation, and the design of statewide higher education policy. Recently, I have brought these extremes together through my work with several institutions in planning, program development, and evaluation designed to improve the lives of children from low-income and racially and ethnically diverse backgrounds, and to address national and state concerns and policies.

As is true for many of us, my original vision of higher education's potential for transforming individuals and informing societal change grew out of my own formative years, first in college and then in graduate school in the 1960s and 1970s. This vision encompasses first of all an educational environment that challenges young people to stretch their intellectual abilities, to discover a love of learning with the concomitant rewards of delving into the academic inquiry process and of exploring new ideas and knowledge. My vision also includes an environment with the primary purpose of guiding students in developing the skills they need in order to fit the knowledge they are acquiring into an explanatory framework or theory and to use their understandings for addressing "real-life" issues. Margaret Miller's definition of the general aims of higher education (2003) captures this vision well. She proposes that the basic goal of the baccalaureate degree is to prepare "college graduates who demonstrate an advanced ability to think critically, communicate effectively, and solve problems" (pp. 5–6).

During my undergraduate years I found my personal locus for the love of learning in the field of anthropology. Cultural relativism is the driving theoretical and analytic framework of anthropology, and the essential work of the discipline consists of documenting and attempting to understand the global diversity of human expression and experience. To come to know another culture, another way of understanding and defining the world, requires a basic respect for the variety of possible human perspectives and ways of living. Anthropology is a discipline that by its nature is concerned with the topics of meaning and purpose, values and beliefs, the spiritual and the secular. For me the study of other peoples and cultures has provided an opportunity to unify my love of academic inquiry and my deeply held personal value, learned through my Quaker upbringing, of honoring the essential worth of all individuals.

In contemplating my core commitments in higher education, I am reminded of key factors for understanding human behavior from a lifelong perspective that have been proposed in the field of human development: (1) historical context, (2) dominant social influences, and (3) individual psychological characteristics. I view my own professional odyssey in higher education as strongly influenced by the interplay of these three factors. My early explorations of professional calling were framed by the prevailing societal definitions of women's roles and women's work during the time I was coming of age at the end of the 1950s and during the 1960s. Because I had very few personal experiences with women professionals, I did not have a clear idea of what I wanted to achieve from my college education. To a large extent because of the social constraints of the time period, many colleges, particularly on the East Coast where I lived, were single-sex institutions. I therefore chose to attend a women's college without having any recognition of the profound effect this choice would have on my subsequent commitment to the academy. Reflecting the fact that this was a women's college, there were more women faculty than was the norm in higher education at that time. As a result, my fellow students and I encountered strong role models of academic women, many of whom had chosen the academic life over the more accepted roles of wife and mother. These faculty role models, as well as a college culture that valued academic inquiry above all else and promoted a sense of personal responsibility for using one's abilities to the fullest, significantly influenced my professional choices, in part by providing me with the confidence to pursue my love of exploring ideas and knowledge at the graduate level.

A second major influence on my life purposes and values was the emergence of the largely youth-driven counterculture of the 1960s and 1970s, which to a large extent was centered on college and university campuses. I learned directly about these young people's movements from my friends and fellow students who were on the front lines of the civil rights, antiwar, and free speech movements and the emerging Students for a Democratic Society (SDS). As I began to join with demonstrators seeking to change the directions of society, my own commitments to the causes of social justice and world peace took root and flourished. A significant part of our education at that time was not through classes and books but at the demonstrations and through the long debates about politics, social change, and altering the university structure, held at the student union or the local pub or sitting around on mattresses on someone's living room floor.

During my student years, the study of women as a topic of serious research was not yet recognized, and there were no full-scale ethnographic studies of women; despite this, my early ethnographic field research centered on studies of women's roles and women's concerns. For one study, I lived in North Africa for a year-and-a-half and conducted field research on Muslim women's roles. My resulting analysis focused on defining the dynamics of women's domestic power. I subsequently became involved in contributing to the emerging field of women's studies, including participating in the development of the women's studies program at the university where I was a faculty member, and in advancing a range of initiatives to promote increased opportunities and support for women students and faculty.

Similar to many faculty members, I was not particularly focused on the educational process but on teaching about and conducting research in my discipline. With my subsequent transition from the faculty role to an administrative one working for a state board of governors for higher education, I came to recognize my personal commitment to promoting accessibility to educational opportunities for all young people. As a senior administrator in a state department of higher education between 1986 and 2000, I had the opportunity to foster standards of quality for institutions of higher education and to contribute to the development of regional and state programs and policies to improve the state's public education and employment training, health care, and other services, particularly those for children and youth and their families. My underlying goal was to more fully utilize the expertise of college and university campuses, bringing it outside the academy to address the needs of society.

A number of my professional choices were mediated by prevailing societal expectations and practices regarding women, including the ambiguities of combining women's roles as mothers and wives with a professional life. The unspoken barriers for women in the academy became clear to me as I began looking for a faculty position in the early 1970s and faced several instances of discrimination. One of the most difficult and painful decisions of my professional life occurred in the early 1980s when my academic career was beginning to flourish through the presentation and publication of my research. At that time the academy was beginning to emphasize professional preparation over a liberal education, and for many of us in the liberal arts disciplines, it was increasingly difficult to find the type of positions we wanted. Faced with the difficulties of the job market and the demands of becoming a single parent, I decided to leave the academy. In the process of seeking other professional directions, I came to understand my deep personal dedication to the educational process, and through my work in state-level higher education discovered a whole new professional field and pathway for putting my values and purposes into practice.

Although my professional endeavors for some years have involved higher education administration, planning, and assessment, the underlying objective of all my work has been to ensure quality education and to promote institutional practices that encourage high educational attainment for all students to attain their personal and professional goals. Above all else, it is always my hope that the collegiate experience will spark the excitement of learning that became the foundation of my own professional commitment to higher education. As we will discuss more fully in later chapters, history has affirmed the profound impact on American society, including in modes of religious expression, of the hopes and dreams for a more just society expressed by my student cohort, in some cases through obstruction and even violence. The values and beliefs publicly expressed by many of us at that time, through large demonstrations in Washington and numerous smaller actions on our own campuses, appear to have faded in subsequent years, during which societal structures seem to support individual gain and consumption rather than the public good. For many of us, however, the promise of a better society and the personal values we developed in the 1960s and 1970s remain our essential core. I join my colleagues Arthur Chickering and Jon Dalton in challenging higher education to again become a center of dialogue and debate about human purpose and values and to use the great intellectual capacity and knowledge of the academy to become a partner in helping young people shape their own authenticity and pursue spiritual growth in whatever ways speak to their particular condition.

—⁓—

We hope these personal statements give you a sense of where we come from as we tackle this work. We also share a strong sense that encouraging authenticity and spirituality in higher education is critical if we are to respond to significant societal needs.

THE NEED

The fundamental argument of this book is that we need to temper our current heavy emphasis on rational empiricism and professional and vocational preparation with increased efforts to help students address issues of authenticity and spiritual growth. Certainly the scientific research done in our colleges and universities has made huge contributions to improved health and longevity, to the development of wide-ranging technologies that enhance our quality of life, to our understanding of our global environment and the complex interactions among human and natural elements, and to our sophistication concerning human behavior. We have put men on the moon, explored Mars, and split the atom, and we are coming to understand and manipulate our own genetic structures. You can make your own list.

And of course, logical analysis, cognitive complexity, and rational processes are critical for a productive career, effective citizenship, a satisfying marriage, and a mutually supportive, loving family. But it seems clear to us that our institutions of higher education need also to address issues of affective complexity and social responsibility.

There are four major contexts that cry out for significant growth in these areas:

1. Our global and national condition, whose problems higher education has an important role in addressing
2. Our institutions, which need to do more than provide professional and occupational training
3. Our students, whose needs should drive our educational policies and practices
4. We professionals, who need to invest our time, energy, and emotion in purposes larger than our own advancement

Our Global and National Condition

My international experiences consulting and traveling in Canada, Latin America, Europe, and the Far East during the last twenty years suggest that things are getting worse, not better. Many persons are experiencing life as more stressful and less meaningful than even during the cold war in the early 1960s. Our economic interdependence and ability to move jobs to take advantage of cheap labor create employment problems in the countries where jobs leave and social dislocation and disruption in receiving countries. Our global communication systems let hackers in one location cause widespread disruption across national boundaries. A SARS outbreak in China becomes an international threat. Starvation and disease increase despite dramatic increases in food production capacity. Intercultural, inter-tribal, interregional, and interreligious conflicts flame up and seem immune to peaceful resolution. Politically driven misinformation and disinformation renders informed decision making almost impossible.

Each reader will have a different list of challenges and different priorities, but few persons think that everything is just fine on our special planet.

Here in the United States we have become almost numb to the litany of problems we face:

A two-tier society in which the gap between the rich and the poor has increased dramatically during the last thirty-five years

Recurrent violence and crime, some driven by drugs, some apparently random expressions of rage and frustration

Moneyed special interests dominating our elections and political decision making, accompanied by apathy and declining civic engagement

Increasing costs for health care, schooling, and higher education that are significantly outrunning inflation

No significant federal responses to address the challenge of maintaining Medicare, Medicaid, and Social Security as the baby boom generation reaches retirement age

Recurrent corruption in politics, corporations, and financial institutions

Persistent environmental exploitation and degradation

In the last thirty to forty years our "social health" has dropped precipitously. Fordham University's Institute for Social Policy has an Index of Social Health based on sixteen variables that include infant mortality, teenage suicide, school dropout, drug abuse, homicide, food stamp use, unemployment, traffic deaths, and poverty among the elderly. On a 0–100 scale, after rising to a high of 71 during the 1950s and 1960s, from 1970–1992 the index showed a decline from 71 to 41.

Much of that drop in social health results from our unbalanced priority given to work. Joe Robinson (2003, p. 13) put it this way:

How do Americans do it? Asked the stunned Australian I met on a remote Fijian shore. . . . The feat he was referring to is how Americans manage to live with the stingiest vacation allotment in the industrialized world—8.1 days after a year on the job, 10.2 days after three years, according to the Bureau of Labor Statistics. . . . In this country, vacations are not only microscopic, they're shrinking faster than revenues on a corporate restatement. . . . A survey by the Internet travel company Expedia.com has found that Americans will be taking 10% less vacation time this year than last—too much work to get away, said respondents. This continues a trend that has seen the average American vacation trip buzzsawed down to a long weekend. Some 13 percent of American companies now provide no paid leave, up from 5 percent five years ago. . . . In Washington state, a whopping 17 percent of workers get no paid leave. . . . The result is unrelieved stress, burnout, absenteeism, rising medical costs, diminished productivity, and the loss of time for life and family. . . . Vacations are being downsized by the same forces that brought us soaring workweeks: labor cutbacks, a sense of false urgency created by tech tools, fear, and, most of all, guilt. . . . Guilt works because we are programmed to believe that only productivity and tasks have value in life, that free time is worthless, although it produces such trifles as family, friends, passions—and actual living. But before the work ethic was hijacked by the overwork ethic, there was a consensus in this country that work was a means, not an end, to more important goals.

Overwork does not just cost us workers. Businesses pay $150 billion a year dealing with job stress, despite the fact that vacations alleviate burnout, the worst form of stress, by helping us recover our emotional resources. But it takes two weeks, not just a long weekend. Further, annual vacations cut the risk of heart attack by 50 percent. Certainly "time is money."

But time itself is our most precious currency. It is finite and limited. Investing it in ourselves, our families, our friends, and our neighbors will yield richer dividends than all those extra hours on the job. Re-creating that better balance will nourish our souls as well as our minds and bodies.

Let me be clear that we are not harking back to some "Golden Age" of the United States. We have come a long way in the past hundred years. Corporate greed was alive and well at the turn of the century.

The required work week averaged forty-nine hours in the 1920s. Women and African Americans could not vote. We have Social Security, more widespread access to health benefits, a twenty-five-year increase in the life span, and better standards of living. These changes flow largely from the theory building and empirical research carried out in our higher education institutions. This research has fostered systematic application of results to policies and practices that generated these changes. But our current "age" has a full platter of daunting problems we need to address. No other social institutions are better positioned to address those problems than our two- and four-year colleges and universities. To realize that potential we need to redress some of our own imbalances.

Our Institutions

Up until the 1990s, higher education had gone from an aristocratic, through a meritocratic, to an egalitarian orientation. With the success of the community college movement that began in the 1960s and the federal grants and loans programs created in the early 1970s, a college education became accessible to a high proportion of the population. Professional and vocational preparation became almost universally available. Unfortunately, during the 1990s and continuing today, that trend and social orientation have shifted. Higher education increasingly has come to be perceived as a private benefit rather than as a public good worthy of tax support. Many of us remember when education at state colleges and universities was basically free. Now, in many states tax support equals only 25–35 percent of total revenues; each cut in state support is accompanied by authorizing tuition increases, which our institutions adopt simply to stay even.

The cuts in support for higher education are occurring while the complexity of the problems our society faces seems to be growing faster than our capacity to deal with them at either the state or federal level. Colleges and universities are the only social institutions that can help educate a citizenry able to function at the levels of cognitive and affective complexity the problems require. They are the only social institutions that can help create the courageous followers, the "servant leaders" our distressed globe requires. Ten capacities of servant leaders include listening, empathy, healing, awareness, persuasion, conceptualization, foresight, stewardship, commitment to the growth of people, and building community No other educational institutions can do as much to enhance these human competencies and personal qualities. But higher education is not succeeding in these tasks.

To redirect our priorities to enhance authenticity and spiritual growth requires major institutional amplification. How can our institutions—supported by a capitalist economy, collaborating with and supported by local, regional, and national corporations—provide the critical research and reflection necessary for the common good?   As the market mentality and its associated values triumph nationally and globally, critical analysis of its intended and unintended consequences becomes ever more important. But instead we reduce ourselves to dispensing information and knowledge, credit hours and degrees—commodities to be delivered with maximum speed and efficiency, as though we are an educational Federal Express or United Parcel Service. Administrators and faculty members become producers, and students become consumers. Chapter Six discusses further the impact of the student-as-consumer mentality on higher education. Student affairs professionals put out fires, cool out the unruly, and struggle with students' use of drugs and alcohol to keep things running smoothly. A faculty caste system is alive and growing, with a few highly paid star aristocrats at the top, a modest middle class of tenured and tenure-track professionals who work long hours and are stretched thin across multiple responsibilities, and, outnumbering both these groups, masses of minimally paid adjuncts

In response to these conditions state legislators concerned about crime, drugs, voter apathy, and public morality withhold support for educational alternatives that foster critical thinking, multicultural understanding, and civic responsibility, in favor of professional and vocational certification.

There is a big difference between preparing for a job and preparing for a satisfying and productive career. The latter requires, first and foremost, interpersonal competence and the ability to work with others diverse in race, ethnicity, gender orientation, and national origin. It requires skills in identifying and solving problems. It requires a sense of purpose and the confidence that you can act in ways that make a difference. These are the same competencies and personal characteristics required to become an effective citizen, to create a lasting marriage, and to raise a healthy and happy family. They are the characteristics that need to accompany spiritual growth if we are to act in the world in ways consistent with our beliefs, whatever our faith. So if we focus only on specific professional and vocational preparation, we sell both our students and our society short.

Our heavy concentration on objectivity and empirical rationality and on professional and vocational preparation indeed can work against encouraging authenticity and identity, integrity and spiritual growth. Parker Palmer (1994) puts it this way:

> The mode of knowing that dominates higher education I call objectivism. It has three traits with which we are all familiar. The first of these traits is that the academy will be objective. This means that it holds everything at arms length. . . . Secondly, objectivism is analytic. Once you have made something into an object (in my own discipline that something can be a person), you can chop that object up into pieces to see what makes it tick. You can dissect it, you can cut it apart, you can analyze it to death. . . . Third, this mode of knowing is experimental. . . . I mean by experimental that we are now free with these dissected objects to move the pieces around to reshape the world in an image more pleasing to us, to see what would happen if we did. . . . Objective, analytic, experimental. Very quickly this seemingly bloodless epistemology becomes an ethic. It is an ethic of competitive individualism, in the midst of a world fragmented and made exploitable by that very mode of knowing. The mode of knowing itself breeds intellectual habits, indeed spiritual instincts, that destroy community. We make objects of each other and the world to be manipulated for our own private ends [pp. 41-42].

Parker's view may seem a bit extreme for some of us. But recall the difference between Lockean and Kantean models in science. Kantean theoretical models propose an active organism, and questions of meaning and purpose are legitimate concerns. Lockean models presume that the organism is passive, a machine; issues of purpose or meaning are irrelevant. So our problem is not with scientific methods and research or with rational inquiries concerning human nature. Instead the problem is that we tend to assume that objective methods require us to eliminate questions of purpose, value, and meaning, and to assume that we humans are only machines or collections of molecules or interacting subatomic particles.

For me Palmer's comments and the Kantean-Lockean distinction indicate why we need to achieve a better balance of intellect and spirit within our two- and four-year colleges and our universities.

The emphasis on rational empiricism, on conceptions of truth as objective and external, and on knowledge as a commodity delegitimizes active, public discussion of issues of purpose and meaning, authenticity and identity, spirituality and spiritual growth. Meaningful dialogues concerning these issues require communities of trust, openness, and candor, where participants can expose vulnerabilities, knowing they will be heard and supported in their searching. Limited self-understanding and self-reflection, and fear of being vulnerable in competitive, individualistic environments leave us swamped with conflicting impulses and ambivalent about appropriate actions. (Chapter Seven examines why a sense of community is so often lacking and how it can be created.)

We must tackle these issues. Society requires it. Many of our students want us to. All of them need us to redress the current imbalances.

Our Students

An April 13, 2005 press release shared results from the College Student Beliefs and Values Survey carried out by Alexander and Helen Astin and their colleagues at the University of California at Los Angeles Higher Education Research Institute (HERI).

"Today's entering college students report high levels of spiritual interest and involvement. Four in five indicate 'having an interest in spirituality' and 'believing in the sacredness of life' and nearly two-thirds say that 'my spirituality is a source of joy.' Many are also actively engaged in a spiritual quest, with nearly half reporting that they consider it 'essential' or 'very important' to seek opportunities to help them grow spiritually. Moreover, three-fourths of the students say that they are 'searching for meaning/purpose in life' and similar numbers report that they have discussions about the meaning of life with friends. . . . The entering freshmen also show a high degree of involvement in religion. About four in five report that they attended religious services in the past year and that they discussed religion/spirituality with friends and family. More than three-fourths believe in God, and more than two in three say that their religious beliefs/spiritual beliefs 'provide me with strength, support and guidance.' Four in ten consider it 'essential' or 'very important' to 'follow religious teachings in everyday life. . . .'

Despite their strong religious commitment, students also demonstrate a high level of religious tolerance and acceptance. For example, most students agree that 'non-religious people can lead lives that are just as moral as those of religious believers' (83%) and that 'most people can grow spiritually without being religious' (64%). Similarly, nearly two-thirds of the students (63%) disagree with the proposition that 'people who don't believe in God will be punished'.

While today's entering college freshmen clearly expect their institutions to play an instrumental role in preparing them for employment (94%) and graduate or advanced education (81%), they also have high expectations that college will help them develop emotionally and spiritually. About two-thirds consider it 'essential' or 'very important' that their college enhance their self understanding (69%), prepare them for responsible citizenship (67%), develop their personal values (67%) and provide for their emotional development (63%). Moreover, nearly half (48%) say that it is 'essential' or 'very important' that college encourage their personal expression of spirituality." (Higher Education Research Institute, April 13, 2005.)

In Chapter Three Liesa Stamm summarizes findings from several studies that documents students' eagerness to explore their spiritual concerns. And in Chapter Six Jon Dalton shares data from student affairs leaders across the country who report rising interest in spirituality among their college students.

These findings make it clear that our students need more opportunities to engage issues of spirituality, purpose, and meaning and that our institutions need to respond.

Some students are acting on these concerns, creating their own initiatives within diverse institutions. The Self Knowledge Symposium (SKS), one of the most energetic and sophisticated student-led initiatives, provides a striking example. Started at North Carolina State University back in 1989 by students who were inspired after hearing a lecture by Triangle entrepreneur Augie Turak, the SKS quickly caught on at UNC-Chapel Hill and Duke, eventually incorporating as a 501(c)(3) foundation in 1999. According to Ed Cheely, the coordinator and a Duke 2000 alumni,

SKS provides a community for the positive spiritual transformation of college age students, as well as an ongoing community for adults looking for further spiritual transformation. It provides not only a community, but also a wealth of mentors, resources, philosophy, and programming to help students in their quest for "the life worth living." Spiritual transformation as practiced by the SKS typically falls into one of three areas:

1. The quest to be a genuine, or authentic person.

2. The discernment of vocation.

3. The spiritual search for Truth.

Within each of these three components lies a strong emphasis on leadership, character, and integrity, because without these qualities, it is impossible to live out the discovery of authenticity, vocation, or truth [E. Cheely, personal communication, June 12, 2004].

Ed reports that the backbone of SKS activities are weekly meetings, where they use "anything from readings to movies to thought-provoking questions to get students to examine their lives and share their experiences, while also teaching the SKS fundamentals of character development, self-knowledge, service, etc." They put on lectures, workshops, and retreats where students work together and "where they are exposed to dynamic teachers and mentors from a wide range of background and perspectives." They have a journal, *The Symposium,* in which students share stories and interview well-known spiritual leaders. They have taught classes, such as What is Zen? Authenticity 101, and Thinking the Unthinkable: An American Nekyia. They take alternative spring break programs to Trappist and Buddhist monasteries and to meditation centers, "which sell out every year." And "we do anything else we can think of—skydiving, rock climbing, etc., to help students get out on the edge." One of their most ambitious ventures was an Inward Bound Conference held in October 2002, which brought together three hundred students from sixty institutions around the country.

When I asked Ed about their plans for the future, he said:

We believe that the SKS chapters, which introduce hundreds and often thousands of students to spirituality each year, along with the Inward Bound Conference, have proven two things: there is a tremendous need for authentic spirituality among college students and the SKS has a model (not at all perfect!!!) that can meet that need. We want to use these "test cases" to find other people, organizations, and foundations who are interested in bringing authentic spirituality to young people, and who would want to work with us to reach young people on a much larger scale than we can do on our own. We are developing curricula that could be replicated on other campuses, and we just recently had a wealthy local benefactor and business person outside of the SKS donate free office space and a great deal of free housing downtown, where we could potentially host summer or year long spiritual leadership programs. We would like to work with others who have proven models for transformation, and we would also like to work with others who can bring resources of marketing or funding.

This kind of action initiative illustrates students' flesh-and-blood, concerted efforts and personal commitments that lie behind HERI's survey results.

We Professionals

Ernest Becker (1970, p. 291) says, "The distinctive human problem from time immemorial has been the need to spiritualize human life, to lift it onto a special immortal plane beyond the cycles of life and death that characterize all other organisms." Higher education needs to create conditions under which all of us professionals, as well as our students, can address this fundamental existential problem.

The first definition of *soul* in *Webster's New Collegiate Dictionary* reads thus: "An entity conceived as the essence, substance, animating principle, or actuating cause. It is correct of life, esp. of individual life manifested in thinking, willing, and knowing." This definition captures what I believe many of us higher education professionals feel we have lost, or are losing. The "essence, substance, animating principle, or actuating cause" that brought us to this calling, which has sustained us throughout the ups and downs of challenging careers, seems increasingly out of tune with the dominant directions of change in our organizational cultures; in our institutional priorities, policies, and practices; in our departmental norms; in our collegial relationships. I believe reclaiming our professional souls is essential if we are to address successfully the daunting social problems we face. It is essential if we are to achieve the amplification of higher education required for our colleges and universities to generate graduates who can function at the levels of cognitive and affective complexity to address those problems.

The major amplifications required to reclaim our institutional soul cannot be achieved unless our professional souls are respected, supported, and celebrated. They cannot be achieved with organizational cultures, institutional policies and practices, departmental norms, and collegial relationships that view administrators, faculty members, and student affairs professionals as instruments for production used to achieve competitive advantage in a market-driven enterprise. They cannot be achieved if students are simply consumers generating credit hours and credentials.

Diana Chapman Walsh (1999) put the issue well for us faculty members: "We know intuitively that ineffectual, dispirited, and alienated faculty are unlikely to be teaching well, unlikely to be providing their students with the inspiration and guidance they need at a time when we need students to be inspired. If the task of a college or university professor is, as I think we can agree, to inspire students with a love of learning that will companion them throughout their lives . . . then surely we need faculty themselves on fire with a passion for their work" (Glazer, 1999, p. 5).

In *Let Your Life Speak,* Parker Palmer (2000) suggests the orientation we need:

> There is a simplistic brand of moralism among us that wants to reduce the ethical life to making a list, checking it twice—against the index in some best-selling book of virtues perhaps—and then trying very hard to be not naughty but nice.
>
> There may be moments in life when we are so unformed that we need to use values like an exoskeleton to keep us from collapsing. But something is very wrong if such moments recur often in adulthood. Trying to live someone else's life, or to live by an abstract norm, will invariably fail—and may even do great damage. . . .
>
> Vocation does not come from willfulness. It comes from listening. I must listen to my life and try to understand what it is truly about—quite apart from what I would like it to be about—or my life will never represent anything real in the world, no matter how earnest my intentions.
>
> That insight is hidden in the word *vocation* itself, which is rooted in the Latin for "voice." Vocation does not mean a goal that I pursue. It means a calling that I hear. Before I can tell my life what I want to do with it, I must listen to my life telling me who I am. I must listen for the truths and values at the heart of my own identity, not the stan-

dards by which I *must* live—but the standards by which I cannot help but live if I am living my own life [pp. 3–6].

Parker's emphasis on listening for our own identity, for our own standards, suggests some specific things we and our colleagues can do to start reclaiming our professional souls.

As individuals we can seek out trusted colleagues and create times and spaces to share our experiences, our feelings, our conflicts and ambiguities, and our ideas about how to find some better resolution. We can legitimize such conversations between ourselves and our students, and among our students. We can encourage students to organize such activities as a way to show the university system what they truly value. We can read pertinent literature, write for ourselves and for others, and speak about these issues in public settings when given the chance. We can undertake systematic inquiry concerning our own institution or our own unit as to the gaps between ideals and realities, between espoused values and values in use.

Collectively we can work with regional and national organizations to bring to the surface and explore these concerns. We can survey the higher education landscape and aim for a vision of what it might become, in terms that are relevant and tangible for our diverse institutions and constituents. We can tackle the cultures of our graduate schools to help future professionals recognize the importance of addressing issues concerning purpose and meaning, authenticity and identity, spirituality and spiritual growth. We can create a series of publications, principles for good practice like those articulated in Jon Dalton's final chapter, and state-of-the-art reports. We can create a national teleconference that brings some of our most thoughtful and active leaders together with professionals from diverse institutions. We can recruit some high-profile presidents and administrative leaders to help create a political and multi-institutional inquiry and action base for sustained effort. We can bring these issues to the attention of larger audiences outside higher education, to explore their significance for the larger cultural context within which we work. Bolman and Deal (1995) put it well for me:

Perhaps we lost our way when we forgot that the heart of leadership lies in the hearts of leaders. We fooled ourselves, thinking that sheer bravado or sophisticated analytic techniques could respond to our deepest concerns. We lost touch with our most precious gift—our spirit.

To recapture spirit, we need to relearn how to lead with soul. How to breathe new zest and buoyancy into life. How to reinvigorate the family as a sanctuary where people can grow, develop, and find love. How to reinfuse the workplace with vigor and élan. Leading with soul returns us to ancient spiritual basics reclaiming the enduring human capacity that gives our lives passion and purpose [p. 21].

So, despite the obstacles, there are individual and collective initiatives we can pursue to reclaim our souls, to reclaim the "essence, substance, animating principle, or actuating cause" that brought us to this calling. Momentum is building. We hope this book adds weight to current initiatives.

CHAPTER TWO

The Dynamics of Spirituality and the Religious Experience

Liesa Stamm

———

Religion is the conceptual framework and the recognized institution within which a society's deep moral values and the rules governing what is defined as correct behavior for individuals are generally associated. *Religion* is the term most frequently used by Americans and in the popular media as well as in scholarly analyses to encompass the complexity of beliefs and practices delineated by established denominational institutions and framed through defined doctrines, theology, and historical narratives or myths accounting for the establishment of these doctrines and practices. Chapter Three illustrates the profound influences of religious institutions on the social history of the United States and on American higher education. As discussed in this chapter and further delineated in Chapter Three, in the past fifty years a major transformation has occurred in the definitions and practices of religion among the American population. No longer comfortable with the constraints associated with organized religion, many Americans are now focused on a more personal experience of religious faith and practice and prefer to define their experiences as *spiritual* rather than *religious*.

In Chapter One, we recognized the difficulty in defining the religious and spiritual experiences of individuals. We suggested a definition with which we are comfortable and which has increasingly common usage among Americans, particularly on college and university campuses. Our definition distinguishes religion from spirituality, with the term *religion* encompassing an affiliation with and practice of an established denominational tradition and *spirituality* marked by a highly personal search for ultimate meaning, purpose, and values wherever they may be found.

Although religion has most frequently been defined in terms of established institutional beliefs and practices, the experience of religion and spirituality is ultimately personal and varies in relation to an individual's cognitive, social, and emotional characteristics, as well as his or her personal narrative. Beginning in the early twentieth century with William James's groundbreaking work, *The Varieties of Religious Experience* (1902), a range of scholars and scholarly disciplines has developed a variety of theories and models to better understand the religious experience of individuals as one of the basic elements of human existence. As a framework for our exploration in Part Two of practical approaches for strengthening authenticity, spirituality, meaning, and purpose on our campuses today, this chapter examines the complexity of defining and understanding individual experiences of religion and spirituality. Note that throughout most of this chapter the term *religion* is used without distinguishing the experiences of religion and spirituality. This usage was adopted to correspond most closely to the scholarly work being cited.

Our concern to promote campus environments that support examining individual values, meaning, and purpose as an essential component of the educational mission rests on our recognition that the college experience can have a major impact in shaping students' lives. Late adolescence is "a time of great potentiality and vulnerability in development, when concerns about individual purposes, meaning, and commitment interact with forces of cognitive development, maturation, and social expectations" (Dalton, 2001, p. 18). In recommending measures to support students' spiritual growth as well as their intellectual advancement, it is important to understand the complexity and great variety of individual religious and spiritual experiences.

THE MULTIDIMENSIONALITY OF RELIGION AND SPIRITUALITY

The religious experience is highly complex. This complexity is dramatically demonstrated by the range of definitions proposed by scholars grappling with delineating and codifying the phenomena they are observing. The difficulty arises from the fact that the experience of religion as expressed in the lives of individuals is what my colleagues Arthur Chickering and Jon Dalton have referred to as "the ineffable." J. Milton Yinger has expressed it well: "Any definition of religion is likely to be acceptable only to its author" (1967, p. 18). Or as Batson, Schoenrade, and Ventis (1993) have suggested, "Never discuss politics or religion. Far from indicating a lack of interest in these topics, this familiar maxim suggests much interest but much difference of opinion" (p. *v*).

William James signaled the complexity and varieties of religious experience when he admonished, "Let us not fall immediately into a one-sided view of our subject, but let us rather freely admit at the outset that we may very likely find no one essence, but many characters which may alternately be equally important to religion" (1902, p. 27). And Gordon Allport (1950), another early psychologist attempting to understand the nature of the religious experience, similarly resists the attempt to generalize: "The subjective religious attitude of every individual is, in both its essential and non-essential features, unlike that of any other individual. The roots of religion are numerous, the weight of their influence in individual lives so varied and the forms of rational interpretation so endless, that uniformity of product is impossible" (p. 26). Rather, Allport recommends that we "refer the task of characterizing the religious consciousness to the only authorities capable of knowing what it is—namely, individuals who experience it" (p. 6).

In examining the phenomena of religious experience, James Fowler (1981, 1996) provides a more theological perspective. He distinguishes between the concepts of faith, belief, and religion. He proposes that the concept of *religion* embodies a cumulative tradition composed of myriad beliefs and practices that form the basis of individual belief and faith. In Fowler's definition, *belief* refers to the acceptance by individuals of the truth of the doctrines or ideological claims of a particular religious tradition or denomination. *Faith,* in contrast, is more personal and existential. Faith is not always religious in its content or context. It is a generic feature of human life and is "foundational to social relations, to personal identity, and to the making of personal and cultural meanings" (1996, p. 55). Human action always involves responses and initiatives, and faith "is our way of finding coherence in and giving meaning to the multiple forces and relations that make up our lives. Faith is a person's way of seeing him- or herself in relation to others against a background of shared meaning and purpose" (1981, p. 4). It should be noted that in many respects Fowler's conception of faith is similar to the understanding of spirituality, in contrast to religion, in common usage among Americans today.

Sharon Daloz Parks's definition of religious and spiritual experiences is an outgrowth of her theological background combined with years of working with college students. Similar to Fowler, she focuses attention on the concept of faith rather than on that of religion. She suggests that the basic capacity and necessity among humans to make meaning in their lives is associated with faith. "Faith goes far beyond religious belief. . . . Faith is more adequately recognized as the activity of seeking and discovering meaning in the most comprehensive dimensions of our experience. Faith is a broad, generic human phenomenon. To be human is to dwell in faith, to dwell in the sense one makes out of life—what seems ultimately true and dependable about self, world, cosmos" (2000, p. 7). Religion, in Parks's understanding, is a "shared way of making meaning" (p. 197). In her focus on the spiritual development of young people, Parks recognizes that faith communities in the traditional sense of religious organizations are undergoing great changes in today's complex society. In general, organized religion no longer serves the central role in mentoring young people to seek their own values, meaning, and purpose that it did in the past.

Through many years of studying the psychology of religion, Bernard Spilka has continued to refine his understanding of the religious experience. In collaboration with Hood and Gorusch (Spilka, Hood, & Gorusch 1985), for example, Spilka emphasizes "the almost unbelievable breadth and variety of religious phenomena and expressions," and the range of perspectives from which the religious experience has been studied, including that of theologians, psychologists, and sociologists. To illustrate this range, Spilka et al. indicate that from an "outside" orientation, both the experience and study of religion are focused in such institutions, practices, and beliefs as theological doctrine, sacred writings, church dogma, liturgy, and ritual. In contrast, psychologists study religion from an "inside" perspective, focusing on the personal and subjective experience of religious belief and faith. In emphasizing the multidimensionality of religion, Spilka et al. indicate that personal and social religion is many faceted and that participation in or expression of one facet does not necessarily imply involvement in others. In preparing the third edition of his book on the psychology of religion, Spilka (personal communication, Feb. 19,

2002) has revised his basic definitions to reflect the increasing emphasis among Americans on spirituality in contrast to religion.

The Variety of Expressions of Religiousness and Spirituality

The complexity and multidimensionality of religious experiences are further illustrated through a series of questions posed by C. Daniel Batson, Patricia Schoenrade, and W. Larry Ventis in *Religion and the Individual* (1993).

WHAT DO WE MEAN BY RELIGION? In addressing this question, Batson et al. (1993) differentiate religion as "a self-contained set of beliefs or an institution in society" (p. 5) from religion as experienced by individuals. As will be discussed later in this chapter, today Americans tend to define their individual experiences of religion as *spiritual*. In examining the nature of religious experiences, Batson et al. suggest that, in contrast to other life experiences, religious experiences can be characterized by their uniqueness, their complexity, and their diversity. "Religious concerns seem to differ from everyday concerns both in the *comprehensiveness* of their scope and in their personal *centrality*. . . . Religious concerns and experiences are unique in that they *do* affect central perceptions about oneself and life itself; they *are* likely to change your notions of who you are and whether your life has any ultimate meaning and purpose" (pp. 6-7). Religious experience is psychologically complex, composed of an array of psychological categories including emotions, beliefs, attitudes, behaviors, and social environments. And most significantly, the religious experience is different for different individuals. It is therefore impossible to provide a definition that adequately describes all the forms that religion takes. The difficulty of defining the diversity of religious beliefs and practices is further compounded by the fact that today many people pursue religious concerns outside the structure of recognized religious traditions.

Given the variety of forms and expressions of religion and spirituality in the lives of individuals, Batson et al. (1993) propose a functional definition of religion that they suggest accounts for the uniqueness, complexity, and diversity of the religious experience. In contrast to the many scholars of religion who have argued for some apprehension of, or belief in, a transcendent, divine reality as a necessary component of religion, Batson et al. define religion as whatever we as individuals do to come to grips with the ultimate existential questions: "What is the meaning or purpose of my life? How should I relate to others? How do I deal with the fact that I am going to die? What should I do about my shortcomings?" (p. 8).

WHO IS RELIGIOUS AND WHO IS NOT RELIGIOUS? Batson et al.'s functional definition emphasizes that religion is an integral and dynamic part of human life. "By providing a new sense of reality and of one's own place within reality, religion is both a response to and a contributor to the individual's personality and social life" (1993, p. 12). They further suggest that this definitional focus on the function of religion in the life of the individual has a transcendent dimension, but not in the usual sense. Rather, in their definition, religion is the dimension through which "the individual transcends everyday matters to deal with existential concerns" (p. 12). According to this definition, therefore, anyone is religious when he or she is grappling with the ultimate questions of meaning and purpose in his or her life.

ARE YOU RELIGIOUS? Responding to this question gets to the heart of the complexity of the religious experience. As suggested by the diverse approaches to defining religion outlined so far, there are clearly many different ways of being religious, for any one individual as well as among different people. This is true within one religious tradition as well as across different traditions, different societies, and different cultures. Kenneth Pargament (1997) summarizes the diverse purposes that religion has served in people's lives. Religion is a system that provides order, reason, and beauty in the world; it gives meaning to the ongoing life experience. Religion offers protection from the dangers of the world and from the human impulse—from pain, guilt, and self-doubt. Religious beliefs and practices afford some shelter or respite from life's tensions and anxieties, whether internal or external in nature. Religion encourages people to moderate and control their impulses. At the same time, "fearsome images of hell, vengeance, and slaughter seem to be as plentiful in the religious literatures of both East and West as soothing ones" (p. 51). Religion serves as a pathway in the search for self and for self-growth. Religion is called on in times of physical illness and represents a source inspiration for those seeking psychological and emotional well-being. Religion provides a sense of community, of belonging, and of intimacy with others. Religion is an avenue for those seeking a better world through improving the lives and social conditions of others. Chapter Seven illustrates the diverse purposes of religion in peoples' lives through its focus on the interrelationship of religion, spirituality, and community in the higher education setting.

Peter C. Hill and Ralph W. Hood Jr.'s encyclopedic volume (1999) provides a further illustration of the great variety of theoretical and conceptual frameworks developed by researchers attempting to delineate and analyze religiosity and spirituality. This work reviews 126 scales designed by psychologists of religion to empirically measure the following dimensions of religious and spiritual experience.

Religious attitudes	Religious beliefs and practices
Religious commitment and involvement	Religious coping and problem solving
Religious development	Views of death and the afterlife
Divine intervention and religious attribution	Religious experiences
Forgiveness	Religious fundamentalism
God concept	Institutional religious attitudes
Religious and moral values or characteristics	Religious orientation
Spirituality and mysticism	Related constructs, such as purpose of life

The Multidimensional Measurement of Religiousness/Spirituality for Use in Health Research (1999), recently developed under the auspices of the Fetzer Institute and the National Institute on Aging (NIA), offers another example of the complexity involved with accounting for the religious experience. The panel of scholars convened by the Fetzer Institute and the NIA addressed the challenge of measuring the range of individual religious and spiritual beliefs and practices by developing scales to assess the following key domains.

Beliefs	Commitment
Daily spiritual experiences	Forgiveness
Meaning	Organizational religiousness
Private religious practice	Religious/spiritual coping
Religious/spiritual history	Religious preference
Religious support	Values

Additional aspects of religiousness and spirituality identified by the group include spiritual maturity, mystical experiences, compassion, hope, prayer, and spiritual integration.

Religious Orientation

Although religious beliefs and practices are potentially as varied as the individuals who adhere to them, studies of the religious experience provide evidence that there are identifiable patterns or categories of religious expression and motivation that psychologists have termed *religious orientations.* Pargament (1997) conceives of these orientations as pathways for achieving the wide range of purposes that individuals seek in religion. The concept of distinct religious orientations, or patterns of being religious, was first delineated in Gordon Allport's highly influential work *The Individual and His Religion* (1950). Growing out of his own research on the authoritarian personality and drawing on other psychological studies of religion at that time, Allport concluded that although individuals may engage in similar religious behavior, such as church attendance, their underlying motives may differ significantly. Allport synthesized the possible range of individual religious motivations into two basic patterns of being religious, which have become known as *extrinsic* and *intrinsic religious orientations.* These conceptual frameworks for understanding religious experience have been refined over the years through ongoing research and are now standardized frameworks of analysis in the psychological study of religion.

The term *extrinsic religious orientation* is generally used by researchers to refer to "utilitarian" motivations for religious behavior. As Allport and Ross (1967) suggested in developing the Religious Orientation Scale, an extrinsically oriented individual adopts specific religious views and engages in religious acts only to achieve purely utilitarian ends. Religion provides security, comfort, status, or social support; it is not valued in its own right but as a means to an end. In contrast, an *intrinsic religious orientation* is not instrumental, but subordinates all other needs to an overarching religious commitment. "In internalizing the total creed of his religion the individual necessarily internalizes its values of humility, compassion, and love of neighbor" (p. 441). In this definition, religion is an end in itself. In essence, the extrinsic and intrinsic orientations distinguish between a *religion of means*—a device, an instrument, a tool—and a *religion of ends*—lived, internalized, totally directive. The concepts of extrinsic and intrinsic religion have come to be understood in terms of the polarization between means and ends. "Perhaps the briefest way to characterize the two poles of subjective religion is that the extrinsically motivated person *uses* his religion, whereas the intrinsically motivated *lives* his religion" (p. 434).

As a result of research originally conducted by C. Daniel Batson, a third construct for delineating religious orientation, known as *quest*, has become widely accepted by psychologists. In grappling with the extrinsic and intrinsic frameworks in their own research, Batson et al. (1993) concluded that particularly Allport's concept of intrinsic religious experience is too rigid and dogmatic and leaves little room for other factors crucial to religious experience: complexity, doubt, and tentativeness.

> These characteristics of complexity, doubt and tentativeness suggest a way of being religious that is very different from either the extrinsic or the intrinsic; . . . they suggest an approach that involves honestly facing existential questions in all their complexity while resisting clear-cut, pat answers. An individual who approaches religion in this way realizes that he or she does not know, and probably never will know, the final truth about such matters. Still, the questions are deemed important and, however tentative and subject to change, answers are sought. There may or may not be a clear belief in a transcendent reality, but there is a transcendent, religious approach to the individual's life [p. 166].

Batson et al. label this open-ended, questioning approach to religion as *quest*. Quest is a religious orientation that is basically cognitive in nature, emphasizing the way in which beliefs are formed and held. In this orientation, questions are much more central to the religious experience than answers. It involves a willingness to actively confront and struggle with tough issues, to remain open and flexible to learning, and to look with doubt upon simple solutions to difficult problems. In sum, a quest orientation to religion results in a complex, highly differentiated framework for viewing the world that leads to a search for truth and for meaning in life.

Reflecting his own research and that of other psychologists of religion, Pargament (1997) suggests that "there are empirical and theoretical reasons to suspect that there may be more than three religious

orientations. Some empirical study indicates that these three orientations oversimplify the intricacies of religious means and ends" (p. 66).
Pargament proposes, for example, that the polarization of extrinsic
and intrinsic orientations into means and ends ignores important differences in the *kinds* of religious pathways and destinations that individuals pursue. Rather he concludes that these two orientations do
not contrast a religion of means with a religion of ends but a religion
of one set of means and ends with another. Further, he asserts that the
basic religious orientations identified through psychological research
are "general dispositions to use particular means to attain particular
ends in living" (p. 59). To fully account for an individual's religious
orientation, Pargament stresses the importance of understanding the
social dimension of religion as well as the cognitive, behavioral, and
emotional. He delineates a number of possible religious destinations
or ends that are not encompassed within the current constructs of religious orientations, such as the desire for physical health, the search
for intimacy and connectedness, the yearning for a radically improved
world, religious obligation as a sense of duty or guilt, and the use of
religion as social gain, to raise one's social standing and self-image.
Further, Pargament contends that some religious pathways may be
fundamentally disorienting, leaving people lost, confused, and headed
toward dead ends.

Distinguishing Between Religion and Spirituality

In an attempt to identify the fundamental characteristics of religion
and spirituality as conceptualized by scholars and researchers, and to
account for the definitional distinctions and overlaps, Peter Hill, Kenneth Pargament, Ralph Hood, Michael McCullough, James Swyers,
David Larson, and Brian Zinnbauer (2000) recently undertook a comprehensive analysis of research on these two phenomena from the perspective of a number of disciplines. Their contribution to the search
for a core understanding of religion and spirituality is particularly significant because the "veritable flood of interest in spirituality witnessed
in the popular culture during the past few decades has resulted in disagreements and perhaps even confusion about what is meant by such
terms as religion and spirituality" (p. 52).

Reflecting the current research by psychologists and sociologists,
Hill et al. differentiate the conceptualization and experience of spirituality from that of religion. *Spirituality* in the current definitional

approaches is associated with some of the components formerly included as part of religion and is used to describe individual experiences identified with personal transcendence and meaning. As a result of this changed understanding, definitions of religion have become narrower and less inclusive, with religion more often identified with structured religious institutions that are frequently considered to restrict or limit personal potential. "Whereas religion historically was a 'broad-band construct' that included both individual and institutional elements, it is now seen as a 'narrow-band construct' that has much more to do with the institutional alone" (p. 60).

The authors conclude that despite the tendency among scholars and researchers to distinguish between spirituality and religion as understood and practiced by individuals, these phenomena are inherently interrelated. They further contend that "given our limited understanding of contemporary religion and spirituality, it is perhaps premature to insist on a single comprehensive definition of either term" (Hill et al., 2000, p. 52). As evidence of the complexity of these phenomena and the difficulty in arriving at satisfactory definitions that encompass the range of attitudes, beliefs, and practices that we include within our use of these terms, the authors identify the conceptual overlap between religion and spirituality, defining spirituality as "a central and essential function of religion" (p. 70). They further recognize, however, that spirituality also may be experienced outside the context of religion and can therefore be understood as a separate phenomenon.

One of the primary contributions of Hill et al.'s analysis is their emphasis on the concept of the *sacred* as a central definitional construct of both spirituality and religion. They describe the sacred as "a person, an object, a principle, or a concept that transcends the self" (2000, p. 68). The occurrence of the sacred is highly personal and may be invested in a wide range of life events, experiences, and entities. Music might be the source of the sacred for one person; for another it may be a religious text or liturgy, or it may reside in the beauty of the natural world.

Further, the authors posit that both religion and spirituality involve a process of individual *search* to identify what is held as sacred and therefore worthy of devotion or commitment.

Hill et al. conclude their examination of the religious and spiritual phenomena by proposing the following criteria for distinguishing and defining religion and spirituality:

1. Religion and spirituality are both understood by individuals to include "subjective feelings, thoughts and behaviors that arise from a search for the sacred" (p. 68).

2. Religion is distinguished from spirituality in that it may include a search for nonsacred goals, such as social identity, affiliation, and health and wellness, within a context that has as its primary goal the facilitation of the search for the sacred—for example, membership in a church.

3. Religion involves the means and methods, such as rituals or other prescribed behaviors, through which the search for the sacred is validated by and receives support from a recognized group. Spirituality in contrast may not require external validation.

Our Societal Transformation from Public to Private Religion and Spirituality

Sociologists such as Wade Clark Roof and Robert Wuthnow approach the study of the religious experience through very different methodologies and analytic frameworks from those of the psychologists. Their research on the changing trends in the religious orientation of the American population during the past fifty years, however, has resulted in definitions of Americans' religious and spiritual experiences that are very similar to those of the psychologists. One primary example is the emphasis they place on spiritual seeking as a dominant religious orientation among Americans today. These findings parallel and confirm Batson et al.'s quest theme (1993) and the work of Hill et al. (2000). As discussed in Chapter Three, both Roof (1999) and Wuthnow (1998) have documented the current diversity of religious discourse in the United States, the extent to which Americans now presume personal religious choice rather than adhere to prescribed religious practices, and Americans' reliance on "self-cultivation" and "self-monitoring" of their religious beliefs and practices. As Roof suggests, "Many individuals consider their own personal religious narratives as evolving, as open-ended and revisable" (1999, p. 78). Religious doubt is not only openly accepted but "even endowed with potential theological significance" (p. 78). In addition, the instrumental aspects of religion, such as personal happiness and spiritual well-being, which were once considered latent benefits, are now highly vocalized and sought after. Similar to Batson et al., Roof emphasizes the transforming force of religion in both personal and social life as a fundamental feature of the human quest. He suggests that religion represents a source of hope in an indeterminate future. "Openness to that future is enshrined in all the great religious traditions as virtues and what ultimately sustains human life: to wait, to meditate, to pray, to expect, to dream, to seek" (1999, p. 295).

Robert Wuthnow's understandings of the religious and spiritual experiences of Americans grew out of many decades of research through which he documented the shift in commitment from what he considers the public side of religion to the "equally profound developments in the ways people express their personal relationships to the sacred—in spirituality" (1998, p. vii). Wuthnow's path to discovery in many ways mirrors the general shift in religious orientation that has occurred in the United States since the 1960s, from the more public expression of religion to the more private and personal. This shift also suggests why defining the religious and spiritual experience is so complex. Wuthnow essentially defines a change in orientation from what he calls "a spirituality of dwelling," the practice of religion within and through the doctrines of organized denominations, to a "spirituality of seeking." His concept of the "spirituality of seeking" is similar to Batson et al.'s concept of quest. Wuthnow proposes that a "spirituality of seeking emphasizes *negotiation*: individuals search for sacred moments that reinforce their conviction that the divine exists, but these moments are fleeting; rather than knowing the territory, people explore new spiritual vistas, and they may have to negotiate among complex and confusing meanings of spirituality" (p. 4). He further suggests that "at its core spirituality consists of all the beliefs and activities by which individuals attempt to relate their lives to God or to a divine being or some other conception of a transcendent reality. In a society as complex as that of the United States, spirituality is expressed in many different ways. But spirituality is not just the creation of individuals; it is shaped by larger social circumstances, and by the beliefs and values present in the wider culture" (p. viii).

As demonstrated in Chapter Three, both Roof and Wuthnow are concerned with understanding religious orientation in a social historical context as well as in terms of the experience of individuals. Roof's research (1999) on the changing modes of religious discourse and practice in the United States leads him to conclude that religion is a social construct that is constantly being reproduced and changed.

"Religion in any age exists in a dynamic and interactive relationship with its cultural environment. . . . Far from being handed down by the heavens, religious symbols, beliefs, and practices are created and then maintained, revised, and modified by the often self-conscious actions of human beings" (p. 79). The changing forms and styles of religion that are observed over time are "a product of a complex set of factors—changing interpretations of religious heritage, social location and influences, new leadership, groups contending for power and control within a religious tradition. . . . Even our notions of the sacred and of life's deepest meanings are in a process of continual social conditioning" (pp. 78–79). "Religion in its most basic sense is a story involving symbol, metaphor, and language, all having the power to persuade and to fan the imagination. Symbol, metaphor, and language are in fact the means by which human beings come to self-awareness and articulate a sense of self in relation to others" (p. 297).

To fully understand the process through which religion is created and re-created in society, Roof (1999) advocates a focus on the actual religious and spiritual narratives of individuals, to let people speak for themselves. We must view "lived religion" as "strategies of religious action" that are open-ended and through which individuals seek greater fullness and draw from a "rich array of beliefs, symbols, imageries, techniques, and popular discourses" (p. 295). "Symbol, metaphor, and language are creative resources undergirding not just cognition, but emotions and bodily experience. Whatever else it might suggest, the spiritual implies the transforming presence of the sacred, a presence made real, indeed created, through the persuasive power of narrative and symbol" (p. 297).

THEORIES OF RELIGIOUS AND SPIRITUAL DEVELOPMENT

Examining Batson et al.'s question (1993), "What leads a person to be religious?" provides a useful framework for developing approaches to strengthen higher education's commitment to nurturing authenticity and spirituality as essential to its educational mission. Social psychologists and sociologists have proposed a range of theories to account for the individual's religious attitudes, beliefs, and practices. The external social environment in which an individual interacts represents one major context for the development of his or her religious beliefs and practices. Chapter Three documents the impact of social institutions, expectations, and practices on Americans' current religious attitudes and practices and describes the historical influence of religious institutions on the development of American higher education. As Batson et al. (1993) suggest, however, social influences are only partially responsible for development of the individual's religious orientation and experience. They argue that the source of religious experience is, in fact, a complex interaction among an individual's social background and social influences and his or her physical, intellectual, and psychological characteristics and developmental processes.

The Impact of Social Learning and Psychosocial and Cognitive Development

Social learning theory, originally developed by Albert Bandura (1978), provides one useful approach for more fully understanding the processes by which individuals acquire their religious and spiritual beliefs. Although not specific to the religious experience, the basic focus of social learning theory on the cognitive development of new beliefs and behavior is relevant to religious development. Bandura's (1978) interactionist model of cognitive development is premised on a three-way "reciprocal determinism" composed of the individual's own cognitive processes, the physical and social environment, and his or her behavior. "Because people's conceptions, their behavior, their environments are reciprocal determinants of each other, individuals are neither the powerless objects controlled by environmental forces nor entirely free agents who can do whatever they choose" (pp. 356-357). Social learning theory emphasizes the active role of the learner in the developmental process: "the learner is not simply a passive recipient of information and values but one who actively seeks to know and to understand, learning by observing other people's behavior and its consequences, as well as learning by observing the consequences of his or her own behavior" (Batson et al., 1993, p. 54).

Although clearly important for understanding the development of individual behavior and beliefs, social learning theory cannot fully account for the complex processes involved with human development. "Social learning theory focuses on how the individual acquires new ideas and behaviors, new cognitive content. But cognitive development involves more than changes in what the person knows, thinks, and believes. At even the most fundamental level, cognitive development involves change in *how* the person knows, thinks, and believes. These changes in the cognitive structures produce new assumptions about the nature of reality and new ways of thinking about experience" (Batson et al., 1993, p. 57).

The important body of work focused on understanding the processes of psychosocial and cognitive development provides powerful frameworks for examining the developmental pathways through which individuals arrive at their own religious and spiritual definitions and beliefs. Building on the groundbreaking work of Erik Erikson (1950) and Jean Piaget (1926, 1953), during the past forty years psychologists have developed a range of theories to account for the complex processes that shape the individual's understandings of the world and his or her attitudes, feelings, and behavior at different stages of maturation, including physical, cognitive, and emotional development. Although much of the work on human development has not focused specifically on issues of religious and spiritual development, it has broad implications for understanding religious development. Through his biographies of Martin Luther (1958) and Mahatma Ghandi (1969), Erik Erikson, for example, explored the implications of his model of psychosocial development for understanding religious life. Building on and extending the understandings of human development derived from psychosocial and cognitive theories, such researchers as Ronald Goldman (1964), Lawrence Kohlberg (1969, 1976), William Perry (1970), Carol Gilligan (1982), and Robert Coles (1990) have posited major theoretical constructs for understanding the process of moral and religious development. James Fowler (1981, 1996) and more recently Sharon Daloz Parks (2000) have developed theories describing the stages of religious development that draw on and are intended to reinforce the major theories of human cognitive and psychosocial development.

As suggested in Chapter Six of this volume, the mission of student affairs in American higher education has always been concerned with the inner lives of students and their holistic learning and development. Theories of human development serve as a critical underpinning for the work of student affairs professionals in supporting student development. In their effort to attend more fully to students' spiritual growth, student affairs professionals may benefit from a consideration of the theories of religious and spiritual development formulated by James Fowler and Sharon Daloz Parks.

James Fowler's Stages of Faith Development

Fowler's theories of faith development are widely considered to be seminal in the field of the psychology of religion. His theories explicitly build on the foundations set by Erikson's theories of psychosocial development, Piaget's theories of cognitive development, and Kohlberg's theories of moral development, and are intended to parallel and elaborate these theories.

Fowler's interest in faith development grew out of his early work as a minister. When he began teaching applied theology at the Harvard Divinity School, he sought to combine his experiences of the varieties of individual faith with the major theological perspectives of the time. Through his exploration of the interaction of faith with human formation and transformation, his own theories of faith development began to emerge. He was introduced to Lawrence Kohlberg, also at Harvard, and, as Fowler describes it, through his friendship and colleagueship with Kohlberg, "a citizen reared in the land of theology began to try to earn dual citizenship in the new world of the psychology of human development" (1981, p. 38).

In Fowler's view, faith is a human universal; it is an innate capacity present in humans from the time of birth. "How these capacities are activated and grow depends to a large extent on how we are welcomed into the world and what kinds of environments we grow in. Faith is interactive and social; it requires community, language, ritual, and nurture. Faith is also shaped in initiatives from beyond us and other people, initiatives of spirit or grace. How these latter initiatives are recognized and imaged, or unperceived and ignored, powerfully affects the shape of faith in our lives" (1981, p. xiii).

Fowler's theory of faith development involves six stages and a prestage of Undifferentiated or Primal Faith that is characteristic of the first two years of life. According to Batson et al. (1993), Fowler draws on Erikson's theories of psychosocial development to provide the "deep structure" of his own theories of faith development, and uses Kohlberg's model of moral reasoning as a template for a developmental stage analysis (p. 72). Fowler maintains that his faith stages, like Kohlberg's moral stages, form an invariant sequence, with each new stage integrating and carrying forward the operations of the previous stage. A person may progress through only three or four faith stages in a lifetime, but the stages are always experienced in the same order, and none can be left out.

PRIMAL FAITH (INFANCY). According to Fowler, all humans are born with innate spiritual capacities. The initial experience of faith is prelinguistic and occurs as the child builds trust in the world based on his or her early dependency on parents and other caregivers. Fowler indicates that his concept of the formation of basic trust that typifies this stage was strongly influenced by Erikson's depiction of the struggles against a sense of anxiety and basic mistrust that occur in the first year or year-and-a-half of life. "If we emerge from that first year or so of life with a balance, on the whole, of trust over mistrust, then a basic *virtue* emerges—a basic strength of selfhood and faith, which Erikson calls the strength of *hope*" (Fowler, 1996, p. 22). In Erikson's theory of development another pivotal life crisis emerges between eighteen and thirty-six months, at which time children begin to experience *autonomy* while maintaining sufficient connectedness to avoid feeling powerless. This autonomy helps the child avoid what Erikson calls "shame and doubt" in the self. Through this struggle to overcome shame and doubt, according to Fowler, "there emerges the virtue or the strength of personhood and faith that Erikson calls *will*—the ability to assert oneself" (1996, pp. 22–23).

The work of Jean Piaget (1926, 1953) also contributed to Fowler's formulation of this stage of faith development. According to Piaget, the early awakening of the child's mind and reasoning initially occurs during the first year-and-a-half of life through the ordering of bodily experience of the world, a stage Piaget calls *sensory-motor knowing*.

Following the stage of primal faith, individuals progress over the course of their lives through the following six stages of increasingly mature faith.

STAGE 1: INTUITIVE-PROJECTIVE FAITH (EARLY CHILDHOOD). From approximately three to seven years of age, the child's faith is fantasy filled, imitative, and heavily influenced by examples, actions, and stories provided by the adults in their lives. Fowler's conception of faith during early childhood closely corresponds to Piaget's stage of *preoperational knowing and thinking*. In Piaget's developmental model, by eighteen months a child's linguistic abilities are emerging, which in turn reinforce the importance of language in shaping and communicating his or her experiences of the world. Fowler's Intuitive-Projective Stage also draws on Erikson's *initiative versus guilt* stage of crisis, which occurs as the child begins to compete with others, particularly for the attention of parents, and must acknowledge that he or she is not the exclusive partner of the parent of the opposite sex. The child's growing sense of freedom and initiative gives rise to the virtue of *purpose* and the emergence of the aspect of *conscience* that involves the internalization of the norms and values of the community in which the child is embedded (Fowler, 1996, p. 23).

Incorporating the theories of both Piaget and Erikson, Fowler proposes that as a result of the child's budding linguistic abilities, an early awareness of the self materializes as well as early awareness of death, sex, and the strong taboos associated with these life occurrences. The emergent strength of this stage of faith is intuitive understanding and imagination. This stage also holds the dangers of the imagination becoming overpowered with visions of destruction, prohibited behavior, and severe moral demands.

STAGE 2: MYTHIC-LITERAL FAITH (MIDDLE CHILDHOOD AND BEYOND). This stage occurs at Piaget's stage of *concrete operations* (between ages seven and eleven). The child now appropriates the stories, beliefs, and practices that symbolize belonging to his or her community of faith. Earlier episodic perceptions of experience give way to logical construction of experience employing sequence and order to provide meaning. There is an increased ability to take in the perspective of others. Interpretation of stories, drama, and myth, though important for understanding experience, are concrete and literal rather than abstract and symbolic.

STAGE 3: SYNTHETIC-CONVENTIONAL FAITH (ADOLESCENCE AND BEYOND). With the emergence of early formal operational thinking, young people develop the use and appreciation of abstract concepts. Life is now more diverse, and faith must interpret this diversity. The individual begins to define self-identity, to establish the meaning of various narratives for self and others, and to synthesize an individual life story, particularly in relation to others. To provide stability, deeply held beliefs and values may be sought, often by identifying with authority figures or peer role models. These beliefs and values take the form of an "ideology," an uncritically embraced worldview that the individual fails to recognize as only one of many other possibilities.

STAGE 4: INDIVIDUATIVE-REFLECTIVE FAITH (YOUNG ADULTHOOD AND BEYOND). For this stage to emerge, the individual must begin to assess the firmly held beliefs established during the previous stage. The individual assumes responsibility for his or her own commitments, lifestyle, beliefs, and attitudes; the self becomes more integrated, less a composite of roles and meanings of others. The emerging faith associated with this stage involves the capacity for self-reflection, the recognition of the relativity of one's inherited worldview, and the rejection of literal interpretations of faith stories and myths. The emergent strength of this stage of faith is its capacity for critical reflection on oneself and one's worldview; the danger is an overreliance on critical, analytic thought.

STAGE 5: CONJUNCTIVE FAITH (EARLY MIDLIFE AND BEYOND). This stage of faith may emerge sometime during the midlife period. In this developmental stage, individuals become sensitive to the pattern of interrelatedness in the universe. There is a "second naïveté," an opening to the voices of one's "deeper self," including the myths and ideals one has inherited from one's social class, ethnic background, and religious group. The individual develops connections that transcend differences; and reliance on "a spirit of love and acceptance, of healing and forgiveness, beyond the powers of humans alone" emerges. Effort is made to accept and unify apparent opposites. The dangers of this stage are paralyzing passivity, complacency, and cynical withdrawal.

STAGE 6: UNIVERSALIZING FAITH (MIDLIFE AND BEYOND). The structuring of this stage derives from the radical completion of a process of decentralization from self that proceeds throughout the sequence of stages. Gradually the circle of "those who count" in faith, meaning making, and justice has expanded until at the Conjunctive stage it extends well beyond the bounds of social class, nation, race, gender, ideological affinity, and religious tradition. In Universalizing Faith this process comes to completion. The authentic spirituality of the Universalizing stage avoids polarizing the world. People at this stage are as concerned with the transformation of those they oppose as with bringing about justice and reform. They have become the incarnation of the spirit of an inclusive and fulfilled human community, and they work to liberate humanity from the "shackles" of social, political, economic, and ideological expectations and constraints. Just as Kohlberg claimed that his highest stage of moral reasoning is rarely reached, Fowler indicates that it is fairly unusual for individuals to achieve this stage of faith development.

—⁓—

Fowler proposes that his approach to understanding faith development is intended to be inclusive of all faith traditions and orientations and therefore is not content specific. "The stages aim to describe patterned operations of knowing and valuing that underlie our consciousness. The various stages can be differentiated in relation to the degrees of complexity, of comprehensiveness, of internal differentiation, and of flexibility that their operations of knowing and valuing manifest" (1996, p. 57). Fowler further maintains that the faith stages and their associated developmental changes take into account the complex interplay of "biological maturation, emotional and cognitive development, psychosocial experience, and religio-cultural influences. . . . Because development of faith involves aspects of all these sectors of human growth and change, movement from one stage to another is not automatic or assured. Persons may reach chronological and biological adulthood while remaining best defined by structural stages of faith that would most commonly be associated with early or middle childhood or adolescence" (p. 57).

In assessing Fowler's theory of faith development within the broad context of social psychological research on the religious experience, Batson et al. (1993) suggest that this model is clearly normative, reflecting "a prescription of what Fowler thinks should be" (p. 73). They assert that as a liberal Christian theologian, Fowler envisions Stage 6 as the ideal and believes that the closer one comes to attaining this stage, the stronger and more complete one's faith will be. In reviewing Fowler's own research data, which in part formed the basis for his theory of faith development, Batson et al. conclude that "it may be more appropriate to speak of styles of faith, as Fowler sometimes does, not stages. One style involves orthodox adherence to traditional religious beliefs; a second involves critical analysis and believing for oneself; and a third involves a symbolic and paradoxical interpretation of religious concepts" (1993, p. 75).

Sharon Daloz Parks's Theories of Faith Development for the College Years

Drawing on over thirty years of teaching, counseling, and research focused on young adults, Parks has formulated a theory of faith development specific to the young adult years of the college-age population. She defines her theory of faith development as standing within and critically elaborating on Fowler's stages of faith development. Her amplification of Fowler's theory derives from her concern with fostering the spirituality of college students. She recognizes that "not only the quality of individual young adult lives but also our future as a culture depends in no small measure upon our capacity to recognize the emerging competence of young adults, to initiate them into big questions, and to give them access to worthy dreams" (2000, p. xi). Parks's concern reflects the fact that the young adult years are generally the time when individuals build their own systems of faith and begin to establish their own understandings of life meanings.

Parks defines the process of faith development as a spiritual quest to make sense out of life experiences and to seek patterns, order, coherence, and relation among the disparate elements of human living. Like Fowler, Parks builds on the work of the developmental psychologists, particularly that of Piaget, Erikson, Perry, Levinson, Kegan, Gilligan, and Belenky and her colleagues. And, similar to that of Fowler, her model of faith development incorporates her own insights from the study of religion, theology, leadership, ethics, and her work as a minister. Her work is therefore well grounded in traditional student development theory as well as in a knowledge of theology and faith in practice.

Fowler's concept of transferring authority from others to the self as faith matures serves as the starting place for Parks's thinking. "Fowler's attention to shifts in the locus of authority in the maturing of faith provided a key girder for building a bridge in my own thought between the formation of faith and human development in the young adult years" (Parks, 2000, p. 45). Reflecting her concern about the young adult years, Parks refines Fowler's theory by defining an additional stage of faith development between adolescence and adulthood that she identifies as *young adult faith*. Her theory of faith development therefore includes two separate stages within Fowler's fourth stage of Individuative-Reflective Faith. The first additional stage in her model is a *young adult stage* of faith development, which she suggests occurs between the stages of adolescence and adulthood as described in most developmental theories. She further differentiates adulthood into what she calls *tested adults* and *mature adults*. The result is a four-stage model of faith development, beginning with adolescence, consisting of (1) adolescent, (2) young adult, (3) tested adult, and (4) mature adult faith. Parks sees the need for such a model because most stage-related developmental theories jump directly from adolescent experiences to the adult years without addressing the variables and nuances involved in reaching adulthood.

Parks's model defines faith development during the young adult years as encompassing three interactive components: *forms of know-*

ing (cognitive aspects of faith development), *forms of dependence* (affective aspects of faith development), and *forms of community* (social aspects of faith development). Within her conceptual framework, the process of faith development involves a series of transformations from "authority-bound forms of meaning-making anchored in conventional assumed community, through the wilderness of counterdependence and unqualified relativism, to a committed, innerdependent mode of composing meaning" (Parks, 2000, p. 102). Love (2001) suggests that Parks's concept of forms of knowing is well grounded in the work of Perry and in other cognitive-structural theories. The components of her theory that focus on forms of dependence and forms of community draw on the work of Piaget, Erikson, and "especially on Kegan, who is the only other major student development theorist proposing a theory that integrates the cognitive, affective, and social aspects of development" (Love, 2001, p. 9). Love further suggests that Parks's theories emphasize the relative significance of dependence on authority at different stages of spiritual development and draw on such developmental theorists as Baxter Magolda and Belensky, Clinchy, Goldberger, and Tarule, who have examined the importance of dependency in understanding adolescent development (Love, 2001, p. 11).

STAGE 1: ADOLESCENT OR CONVENTIONAL FAITH. At this stage, faith is characterized by *authority-bound, dualistic (tacit)* forms of knowing; *dependent/counterdependent* forms of dependence; and *conventional* forms of community. The individual's faith is focused in forms of authority outside the self, such as churches, the Bible, parents, clergy. The adolescent's sense of self and truth are dependent on his or her immediate relational and affectional ties. The experience of community is defined by enforcement of conformity to cultural norms, interests, and assumptions of the group.

As the individual's faith matures, the absolute form of knowing breaks down, and he or she recognizes the perspectives of others, a form of knowing that Parks labels "unqualified relativism," the recognition that knowledge is shaped by context (2000, p. 57). With the growth of self-awareness, the individual may resist authorities through counterdependence, a movement in opposition to authority. The definition and experience of the community become more diffuse, the individual becomes more open to other communities of interest, and the commitment to a particular community weakens.

In summary, the ways in which an individual makes sense of the world and answers the existential questions during adolescence usually begin with simple answers representing an uncomplicated view of a straightforward and knowable world. As an individual matures during this stage, authorities are found to be in error, undependable, or in conflict. The individual discovers and recognizes new types of community as having value and worth. These experiences may result in a loss of faith that is in fact a developmental movement forward.

STAGES 2: YOUNG ADULT FAITH. Parks characterizes Young Adult Faith in terms of *probing commitment (ideological)* forms of knowing; *fragile inner-dependent* forms of dependence; and *mentoring* forms of community. Most developmental theorists define this stage as a transitional period rather than a fully recognized stage of development in itself. In postulating a young adult stage, Parks asserts that in the young adult years individuals begin to recognize the need to define a path that shapes their future within the complex and contextual nature of the world. They begin to construct meaning and faith. At the same time, the young adult remains semidependent on parents and other authorities so that the developing self-identity remains fragile. Parks identifies a "mentoring community" as the ideal form of community needed by young adults to help them develop a complex adult faith. She maintains that the growth that comes with critical self-awareness must be grounded in the experience of a supportive social group. Such a mentoring community "offers a network of belonging in which young adults feel recognized as who they really are, and as who they are becoming. It offers both challenge and support and thus offers good company for both the emerging strength and the distinctive vulnerability of the young adult" (Parks, 2000, p. 95).

The Young Adult stage is typical of college students. During this period, the individual challenges established ideas and identifies new authorities through a variety of curricular and cocurricular experiences, as well as through the influence of peers and of professors and other college personnel. The person's emerging sense of inner-dependence is tested and new commitments are made, particularly in the context of one or more mentoring communities.

STAGE 3: TESTED ADULT FAITH. This constitutes the second refinement of Fowler's Individuative-Reflective Faith and occurs following the young adult stage. It is distinguished by *tested commitment (systemic)* forms of knowing; *confident inner-dependent* forms of dependence; and *self-selected class/group* forms of community. The forms of knowing at this stage are based on the individual's coming to terms with an understanding and acceptance of his or her commitments and meanings and, ultimately, with his or her faith. Faith development moves from a focus on external authority to an internal focus (inner-dependence), to an interaction and healthy integration of the two (confident inner-dependence), and finally to recognition that throughout one's life there has existed interdependence. As an individual's faith develops, he or she begins to associate with others who share similar meanings and have similar socioeconomic, political, religious, and philosophical views (self-selected groups). There is a disciplined openness to multiple truths. Parks suggests that although some undergraduates may reach the Tested Adult stage, individuals at this stage are more likely to be postgraduates, graduate students, or beyond.

STAGE 4: MATURE ADULT FAITH. This stage, according to Parks, is typified by *convictional commitment (paradoxical)* forms of knowing, *interdependent* forms of dependence, and *openness to other* forms of community. In moving toward mature adult faith, an individual becomes comfortable interacting with and belonging to the broader world. He or she recognizes interdependence and interconnectedness with communities and individuals outside the immediate environment. Mature Adult Faith involves becoming open to the ambiguity and doubt that exist even within tested convictions. Parks suggests that a mature adult faith is rarely evident before midlife.

Analyses of Stage Models of Development

Parks asserts that although her model appears to represent the evolution of faith as linear and fixed, her model of faith development, in contrast to Fowler's theory, represents a "dynamic, multidimensional, creative process" (2000, p. 102). Because her theory builds on and is intended to elaborate Fowler's stages of faith development, however, it does not address the serious questions that have been raised by a number of researchers concerning the ultimate validity of stage models of development in defining human experience. In acknowledging the limits of such sequential models for understanding student development, for example, Chickering and Reisser (1993) suggest that stage theories are premised on the basic assumption that each stage represents a "qualitatively different and more comprehensive system of mental organization and a different conception of right and wrong. Progress occurs in an invariant sequence, with thinking becoming less concrete and more abstract" (p. 18). Chickering and Reisser further assert that "[D]evelopment for college students, which today includes persons of virtually all ages, is a process of infinite complexity. Just as students are notorious for not proceeding through the institution according to schedule, they rarely fit into oversimplified paths or pigeonholes" (p. 34). Further supporting their conclusions, Chickering and Reisser cite the work of King (1990), who argues that the description of cognitive processes typical of most stage theories are oversimplified and not consistent with many research findings.

> For example, people don't seem to change from the exclusive use of one set of assumptions to the exclusive use of those of the next adjacent stage; rather, the use of assumptions characteristic of several stages at once often has been found. Stage usage seems to be influenced by a variety of individual factors (e.g., consolidation of existing structures, fatigue, readiness for change) and environmental factors (e.g., whether one is asked to create one's own solution to a problem or to critique someone else's solution, explaining one's beliefs verbally or in writing) [quoted in Chickering & Reisser, 1993, p. 36].

As an anthropologist, I would add to other critiques of stage theories a fundamental question concerning their universal applicability across cultures. Few studies have been conducted that document the applicability of stage models of development in other cultures. In raising questions about Fowler's theory, Batson et al. (1993) cite its emphasis on liberal Christian theology. To take this thinking a step further, I would suggest that stage theories in general are premised on American values of individualism and autonomy. They assume that progressive development occurs as individuals engage in an increasing level of independent thinking, become more autonomous and less embedded in family ties, and reject authority. In contrast, many other societies around the world place a higher value on community than on individualism, and define maturity as developing the ability to subsume individual urges and needs to the agreed-on common good. Fowler's and Park's theories refer to such a possibility as the highest stage of faith development, but they also contend that the ability to reach this stage is rare, thereby implying that it is the exception rather than the norm.

Robert Kegan's (1982) model of cognitive development provides an important corrective to other developmental frameworks that are premised on the supposition that development is a linear and invariant sequential series of accomplishments, with differentiation, separation, and increasing autonomy as the desired result. In his view, these developmental models lose sight of the fact that adaptation is equally about integration, attachment, and inclusion. Kegan's analyses lay the groundwork for exploring new approaches for understanding the developmental process. His theory emphasizes the interaction between intimacy and autonomy as a critical developmental process, specifically the dynamic between "the yearning to be included, to be part of, close to, joined with, to be held, admitted, accompanied [and] the yearning to be independent or autonomous, to experience distinctiveness, . . . one's individual integrity" (p. 107). In proposing frameworks for understanding student development Chickering and Reisser (1993) also emphasize the importance of accounting for the complex "interplay between autonomy, interdependence, and intimacy" and the importance of interpersonal relationships in accounting for student development. In their revision of Chickering's earlier seven vectors of student development, Chickering and Reisser give greater emphasis to the importance of developing *mature interpersonal relationships*. Rather than a predetermined, linear sequence, Chickering and Reisser define "the seven vectors as maps to help us determine where students are and which way they are heading. Movement along any one can occur at different rates and can interact with movement along others" (1993, p. 34). The developmental process itself consists of the acquisition of skills and strengths within each of the seven vectors. Further, unlike the majority of developmental theories, Chickering and Reisser's theory "assumes that emotional, interpersonal, and ethical development deserve equal billing with intellectual development" (1993, p. 39).

CONCLUSIONS

Despite some significant questions about the universal applicability of Fowler's and Park's theories of faith development, they represent the most thorough investigations to date into how individuals develop their religious and spiritual attitudes and beliefs, and as such provide useful heuristics for guiding the work of student affairs professionals. Students in our classes will vary in their faith development or faith orientation. And individual differences in faith development or orientation can have significant implications for students' understanding of curricular content and their response to pedagogical practices. As an example, using Fowler's formulation, a student with a "Mythic-Literal Faith" will be affected by the college experience in very different ways than will one whose faith is "individuative-reflective", "conjunctive", or "universalizing". In Parks's terms, one who holds "adolescent or conventional faith" will respond very differently from one who holds "tested adult" or "mature adult faith". Our ability to deal with this diversity of faith orientation sensitively and helpfully will be enhanced by understanding the key theories concerning faith development.

Parks's emphasis on what she calls *community*, or the social environment, as one of the three interdependent components of her model of faith development, is an area that has received relatively little attention in other developmental models, which focus primarily on defining and understanding the cognitive and affective components of development. Extrapolating from the component of community in her model, Parks proposes that the college environment presents a significant opportunity for fostering the faith development of young adults. Higher education is "distinctively vested with the responsibility of teaching critical and systematic thought and initiating young lives into a responsible apprehension first of the realities and questions of a vast and mysterious universe and second of our participation within it. Higher education is intended to serve as a primary site of inquiry, reflection, and cultivation of knowledge and understanding on behalf of the wider culture" (2000, p. 10). Because of their potential to serve as mentoring environments, institutions of higher education can play a powerful role in the process of faith development among young adults. Parks encourages educators to become more mindful of their role in preparing young people not only in their intellectual development and to enter the world of work but also in their quest for and practice of faith. "Spiritual formation and religious faith development happen best in tandem with the whole flow of one's life. This means that young adults need access to religious faith communities" while they are engaged with the academy (p. 199).

The multiple perspectives presented in this chapter for understanding what religious and spiritual experiences mean in people's lives underline the complexity of the task we face in advocating a renewed engagement at our institutions with issues of authenticity, meaning, and purpose—*and* with religion and spirituality. Given the historical prominence of religious values and religious institutions in shaping the social, political, and economic lives of Americans and of our institutions of higher education, we cannot ignore the importance of religion in today's culture. And on our campuses, we must not continue to overlook the controversies associated with diverse religious positions and the heat that these generate when the conversation turns to issues of authenticity and spirituality, purpose, meaning, and values. These controversies are uncomfortable because they usually involve deep personal and emotionally held beliefs, values, and systems of meaning. As illustrated in Chapter Three, religious beliefs and values are generally closely associated with social values and personal social choices: where to live, who one's friends will be, what political candidate to support, what job to choose. We now live in a religiously pluralistic society. Just as we have embraced multiculturalism to respond to the diverse racial and ethnic composition of our population in the twenty-first century, we now need to create safe spaces for expressing and appreciating the diverse religious perspectives of our students, faculty, administrators, and staff members.

CHAPTER THREE

The Influence of Religion and Spirituality in Shaping American Higher Education

Liesa Stamm

The history of American higher education is integrally linked to the dominant role of Christian churches in shaping American social and political institutions. From the early colonial period until well into the twentieth century, a growing number of colleges and universities were founded throughout the country by a range of Christian churches, with the declared purpose of promoting Christian values and morality. As Marsden (1992) indicates, during most of its history, American higher education "was thought of as a religious enterprise, as well as a public service" (p. 10). Values formation and cultural learning, in addition to professional preparation, were considered vital societal functions provided by institutions of higher education.

In defining our understanding of authenticity and spirituality in Chapter One, we contrasted religion, which refers to "belonging to and practicing a religious tradition," with spirituality, which can be understood as "a personal commitment to a process of inner development that engages us in our totality" (Teasdale, 1999, p. 17). Although many Americans today are more comfortable with spiritual seeking than with engaging in the practices of traditional religious institutions, the basic values and beliefs of America's religious establishments still influence the public discourse, as well as the private experiences, of a great number of Americans.

Religious and spiritual experiences are a fundamental aspect of human existence. All societies at all periods of history have developed systems of shared values and practices that guide personal morality and are grounded in traditions of belief in powers that transcend the individual, regardless of whether these are defined as God, gods, saints, the Buddha, Brahman, or the spirits of the natural world or of the ancestors. As organized bodies of belief and practice, formal religions and religious institutions provide their followers with definitions and categories for interpreting the world around them, with systems of personal and collective meaning and purpose for understanding their life experiences, and with the basis for personal and societal decision making.

Religious beliefs and practices and the institutions that maintain and promote them have determined many of the major events in world history and continue to have a significant influence in many parts of the world today. It is impossible to comprehend the history of the United States, for example, without reference to the profound impact of formal religious institutions and religiously defined morality on the development of American culture and society. And for us to examine the potential of higher education to engage in deeper questions of authenticity, spirituality, meaning, and purpose, it is critical to understand the wider social and historical context of religious and spiritual beliefs and practices in the United States in which institutions of higher education are embedded.

FROM DENOMINATIONALISM TO DIVERSITY: THE CHANGING NATURE OF AMERICAN RELIGIOUS AND SPIRITUAL LIFE

Historically, Christianity, particularly what has been called "Mainline Protestantism," was a powerful force in determining American social, economic, and political life until well into the twentieth century. The early history of European settlement and the establishment of the American colonies laid the foundation for the significant influence that religious institutions have exerted on American life until the last half of the twentieth century. A large proportion of the first European settlers were religious dissidents seeking new opportunities to live out religious beliefs and practices that were banned and persecuted in their own societies. These early settlers founded new societies in the colonies based on their religious laws and practices. Ironically, as the new societies developed and prospered, they excluded from full participation, and in some cases persecuted, those who did not accept membership in the official religious denomination. The legacy of these early settlers remains an aspect of American culture today, for example, in the undercurrents of "Puritan morality" and in the "Protestant ethic" that continue to define our attitudes toward work.

Although the waves of European immigration in the second half of the nineteenth and early twentieth centuries brought increasing populations of Catholics and Jews to the United States and greater religious diversity to our country, these groups generally remained on the margins of influence and power, due in part to their initial poverty and working-class status. It was not until World War II, for example, that the term *Judeo-Christian* came into use to describe the religious underpinnings of American society. Even into the post-World War II era there remained numerous subtle and not-so-subtle barriers to the full participation of Catholics and Jews in the economic, social, and political life of the United States. Catholics and Jews, for example, faced restrictions on the jobs for which they would be considered and on the neighborhoods in which they could find housing. Many colleges and universities, including some of the most prestigious institutions, maintained quota systems that limited the number of Catholics and Jews who were admitted.

During the past fifty years a profound revolution has occurred in the religious practices in the United States, and, as portrayed by Roof (1999), "the images and symbols of religion have undergone a quiet transformation" (p. 3). Americans' expressions of religiosity and spirituality appear to be moving away from the historical traditions of Protestantism, Catholicism, and Judaism, and as Americans struggle to invent new language to describe their faith, their beliefs are becoming more eclectic, and their commitments are often becoming more private (Wuthnow, 1998; Roof, 1999; Hoge, Dinges, Johnson, & Gonzales, 2001). The essence of this transformation centers on a basic shift in the experience of everyday religious life from established religious institutions and their associated theologies, doctrines, and prescribed practices to a focus on the self and the personal spirituality of seeking. A growing majority of Americans today "piece together their faith like a patchwork quilt; . . . spirituality has become a vastly complex quest in which each person seeks his or her own way" (Wuthnow, 1998, p. 2).

Transforming America's Religious and Spiritual Landscape

Scholars of the American religious experience concur that the enormous cultural transformation growing out of the tumultuous period of social change beginning in the late 1950s and continuing through the 1960s and into the 1970s produced a profound alteration in Americans' most basic conceptions of religion and spirituality, their understanding of traditionally accepted religious beliefs and practices, and even their interpretation of the sacred itself. In previous decades Americans sought *social belonging* through their association with churches and synagogues, and practiced religion in terms of socially defined expectations and beliefs, what Wuthnow calls a *spirituality of dwelling.* The majority of Americans today focus their religious energies on the development of *personal meaning,* on individual religious and spiritual seeking, and on private interpretations. Americans are asking such questions as, "Does religion relate to my life?" "How can I find spiritual meaning and depth?" and "What might faith mean to me?" (Roof, 1999, p. 7).

Symbolic of the shift in the locus of American spirituality from dwelling to personal quest, a large percentage of Americans no longer belong to or attend churches or synagogues. The established Protestant and Catholic churches are losing their historical religious control of the American population, and the so-called alternative spiritualities are flourishing. "Many Americans now find inspiration at counseling centers and from popular authors and spiritual guides. Growing numbers of people shop for spirituality at New Age and recovery bookstores or pick up spiritual tips from films, talk shows, and news specials on television. . . . Many people take classes that expose them to science, secular philosophy, and the teachings of world religions" (Wuthnow, 1998, p. 2).

The approach to religious experience as *spiritual searching or quest* is now pervasive throughout American society. Reflective of the dominant cultural theme of self-fulfillment of the 1960s and 1970s, an emphasis on self-understanding or *self-reflexivity* is now of primary importance among the various themes in the search for spirituality. The majority of Americans today consider their own religious narratives as evolving, open-ended, and revisable. Religious authority lies in the individual believer, rather than in the church or in the Bible. It is a deeply personal and intentionally self-conscious spiritual style, not just in the obvious psychological sense but also theologically and metaphysically. "In a radically relativistic and individualistic culture, the authority of personal experience has become one of the few certain norms for authenticity—spiritual or otherwise" (Hoge et al., 2001, p. 173).

The focus on spiritual seeking rather than on religious dogma and theology is not just on the margins of society but is typical of the mainstream, across social classes and ethnic and cultural enclaves. By the late 1980s, large sectors of the population, including mainline Protestants, Catholics, Jews, born-again Evangelicals, and New Agers, were deeply focused on developing their own understandings of spiritual matters regardless of whether or not they attended churches and synagogues (Roof, 1999). Hoge, Johnson, and Luidens's study of American Protestants (1994), for example, found that although relatively few individuals express hostility toward the churches in which they were raised, there is a general lack of interest in denominational or ecumenical organizations. Rather, most Protestants have a market view of churches; they see churches as selling a product that they can buy or not, and they feel perfectly free to change from one supplier to another if there is a reason to do so. In fact, the majority of individuals in this study expressed no obligation to participate in churches at all, either because they were skeptical about one or another church teaching or because they were convinced that "you don't have to go to church to be a good Christian."

The Emergence of the Spiritual Marketplace

Of particular significance, the more intentional, self-conscious spiritual style that gained precedence in the United States by the 1980s is found both inside and outside religious establishments. Spiritual reflexivity is not just an individual trait. Established religious institutions also engage in interpretative and monitoring processes. With the shifting social demographics of religious constituencies, religious and spiritual leaders have begun to envision beliefs and practices appropriate to changing social and cultural circumstances. The resulting alterations in the practices of traditional religious bodies in the United States reflect what Roof defines as an open, competitive religious economy, which like any marketplace must be understood in terms of demand and supply. In Roof's interpretation, to stay "in business," the traditional Protestant and Catholic churches, for example, have designed services that meet the interests of a population more focused on personal spiritual fulfillment than on socially motivated church participation. Older religious language has been redefined to make it more acceptable in the new climate of "quest culture," and the concept of spirituality has been incorporated as a revitalizing religious form.

In addition to producing major revisions in the practices of established religious bodies, the orientation toward spiritual quest established by the 1980s created an environment ripe for "new suppliers" catering to the emerging quest themes predominant among the American population. According to Roof (1999), the development of this "spiritual marketplace" reflects the shift in religious narrative style from the hands of theologians and established religious leaders into those of ordinary people. The new religious suppliers take religious pluralism for granted and play to themes of choice, individuality, and the desirability of a cultivated and spiritually sensitive self.

As individuals increasingly take a more active role in shaping the meaning systems by which they live, they also are faced with a widening range of suppliers, all contending with one another in creating symbolic worlds. Outside the established churches and synagogues, seeker themes find eclectic expression in a variety of workshops, seminars, conferences, and retreat centers. The spiritual marketplace is reflected in a proliferation of newsletters, meditation cassettes and videos, psychic phone lines, self-help groups, books, magazines, and music. And spiritual seekers frequently engage in and weave together the belief structures of a range of religious suppliers, creating their own practice of religion and spirituality. Unlike the religious doctrines of the past, the new spirituality does not imply the necessity of a unitary faith and practice. "Boundaries separating one faith tradition from another that once seemed fixed are now often blurred; religious identities are malleable and multifaceted, often overlapping several traditions (Roof, 1999, p. 4).

These trends, which originated with the baby boomers, have continued into the current "Millennial Generation." As Michael Coomes (2004) suggests, the turning of the millennium has been accompanied by an increased interest in spirituality as distinctly separate from formal religious institutions. There is a "pick and choose" approach to faith that "empowers seekers to borrow the most useful doctrines and practices from a range of faith traditions; a continuation of the movement of spirituality into other areas of life, including work and education; and the polarization of faith" (pp. 22–23). In addition, Coomes confirms the connections between faith and popular culture suggested by the studies of Hoge et al., Wuthnow, Roof, and other sociologists of religion. He concludes that in becoming a primary conveyer of common culture, entertainment will increasingly compete with religious groups in the delivery of religious insight.

Summary and Conclusions

To summarize, the current religious and spiritual climate in the United States can be characterized not so much by a loss of faith but as experiencing a qualitative shift from unquestioning belief to a more open, questing mode. Although established religious institutions and their doctrines and practices are no longer the center of Americans' religious and spiritual life, the evidence clearly demonstrates that high levels of religious individualism do not necessarily undermine spiritual vitality. The multiplicity of new religious and spiritual approaches is transformative and pluralistic.

Although many of the old structures remain, "the meaning of religious community has itself undergone major transitions over the course of American history—moving generally from a singular, homogeneous community toward more diversity. . . . What we witness today is the rise of the 'participatory congregation'—the demand of laypeople to participate within [established congregations] on their own terms" (Roof, 1999, p. 299). The accommodation of the established churches to the current religious and spiritual orientations of their constituencies represents an adaptation to the larger culture by "institutionalizing a serious encounter between the religious and the secular" (p. 299). . . . " 'Religious capital', like 'social capital', is not exhausted by any single set of institutional forms. . . . [Individuals] are expressing their deep concerns about children and families, about social injustices, about the environment and other causes in organizations and networks that may look different but actually have goals not unlike those of an older type of voluntary organizations" (Roof, 1999, p. 301). In America today, the quest culture opens the possibility of articulating in new ways and through new commitments the experience of the sacred that is basic to human existence.

THE RELIGIOUS FOUNDATIONS
OF AMERICAN HIGHER EDUCATION

Reflecting the centrality of churches in American society during most of our history, it was considered only natural for education to be closely tied with the church. Beginning with Harvard College, established in 1636 to prepare Congregational (Puritan) ministers to nurture the burgeoning communities of New England with knowledge and respect for the Christian gospel, the nine colonial-era colleges set the pattern for church influence in guiding the directions and setting the standards for American higher education until the late nineteenth and early twentieth centuries. Each of the first nine colleges was founded by the dominant Christian denomination in the region, which maintained close ties with and supported the institution's operations during its early history. Yale College was established in 1701 as a result of dissent within the Congregational establishment over the appropriate preparation for ministers, and Dartmouth College was founded in 1769 by a Yale-educated Congregational minister following his calling for "the laudable and charitable design of spreading Christian Knowledge among the Savages of our American Wilderness." Brown University (originally Rhode Island College) was founded in 1760 by the Baptists. The Anglican (Episcopalian) Church founded William and Mary in 1693, the University of Pennsylvania (originally the Charity School) in 1740, and Columbia University (originally King's College) in 1754 to serve Virginia and the Middle Atlantic colonies. Princeton University (originally the College of New Jersey) was founded in 1746 to serve the Presbyterian congregations of the Middle Atlantic colonies, and Rutgers University (originally Queens College) was founded in 1766 by the Dutch Reformed Church to serve its congregations in these same colonies (Burtchaell, 1998, pp. 1–8). Despite the pervasive interconnections between America's colleges and universities and the religious institutions that founded them, however, the circumstances and actual authority of these religious affiliations varied considerably, particularly among the colleges founded during the great expansion of American higher education in the nineteenth century. Some colleges, for example, were established at the initiative of local communities, others at the instigation of national denominational organizations, still others through the combined efforts of local citizens and the local church, and a few by a single benefactor to fulfill the goals of a church or denomination. The vast majority of American colleges, although founded by churches, received support from state or community taxes.

The Tensions Between Religious and Educational Purposes

As expressed by the sponsors of Davidson College in 1845, the espoused mission of most of America's colleges was "for securing the means of Education to young men within our bounds of hopeful talents and piety, preparatory to Gospel ministry" (quoted in Burtchaell, 1998, p. 820). Even during the early history of American higher education, however, there existed an initially unacknowledged tension between the institution's religious and educational purposes. Educators were aware that their student bodies were not necessarily called to the ministry in droves. And no institution restricted its student body to members of the affiliated church or denomination. In fact, most legislatures in granting institutional charters imposed religious nondiscrimination as a condition of the charter. From the beginning, therefore, American colleges and universities served to prepare young men interested in law, medicine, and other professions, as well as for the ministry.

The college curriculum exemplifies the historical tension between the religious and secular purposes of higher education. On the one hand, until the rise of the modern American university in the late nineteenth and early twentieth centuries, religious and moral instruction were considered basic to a college education. "Educators often assumed that religious principles and Biblical knowledge were coextensive with science, history, and language" (Cherry, DeBerg, & Porterfield, 2001, p. 2). On the other hand, the classical European curriculum formed the foundation of college instruction through the late nineteenth century, and the Christian faith was not studied as a form of academic inquiry. The religious elements of American colleges were those of piety and moral discipline, not religious theology. The theological conflicts that began to arise in the late nineteenth century, for example, generally occurred within the divinity schools and seminaries, not the colleges. Students were not encouraged to examine and deepen their faith as part of their college education. Rather, they generally were presented with Christian moral philosophy through lecture series, customarily delivered by the college president (Burtchaell,

1998). As Burtchaell suggests, "It is fair to say that while . . . [American] colleges [were] from the start identified with a specific church, denomination, or movement, there was no manifest intensity in that identification, no very express concern to confirm or to be intellectually confirmed or critical within the particular faith of their communion. There was hardly any expectation that the *quality* of faith in the church stood to be strongly served by its colleges" (p. 823).

Maintaining the Dominance of Christian Values

Although America's colleges and universities did not directly promote a particular denominational theology, all campuses until the early twentieth century defined themselves as Christian institutions, with the propagation of Christian faith and values as an essential component of their missions. Historically even public institutions, although founded as nonsectarian, were distinctly Protestant institutions. Clergy presidents and faculty were the norm, daily chapel attendance was required, and courses such as Evidence of Christianity and Natural Theology were frequently mandatory. This was true of such major public institutions as the University of Michigan, University of Wisconsin, University of Illinois, University of Indiana, and Ohio State University. As late as 1890, for example, James B. Angell, president of the University of Michigan, then the leading state university in the nation, reflecting his theological training, worked fervently to promote the advantages of Christianity as part of a Michigan education: "The State as the great patron and protector of the University has a right to ask that . . . the Christian spirit, which pervades the laws, the customs, and the life of the State, shall shape and color the life of the University" (quoted in Longfield, 1992b, p. 50).

By the end of the nineteenth century, the religious tenor of the public Midwestern universities changed significantly. Faced with the combined pressures of secularization resulting from the increasing emphasis in higher education on research, vocationalism, and specialization, and the growing pluralization in society, the required courses in Christian theology, mandatory chapel, and prayer before class were largely eliminated. The essential Christian influences and concerns, however, did not disappear (Longfield, 1992b).

Many of the broad religious and moral concerns encompassed in the previously required courses in moral philosophy were incorporated into the emerging disciplines of the social sciences and in the new approaches to philosophy. "The discipline of moral philosophy, which had been a means of teaching non-sectarian religion in the public forum, spawned such fields as economics, sociology, and psychology. Under the guise of philosophy and the social sciences, many professors at the public Midwestern schools, which envisioned themselves as the custodians of democracy and Christian civilization, advocated the values and beliefs of liberal Christianity and Social Gospel" (Longfield, 1992b, pp. 56–58). In the 1880s, for example, the emerging disciplines of modern economics and of sociology were correlated with the social reform movement, which in turn was defined as an expression of Christian values and beliefs.

As asserted by Richard T. Ely, for example, a faculty member at the University of Wisconsin and a national leader of the "new school" of economics, "Christianity is primarily concerned with this world, and it is the mission of Christianity to bring to pass here a kingdom of righteousness and to rescue from the evil one and redeem all our social relations. . . . It is as truly a religious work to lead a crusade against filth, vice, and disease in the slums of cities, and to seek the abolition of the disgraceful tenement houses of American cities, as it is to send missionaries to the heathen" (quoted in Longfield, 1992b, p. 59). Ely further insisted that reform of children's and women's labor, provision of public playgrounds, the redistribution of wealth, and the fight against political corruption were all religious subjects.

John Dewey, a member of the philosophy faculty at the University of Michigan between 1884 and 1894, provides another prominent example of the strength of liberal Christianity in shaping the new educational approaches emerging in the late nineteenth century. Although his perspective subsequently changed, at this point in his career Dewey insisted that Christianity formed the basis of the teaching and scholarship of philosophy. He maintained, for example, that "Hegelianism in its broad and essential features is identical with the theological teachings of Christianity." And he argued that "There is an obligation to know God, and to fail to meet this obligation is not to err intellectually but to sin morally. . . . Science or philosophy is worthless, which does not ultimately bring every fact into guiding relation with the living activity of man, and the end of all his striving—approach to God" (quoted in Longfield, 1992b, p. 62).

As illustrated by Richard Ely and John Dewey, the Christian faith of faculty greatly contributed to maintaining the influence of Christianity in higher education at a time of major transformations in its educational purposes and its curriculum. In spite of the fact that increasing emphasis on academic specialization and research moved teaching in a secular direction, Christian commitment remained a primary concern in hiring faculty. At the University of Michigan, for example, Angell advocated care in the selection of faculty "to secure gifted, earnest, reverent men, whose mental and moral qualities will fit them to prepare their pupils for manly and womanly work in promoting our Christian civilization" (quoted in Longfield 1992b, p. 55).

As moral teaching was eliminated from the curriculum, student associations became a major focus on most campuses for the expression of Christian sentiments through religious work. "But as America became more pluralistic and secular, and as an increased stress on research, specialization, and vocationalism and an expanded curriculum worked to further the secularization of higher education," most institutions "would abandon their earlier efforts to serve God and simply pursue a mission of service to the nation" (Longfield, 1992b, pp. 65–66).

THE SECULARIZATION OF THE ACADEMY

Although the historical tension between the religious foundations of American colleges and universities and their more secular educational purposes existed throughout the history of American higher education, the process of uncoupling the academy from its foundational Christian mission has been gradual, and provides evidence that despite the ivory tower imagery, institutions of higher education at any given time period are formed by and promote the current cultural and social norms. Numerous factors contributed to the declining influence of religion on America's college and university campuses. As indicated by the examples from the Midwestern public universities, particularly in the years between the Civil War and World War I, higher education in the United States underwent a major revolution. Until the mid-nineteenth century, postsecondary education in the United States was largely in the hands of church-affiliated colleges run by clergy presidents with a predominantly clergy faculty. By the 1920s, the rise of the research-oriented university was rapidly transforming the shape and nature of higher learning. Whereas nineteenth-century colleges and universities had the express purpose of promoting the intellectual and character development of their students through moral philosophy and required participation in religious services, the new universities being established after World War I stressed research, disciplinary specialization, and a diverse curriculum. "New private universities—such as Johns Hopkins, Stanford, and the University of Chicago—founded by industrial ty-coons, the growth of state universities under the Morrill Act, and the transformation of former colleges—notably Harvard—into centers of scientific research all worked to promote the ideal of the research uni-versity. Religious influences had accordingly been moved more and more from the center of the academic enterprise to its periphery" (Longfield, 1992a, pp. 155-156).

Transformation into the Multiversity

The gradual disengagement of American higher education from its religious roots ultimately resulted in a rejection by most colleges and universities of their self-definition as Christian institutions. Whereas theological training represented a central feature of faculty prepara-tion during the early history of American higher education, after the Civil War more and more faculty received graduate training in acad-emic disciplines, libraries and laboratories were enlarged, and learned societies nurtured disciplinary guilds. In response to the increasing emphasis on scholarship and the concomitant advancement of voca-tional prospects for students tied to these newer areas of study, aca-demic disciplines began to expand and demand more attention within the student curriculum (Burtchaell, 1998). The growing adherence in the academy to a scientific research-based approach to learning and teaching and to the development of new areas of knowledge propelled the transformation of American higher education toward seculariza-tion and total disengagement from its Christian foundations.

As reflected in the early American Ph.D. programs, the scholar came to be defined as a disciplinary specialist and, as a result, no longer had responsibility for addressing the broad interests of the public. Mars-den (1992) suggests that the ideal of academic freedom that emerged as the most sacred of all principles within the new academic profes-sions provides a powerful symbol of the profound impact exerted by the newly independent territories of knowledge on the structure of the academy. The establishment of the American Association of Univer-sity Professors (AAUP) in 1915 illustrates higher education's transfor-mation as faculty with advanced degrees and significant specialization in their disciplines began to replace faculty who were generalists. In its 1915 statement of principles, the AAUP confirmed the "sacred status of scientific knowledge and free inquiry" and confirmed that "if education is the corner stone of the structure of society and if progressing in scientific knowledge is essential to civilization, few things can be more important than to enhance the dignity of the scholar's profession" (quoted in Marsden, 1992, pp. 18–19).

The triumph of the practical emphasis in American higher education after World War II represented the culmination of the growing association between colleges and universities and the increasingly technological society that began to emerge in the 1870s. Marsden (1992, p. 20) postulates, "More than anything else, what transformed the small colleges of the 1870s into the research universities of the 1920s, and then into the multiversities of the late twentieth century was money from industry and government for technical research and development. Universities became important in American life, as earlier colleges had not been, because they served the technological economy, training its experts and its supporting professionals, and conducting much of its research. At least as early as the Morrill Act of 1862, the demand for practicality had been re-shaping American higher education."

Higher education's pragmatic mission was reinforced by the ever-increasing percentages of university budgets provided through government and business research grants. As universities came to promote technical skills over education in the humanities, the academic disciplines were increasingly fragmented into subdisciplines. The growing emphasis on research as necessary for professional advancement resulted in rewarding faculty who were more loyal to their academic disciplines than to the institution and who gave precedence to research and professional involvements over teaching.

Finally, the great social and cultural upheavals beginning in the 1950s and culminating in the 1960s and 1970s had an immediate impact on institutions of higher education. The youth-based counterculture with which these social movements are closely associated was largely initiated at and fostered through America's colleges and universities. The civil rights legislation enacted through the 1964 Civil Rights Act and the 1965 Voting Rights Act resulted in expanded economic, political, and social opportunities for American minorities. Colleges and universities responded with programs and policies to ensure increased educational access for minority populations and to promote greater knowledge of the rich diversity of racial and ethnic cultural traditions in the United States. The resulting major changes in educational access for American minorities and the increased multiculturalism of family backgrounds now typical of the American population are reflected in the diverse student bodies of today's colleges and universities. And significant progress has been made in including an understanding of American multiculturalism as an essential component of higher education's mission. Coincident with the major civil rights legislation, the passage of the landmark Immigration Act in 1965 opened America as never before to non-European immigration and to a new chapter in American racial, ethnic, and *religious* pluralism. The religious profile of American colleges and universities now has changed just as radically as their ethnic and racial profiles. It is clearly time for American higher education to focus greater attention on the religious diversity of its campuses.

The Triumph of Scientifically Based Knowledge

In accounting for the separation of Protestant churches from the many colleges and universities that they founded, Sloan (1994) focuses on the relationship between faith and knowledge. It is his thesis that the faith-knowledge relationship lies at the center of the church's endeavors in higher education. The church's claim to have a legitimate voice in higher education depended on the ability to demonstrate an essential connection between the truths of scientific knowledge and discursive empirical reason and the truths of faith, religious experience, morality, meaning, and value. Sloan further maintains that the attitudes toward religion in higher education at any given time period are directly correlated with the place of religion within society and culture. He contends that the church affiliations that were preserved in some form by most colleges and universities in the country until the 1960s contributed to keeping alive within the academy a whole realm of knowledge, of human experience and meaning, that cannot be justified by scientific reasoning. The wholesale acceptance by the 1960s of the university as the institutional center for developing the knowledge on which a modern scientific technological society depends eliminated entirely any theological basis for the engagement of churches with higher education. Today the church has become the sole guardian of faith, the college and university the prime champions of knowledge.

In fact, Marsden (1992) suggests, the movement in higher education away from faith-based knowledge toward a scientifically based knowledge came as often from Christians as non-Christians. As an evolutionary process, the secularization of the academy was not considered antireligious but reflected broader American cultural changes.

According to Marsden, the ultimate abandonment by most Protestant denominations of their extensive educational enterprises was a result of the changing nature of Protestantism itself. The ascendance of liberal Protestantism by the early twentieth century, which equated Christianity with social reform and equity, made it "awkward if not impossible to take any decisive stand against the secularizing trends" in higher education (Marsden, 1992, p. 28). Although the ultimate separation of institutions from their religious foundations was forced by their constituencies, the faculty, students, alumni, or other financial supporters, the dynamics of separation were two-sided; the process was equally initiated from within the churches as by the colleges and universities (Burtchaell, 1998). "The mainstream Protestant theologians had come to embrace totally the conventions about knowing and the knowledgeable world dominant in the university and modern culture" (Sloan, 1994, p. 144).

SPIRITUAL SEEKING ON CAMPUSES TODAY

This overview of the social and historical trends in Americans' religious attitudes and practices provides a framework for understanding the current religious climate on college and university campuses. The previous discussion of the changing relationship between religion and American higher education, however, primarily reflects the perspectives of college and university administrators and faculty. It is equally critical to understand how the decisions of administration and faculty affect the attitudes and beliefs of students. In contrast to the rich documentation of how the college experience transforms students' personal and social life, there are few systematic studies of the influence of college on changing students' religious and spiritual beliefs and practices. The studies of Alexander and Helen Astin and their colleagues at the Higher Education Research Institute (HERI) of the University of California Los Angeles provide clear evidence of the potential influence of the college years on students' basic beliefs and values. The HERI studies, for example, have documented the benefit to students of institutional encouragement of and support for the development of multicultural understandings and respect for diversity (Astin, 1993). The HERI research has not focused until very recently, however, on documenting the impact of college on students' spiritual beliefs and values.

With the renewed interest in finding a place for the examination of authenticity and spirituality, personal meaning, and values as part of higher education's mission, a number of recent studies are being conducted on college and university campuses around the country that promise to increase our understanding of this important area of student development. Jon Dalton and I have both conducted studies that provide insights into ways in which students currently define the role of religion and spirituality in their lives. In Chapter Six, Dalton summarizes the findings of his Survey on Trends in College Student Spirituality, which represents the perspectives of student affairs administrators. My study, which I summarize here, focuses on the experiences of campus religious leaders in fostering students' spiritual growth. Cherry et al. (2001) conducted parallel ethnographic studies on four diverse campuses around the country to document students' personal religious orientations and involvements with religious organizations. Carney Strange and Georgianna Martin are conducting research at Bowling Green State University on spirituality and the college experience (2004). Thomas J. Johnson, Jean Kristellar, and Virgil Sheets (2004) at Indiana State University's Center for the Study of Health, Religion, and Spirituality are measuring developmental patterns of students' religiousness and spirituality in relation to religious involvement, search for meaning, experiences of religious distress, openness to spiritual quest, and spiritual well-being. Jenny J. Lee, Aurora Matzkin, and Sara Arthur (2004) conducted a case study of students' religious and spiritual pursuits at New York University. In collaboration with the John Templeton Foundation, Alexander and Helen Astin and Jennifer Lindholm at HERI have initiated a major national College Students' Beliefs and Values Survey. It is designed to provide comprehensive multidimensional and longitudinal information on students' religious and spiritual beliefs and values parallel to the information on other dimensions of students' attitudes and beliefs included in the annual CIRP surveys. Through these and other studies, a sharper portrait of our students' current religious and spiritual beliefs and practices is coming into focus. Here are a few examples of this work.

A Comparison of Four Diverse Campuses

In response to the increasing interest in better understanding religion and spirituality in higher education, between 1996 and 1998 Cherry et al. (2001) conducted research on four diverse campuses around the country to assess the extent to which religion was a component of the undergraduate experience. The four institutions, which are identified by their geographic locations, not their real names, are as follows: West University, a large public research university with no claims of a religious tradition, which enrolls over thirty thousand students in ten colleges and offers a comprehensive range of academic programs and degrees; South University, an Historically Black private institution previously affiliated with the Presbyterian Church, which currently enrolls approximately thirteen hundred students, most of whom are African American; East University, a large Jesuit institution with a range of academic programs and degree offerings in a Northeastern city; and North College, a Lutheran-affiliated private undergraduate college in the Midwest with three thousand students.

In a number of respects, Cherry et al.'s findings (2001) parallel those of such sociologists as Wuthnow, Roof, and Hoge concerning changes in religious beliefs and practices among the American population as a whole since the 1960s. All four campuses demonstrate that the forms of religious practice on campuses today differ from those of the past in their strong tendencies toward religious pluralism and freedom of religious expression and in the shift away from denominational orientation. Religious practice, however, is not taken less seriously because it is voluntary. "If anything, the ethos of religious choice seemed to stimulate religious interest and religious enthusiasm" (p. 294). Further, Cherry et al. conclude that the increasingly diverse composition of the student bodies on all four campuses has had a significant impact on creating a climate of openness toward religious pluralism. Most undergraduates at all four campuses are "spiritual seekers rather than religious dwellers, and many of them were constructing their spirituality without much regard to the boundaries dividing religious denominations, traditions or organizations" (pp. 276–277). The researchers also found strong connections on all four campuses between personal spirituality and volunteer social service. Although in many cases students' involvement in volunteer social service was defined as an expression of their spiritual beliefs, the researchers found that "the influence also often flows the other way, from service back to religion, with volunteer work deepening and expanding personal spirituality" (Cherry et al., 2001, p. 279).

Despite the strength of Cherry et al.'s findings regarding a general acceptance of religious diversity, three of the four institutions have an explicit Christian ethos. As illustrated in the following examples, diversity on these campuses therefore appears to be defined as a tolerance for differing practices of Christianity rather than as a broad tolerance for religious pluralism.

EAST UNIVERSITY. Porterfield found that even though the students, faculty, and administrators at East University expressed a variety of conceptions concerning the nature and meaning of religion and the appropriate role of religion in shaping the institution, "interlocking Catholic attitudes toward sacramentality, personal purity, poverty, and secularization permeated campus life" (Cherry et al., 2001, p. 217). The pervasive respect for these Catholic attitudes is exemplified by the extent to which the sizeable minority of non-Catholic students and faculty clearly accepted and were shaped by them, including the self-discipline epitomized by the Jesuits on campus and a generalized negativity toward secularization. Many non-Catholic students, for example, participated in Catholic religious activities, including liturgies, and they reported that these activities enhanced their religious lives.

SOUTH UNIVERSITY. Cherry's research at this Historically Black college led him to conclude that despite the college's public image as a secular institution, "the presence of religion on campus was unmistakable" (2001, p. 140). South University students preferred to describe themselves and their campus as "spiritual" rather than "religious." Nonetheless, reflecting the Baptist and Pentecostal backgrounds of a large majority of students, the religious orientation of the campus was distinctly African American evangelicalism. Cherry found, for example, that Christian practice permeated all public events. "Founders Day, freshman investiture, commencement, convocation, and the coronation of the homecoming queen were framed as orders of worship, included the presence of the [Presbyterian] chaplain, were saturated with religious music, and focused on religious messages" (2001, p. 141).

NORTH COLLEGE. This institution is a legal corporation of the Evangelical Lutheran Church in America, and the majority of students identified themselves as Lutherans. Nonetheless, Cherry, who studied this institution, found that in contrast to the avowed respect of the Lutheran Church for religious diversity, "The practice of religion at the college demonstrated both the limits that can be placed on religious diversity and the tensions that can ensue between practicing Christians" (2001, p. 272). There is no religious practice on the campus other than Christian, although a very small minority (approximately 2 percent) of the students was non-Christian. Tension existed, however, among students with differing Christian traditions, particularly on the part of the sizeable group of evangelical students who were seeking a religious practice that was more "upbeat and emotional" than that offered through the college's Lutheran congregation and daily chapel services. And the college's required Bible course created strains among faculty members with different perspectives on the teaching of religion.

WEST UNIVERSITY. In a number of respects, West University, the large public research university included in the study, is more broadly representative of higher education than the other campuses. In summarizing her findings at West University, DeBerg concluded that in economic terms, religion at the university was "healthy on supply and weak on demand." Of the approximately 350 student organizations on campus, over 30 religious organizations provided students with diverse forms of religious practice and wide choices for spiritual quest. The university's administration, in response to recent Supreme Court decisions (outlined in Chapter Four), ensured that the religious organizations on campus were eligible for official recognition by the student government and Office of Student Affairs. This recognition allowed them to use campus facilities and to receive financial support from student activity fees. Despite the campus's openness to diversity, the majority of the campus religious organizations were Christian, with about half representing varieties of conservative or evangelical American Protestantism, including Campus Crusade for Christ and InterVaristy Christian Fellowship. The "mainline" religious organizations included campus ministries representing nine Protestant denominations, as well as the Catholic Newman Center and the Hillel Jewish Student Center. In addition, students were able to learn about and practice Islam, the Baha'i faith, Zen Buddhism, Eastern Orthodox Christianity, and neopaganism. Notwithstanding the many opportunities for students to explore religious faith and practices, fewer than 10 percent of the students at West University participated in any of the programs offered by the campus's religious organizations. The students who were involved in religious activities did so as much for social reasons as religious ones. And the vast majority of these students were not interested in "church" or "religion" but expressed a strong interest in "spirituality."

Fostering Students' Spiritual Growth: The Perspectives of Campus Religious Leaders

To obtain a broad picture of the current climate of students' religious and spiritual interests and involvements, in 2002 I conducted a series of interviews with chaplains, deans of religious life, and representatives of national organizations that support campus ministries and religious life programs. This study was part of a larger survey of research on the dimensions of spirituality and religion in the American population in general and in higher education in particular, conducted in conjunction with the Templeton Foundation (Schwartz & Stamm, 2002; Stamm, 2003). Through an analysis of the observations of the campus religious leaders whom I interviewed, I identified the following themes that define the religious and spiritual interests and practices of today's college students.

SPIRITUAL SEEKING. Today's students can be typified as spiritual seekers. The renewed student interest in religion observed on campuses around the country, however, is not a return to traditional religious practices associated with established churches or synagogues. Although a large percentage of students are interested in discussing issues of spirituality, they are not interested in exploring the religions of their parents and grandparents. In the words of one religious leader, "Students are hungry for spirituality, but not the faith and practice of a specific denomination." And as depicted by another leader, "Students are on a spiritual quest, but they find the rituals of religious institutions too traditional and no longer relevant to meet their needs."

In fact, today's students frequently have minimal experiences with an established faith tradition to guide their quests. They tend to express an "amorphous spirituality." As one college chaplain indicated, a common comment from the children of the baby boomers is, "My parents didn't give me anything to reject." Another chaplain concluded that "Today's students reflect a post-denominational era." Students are often uncomfortable with the idea of "religion," because this connotes rigid beliefs and practices organized within an established church or synagogue. The nondenominational emphasis of today's students is mirrored in the orientation of many of the primary campus ministries. The evangelical Christian organizations, for example, although espousing prescribed belief systems based on the messages of Jesus and the Bible, are not associated with a specific Christian denomination. Although it is the mission of Hillel to help Jewish students develop a relationship with God and a deeper understanding of the religious traditions of Judaism, Hillel leaders have found that many students do not believe in God or formal religious practice. Most Hillel campus centers, therefore, encourage students to understand their connections with the world Jewish community. Catholic colleges and universities around the country are grappling with how to foster spiritual development "in the Catholic tradition" for students who no longer identify their spirituality with the traditional Catholic rituals and practices.

DIVERSITY AND RELIGIOUS PLURALISM. Having moved away from the denominational ties of previous eras, the spiritual life at most colleges and universities reflects the broader campus orientation toward promoting diversity and pluralism. This orientation reflects both the spiritual seeking of students and the diverse ethnic backgrounds of the current student population. As one interviewee put it: "The college campus provides a pool of worldviews that leave many students actively searching for some absolute truth. This generation of students has been raised in a society where situational ethics and relative morality have softened the spiritual foundation that was secure for past generations."

Further, a number of campus chaplains and leaders of religious life and religious organizations indicated that students frequently are interested in exploring spiritual pathways outside of traditional Judeo-Christian beliefs and practices. In their spiritual seeking, students have a great curiosity to learn about something new, to "dabble" with a range of practices. They express a great interest in learning about the "exotic." One college chaplain reported, for example, that courses in Eastern religious traditions such as Buddhism and Hinduism are now very popular, and the Judaic Studies department was eliminated. Reflecting this interest, a number of colleges and universities now have multifaith centers that support student-run spiritual activities and the worship services of a range of faith traditions.

SOCIAL JUSTICE AND COMMUNITY SERVICE. Reflecting a long-standing component of most religious traditions in the United States, many students experience service as "faith in action." Students are strongly committed to involvement in activities to promote social justice and community improvement and often define this service as an expression of their spirituality.

Dimensions of Students' Religiousness and Spirituality at Indiana State University

Johnson et al. (2004) initiated a study of the different dimensions of students' religiousness and spirituality in 2000 as part of their research on the relationship between alcohol use and religion and spirituality in college students. As educators and clinicians, the authors also were interested in students' intellectual, social, emotional, and spiritual development during their college experience. Their study therefore included two samples of Indiana State University students: a cross-sectional sample comprising separate groups of freshman, sopho-mores, juniors, and seniors; and a prospective or longitudinal sample of the same group of students prior to entering college and at the end of their freshman year. These two samples included a total of 515 students, of whom 61.6 percent were females and 88 percent were white, reflecting the overall proportions of women and minorities at the university. All students were under 26, with a mean age of 20.6 years. Approximately 94 percent of the students identified themselves as Christians. Because of the relative lack of diversity in this study, the authors caution that their findings about students' perspectives on religiousness and spirituality may "not translate to students from other parts of the country or from other religious or spiritual backgrounds" (Johnson et al., 2004, p. 1).

One of Johnson et al.'s primary findings was that most students viewed the concepts of religiousness and spirituality as separable but significantly overlapping; for example, most students defined themselves as either high in both religiousness and spirituality or low in both (2004, pp. 7–8). In their analysis of the prospective sample, the authors found evidence of the following developmental changes in religiousness and spirituality that resulted from the college experience. The measurements of students' religious involvement indicated a decrease in public participation in religious activities from the summer before college to the end of the freshman year. In contrast, involvement in private practices and experiences of religiousness and spirituality increased during the freshman year.

Unlike the measures of religious involvement, which showed significant differences between the beginning and end of the freshman year for all students, the measures of what the authors refer to as religious distress, feeling abandoned by God or doubting God's existence, demonstrated significant differences by gender: men did not change appreciably, whereas women's responses showed a decrease in religious distress during their freshman year. Negative affect, in contrast, showed an increase for all students, as did most measures related to alcohol use.

Students' responses to measures related to spiritual well-being—inner peace, a feeling that life has meaning and purpose, connectedness to others and God or a higher power, and hopefulness about the future—demonstrate a decrease during the first two years of college but a steady rise following the sophomore year. Men's responses to measures of spiritual well-being were consistently lower than women's throughout the college experience (Johnson et al., 2004, pp. 10, 14–15).

In analyzing these findings Johnson et al. propose some tentative hypotheses concerning patterns of developmental change among Indiana State University students as a result of their college experience. There appears to be a slight increase in private practices of religious involvement from the summer before college to the end of the freshman year, but no major changes subsequently. Utilizing longitudinal data from other dimensions of religiousness/spirituality included in their research, the authors suggest, however, that the quality of religious involvement may in fact be more complex. "Spiritual Well-Being may decrease from the summer before college into the first two years, bottoming out in the sophomore year and then rising steadily. Interestingly, Religious Distress and Search for Meaning may also increase from the sophomore year to the junior year, but while Search for Meaning may remain stable into the senior year, Religious Distress may decrease from the junior to the senior year" (2004, p. 14).

In analyzing these observations, Johnson et al. suggest that some of the patterns demonstrated by their findings may be consistent with aspects of the developmental models of Fowler and Parks (see Chapter Two). They indicate, for example, that "for many of our students, coming to college leads to some separation from their old social network, including their religious network. Some students may react to the loss of religious social experiences by turning inward and engaging in private practices, such as increasing their frequency of prayer" (2004, p. 14). Johnson et al. (2004, p. 14) propose that this finding may be explained by Parks's theory that "the transition into and out of Young Adult Faith is facilitated by the availability of some form of connection to a community that can nurture and mentor faith development." The authors further hypothesize that stresses resulting from the major life transitions experienced by students during their first year of college may account for the decline in spiritual well-being and may be consistent with Parks's description of the fragility of the faith that young adults begin to construct for themselves. The observed decline in spiritual well-being, combined with the new knowledge gained through their college experiences as they enter the second half of their college years, may lead students to question their religious beliefs. Additional challenges such as the pressure to make career choices and decide about future directions may contribute to students' decrease in public religious involvement. These combined factors may also account for the observed increase into the junior year in both religious distress and the search for meaning.

In proposing these explanatory hypotheses Johnson et al. emphasize the preliminary nature of their findings, particularly from the prospective data. They point out, for example, that "while there may be some utility to making generalizations about developmental trends in religiousness and spirituality in college, descriptions of how an entire group of students changes (or does not change) may mask the fact that religiousness and spirituality could increase in one group of students, decrease in another, and yet remain unchanged in a third" (2004, p. 15). For this reason, they are currently exploring such techniques as Growth Mixture and Modeling "to identify groups of students that show unique patterns or trajectories of developmental change in religiousness and spirituality" (p. 15). Finally, Johnson et al. indicate that their findings suggest a number of important questions for further research. Continuing investigation clearly is needed to more fully understand the range of students' perspectives on religion and spirituality, particularly the impact of college in furthering their development in these areas, and the potential differences among students of diverse backgrounds.

SUMMARY AND CONCLUSIONS

As these studies suggest, there is a great need to continue the work of documenting the complexity of our students' current religious and spiritual attitudes and practices. Our emerging knowledge about the religious and spiritual climate on today's campuses demonstrates that, similar to previous historical periods, today's expressions of religious and spiritual beliefs and practices very much reflect those of the larger society. The themes of quest and reflexivity documented by Hoge, Roof, and Wuthnow, for example, are echoed throughout the portraits of students' religious and spiritual beliefs and practices currently being compiled through a variety of research initiatives. Students are actively engaged in piecing together their own spiritual homes from the diverse array of world religious practices and beliefs and from other spiritual sources, such as inspirational literature, films, workshops, conferences, retreats, and self-help groups. They are less interested in, and often distrust, organized religion, finding spiritual growth through their personal quests for meaning and purpose in their lives.

In reviewing the historical changes in the role of religion in higher education, Marsden (1992) cautions against the tendency to criticize higher education's secularity and to advocate for the return to a "lost Golden Age" of religiosity. While arguing for a renewed place for religion and religious perspectives in the academy, Marsden indicates that the practices of the past were part of a Christian establishment "that provided Christianity with an unjustly privileged social and political position and attempted to promote the faith by associating it with power and coercion" (p. 12). In fact, there is ample evidence that the secularization of higher education has not necessarily resulted in the extinction of the religious and spiritual impulse. Rather, within the truly pluralistic society that the United States has become, there is a place in the academy for a continued search for greater authenticity, meaning, and purpose through spiritual and religious means, as well as through intellectual analyses. The ground is fertile—as educators we must provide the sunshine, the rain, the nutrients, and the encouragement and support for our students to pursue wholeness as essential to their education.

PART TWO

Institutional Amplification

*I*nstitutional amplification??? What's that? Someone said that the beginning of wisdom is to call things by their right name. (An admonition worth remembering in this age of mis- and disinformation!) *Institutional change* is a tired phrase and lacks any sense of direction, good or bad, more or less. *Transformation* has recently been favored. It implies change in form or structure. *To amplify* means "to make larger or greater as in amount, importance, or intensity." That's much closer to what we advocate in this volume. We do not argue for a different form or structure. We do not suggest forgoing rational discourse or empirical research. We do not discount the importance of knowledge and critical thinking. We *do* argue that these are no longer sufficient. We believe that the academy needs to give greater importance to issues of spiritual growth, authenticity, purpose, and meaning. It needs to increase the intensity with which these issues become built into our cultures as legitimate concerns, not only for students but for faculty, student affairs professionals, staff members, and administrators. So, though the term is a bit polysyllabic, *institutional amplification* best expresses the kind of changes we propose.

Our basic position is that strengthening authenticity, purpose, meaning, and spiritual growth will not result from tinkering around the edges, from adding additional special courses, new majors, and student activities. These supplementary efforts are increasingly under way at diverse institutions across the country. They make a contribution for those particular students who choose to pursue them. But they leave all the rest of the students unaffected, and the rest of the faculty members, administrators, and student affairs professionals disengaged. To have significant impact, and to ultimately amplify the institutional culture, we need changes that penetrate all aspects of the student experience and that engage all administrators, faculty, student affairs professionals, and staff.

We recognize that this is a tall order. It is a distant goal, a daunting aspiration, but it's what we must aim toward. Over time—five to ten years—that goal, that condition can be achieved by the cumulative consequences of small steps. Part Two suggests ways to begin. Most chapters go beyond rhetorical admonitions and provide working examples that can be adapted to the particular characteristics, resources, and orientation of an interested institution. These detailed examples aim to demystify this complex and emotionally charged arena and show practical ways we can act to effect the outcomes we desire.

Chapter Four reviews Supreme Court decisions that demonstrate that there is no legal bar to acting on the recommendations in the subsequent chapters. It argues that a clearly articulated institutional policy can be the cornerstone for initiatives to amplify institutional practices.

Chapter Five emphasizes the necessary interdependence between content, teaching practices, and student-faculty relationships. We argue that all the disciplines and professional preparation programs have content that can help students become aware of, and examine, their own mental models, beliefs and values, metaphysical assumptions, and future plans and aspirations. But this content will not generate that awareness and enable that examination unless it is accompanied by appropriate pedagogical strategies. Most important, both the curricula and teaching practices need to be accompanied by teachers who are themselves authentic, who are open and candid, who share their own searching, their own concerns, and their own struggles, past and present. Appendix B contains detailed syllabi that demonstrate this orientation.

Chapters Six and Seven address two other interdependent areas that go beyond courses and classes. In Chapter Six, Dalton reflects on the roots and legacy of holistic education, which has guided student affairs practice but which has, since the 1960s, largely ignored the place of religion and spirituality in the lives of college students. He examines the current movement and outlines what student affairs staff can do to reclaim its advocacy for the place of spirituality in college student learning and development.

In Chapter Seven, Dalton explores the meaning of community in the higher education setting and why social relationships and the communal forms, symbols, rituals, and meanings created by colleges and universities can nurture or demean students' spiritual impulses. Dalton argues that spirituality is deeply connected to a sense of community and that colleges and universities that seek to respond to students' search for spiritual fulfillment must be able to create and sustain nurturing communities. He describes the efforts of some colleges and universities that are seeking to promote community on campus and offers a number of recommendations on useful community development practices.

We hope the general propositions and specific examples set forth in Part Two suggest initial steps we can take to start this challenging journey.

Policy Issues: Legislative and Institutional

Arthur W. Chickering

In Chapter Three, Liesa Stamm documents the profound impact of religion, particularly Christianity, in determining the development of American social and political institutions until well into the twentieth century and in shaping the history of American higher education. Her chapter makes clear that the profound revolution in the religious practices in the United States in the past fifty years is reflected in the dramatic shift in our colleges and universities away from their original mission of values formation and cultural learning in combination with professional preparation. And these shifts are still under way.

Nationally, and at the state and institutional levels, we face a daunting dilemma. Here in the United States we have long-standing white, Anglo-Saxon Protestant and Catholic religious assumptions and habits embedded in our psyche and expressed through our symbols and rituals—our currency, Pledge of Allegiance, legal holidays, presidential inauguration, and court practices. Since World War II the United States has become increasingly diverse in its belief systems and religious orientations, resulting from significant immigrations from the Far and Middle East and from our own spiritual quests for other alternatives. But until fairly recently the Protestant foundations for our culture have gone largely unexamined in our schools, colleges, and universities.

But the challenges of religious pluralism and of extremist elements around our reeling globe and here in the United States are having a daily impact. Most of us know little about the belief systems, values, assumptions, and behaviors associated with other religious traditions. This ignorance leaves us without the understanding and sophistication we need to meet the complex global challenges we face. Without the necessary background and prior experiences, we easily succumb to stereotypes. Extremist appeals to our emotions override logic and common sense. We become suspicious of, and nervous about, community members who formerly were well-accepted and integrated participants in varied school, neighborhood, economic, and political activities. Even some of our social relationships can become strained when hit by these appeals.

When these divisions become enflamed, conflict follows. In *When Religion Becomes Evil,* Charles Kimball (as quoted in Nash, 2004, p. 8) estimates "that more wars have been waged and more people injured, killed, captured, or missing for religious reasons alone throughout the second and third millennia than for political, geographical or military reasons." We need to recognize that when a war becomes "holy," whether carried out by crusading Christians, Muslims, Hindus, or others, religion is corrupted. Recall the long and recent history of Northern Ireland, where Catholics and Protestants killed one another. Recall the millions of Hindus, Muslims, and Sikhs who killed each other during the late 1940s when India was becoming free from British rule; provocative incidents still trigger major violence in that region. In 1993, in Bosnia and Kosovo, Serbian Christians organized mass rapes, executions, and "ethnic cleansing" of Muslim women and children. And of course we have the ongoing, intransigent conflicts between Jews and Arabs in the Middle East.

For me, Nash (2000) lays it on the line accurately:

> At the beginning of the twenty-first century, the reality of religious pluralism hits each of us where we live. We must learn to deal with this new awareness with openness, respect, and critical understanding, or it could very well kill us. For Americans to be ignorant of militant Islamic fundamentalism, or of ultra-nationalistic Judaism, or of radical Hinduism, or of the proliferating extremist evangelical fundamentalist denominations of Christianity throughout the world, for example, is to court disaster.

Our earlier provincial and isolationist American world view, particularly its religious, political and cultural elements, have been thrown into turmoil. We have seen first hand what happens whenever starkly opposing religio-political conceptions of the world and human life collide. Whatever our views on world religions such as Islam might have been in the past, at the present these religions signify something dramatically different and real for all of us. Whenever these religions remain true to their original, humane ideals, then they are a force for good in the world. But whenever they serve as engines for the escalation of cruelty and violence, then they are an indisputable force for evil [p. 5].

If we are to avoid continued local, regional, and global religious strife, if we are to respond to terrorist acts with more than counter-strikes, we must become more knowledgeable about, and understanding of, the varied religious and cultural traditions whose extremists drive such behaviors.

This educational imperative is especially significant for the nation's colleges and universities. It is critical because religious diversity characterizes students, faculty members, administrators, and staff at all our public institutions and the vast majority of the private ones. To work well together, with understanding and mutual support, we need to create an institutional culture and educational environment where all of us can become more sensitive to the behavioral norms, underlying belief systems, and religious practices that characterize our varied community members. In the next chapters of Part Two we suggest specific implications for curricula and teaching, for student affairs, and for community relationships. In Part Three we consider implications for planned change and professional development, for assessment, and for leadership. But, as we discuss in this chapter, for the suggested institutional amplifications to be created—openly, thoughtfully, and in coordinated and coherent fashion—they need to be legitimized and supported by explicit policy statements. Ideally, we need explicit statements at the national and state levels that recognize the significant range of religious orientations among our citizens and the critical importance of learning about those in our schools, colleges, and universities. In the absence of those, we need to take initiative ourselves, in our own institutions.

Confusion and uncertainty about legal issues concerning the separation of church and state as they relate to educational policies and practices are major barriers to developing clearly articulated policies at the state and institutional levels. The following section outlines where things stand on some key decisions regarding college and university policies and practices.

THE CONSTITUTION

Two provisions of the First Amendment apply to issues of religion and spirituality: the establishment clause and the free expression clause. The establishment clause says, "Congress shall make no law respecting an establishment of religion." The free expression clause immediately following says, "Congress shall make no law . . . prohibiting the free exercise thereof [religion]." These constitutional provisions apply differently to state-supported and private institutions. As the word *Congress* implies, the clauses apply to governmental actions, not those of private organizations or individuals. But Congress has passed laws that apply to private institutions, the Civil Rights Act of 1964 being perhaps the most significant. This act interacts with the First Amendment provisions and has been applied in issues involving religion. But the provisions of the Civil Rights Act and the First Amendment are subject to interpretation, because both state that religious beliefs must be "reasonably accommodated." And reasonable accommodation depends heavily on the particular circumstances and contexts involved. *Lemon v. Kurtzman* (1971) helped clarify whether a law supports limits on religious expression by a sectarian college. The Supreme Court articulated three tests: "First, the statute must have a secular legislative purpose; second, its principal or primary effect must be one that neither advances nor inhibits religion; . . . finally the statute must not foster an excessive government entanglement with religion." Here are some decisions relevant to diverse practices in colleges and universities that apply these tests.

Teaching

There is no constitutional bar to teaching about diverse religions. In 1963 when the Supreme Court outlawed school-sponsored prayer, in *Abington School District v. Shempp*, Justice Clark said, "Nothing we

---

The legal issues and cases described in this section come from Clark (2001).

have said here indicates that such study ... when presented objectively as part of a secular program of education may not be effected consistently with the First Amendment."

In *Bishop v. Aronov* (1991) a professor occasionally referred to his personal religious beliefs as part of his lectures. The program chair directed him to refrain. The professor sued, claiming that the directive inhibited his right to freely exercise his religious beliefs and constituted an establishment of religion. The U.S. Eleventh Circuit Court of Appeals found that the ban on the professor's speaking about personal religious beliefs in class was directed to his teaching practices, which, along with the content of classroom teaching, institutions have the authority to control. Therefore the directive did not violate his exercise of religious beliefs nor did it establish a religion. Note that this case does not preclude discussion of personal beliefs in classrooms or through varied student affairs programs.

Student Activities Fees

Campus Crusade for Christ sought university funding to sponsor campuswide Bible study to reach out and inform students about gospel messages. University policy prohibited funding any sectarian program by a recognized organization unless the request (1) was for a secular purpose, (2) neither advanced nor inhibited religion, and (3) avoided excessive entanglement with religion. The U.S. Ninth Circuit Court (*Tipton v. University of Hawaii*, 1994) held that colleges have wide discretion in policies regarding the limited funds available to student organizations and that there was no violation, because the policy was consistent with *Lemon v. Kurtzman*. Thus colleges can establish reasonable policies for funding student organizations. They may also adopt policies that encourage discussion of issues concerning faith and spirituality by funding groups that explore these issues nondenominationally.

Supporting Offensive Personal Beliefs

University of Wisconsin students alleged that the university must let them refuse funding for registered student organizations that expressed religious or ideological views offensive to their personal beliefs. In *Board of Regents of the University of Wisconsin System v. Southworth et al.* (2000), the Supreme Court found that a public university can charge its students an activity fee used to fund programs to facilitate extracurricular student speech as long as the program is "viewpoint-neutral," that is to say, so long as the funding is not provided on the basis of the subject matter of the program. The court said, "if a university determines that its mission is well served if students have the means to engage in dynamic discussion on a broad range of issues, it may impose a mandatory fee to sustain such dialogue."

Using Facilities

Supreme Court decisions permit state-operated colleges to give equal access to groups even when meetings are for religious or spiritual purposes so long as policies allocating campus space are neutral as to religion. "The Constitution requires governments to treat religion and spirituality neutrally and the same when individuals and groups are similarly situated. . . . These cases present examples of how student affairs staff can assist students in exercising their faith within the campus community. This not only benefits the individual(s) involved but also exposes others to alternative faith beliefs and practices—something desirable for a liberal arts education and a well rounded individual" [Clark, 2001, p. 44].

Student Housing

Orthodox Jewish students said that a sexually free atmosphere in required residential housing offended their religious traditions and asked to be exempted from housing requirements. The U.S. Second Circuit Court, under the Fair Housing Act, denied the claim. Although colleges must not discriminate against students on the basis of religion, they cannot be expected to alter campus culture to fit varied religious dictates.

The basic point underlying these Constitutional decisions is that there is no legal constraint on articulating clear policies at the state and institutional levels. But as the dates of the aforementioned judgments indicate, this continues to be an unsettled arena. As we write, the Supreme Court has agreed to hear a case challenging the reference to "under God" in the Pledge of Allegiance. By the time you read this chapter, that case probably will have been settled one way or the other.

It is still unsettled. The controversies concerning teaching evolution versus "creationism," which have recurred periodically since the Scopes trail in Dayton, Tennessee, are further evidence that these issues remain unsettled.

I believe that the fluidity and uncertainty concerning these issues of church-state relationships are arguments for articulating policies. Whatever our religious or spiritual persuasion, we all need to be sophisticated participants in these dialogues as the issues are debated. Our sophistication will be enhanced if we articulate policies that describe our institutional orientation and lay out ground rules consistent with the constitutional tests and legal precedents. But, unfortunately, the heat that accompanies this particular legislative potato will probably forestall any such statements, at least for the near future.

If that assessment of our political climate is accurate, we have a chicken-and-egg problem. Any legislative initiative is likely to be met with loud opposition fueled by the special interests of those invested in preserving and strengthening a single dominant religious orientation, supported not only by those who identify with that position but by others ignorant of the alternatives. It will be difficult to respond to that opposition until the citizenry becomes sufficiently aware of, and sophisticated about, the importance of our religious pluralism to our ability to function as a world leader for democracy and for basic human rights and dignity. That sophistication will become widespread only as our educational institutions address this challenge. This means that the initiative lies with us, that our colleges and universities must lead the way. To do so we need to formulate our own particular policy statements that are consistent with our missions and our constituents.

FORMULATING INSTITUTIONAL POLICIES

Formulating such policies will not be easy. More than a few of our institutions have religious bigots and narrow minds on campus and among their stakeholders. Students complain to deans about faculty members who encourage examination of points of view that challenge preconceptions and create discomfort. Asking students to read and discuss the Quran provokes an uprising. Tackling these issues requires the kind of sophisticated leadership Stamm articulates in Chapter Ten. It also requires courageous followers willing to stand up and be counted when it comes to supporting intellectual inquiry and creating honest, open dialogue about diverse religious belief systems and varied approaches to creating lives of authenticity, purpose, meaning, and spiritual growth.

But we do have prior experiences and prior learning to build on. Developing institutional policies to encourage and support intellectual inquiry and open dialogue about diverse religious belief systems spiritual growth should not be viewed as a radical departure. We have created similar policies and programs in response to other significant social and legal challenges in the past thirty-five years. The advent of the civil rights movement more than fifty years ago and the subsequent victories of the 1964 Civil Rights Act and the 1965 Voting Rights Act triggered programs and policies to ensure increased access for racial and ethnic minorities and to promote greater knowledge about, and appreciation for, the diverse racial and ethnic cultural traditions in the United States. We have made significant advances in recognizing American multiculturalism as an essential component of higher education. Institutions have established policies, for example, that have incorporated courses on multiculturalism as part of general education requirements. They have provided incentives to departments and faculty members across the disciplines to incorporate multicultural components into their courses. Ethnic studies programs, such as African American studies, Hispanic/Latino studies, and Asian American studies, are now an established part of the curricular offerings at most large institutions and at many small colleges and universities. Institutional support for African American student centers, Hispanic student centers, and Asian American student centers is considered a standard part of campus life. Similarly, with the advent of the feminist movement in the 1970s and legal measures against gender discrimination, women's studies and women's centers have become regular components of curricular offerings and student experiences. Institutional policies encourage departments across the disciplines to include women's perspectives in their courses and to develop courses specifically focused on examining this area.

It is now time to give the same attention to creating campus environments that encourage the understanding and appreciation of the religious diversity and pluralism of American life and of peoples around the world. We need to create learning environments that promote spiritual and religious understanding and that address issues of authenticity and values. We need to use our considerable faculty and staff resources to help students examine, clarify, and strengthen their religious and spiritual understandings. We need to broaden their, and our own, knowledge about global religious diversity and spiritual seeking. Curricular and cocurricular experiences need to subject diverse religious and spiritual experiences to the same analytic and critical processes that are applied to other academic subject matter.

The rigorous research methods and analytic frameworks we use to understand other critical social, psychological, and cultural issues need to be applied to helping us professionals understand students' spiritual experiences and their development of values and personal beliefs. But our experiences incorporating similar concerns for multiculturalism and women's perspectives into our institutional missions and educational enterprises demonstrate that such research and analysis will happen only as a result of explicit institutional policies and institutional support for initiatives of individual faculty and student affairs professionals. The next section includes three policy statements that illustrate different institutional approaches.

Illustrative Policy Statements

With help from Peter Laurence I have found three examples of institutional policy statements. They come from the University of Massachusetts Amherst (UMass), from the University of Missouri—Columbia, and from Earlham College, a faith-based institution. The UMass and Earlham statements appear here; that of the University of Missouri—Columbia is in Appendix A. I submit that these are adaptable by many other institutions, public or private, secular or faith based.

UNIVERSITY OF MASSACHUSETTS AMHERST. Let's look first at the UMass policy statement.

UNIVERSITY OF MASSACHUSETTS AMHERST
DEAN OF STUDENTS OFFICE
GUIDELINES FOR RELIGIOUS ORGANIZATIONS AUGUST, 1994

As a public institution, the University of Massachusetts affirms the right to the free exercise of religion by all its members. The University may not abridge the rights of individuals to believe and worship as they please, nor may it sanction particular forms of religious expression to the exclusion of others. The University has, however, an obligation to insure that religious groups using the facilities of the University are willing to abide by those standards and values which apply to all groups. Such values are rooted in the University's commitment to free inquiry, respect for diversity, and freedom from coercion, and are related to its primary mission of offering an educational environment in which the pursuit of truth and knowledge is honored and affirmed.

Members of the University community, be they people of faith or of no faith, are encouraged to discuss with one another the richness of their own heritage, values and beliefs. In doing so, we affirm the worth of each individual and of the principles which he or she holds dear. We recognize that, in discussing topics of deeply held conviction, some offense is always a risk. Such a dialogue requires sensitive listening and humility. It is through the work of communicating about our intensely held values that we will learn to appreciate one another and to live with our most significant differences.

Groups promoting particular religious traditions express their beliefs and serve students, faculty and staff as participants in the greater community of the University. These groups may have access to, and use of, University facilities and services at the discretion of the University. Groups wishing registration as student organizations may seek to be recognized by Student Government/Graduate Student Senate and the Student Activities office. The Office of the Dean of Students publishes annually a listing of campus religious organizations.

It is with the goal of heightened communication that we offer the below listed guidelines. The list of behavior is stated negatively for convenience, but the positive and correlated behaviors are implied.

Behavior Which Is Not Acceptable

Any behavior that demeans individuals and their religious conviction is unacceptable. Such behavior includes:

1. The issuing of materials which threaten, undermine or distort the integrity of another person's or group's beliefs. This is not a prohibition of the free expression of ideas, but a commitment to present all opinions in a way respectful of others.

2. Sharing one's faith with anyone without appropriate sensitivity to that person's integrity and freedom to make his or her own decisions in matters of faith and identity.

3. Intruding by phone, by mail, or by visitation in residence halls, on the privacy of individuals without their explicit permission.

4. The issuance of misleading or false publicity.

5. Actions which are designed to coerce, either physically or emotionally, or which clearly damage the student's academic pursuits, financial status, relationships with parents or peers.

6. The use of language in private and public contexts which is clearly denigrating of or unrespectful of another's beliefs, traditions and/or person.

GUIDELINES FOR UNIVERSITY OF MASSACHUSETTS CAMPUS RELIGIOUS ORGANIZATIONS

The Dean of Students will appoint the University Religious Affairs committee composed of:

a. The Assistant Dean of Students (ex officio)

b. One representative from the campus ministers representing the Newman Center

c. One representative from the Hillel House

d. One representative from Chabad House

e. One representative from the Ark

f. One representative from the United Christian Foundation

g. One representative of Campus Crusade for Christ

h. One representative from Intervarsity Christian Fellowship

i. One representative from Alliance Christian Fellowship

Please note that other campus groups will be welcome to become part of the committee as well.

This group meets at least four times each semester to review the state of activity by campus religious groups; to consider the degree to which such groups are abiding by the principles below; to provide a forum for mutual consultation among campus religious groups; and to receive from the University administration information or requests relevant to its purpose. Responsibility for calling these meetings will rest with the Dean of Students Office.

In order to promote the appropriate expression of religious freedom at the University of Massachusetts, the following principles and guidelines have been adopted, and agreed to, by the undersigned representatives of campus religious groups and organizations. Other such groups which may come to the University in the future will be asked to join in this agreement. We agree that:

a. Our activities involving University members shall be carried out in accord with the Policy for Religious Groups at the University of Massachusetts (adopted 1994).

b. All on-campus meetings of religious groups shall be open at all times to any interested person. Further, all advertising of these programs, services, etc., will clearly identify the sponsoring religious organization.

c. The involvement of student members of the University in the activities of religious groups shall be judged against the standard of their primary reason for attendance at the University, that is, to be engaged in the educational process of teaching and learning. Thus, students shall be free and encouraged by the leaders of religious groups to maintain a high degree of involvement in their academic pursuits and obligations as members of the wider community, and shall not be coerced into religious participation which detracts from such involvement.

d. The presentation of religious ideas shall always be subject to the freedom of individuals to accede to, or reject, such ideas in an atmosphere of openness and respect for their integrity, beliefs, and all the differences which characterize the University community.

e. Groups will not require, explicitly or implicitly, any financial contribution in order for an individual to participate fully in the regular activities of a campus religious group.

f. Members of the groups will respect one another's traditions and efforts in ministry, and insofar as possible, be supportive of one another. They will refrain from publicly or privately demeaning the beliefs and practices of groups or individuals which differ from their own, and seek to represent the beliefs of other faiths accurately.

g. In all activities there shall be no misrepresentation of ideas, methods, or purposes.

h. Religious groups will be guided in their efforts by a commitment to enhancing the religious and moral life of the community and its members, and by a willingness to allow their values and beliefs to be openly challenged, tested, and affirmed.

i. All disagreements over the observance or violations of these guidelines and/or the policy on religious organizations will be subject to review by the University Religious Affairs Committee. Should a group feel that it has been unfairly or inappropriately treated, it may ask the committee to provide a forum for discussion and resolution of the issue. Recommendations for University action will be forwarded to the Dean of Students.

This policy statement and its guidelines make clear that UMass Amherst recognizes and respects the religious diversity among its students, faculty members, student affairs professionals, staff, and other stakeholders. The university explicitly values the educational potentials that lie in this diversity and encourages sharing those varied perspectives. It is clear about both positive and negative behaviors and allocates responsibility for oversight to a broadly representative group.

EARLHAM COLLEGE. In his inaugural address in spring 1998, Douglas C. Bennett said, "We have no small or ordinary mission at Earlham. We do not merely seek to give those who come better skills and improved capabilities. . . . We seek to transform lives, and we will be satisfied with nothing less." In *Quaker to the Core: Welcoming All* (Bennett, 2000) he says, "The faith and practice of Friends at Earlham also supports our creating a plural community, in religious and other terms. There is 'that of God' in every person, not just within those who are drawn to Quaker beliefs. . . . But can we remain true to our Quaker foundations and also welcome all who come to seek the truth in our learning community? Could we write a statement that both reassured us that this was possible and also provided guidance for making this so?" His article describes the team and the process by which they addressed that challenge. Here is their product.

RELIGIOUS LIFE AT EARLHAM COLLEGE

Earlham is a crossroads college. We are a meeting place of different cultures, different academic disciplines, and differing perspectives. Religious life at Earlham is constituted by four overlapping communities.

A Quaker Community

Earlham is a Quaker college rooted in principles derived from the teaching of the Religious Society of Friends; we try to respect every individual, to be truthful and act with integrity, to pursue peace and justice, to seek consensus in making decisions, to live simply. For Quakers these principles are religiously based in Friends' faith and practice and grounded in worship. For all people at Earlham, Quaker and other-than-Quaker, believer and non-believer, these principles are not merely exhortations. They are standards by which we try to live. To assure that there is always a living Quaker presence at Earlham, we actively recruit Quaker faculty, staff, and students as an important part of our religiously diverse campus.

A Multi-faith Community

Earlham College is made up of people of various faiths and religious practices and people of no religious faith. We recognize that there should be time for Catholics to be together with Catholics, Muslims with Muslims, Quakers with Quakers, Jews with Jews, Bahais with Bahais, and so on. We are committed, therefore, to making it as easy as possible for students, faculty, and staff to celebrate their own holy days, hold their own retreats, and say their own prayers together. Whenever possible we provide special places for these observances—for example, Beit Kehilla, Stout Meetinghouse, and Interfaith House. We believe there must be occasions and places where each religious group feels itself to be the norm, where most of the participants are literate in the practices in a unique faith tradition. We do not impose our particular religious practices on others; at the same time, we welcome friends and visitors at all our activities. We facilitate participation of Earlham students in religious communities beyond the campus, and welcome our neighbors to religious practices and celebrations on campus.

A Rational Community

As a college of liberal arts and sciences, Earlham expects its students and faculty to develop their intellects to the greatest extent possible. Through our curriculum and through many activities outside the classroom, we seek to strengthen the disciplines of reason and the interconnections among them. We are a college committed to the view that the intellect can most fruitfully develop in an environment where there are plentiful opportunities for spiritual seeking and religious life. We hope the possibility of spiritual wonderment, of awe, is never absent from the classroom, our laboratories, our libraries. We do not ask members of the community to relate intellect and spirit in any particular way, but we do intend to create many opportunities for making the connection. We are a crossroads of the intellect and the spirit.

A Community of Dialogue

Our goal is to become good guests and good hosts within our various religious traditions. We want to become good students of one another's cultures and practices. Over the course of a year we hope our concerts, lectures, and other public events and celebrations represent the full religious pluralism of the Earlham College community. While we recognize the need for each group to spend time apart from others, we also recognize the need to get to know each other better, to enrich our lives by learning from people whose religious practices differ from ours and people who do not identify themselves with an historical religious community. Just as we discourage unwelcome proselytizing, we discourage continuous isolation within religious enclaves. Dialogue can sometimes be painful; the legacies of intolerance run through all our religious histories. Respectful dialogue, nevertheless, is the first step in modeling a peaceful world, in making new friends, and in deepening our spiritual lives [Bennett, 2000, pp. 190–191].

This statement was approved by the faculty in April 1999 and by the board of trustees in June 1999. President Bennett closes his article noting some "issues for the future." He says, "First, we need to live up to the statement. In drafting it, we were not trying to make new policy, only to state as clearly as we could what our intentions already were. But in drafting it we also realized that we were not fully living up to all that this policy asks of us. We are using the statement to improve our practice" (2000, p. 193).

This policy statement is clearly anchored in Earlham's educational philosophy as well as in its religious and spiritual orientation. It openly recognizes the need to become more effective in realizing the educational values of religious pluralism. It provides a foundation for improving practice.

Guidelines for Institutional Policy Statements

These policy statements from public and private institutions share some basic elements that can be helpful to other institutions:

1. They make a formal institutional commitment to supporting religious pluralism.

2. They recognize the educational value of open sharing and examination of diverse views, and promote interfaith dialogue.

3. They emphasize the importance of respect and civility.

4. They spell out expected behaviors, both positive and negative.

5. They provide special places and opportunities for religious groups and practices.

6. They discourage the isolation of religious groups into enclaves, even as they recognize the need for groups to have their own places and opportunities.

7. They support celebrating various holy days.

8. They believe everyone should be a good student of others' religions and cultures.

9. They designate a clear locus of responsibility for encouraging the educational values of religious pluralism and for monitoring on-campus activities and behaviors.

CONCLUSION

For me, "living up to all that this policy asks of us"—in other words, improving practice—is the fundamental reason for tackling the difficult task of creating a policy statement. The process itself requires that the institution be clear about what its "intentions already were." Very often that process will identify gaps between espoused values and values in use, between rhetoric and reality. It takes solid leadership and committed faculty, student affairs professionals, and staff to bring those gaps to the surface, own up to them honestly, and admit them publicly. When they have achieved those tasks, they will have laid the cornerstone for institutional amplification.

CHAPTER FIVE

Curricular Content and Powerful Pedagogy

Arthur W. Chickering

I bring two basic premises to this chapter.

First, almost all the content areas that typically characterize college and university curricula have potential for helping students address issues of spiritual growth, authenticity, purpose, and meaning. I include here not only the traditional liberal arts disciplines in the humanities, social sciences, natural sciences, and general education program but also the varied professional preparation programs, such as business, education, engineering, and nursing. Only the most narrowly focused training programs may lack that potential.

Second, realizing the potential of any particular content area requires integrating pertinent pedagogy, experiential learning, and human interactions. Simply presenting relevant readings and lectures and asking students to memorize the content and feed it back may occasionally trigger some reflection and growth, but for most persons the material remains inert, devoid of lasting contribution. Similarly, pedagogical technique, in the absence of judiciously chosen, well-organized resource materials and without rich experiential encounters won't have much impact.

Getting my arms around this range of material is a daunting challenge. Abstract generalizations or principles can be helpful. But when it comes to creating courses and classes that generate learning that lasts—especially when we aim to encourage authenticity and spiritual growth—as well as cover a body of "course content," detailed examples that we can adapt are even more helpful. Addressing and illustrating the range of potential curricular content within the space limitations of a single chapter is difficult. I try to do this by including a few detailed syllabi in Appendix B. Refer to these as you read if they seem tempting.

There is another book to be created that collects, organizes, and comments on a wide range of different courses and programs that help students address issues of spirituality, authenticity, purpose, and meaning. There are many efforts under way among diverse colleges and universities. A strong collection of working examples would help all of us improve our own courses, classes, and programs. All I can do here is offer a few general comments and some examples at various levels of detail to initiate the process.

CURRICULAR CONTENT

Curricular content incorporates the many and varied conditions that are part of human life and thought and, therefore—implicitly and explicitly—encompasses issues of authenticity, spirituality, meaning, and values. Here are some of the content areas that are particularly powerful.

• In every age and country, literature has recorded what it means to be human, to love and to hate, to experience ecstasy and pain, to be good and to be evil, to face death and to seek G(g)od. The poem, counting rhyme, play, and tale came before history, philosophy, science, or math. Reading and discussing literature, reflecting, and writing help students experience new relationships and ideas, new values and lifestyles, with minimal risk. They can observe varied forms of authenticity and fakery and test their own struggles against these.

• Historical trajectories and portraits of key leaders document the moral and ethical dilemmas associated with past times and cultural contexts. They give perspective on current social and political dilemmas and decisions and help inform personal judgments about key issues.

• Basic economic questions present sharp value conflicts. What shall we produce? How much? At what cost to the environment? For whom? How? Each of us is intimately affected by these decisions. Every dollar we spend is a value statement.

• Anthropology introduces us to diverse cultures, alternative belief systems, and exotic ways of being that can seem strange. Often they challenge our culturally bound concepts of human characteristics, social organization, values, and behavioral norms. The concept of metathought—thinking about how we think and where our behavioral habits and mental models come from—encourages the kind of critical self-reflection that can deepen authenticity and strengthen spiritual growth.

• Varied business studies confront us with tough trade-offs as communitarian, humanitarian, and larger social values interact with the individualistic, competitive, and materialistic orientations on which business depends.

• Psychology, social psychology, and sociology all bring us face-to-face with research findings that often challenge conventional wisdom and cultural assumptions. Conceptual frameworks concerning human development, motivation, learning, group processes, and social dynamics give windows on our family and community backgrounds, personal dynamics, and lifestyle choices. Such conceptual frameworks help us address our own purposes and meaning making, our issues of identity and integrity. They can help us move to deeper levels of cognitive and affective complexity so that we are less often "in over our heads."

• Teacher education and human services programs ask us to address various dimensions of intellectual and emotional development. We encounter our own blind spots and stereotypes. We learn, sometimes painfully, about our own strengths and weaknesses in trying to help others learn or cope with serious personal and social issues.

Any of us can go through our institution's course catalogue and program descriptions and identify their potentials for encouraging authenticity and spiritual growth, for clarifying identity and developing integrity, for tackling issues of purpose and meaning. With some thought we can introduce pertinent readings, sharp questions, reflective activities, and experiences and interactions that help our students—and ourselves—wrestle with these lifelong developmental challenges.

Make your own list. Consider your own area of professional expertise, the current focus of your research and writing. What amplifications would encourage authenticity and spiritual growth?

Moments of Meaning at Wellesley College

Religious tradition and spiritual beliefs play an important role in the educational experience at Wellesley College. Victor Kazanjian Jr., dean of religious and spiritual life, has spent the last ten years exploring ways that Wellesley's religious diversity can be a community-building and educational resource. One of his initiatives gives us another perspective on the potential impact of varied curricular content. It started quite simply in spring 1998 when he gathered together a group of students and asked them to share "moments of meaning" they had experienced in their classes. Here is what happened.

> As this program took hold at Wellesley, many students and faculty who do not identify with a specific religious tradition but are spiritual seekers also began to seek out the religious and spiritual life programs. They asked questions about how to integrate the religious or spiritual dimensions of their lives into their learning and their teaching. Their questions challenged some of the most basic assumptions of higher education as a place where one develops the mind separately from the emotional, social and spiritual.
>
> Many of today's students and educators, whatever their religious traditions and spiritual perspectives, are asking for a college community where the life of the mind is not separated from the life of the spirit. I was searching for a way to present a more inclusive vision of education as an integrative process encompassing all of the dimensions of life and learning. The divide between mind and spirit, head and heart is so deeply embedded in western education that it seemed that any attempt to bridge the gap would be futile. But as I sat with these students and listened to their stories, their words provided a bridge to cross this abyss. The students told of moments of meaning, inspiration, connection, wonder and awe in the classroom. The classes in which these moments occurred cut across the entire curriculum, from biology to history, from sociology to theater studies, from ethnic studies to mathematics—story after story of moments when they were awakened to a deeper understanding of themselves, of others around them and of the world which they described as transformational in some way.

One student told of a moment in molecular biology during a lab when she suddenly made the connection between the smallest forms of life and the largest living ecosystems of the planet. Another student related an experience of working on a psychology project with her mentor in which the faculty member's encouragement of the student's research resulted in them co-authoring a paper. A Wellesley sophomore talked about a mathematics class in which her professor introduced the notion of dreams being useful in solving mathematical problems. A political science major shared her experience of her political science studies coming alive during a winter trip to Mexico with her class in which she was able to apply her methods of analysis in the field 24 hours a day.

Students spoke of these transformational moments coming through collaborative work with other students, through service learning opportunities associated with a course, through an encounter with a particular text, through the mentoring of a faculty member. In each case the students talked about these moments as transformational in their lives and often representing a spiritual dimension to their education.

As I listened to students tell their stories, the questions that were foremost on their minds were questions which I consider profoundly spiritual: "What is the purpose to all of this learning? What does it mean to be an educated person? What does my learning have to do with my living? How is my learning relevant to the lives of others?" Buried in these stories and these questions was a vocabulary that seemed to bridge the chasm between the language of spirituality and the language of scholarship. I settled on a definition of spirituality in education as that which animates the mind and body, giving meaning, purpose and context to thought, word and action or the meaning-making aspect of learning.

I decided to approach faculty members with the stories told by their students. I e-mailed faculty members telling them that a student in their class had described having a transformational experience, a moment of meaning which they connected to a spiritual dimension of their education. I then invited these faculty members to a discussion about such moments in the learning and teaching process. Over the course of the next month, 55 faculty members met to discuss transformational moments in the classroom and shared similar stories with one another about such moments from their own learning and teaching. Eventually the discussion centered on the reasons for their original choice to become a scholar and a teacher. Some spoke of a passion for seeking truth, others of a desire to kindle a fire within their students, many told stories of having been affirmed as a person whose ideas were of value by a faculty mentor in their own life. Many spoke of the joy of watching students come alive in their classes as connections between self and world began to be made. After our discussions, even some faculty members who often, in the past, responded with blank stares—occasionally overt expressions of anger—at the presumption of speaking about spirituality and scholarship in the same breath, seemed now to see the connection. Indeed, it was clear to students and faculty that teaching and learning was more than passing out information, that something beautiful, something transformational was happening in the classroom and that we needed a language to speak about it.

The stories told by these students and faculty seemed to awaken in them a vision of education as a place of liberation for the human spirit from the bondage of ignorance. This vision challenges the notion that colleges and universities have become simply dispensers of marketable skills, which, when purchased, enable people to manipulate others in order to gain power, prestige and material wealth. This vision seeks to look beyond education as the imparting of information. It is rather a process of transforming that information into knowledge that will enable us to engage the world in a heartfelt way.

Kazanjian's experiences with students and faculty members at Wellesley College powerfully document the wide-ranging areas of curricular content that can help students address issues of authenticity and spiritual growth, and related dimensions of personal development. They also demonstrate how meaningful it is for faculty members to be engaged with students concerning issues like these as they interact with their varied areas of professional expertise.

Patrick Morton taught mathematics at Wellesley. He participated in some of Victor's Moments of Meaning discussions. He believes that many problems students have with math flow from the absence of connections to their own "inner life" or "wholeness." They need to have experiences that help them recognize that the facts, concepts, techniques, and blind alleys are part of an indivisible reality. They need imagination, spontaneity, and opportunities for exploration because mathematics is so structured and rational. They need to try their own ideas, make choices, suffer mistakes, see what succeeds and what fails. Morton (1999) aims to have the problems "get under their skin . . . so they have trouble keeping them out of their minds. . . . Then the problem becomes a guide helping her discover something new in her own inner landscape" (pp. 74–75).

Morton reaches for his goal with six key learner-oriented pedagogical strategies:

1. Make sure she chooses a topic she really wants to learn about.

2. Make sure the problem is sufficiently large and difficult so as to challenge her imagination and provoke widespread exploration, but also sufficiently circumscribed so that she can make progress.

3. Provide readings and exercises that that supply background knowledge of the subject.

4. Allow time to be playful and to explore, to get stuck and frustrated.

5. Meet regularly to answer questions and discuss the problem.

6. In these meetings, continually plant seeds related to the overall problem.

For me, this is a powerful example of how a thoughtful teacher integrates content and pedagogy in ways that help students connect with their own "inner landscape." It illustrates how good learner-oriented teaching can use almost any curricular content to feed the spirit and nurture the soul. (Given my own limitations, I am tempted to say, "even mathematics.")

A fundamental principle for generating lasting learning that has an impact is to start with a problem that is emotionally, intellectually, or pragmatically important to the learner. The complex curricular content areas that characterize the humanities, social sciences, and natural sciences provide ample and spacious opportunities to make sure each learner tackles something he or she really wants to learn about. Then we can respond to that motivation and the strong energy it generates by supplying resources, personal support, and provocative interventions.

Some Illustrative Syllabi

To illustrate some nuts-and-bolts interactions between content and pedagogy, Appendix B shares some detailed course descriptions. First Year Seminar 13: Erôs and Insight, taught by professors Joel Upton, art history, and Arthur Zajonc, physics, at Amherst College, appeals to me because it seems like an excellent way to help first-year students broaden their perspectives on ways of knowing, and because it illustrates the power of interdisciplinary team teaching. When Zajonc sent me these materials he said, "I don't know what you will make of the syllabus. Much of the technique of the course is invisible. . . . We are trying to really integrate what we call 'contemplative knowing' as a crucial modality of inquiry . . . relating it specifically to content, be it art, poetry, or science. The idea being that we can know more, more fully and deeply, by including contemplative knowing as a legitimate part of our academic work."

The introduction to this course says, "Our central purpose is to introduce a way of knowing: namely, contemplative knowing . . . defined here as attentiveness, openness/embracing the obverse and sustaining contradiction . . . which in turn becomes erôs and insight which together comprise 'love.'"

Upton and Zajonc challenge the separation of "art" and "science" as an arbitrary construction. With self-reflective contemplative knowing, art and science "re-emerge as distinct, but still superficially different ways of knowing, transcended by a commonality of human longing for 'wholeness' from an acknowledged condition of conscious, i.e., mortal fragmentation."

The topic for the first class meeting is "Who are you? Aspirations . . . intellectual, academic, personal?" The first essay (one page) asks students to "Characterize your experience of being silent." At least two preliminary drafts are required for each essay, due at specified dates.

Rembrandt and Kepler are used as "exemplars." Throughout the course there are readings from Goethe, C. S. Lewis, Rilke, Plato, and others. Essay assignments ask students to address similarities and differences and also call for self-reflection. Students are asked to "construct a value and neutral color chart" and then asked to write about how "attentiveness and openness" were instrumental in their construction of the chart.

The last essay assignment (four pages) reads, "How might FYS 13 cause you to re-imagine how you will construct your education from this point forward? Be specific in your accommodation to the enduring dynamic relation of erôs and insight as the basis of contemplative knowing."

This multidisciplinary course exemplifies some basic principles about learning that lasts and that helps students deepen their understandings about reaching for authenticity and spiritual growth. It starts and ends with self-reflection and employs that throughout. It uses diverse readings and exercises and calls for solid academic analyses. And note the similarity to Morton's basic approach and his principles. Appendix B shares the detailed syllabus.

Another creative syllabus comes from a course called Agony and Ecstasy: Spirituality Through Film and Literature, taught by Augie Turak, at Duke University. Some of his introductory language gives the essence of his approach:

The unexamined life is not worth living. —Socrates

To live is the rarest thing in the world. Most people exist, that is all. —Oscar Wilde

Socrates and Oscar Wilde point to something we all sense deep-down: That to stumble through life without thinking, to simply "get through" by bowing to the overwhelming pressure to just do "what everyone else is doing," to not answer the call of Thoreau to "live deliberately," would somehow be the most tragic epitaph that could be applied to a life. Many great and minor figures throughout the ages have made it their life's mission to wrestle with the fundamental questions of life and to bring their insights, or at the very least the "agony and ecstasy" of their struggle, to others.

To see clearly is poetry, prophecy, and religion—all in one. —John Ruskin

One of the most powerful and captivating ways these struggles and insights have historically been brought to life is through the medium of film and of literature. Through a combination of film, literature, discussion, critical thinking and personal exploration, this course will ask you to think critically and evolve your own answer to the questions "What is spirituality?" and "What is *my* movie?" Even more, the course will offer you the opportunity to take up the artist's challenge and wrestle with the fundamental questions of meaning and truth in the context of your own life. As a result, this course will demand that you engage the materials both intellectually *and* personally, a process which can be both difficult and rewarding, exciting and terrifying, *agony* and *ecstasy*, and which in any event will be an adventure you will not soon forget. As Marcel Proust says, "We do not receive wisdom, we must discover it for ourselves, after a journey through the wilderness, which no one else can make for us, which no one can spare us, for our wisdom is the point of view from which we come at last to regard the world."

Their first assignment asks students to "Write down all the spiritual elements/metaphors in *The Matrix*." Other recommended readings and viewings for this course include Plato's *Allegory of the Cave*, Richard Bach's *Illusions: Confessions of a Reluctant Messiah,* and *The Karate Kid.* The course proceeds through a rich mix of films and readings accompanied by both analytic and self-reflective writing and exercises. See Appendix B for the detailed syllabus.

I hope these illustrative courses and pedagogical perspectives suggest what can be done when thoughtful teachers take seriously the goal of strengthening spirituality, authenticity, purpose, and meaning.

An Institutional Initiative

Here is an illustration that suggests what can be done when a major research university takes such outcomes seriously. Rutgers University is the flagship of New Jersey's public higher education system. I quote from a proposal developed by Livingston College of Rutgers University, supplied by Liesa Stamm, who helped create it.

> The curriculum is the heart of the undergraduate experience. For this reason, Rutgers, The State University of New Jersey, proposes to address the gap in higher education by introducing curriculum changes that will educate our students for developing personal meaning, purpose, and values as an essential part of their undergraduate experience. Through the educational innovations outlined in our project description, we will re-engage the earlier mission of higher education to promote the character formation of our students in conjunction with the development of intellectual knowledge and skills. These innovations fulfill Rutgers' institutional vision statement that commits us to:
>
> Creating knowledge and ideas for the improvement of the human condition;
>
> Preparing students to meet the needs of a changing society and encouraging their personal and profession growth;
>
> Advancing the well-being of our communities, state, and nation.
>
> As a large, public, research university, the educational models developed through this project will provide guidance to a diverse range of other institutions around the country.

Rutgers New Brunswick campus, where the proposed project will be implemented, has 25,000 undergraduate students, 10,000 graduate students, and 2,000 faculty members. Given the large number of undergraduates, the university proposes to develop new models for the undergraduate curriculum initially within Livingston College, one of four undergraduate liberal arts colleges. With approximately thirty-five hundred students, Livingston College offers a small college environment. Livingston's historical dedication to academic excellence coupled with a willingness to experiment has had an impact on the wider university, including the development of new majors, departments, and programs. By focusing these innovations in one college, other university administrators and faculty members can monitor the progress of the proposed curriculum changes and ensure a greater impact when they adapt the changes to their students. Then the curriculum changes introduced at Livingston College can serve as models for the other Rutgers colleges, as well as other colleges and universities around the country.

PROJECT DESIGN

1. Educating Students for Meaning and Purpose

To accomplish our goal of creating a significant impact on the undergraduate education of Livingston College students, we are introducing the following model of curriculum change.

- Revision of the required first year course
- Guest Speakers Series
- Advanced course sequences
- Provision of community service opportunities

The central feature of our proposed model is to expand the scope of Livingston College's first year course required of all its undergraduates and to develop advanced course offerings designed to further guide students in deepening their understanding of their own purposes and values. In addition we will provide students with opportunities to apply their values through service in the community. Through the modified and new curricula, we will provide a sequential learning experience for students at Livingston College designed to explore the meaning and purpose of values and spirituality in their lives. As a result of these modifications, all first year students at Livingston College will learn to critically examine issues of personal meaning, purpose, and values and will be encouraged to continue their personal explorations throughout their college experience.

To enhance and reinforce the classroom experiences, a series of guest speakers will engage students in grappling with the larger issues of meaning and purpose, values and beliefs for guiding life choices. Presentations by guest speakers will be open to all Rutgers students, faculty, and staff, thereby expanding the educational impact to the wider campus community.

The Required First Year Course: "Building Community Through Leadership and Understanding." To achieve its goal of offering an undergraduate education that prepares students to think critically and to act responsibly in the contemporary world, Livingston College requires entering students to enroll in a foundation course entitled "Building Community Through Leadership and Understanding." Through this first-year mission course, the College distinctively emphasizes the concepts of interpersonal understanding, leadership, and community building, and fosters a deep appreciation and understanding of the local, national and global communities in which we must all function. This educational focus forms the basis for the development of students' leadership potential, one of the college's highest priorities.

The "Building Community Through Leadership and Understanding" course is taught by approximately 20 instructors per semester and enrolls approximately 600 students per year. Currently students explore their responsibility to and roles as leaders in their local, national and global communities, and examine the development of altruism, as well as the impact of groups on individual behavior and decision-making. Through the class students are encouraged to think about who they are (personal identity), the communities they are a part of (corporate identity) and the role of leadership in building and leading community (personal and corporate responsibility). Students are expected to develop a clear understanding of the relationship between events in the global community and their impact on the national and local communities.

Required reading examines the nature of community, the role of leadership in community and the impact of community on individual behavior and decision-making. The course currently includes a class project that requires students to work in small groups to make a meaningful contribution to the local community. One of Livingston College's objectives is to encourage students to make decisions grounded in sound moral judgement, ethical conduct, honesty, self-respect and compassion for the well-being of others.

Through our proposed project Livingston College will augment the current curriculum with an appreciation of how our lifelong search for meaning and purpose including spirituality enriches not only our individual lives, but the quality of the life of the entire community. The content of the "Building Community Through Leadership and Understanding" course will be expanded to address how a life-long spiritual search can enrich individual lives and the life of the community. The revised course will center on the following basic questions:

- What is the role of spirituality, meaning and purpose in our individual lives?
- How does an understanding of meaning and purpose effect community?
- How do spiritual values unite a community?
- How can spiritual values cause disunity in community?

Students' explorations of these basic questions through class discussions are guided by assigned readings which focus on a variety of topics, such as the confluence of science and spirituality. A unit on the confluence of science and spirituality is particulary significant for our students as we enter the 21st century which is dominated by increasingly rapid technological changes that have a profound impact on our daily lives. Classroom discussions will pose questions such as:

- How do we make meaning of transcendent spirituality in a technological age?
- How do individuals reconcile traditional systems of belief with an increasingly complex and comprehensive knowledge of science?

The required summer reading at Livingston College is James McBride's *The Color of Water.* In this work, McBride addresses the importance of faith in his personal search for values. To this existing core we will add classroom discussions based on readings such as W. B. Drees's *Human Meaning in a Technological Culture: Religion in an Age of Technology,* and P. Hefner's *How Science Is a Resource and a Challenge for Religion: Perspectives of a Theologian.*

Guest Speakers Series. To directly support instruction in the required course, we will establish a guest speaker series that will be held each semester and will be open to a large audience of Rutgers students, faculty and staff. Speakers will be selected to examine and amplify readings and topics presented in each of the courses, and may include the authors of some of the assigned readings. Potential speakers might include the anthropologist Jonathan Boyarin to speak about his spiritual odyssey in Judaism. Raised in a Jewish community in southern New Jersey, Boyarin left behind his home and his faith to pursue academic learning. It was through this learning, however, in particular the study of anthropology, that he regained interest in Judaism and became a committed—and cosmopolitan—practitioner, firm in his own tradition while regarding it as one tradition among many others. To the extent possible, speakers will be invited whose work addresses topics common to all three course additions proposed as part of this project. Such examples include the Arab-American anthropologist Lila Abu-Lugod to speak on women in Islam; Ellen Willis, an African-American woman who describes experiences as a "Baptist Buddhist"; Gary Zukava, author of *The Dancing Wu Li Masters* and *Seat of the Soul,* which examine the traditional western mode of the soul and offer a different perspective on meaning based on understanding the connections between the soul and the physical being; Imam Feisal Abdul Rauf, founder of the American Sufi Muslim Association which is dedicated to creating bridges between the American public and American Muslims; Dr. Robert Coles, author of *The Spiritual Life of Children*; and Rabbi Harold Kushner, author of *When Bad Things Happen to Good People.*

Building on the First Year Experiences. To provide students with sequential learning experiences that deepen their examination of personal meaning and purpose, Livingston College proposes to develop and/or revise advanced course offerings in order to create additional learning opportunities for students.

"Transcendent Values: The Role of Personal Beliefs in Public Behavior." As a follow-up to the initial required course, "Building Community Through Leadership and Understanding," Livingston College is proposing to develop an elective 3 credit course, "Transcendent Values: The Role of Personal Beliefs in Public Behavior." The course will invite students to scrutinize, question, and discuss the role of values in their personal and public lives. In addition to readings, students will

be exposed through guest speakers, films, and visits to art exhibitions and theater productions to leaders and educators, such as Gandhi and Martin Luther King, who have used faith to guide their personal and public decision-making. The course will make extensive use of journal writing and personal essays as a means of clarifying thoughts and opinions. The College projects an enrollment of approximately 60 to 120 students in the course.

Guest speakers for the Transcendent Values course also will participate in the Guest Speakers Series and, therefore, contribute to students enrolled in the other courses included in the project, as well as a larger audience of Rutgers students, faculty and administrative staff. Examples of guest speakers are included in the section that describes our plans for providing a Guest Speakers Series.

Readings for the course will include selections from such works as *This Far by Faith: Stories from the African-American Religious Experience* by Juan Williams and Quinton Dixie; *Abraham: A Journey to the Heart of Three Faiths,* by Bruce Feiler; Ian Barbour's *When Science Meets Religion: Enemies, Strangers, or Partners?;* and *The Active Life: A Spirituality of Work, Creativity and Caring* by Palmer Parker.

Such films as *Becket* and *Gandhi* will provide the basis for examining issues of meaning and purpose that blend the spiritual, the political and the practical in shaping meaning for individuals, and society.

"Values Made Visible: A Service Learning Experience." To expand sequential learning opportunities for its students, Livingston College is proposing to develop a second (1.5 credit) elective course "Values Made Visible: A Service Learning Experience." This will provide an intensive experience for students to apply positive values through community service. The objective of the course is to provide students with a learning opportunity to reflect how engagement with the community relates to individual quests for meaning and purpose, and how individual values can translate into positive action for the community. The College anticipates that between 35 and 60 students will enroll in this learning experience.

2. Preparing Faculty to Engage Students in Examining Meaning and Purpose

Challenging curriculum and inspiring educational goals provide a solid framework to guide the educational process. Effective learning, however, is most fully realized through the strength and dedication of faculty. To insure that instructors fully understand and reflect the goals of the proposed curriculum revisions in their teaching, we are planning to develop a series of seminars and workshops to assist them in designing their pedagogical approaches for educating students in meaning and purpose. Through the seminars and workshops, the instructors will explore readings and research on character development. They will grapple with the challenge of how to address the inner or personal dimension of knowledge with students in a way that honors differences and avoids promoting a single definition and approach. The seminars and workshops will provide guidance to instructors in the difficulties involved with teaching about issues of personal identity, values, and spirituality from a variety of perspectives without endorsing a particular point of view. In addition, instructors will work together on developing reading and writing assignments and will delineate the range of appropriate expectations for students' responses to and analyses of the topics presented in classes and through their readings. Possible readings for the faculty seminars and workshops include: Reverend Scotty McLennan's *Finding Your Religion: When the Faith You Grew Up with Has Lost Its Meaning*; Leon Kass's *The Hungry Soul: Eating and the Perfecting of Our Nature*; and Sharon Daloz Parks's *Big Questions, Worthy Dreams*.

We anticipate that as part of our proposed project at least 20 instructors will be involved in developing new approaches to teaching that encourage students to examine their personal meaning, purpose, and values. The instructors for these courses will include tenured and tenure-track faculty, administrators, professional staff, and graduate students from a range of disciplines. The proposed faculty seminars and workshops are not only critical to insuring the successful achievement of our curriculum innovations, but provide an opportunity to begin to address the findings of the Astins' study (1999) that many college and university faculty are eager to examine issues of personal values, meaning and purpose with their students and colleagues.

The next several pages of the proposal describe complex and comprehensive plans for project evaluation and dissemination. The evaluation plans call for a combination of surveys and focus groups. The surveys include the Higher Education Research Institute's College Students Beliefs and Values Survey and their Faculty Survey, as well as the university's Student Instructional Ratings Survey. Plans for dissemination spell out strategies for sharing results internally with key institutional constituents. They also describe various conferences, presentations, and publications to share the programs and findings with diverse higher education audiences. Appendix C shares these details.

I submit that this is an eminently sound and workable approach to tackling curricular revisions that will strengthen education for meaning and purpose in a large, culturally diverse, public research university that is the flagship for the system. It integrates content and pedagogically powerful strategies. It addresses the general institutional culture with a lecture series. Most important, it provides professional development programs to help faculty members create the changes in curricular content and pedagogical practices that will make for educationally powerful experiences.

I hope these illustrative materials concerning specific content areas and courses—including those in Appendix B—and concerning a major institutional initiative demonstrate that a very wide range of curricular content, accompanied by appropriate pedagogy, can help students address their important issues concerning spiritual growth, authenticity, purpose, and meaning. But these varied content areas need to be accompanied by powerful pedagogy.

TEACHING, LEARNING, AND STUDENT-FACULTY RELATIONSHIPS

When Diana Chapman Walsh, president of Wellesley College, provided an overview for *Education as Transformation,* she said, in part, "To support our students in this process of transformational growth, we need learning environments that integrate into the educational process all of the student experience: curricular, extracurricular, residential, social, inter and intrapersonal. And we must address the central question of how to find greater coherence, meaning, and purpose in academic life. This brings us to . . . the many questions related to pedagogy, broadly defined. . . ." (1999, p. 5).

No matter how rich and provocative the curricular content, it will not generate learning that lasts, nor will it stimulate spiritual growth or raise questions about authenticity, purpose, and meaning, unless it is accompanied by appropriate teaching. A text and lectures, with midterm and final exams, won't cut it.

In the brief space of this chapter I do not aim to synthesize what we now know about effective teaching to create learning that lasts and to encourage authenticity and identity, purpose and meaning, integrity, and spiritual growth. My purpose here is more limited. First, I share some basic distinctions and perspectives. Then I suggest some key pedagogical ingredients that are especially important for encouraging authenticity and spiritual growth.

Some Basic Concepts

Three basic perspectives underlie my orientation: the difference between education and training, research on mental models, and the distinction between "surface learning" and "deep learning."

EDUCATION AND TRAINING. The distinction I make between training and education is a cornerstone for much of my thinking. The purpose of training is to take a collection of diverse persons and make them more alike. It aims to give them a common set of skills; a base of shared information and knowledge and, often, shared values; and identification with some particular cause or purpose. I contrast it sharply with education. The Latin root of the word is *educare,* which means "to lead out or to draw forth." For me, education starts with the learner. It takes a collection of diverse persons and helps each of them become more what she wants to be, to realize her own personal potentials and talents, to achieve her own purposes and aspirations.

Both training and education are important. I certainly would not want to be operated on by an untrained surgeon, flown by an untrained pilot, or represented by an untrained lawyer. But having broadly educated persons who function at high levels of cognitive and affective complexity is critical for addressing the daunting global and domestic issues and the personal and public problems we all face. Most training does not challenge learners to move to those higher levels of complexity.

Both training and education interact powerfully with motivation. When we teach, starting with the learner's interests and purposes, recognizing and building on the individual's prior knowledge and competence, capitalizing on particular talents and strengths while addressing areas for improvement, pretty much guarantees strong motivation for learning. Patrick Morton clearly recognizes this when he uses problems important to the learner in teaching math. But training, unless it is clearly related to a compelling personal interest, seldom generates learning that lasts. Unfortunately, much of our teaching in colleges and universities, where very diverse individuals are asked to learn the same content, at the same pace, with the same resources, using the same activities, to the same performance standards, is much more like training than like education. And that is one fundamental reason why our students often show little motivation, and why retention of content and transfer of competence are so limited.

What we know about learning is pertinent to both training and education. But you will see that some of the key findings apply most powerfully to conditions created for education rather than for training—to the conditions necessary for encouraging authenticity and spirituality.

MENTAL MODELS. "Know thyself." That age-old precept is the cornerstone for effective learning. Socrates said, "An unexamined life is not worth living." Current cognitive psychologists document the powerful ways our prior beliefs, our "mental models," influence how and what we learn. We are all "meaning-making" creatures. From our earliest days we are trying to make sense of our world. The meanings we make—and remake and remake—provide an ongoing, increasingly complex, and increasingly solidified context in which we interpret and assimilate new experiences.

Most of us assume we respond to our experiences like a camera and tape recorder. Sights and sounds that hit our eyes and ears get faithfully reproduced in the brain. Not so. Using new technologies, scientists—neurophysiologists, molecular biologists, neuroanatomists, chemists, and medical researchers—now can directly observe mental activity. They can record how the brain responds to varied stimuli, how it carries out varied tasks. Certainly there is not yet agreement on a comprehensive theory about how the brain functions, but there are findings that help us know more about learning. One major finding, consistent with a substantial body of psychological research, is that the brain does not simply reproduce external reality. Instead, apparently, about 80 percent of what we perceive and think we have understood is in fact rooted in prior attitudes, information, ideas, and emotional reflexes. Only about 20 percent comes from the "external reality." For more details on this topic, see Ted Marchese's *The New Conversations About Learning: Insights from Neuroscience and Anthropology, Cognitive Science and Workplace Studies* (2002).

Learning is a whole-person, whole-brain activity. Intellect and emotion are inseparable. That's why knowing oneself is so important. That's why examining our own prior history, prior knowledge, preconceptions, attitudes and values, and emotional reflexes is critical for significant learning. That's why we must start with our learners, recognizing their diverse backgrounds and prior learning. It's why we need to help them examine their own mental models. Their prior learning, dispositions, preferences, and motives powerfully influence their capacities for learning.

We all are loaded with mental models strongly associated with how we define our identity and how we feel authentic. We have models of appropriate purposes. We have developed strategies for making meaning. We have our own more or less articulated conceptions of spirituality and of how we might pursue spiritual growth. Our challenge is to become more aware of how these built-in reflexes operate so that we can become more intentional about modifying them as seems appropriate for our continued growth and development as we encounter changing circumstances and conditions throughout our life span. Of course, confronting our mental models and the varied biases associated with them can be upsetting. We can be thrown off balance. Significant learning and personal development—in any area—involves our going through challenging cycles of differentiation and integration. Those cycles are often accompanied by concurrent experiences of lost and regained equilibrium. We are thrown off balance and need time and support to recover. These processes will be both especially challenging and especially important if we are to encourage authenticity and spirituality. But we should not shrink from this challenge.

SURFACE LEARNING AND DEEP LEARNING. Recognizing and addressing our mental models means that we need deep learning, not surface learning. Surface learning relies primarily on short-term memorizing—cramming facts, data, concepts, and information to pass quizzes and exams. We know how to do it and how to help our students do it. Highlight texts. Make lists. Create outlines. Develop mnemonics. Rehearse, alone or with friends. Ask questions about things we don't understand so we have the right answers. Surface learning does *not* entail seeking meaning.

It contrasts with deep learning, through which we ask how the texts, ideas, information, concepts, and data relate to our own thinking, our own attitudes, our own behavior in the world. Deep learning asks us to reflect on our particular mental models, our preexisting prejudices. It asks how this new learning builds on, connects with, challenges our prior knowledge and competence. This is the kind of meaning making that is the primary characteristic of deep learning.

Deep learning asks that we create and re-create our own personal understandings. It asks that we apply new information to varied real-life settings and reflect on what those experiences tell us about the validity of the concepts, the limits of their applicability, the shortcomings of our own understandings, and our behavioral shortfalls. It is through engaging in recurrent cycles of such behaviors that we generate deep learning that lasts.

Studies in Scotland, Canada, and Australia find that 90 percent of students' study was characterized by surface learning. From what we know about teaching in the United States, that figure is probably not far off for us as well, because most of our teaching calls only for surface learning. It emphasizes covering large amounts of material rather than examining, applying, and reflecting on a few key concepts. Most course work is required in the same amount, at the same pace, for all students in a class. So students have little choice and little influence on what they are asked to learn, regardless of their prior knowledge and competence or the motives that bring them to the course. Quizzes, exams, assigned papers and projects—all "graded on a curve—create competitive, threatening environments. These approaches to teaching, and the surface learning that accompanies them, also generate anxiety, fear of failure, and low self-esteem.

In *The Power of Mindful Learning,* Ellen Langer (1998), a Harvard psychologist, recognizes the limited value of rote learning, canned assignments, and hurried coverage. Students go into autopilot. With mindful learning we are open to new information; we construct our own categories, recognize and try to reconcile diverse perspectives and points of view. We make choices about how we will pursue our learning, devise our own assignments and challenges, identify our own products and performances, consider how we will evaluate those to ascertain what and how much we have learned.

We also need to emphasize practice. Strong performance depends heavily on tacit knowledge. *Tacit* means "expressed or carried on without words or speech" and "implied or indicated but not actually expressed." Tennis players talk about being "in the zone." That's when everything is flowing smoothly and naturally, when you are not talking your way through a serve, backhand, overhead, or volley. Studies comparing newcomers and experienced workers show that newcomers try to solve problems by reasoning from laws or principles, going to the text. Experienced workers draw on stories, on sharing information with others. They reason from causal models but are always putting those models against their own experiences in practice. Novices are typically trained to produce the "right answers." Experts work from socially constructed, experience-based understandings, appropriate for the specific situations they confront. That kind of tacit knowledge comes from rich experiences in varied situations and from repeated practice over time.

Wayne Gretsky, the star hockey player, distinguished among good high school, college, and professional players: High school players can skate the puck down the ice; college players get to where the puck is; pros go to where the puck will be. High-performance knowledge is always connected to specific activities, contexts, and cultures. To generate that kind of knowledge we need to ask learners to create responses with minimal cues, repeatedly, over time, in varied contexts and applications. We need to ask them to represent information, concepts, and principles in varied formats: diagrams, metaphors, analogies, equations, formulas, and so forth. Theories and abstractions are helpful conceptual organizers, but effective application depends on tacit knowledge. And that comes only with practice.

The distinction between surface learning and deep learning is critical to recognize if we are to teach in ways that encourage authenticity and spiritual growth, if we are to help our students clarify issues of identity, integrity, purpose, and meaning. And we need to recognize that most of our self-perceptions and daily behaviors in these domains flow from tacit knowledge anchored in sustained experiential learning. We therefore need to provide a rich range of experiences that can expose that knowledge and help our students become more mindful about how they wish to modify and strengthen it.

Pedagogical Practices

Research and theory concerning powerful pedagogy have been accumulating for decades. Kenneth Eble and William McKeachie have been major contributors during the 1950s, 1960s, and 1970s. There has been an explosion of work aiming to shift the conversation from a focus on teaching to a focus on learning. Current literature addresses a variety of strategies: collaborative and problem-based learning, case studies, learning teams and research teams, socially responsible learning contracts, criterion-referenced evaluation. All of these strategies strengthen learning that lasts. Since the early 1970s we have increasingly recognized the educational power of experiential learning. Our understanding and uses have been significantly boosted by David Kolb's experiential learning theory (Kolb, 1984). For the aforementioned pedagogical practices to be effective, they need to incorporate all the phases of Kolb's experiential learning cycle. They must provide concrete experiences and structured opportunities for individual and group reflection. They must help learners identify key concepts and principles and apply and test those concepts, principles, and theories in real-life situations.

On campus, student government, student activities, residence hall governance and decision making, and accreditation processes for fraternities and sororities also can play a significant role. Intercollegiate and intramural athletics provide potent contexts for reflecting on social stratification, interpersonal relationships, motivation, and integrity. Off campus, service learning, internships, field studies, and volunteer activities make powerful contributions.

We increasingly respect, recognize, and try to act on the critical significance of individual differences, not only in learning styles but in developmental stage and as a function of gender, national origin, and ethnicity. We know about "levelers" and "sharpeners," "field dependent" and "field independent" learners, and neurolinguistic programming.

Excellent recent general publications include *To Want to Learn: Insights and Provocations for Engaged Learning* (Kytle, 2004), *Creating Significant Learning Experiences: An Integrated Approach to Designing College Courses* (Fink, 2003), *Learning to Listen, Learning to Teach: The Power of Dialogue in Educating Adults* (Vella, 2002), and *Learner-Centered Teaching: Five Key Changes to Practice* (Weimer, 2002).

Clearly there are numerous very helpful resources addressing powerful pedagogical strategies. But here I want to focus on pedagogical practices calling for behaviors that are consistent with our desired outcomes concerning spiritual growth and strengthening authenticity, purpose, and meaning. Perhaps the most powerful is service learning.

By now we have unequivocal evidence concerning the impact of service learning on students. Alexander Astin and his colleagues examined thirty-five measures of student outcomes concerning civic responsibility, academic development, and life skill development. Here are some of their results:

> The most remarkable finding of this longitudinal study was that all 35 student outcome measures were favorably influenced by service participation. In other words, participation in volunteer activities during

the undergraduate years enhanced ... academic development, civic responsibility and life skills. ...

The largest differential change ... occurred with the values "promoting racial understanding," "participating in community action programs," and "influencing social values." ... As a consequence of service participation, students became more strongly committed to helping others, serving their communities, promoting racial understanding, doing volunteer work and working for nonprofit organizations. They also became less inclined to feel that individuals have little power to change society. ...

Service participants, compared to non-participants, were nearly 50% more likely to spend at least an hour per week interacting with faculty. ... Despite the additional time for service participation, students who engaged in volunteer service actually spent more time with studies and homework than did non-participants [Astin & Sax, 1999, pp. 255, 256, 259].

Subsequent studies have shown that service learning has the most powerful consequences when it is integrated with courses and classes.

This research is consistent with studies dating back to the 1960s, which document the powerful impact of student involvement in diverse experiential contexts, many of which are organized and administered by student affairs professionals. But now we also know that the strongest way to maximize student learning is to integrate activities beyond courses and classes with the regular curriculum and to work with appropriate faculty members who teach the courses and design the curricula.

Jim Keen's reflections on the E Pluribus Unum project bring home the particular ways well-crafted service activities and associated interactions can lead to our desired outcomes:

First, these students make a clear connection between inter-religious dialogue and community service. Several students led their own campus religious organizations to join with other religious groups in community service initiatives. In planning and carrying out these initiatives, opportunities for dialogue about their faith traditions arose naturally. ...

Second, while the productive encounters across thresholds of difference often occur naturally, it would be naïve to suggest that such

encounters are inevitably productive of the kinds of insights and outcomes reflected in the previous quotations of comments by students.
On the contrary, the most common responses to such encounters are
discomfort and retreat into stereotyping. Most of us have seen or
heard ample testimony regarding the balkanization of ethnic, cultural,
religious, and other identity groups on our campuses. . . . Because
productive encounters across difference often involve a reconfigura-
tion of one's own sense of identity, they require effort and commitment. Encountering beliefs, practices, and, above all, truth claims
which differ from and challenge one's own requires significant self-
reflection, in order to move past the point of suspicion and into the
realm of appreciation. For most adolescents and young adults, in
most situations, it's easier to go with the flow of "in group, out group"
identification. . . .

If, in the first blush of romance, one carries naïve assumptions that
differences are superficial and we're all "really the same" across such
boundaries, the result can be a sense of betrayal when differences basic
to the identity of those across the boundary continue to persist. Such
a sense of betrayal can lead to retreat and reinforce stereotyping. Transforming "romance" into "precision" requires hard work and is much
more likely to occur in contexts which name the problem and support
young people in stepping up to the challenge of learning to appreciate the differences that make for diversity [2000, pp. 210–211].

Jim Keen's comments make it clear that encountering diverse "others" in service learning contexts and processing those experiences can
have powerful impacts on authenticity, purpose, and meaning. They
also make it clear that those experiences must be accompanied by well-
guided opportunities for thoughtful reflection on the issues they raise
for one's own identity, values, mental models, and meaning making. If
students do not engage in such reflection, the outcomes may be much
more negative than positive.

Cheryl Keen (2000) shares recent research from a Bonner Foundation project that provides service scholarships to students at twenty-
five colleges. "These students value engaging with diversity, they value
dialoging with people from backgrounds different from their own,
and they value the reflective process that generates from the discussions they have with program staff supervisors at the service sites. In
rank descending order, they also value opportunities to work for social

justice, developing international perspectives, maintaining a sense of civic engagement through their service, and furthering their faith development" (p. 231).

For helpful information about service learning and spiritual growth see the January 2005 *Spirituality in Higher Education Newsletter*. An annotated list, "Helpful Resources for Making Service Learning a Spiritual Endeavor," includes, for example, *Everyday Spiritual Practice* (Alexander, 1999), "a compilation of essays exploring everyday practices that strengthen spiritual growth and development," and *The Force of Spirit* (Sanders, 2000), personal essays about the importance of community service for "cultivating the internal spirit."

IT'S MORE THAN TECHNIQUE

My basic point up to now has been that, at a minimum, we need to recognize some critical perspectives and to exercise our best knowledge and competence across a wide range of well-tested pedagogical strategies like those mentioned earlier. But those techniques, effective as they may be for many kinds of outcomes, are not sufficient for encouraging spiritual development, for strengthening authenticity, purpose, and meaning. To achieve these outcomes, we need the perspective and orientation Parker Palmer (1999b) describes so well. "Good teaching isn't about technique. I've asked students around the country to describe their good teachers to me. Some of them describe people who lecture all the time, some of them describe people who do little other than facilitate group process, and others describe everything in between. But all of them describe people who have some sort of *connective* capacity, who connect themselves to their students, their students to each other, and everyone to the subject being studied" (p. 27).

Palmer gets more specific:

But let me reflect on a few dimensions . . . that would transform education if we could embody in our own knowing, teaching, and learning, this simple sense of the sacred.

First, . . . we could recover our sense of the *otherness* of the things of the world—the *precious otherness* of the things of the world.

One of the great sins in education is reductionism, the destruction of otherness that occurs when we try to cram everything we study into categories that we are comfortable with—ignoring data, or writers, or voices, or simple facts that don't fit into our box, lacking simple respect for the ways in which reality is other than we want it or imagine it to be. This fear of otherness comes in part from having flattened our intellectual terrain and desacralized it: people who know the sacred know radical otherness, but in a two-dimensional, secularized culture, we don't possess that sensibility any more. . . .

The second thing that a people who know the sacred would know is the precious *inwardness* of the things of the world. . . . We don't often respect the inwardness of the things we study—and we therefore do not respect the inward transformation that may be in store for us when we have a deep encounter with those things. . . .

Third, by recovering the sacred, we might recover our *sense of community* with each other and with all of creation, the community that Thomas Merton named so wonderfully as the "hidden wholeness." I have become increasingly convinced that this recovery of community is at the heart of good teaching. . . .

Fourth, if we recover a sense of the sacred, we will recover the *humility* that makes teaching and learning possible. . . . It is only with humility—the humility that comes from approaching sacred things, like life on earth, with the simple quality called respect—that genuine knowing, teaching, and learning become possible. . . .

Finally, if we recovered a sense of the sacred, we could recover our capacity for *wonder and surprise,* essential qualities in education [1999b, pp. 23–29].

Personal Authenticity

There you have some general conceptual frameworks concerning what we know about learning and about varied pedagogical strategies. You have Parker Palmer's perspectives regarding knowing, teaching, learning, and the sacred. With that background I want to share some specific examples. Someone said, "God lives in the details." Perhaps examples from experienced practitioners will put flesh and blood on these generalizations.

In Chapter One we said, "the most central tenet of our orientation toward strengthening authenticity and spirituality in higher education is that each and every one of us must be as candid and open as we can about our own orientations, motives, prides, and prejudices." In the syllabus for his course Religion, Spirituality, and Education, Robert Nash, at the University of Vermont, does this more powerfully than anyone else I have encountered. Course participants include undergraduates and graduate students, diverse in age, ethnicity, and religious orientation.

My dear students:

I want at the outset to talk about why I look forward to teaching this course. . . .

I believe that the quest for meaning in life is what a genuine, liberal education should be about. To this end, I will encourage you to engage in what I think of as true liberal learning. I want you to explore your own biases both for and against the content of the course. I also want you to engage in some deep meaning-making for yourself during the term. What is it you believe or disbelieve and why? I anticipate that this course will be intensely personal. This is the main reason why I have come back year after year to offer this course. If this personal approach to religious and spiritual meaning is not your preference at this particular time in your life, then I strongly urge you to choose another course. Please keep in mind that this course is an elective; it is not a requirement.

WHERE I STAND PERSONALLY
ON RELIGION AND SPIRITUALITY

You will soon be reading an article I wrote recently that appeared in the *Journal of Religion & Education*. It is one of the most personal articles I have ever written, particularly about some of the topics under consideration in this course. It ought to tell you what you need to know about my own perspective on the material we will be studying this term. We may or may not have enough time to read the piece this evening. If nothing else, it will help you to decide whether you want to stay in the course for an entire semester, studying this material with someone of my philosophical and pedagogical inclinations. Think of my essay as a truth-in-packaging statement. One way or the other, I would like to talk about it with you before you make a choice to stay in, or leave, this class. . . .

COURSE GOALS

There are five:

First, I want you to learn a lot of new information about a subject matter that most Americans know little about, even though they might have lots of opinions.

Second, I want you, whether teacher or administrator, counselor or lay person, believer or unbeliever, to think about the role that the study of religion and spirituality might play in the education of students of all ages, at all levels, in public and private, secular and parochial, venues. I want you to think seriously and systematically about the risks and benefits, the disadvantages and advantages of teaching this material in secular and private educational settings at all levels.

Third, I want you to reexamine your own biases both for and against organized religion and private spirituality. This process is key to working with, and understanding, others. Its importance cannot be underestimated.

Fourth, I want you to write reflectively, personally, and honestly about this very provocative, often controversial, subject matter.

Fifth, I want you to learn how to talk respectfully and compassionately with one another, including me, about a topic that, throughout history, has caused as much pain, suffering, and division as comfort, joy, and reconciliation.

MORAL CONVERSATION:
THE MOST IMPORTANT COURSE GOAL OF ALL

I am known for conducting classroom discussions in a particular way. Whatever you might have heard, experienced, or read . . . about my conversational process, I ask that you forget it. What is most important about moral conversation is how I actually conduct it, and how you actually engage in it during this semester. Watch me in action. Watch yourselves in action. If it works well, it is because of you. If it doesn't, it is also because of you. After all, you outnumber me 15 to 1. I'll take some credit and blame, of course, for our success and failure as a group, but only a small portion of it. We're all in this together, you at least as much as I.

If doing moral conversation for a whole semester looks as if it might not be what you need this term, I fully understand, and, once again, I bid you a very respectful adieu. My courses have a reputation for being intense. They are, I think, because I value the conversational process as much as the content we will be conversing about. In my mind, they are at least coequal. This disclosure is another truth-in-packaging statement that I think it is important for you to know. . . .

Here is another very important truth-in-course-packaging for you to know: I am a postmodernist. You will learn a great deal about this concept during the semester, particularly when you read my book, so be patient. But for now, here is what a postmodern reading of texts, and listening to personal commentary, is all about: I am more interested in the meanings that each and every one of you is imposing on the readings and on one another than I am in the readings themselves.

I want to know what *you* think and feel about the readings and discussions; what meanings *you* are attributing to course content; what personal narrative *you* are writing for yourself in the areas of religion and spirituality. I do not want to spend a semester guiding you in the process of tearing apart texts, adroitly deconstructing an author's meanings, brilliantly ferreting out hidden assumptions, showing off background expertise and cleverness, or trying desperately to remain impartial and intellectually and emotionally unaffected. All of this, at least for me, is numbingly boring, at this stage in my life. Once again, I am sorry, but this is who I am and what I do not want to experience in a course about this material.

I am going to insist that you probe deeply (in *personal* terms) the readings and conversations that we will be engaging in for 15 weeks. If you are looking for a whirlwind, dispassionate tour through the world's major and minor religions, then please look elsewhere. This is not a comparative religions course. If you are looking for an uncommon spiritual wisdom, eloquent homilies, inspiring metaphysical answers, and money-back guarantees of supernatural or secular truth from your instructor, then you will be sorely disappointed. I am as much at sea over these issues as most of you. Sorry again, but I thought that you should know. . . .

In a seminar such as this, I think that I have the ability to ask the provocative questions, push the appropriate (and sometimes inappropriate) hot buttons, genuinely empathize with your discoveries, doubts, fears, bewilderments, and misgivings, and share some compelling, personal concerns, but this is as far as I am able, or willing, to go. I have no hidden religious or spiritual agendas to push in teaching this course other than to learn more about this material for myself. I also want to get you to talk about this material with me, with the authors, and with one another in a mutually respectful, kind, and generous manner [R. Nash, personal communication, Sept. 13, 2003].

Now, although Nash is teaching a course on religion, spirituality, and education, I submit that this personal authenticity, this kind of "truth in course packaging"—concerning both personal orientations and challenging critical processes—is not only an appropriate but also a necessary part of every course we teach. In their own ways, Patrick Morton, Joel Upton and Arthur Zajonc, and Augie Turak are candid and open about the perspectives they bring to the content and processes they use. As the earlier part of this chapter tried to make clear, all elements of our varied curricula, all our courses, have explicit or implicit value loads, personal preferences and biases, conscious or unconscious mental models. We act responsibly with our students when we do our best to articulate those. We are irresponsible when we don't.

Reflection and Contemplation

Second to the importance of personal authenticity comes clear time for reflection, for contemplation. Contemplation is the cerebral metabolic process for meaning making. The food that we chew and swallow, that then enters our stomach, only nourishes us, only becomes part of our bloodstream, muscles, nerves, and body chemistry when it is metabolized. It makes sense that the second step in Kolb's (1984) experiential learning cycle is reflection, after direct experiences and before abstract conceptualization and active application. Reflection is the absolutely necessary intervening activity that converts input—whatever the experiences are—into meaningful working knowledge that can then be tested in other settings. Without reflection, whatever new experiences we have, whatever new information and concepts we encounter in lectures and texts, end up like the residue from food we don't metabolize. It passes through us and may be excreted for a quiz or exam, but it does not nourish learning that lasts. In academe, time is precious; in our general culture, "time is money." Ironically, "time out" for reflection often can be the best investment we make. In Chapter Seven we discuss ways to create environments on campus that allow for silence, contemplation, and reflection.

Andre L. Delbecq is a University Professor at Santa Clara University. His Spirituality and Business Leadership course provides an excellent example of how a variety of contemplative and reflective practices are integrated with a complex mix of solid resources and diverse learning activities. His syllabus, supplied in Appendix B, gives a good overview of these practices and how they are integrated with other course activities.

CONCLUSION

Perhaps this combination of general principles and specific examples will encourage others to scratch—or dig—more deeply into this significant arena. Because after all is said and done, strengthening authenticity, spirituality, purpose, and meaning depends first and foremost on how individual faculty members are authentically present with their students, individually and collectively, and on the sophistication they bring to the learning environments they create.

CHAPTER SIX

The Place of Spirituality in the Mission and Work of College Student Affairs

Jon C. Dalton

———※———

The mission of student affairs in American higher education has always been concerned with the inner lives of students and their holistic learning and development. Although much of the attention of the profession has quite naturally focused on the external lives of students, such as their conduct, habits, race and ethnicity, social life, and activities, there is an historical legacy of concern for students' internal lives of personal meaning, faith, values, beliefs, and spirituality. Student affairs deans were probably the first college administrators commissioned to give special attention to the general welfare and holistic development of students. When LeBaron Russell Briggs was selected from the Harvard faculty in 1890 and asked to be a dean for students, he was given the broad charge of looking after students and nurturing their overall mental, physical, and spiritual development. Briggs was described as a man who could spot a hungry student clear across the College Yard (Sandeen, 1985).

The creation of a dean for students was important for two reasons: (1) it was a practical acknowledgment that the faculty could no longer provide the necessary personal attention to individual student welfare and guidance, and (2) it symbolized a commitment on the part of

American colleges to preserve the long tradition of concern for the holistic development and welfare of students. This tradition emphasized the humane values that were central to the early faith-oriented American colleges, and it reflected the ideal that higher education should be an intellectual endeavor that was tied inseparably to the personal development of students as moral, physical, and spiritual beings. In Chapter Three Liesa Stamm examined in more depth the role of religion in American society and its unique historical association with the mission of higher education in the United States.

Stamm points out that in the eighteenth and nineteenth centuries it was assumed that students' spiritual lives and faith development were integral aspects of learning and development in college. Horowitz (1987) noted that the evangelical temperament of those times encouraged a close watch over the young, and colleges were expected to monitor and encourage the spiritual growth of their students. Religion and piety were generally regarded as necessary guides to correct behavior for students. In 1838 the president of Davidson College wrote, "Remove the constraints and sanctions of religion, and talents and intellectual attainments can't stay the demons of human depravity" (quoted in Marsden, 1992, p. 10). Rudolf (1977) observed that because higher education was usually thought of as a religious enterprise as well as a public service, it seemed natural for church and state to work hand in hand. Smith (2001) noted that only a century ago almost all state and private colleges and universities had required chapel services and church attendance. The rather rigid segregation of religion and spirituality from academic life that one sees today in much of higher education is a relatively recent development. A great deal of this change, in fact, has occurred in the last fifty years.

The first student affairs deans assumed an educational role that reflected the educational philosophy of the time and was widely supported by educational leaders, parents, and the general public. As the profession evolved, student affairs deans increasingly became the designated campus officials who most embodied the quasi-parental role that was later codified in the legal principle of *in loco parentis*. Their close oversight and responsibility for both behavioral and affective aspects of students' lives made the interconnectedness of students' intellectual, physical, and spiritual development a central tenet of their evolving mission and philosophy. Student affairs leaders formalized their concern for the holistic development of students, including spirituality, in *The Student Personnel Point of View* (American Council on

Education, 1937): "The concept of education is broadened to include attention to the student's well rounded development physically, socially, emotionally, and spiritually, as well as intellectually" (p. 1). Student affairs deans recognized very early that friendships, finances, faith, and fun all played important roles in the academic success of students in college and that these diverse experiences, many of which occurred outside the classroom, contributed in significant ways to the holistic development of students.

The concern for spirituality was one aspect of their wide-ranging charge to oversee the general welfare and development of students. Student affairs deans found themselves with expanding responsibilities for housing, dining, counseling, recreation, jobs, sports, social life, and student conduct and discipline. Their responsibility for almost everything related to students' lives outside the classroom brought them into regular contact with students' religious and spiritual activities and concerns. Student affairs deans did not, as a rule, have to be persuaded of the relevance of spirituality and religion to students' learning and development, as these were routine matters in their interactions with college students and a deeply ingrained aspect of their holistic philosophy of student development.

But despite their holistic philosophy and historical commitment to the spiritual development of college students, student affairs professionals have not been influential advocates for the place of spirituality in the higher education setting. They have often failed to recognize the centrality of spirituality in the identity development of students during the college years and have underestimated the power of students' spiritual quests to help them cope with stress and fragmentation in the college setting. In their desire to avoid the appearance of meddling and moralizing, they have often treated religion and spirituality as primarily private domains and, in so doing, have ignored an aspect of students' lives that is often at the very core of their concerns. Emmons (1999) argues that "Spiritual or religious goals, beliefs, and practices are not only a distinctive component of a person, for many they are the core of personality" (p. 13).

Student affairs staff have given great priority to students' social, emotional, and physical needs, and it may not be overstating it to say that the primary focus of most student affairs organizations is on these aspects of students' learning and development. Ernest Boyer (1990) praised the work of student affairs in addressing serious conduct problems and making the campus more welcoming for students. He wrote,

"Student personnel professionals, who carry most of the responsibility for student conduct, are expected to 'keep the lid on' with no overall strategy to guide them" (pp. 6–7). Student affairs staff do not get sufficient credit for the strong leadership they have provided in addressing social justice issues on campus and making the principles of fairness and equal consideration cornerstones of college student life. In recent years much attention has been given to student affairs' contributions to students' intellectual development and new ways of partnering with academic colleagues in promoting holistic learning. But for all they have done to enhance the quality of student life and learning on campus, student affairs professionals have until quite recently been oddly very silent about the roles of spirituality and religion in the lives of students. The profession has only recently begun in a serious way to address students' spiritual development in the college setting and to integrate this aspect of their development into operating programs and services.

Prior to the 1960s it was common to find student affairs staff who had professional preparation in religion and theology and worked in the chaplaincy, campus ministry, religious activities, and interfaith programs. These individuals were often attracted to higher education because of their interest in the spiritual and religious development of young people. However, as student affairs developed as a profession in the latter half of the twentieth century, it narrowed and formalized its preparation standards, and fewer individuals were hired who had religious and theological training. Professional preparation in religion and theology came to be regarded as a peripheral and even suspect preparation track for the student affairs profession. Administrators in public universities grew increasingly concerned that the appearance of too close an involvement in the religious and spiritual lives of students on campus might be construed as violating the wall of separation of church and state.

Moreover, there was often suspicion that staff who had interests and training in spirituality might be perceived by students and faculty as promulgating religion. Consequently, the student affairs profession gradually lost a group of professionals with educational backgrounds and skills that equipped them in unique ways to understand and work with the spiritual needs of college students. The loss of these staff was compounded by the fact that emerging student affairs training programs did little to incorporate student spiritual development into their graduate study programs. Most graduates of student affairs training programs now working in the field have had very little, if any, formal study of the place of religion and spirituality in college student learning and development. Only in recent years have scholars begun to integrate research on college student spirituality into student affairs preparation programs.

In summary, the student affairs profession grew out of an historical legacy of concern for students' holistic learning that included faith and spiritual development. That legacy continues today in contemporary student development theory and philosophy that affirms the holistic nature of student learning and development and the importance of faith and spirituality. The recent joint report by the National Association for Student Personnel Administrators (NASPA) and the American College Personnel Association (ACPA), *Learning Reconsidered: A Campus-Wide Focus on the Student Experience* (2004), strongly reaffirms the holistic approach to student learning and development: "The new concept of learning recognizes the essential integration of personal development with learning; it reflects the diverse ways through which students may engage, as whole people with multiple dimensions and unique personal histories, with the tasks and content of learning" (p. 3). Moreover, the report also argues for "transformative" learning, which emphasizes reflective processes, internality, personal meaning, and experience: "To support today's learning outcomes, the focus of education must shift from information transfer to identity development (transformation)" (p. 9). This important statement of holistic philosophy once again affirms the importance of the inner realm of students' spiritual lives. It also offers the profession a useful conceptual framework with which to argue for the place of spirituality in college student learning and development.

MEDIATING SPIRITUALITY THROUGH CAMPUS CULTURE

One of the important ways in which the work of student affairs affects the inner lives of students is through its role in constructing and mediating many aspects of student culture. Notwithstanding the very important role student peers have always played in the formation of college student culture, student life on campus is structured and monitored in some very important ways by student affairs staff. For example, student affairs staff organize and authorize many if not most of the activities and experiences that create structure, involvement, and meaning for students in college, especially during the first two undergraduate years.

Allen and Cherry (2000) argue that this mediating role is inherent in student affairs roles: "In the end, we are meaning makers. We structure the reality of college life through our programs, activities, and social-norming approaches" (p. 45). Student affairs staff are the gatekeepers for much of what occurs in the arena of student life on campus. Through sponsorship and authorization of programs, activities, and events; communication of traditions, symbols, and rituals; administration of student life policies and conduct norms; and frequent contact and interaction with undergraduates, student affairs staff shape the form and content of meaning that most students experience in college. Kuh (1991) observed that student affairs staff "have become the de facto caretakers of the undergraduate experience" (p. 83). Their influence is greatly enhanced by the fact that they are more likely to be present with students during many teachable moments that occur outside the classroom.

Unfortunately, too much of student affairs' concern and discussion about campus culture focuses on the excesses of student behavior in such areas as alcohol and drug use, sexuality, human relations, and cheating, and not enough on students' interior lives and their search for authenticity, meaning, purpose, and spiritual fulfillment. When staff are continually preoccupied with "keeping the lid on" student conduct, they can promote a campus culture that places great emphasis on monitoring social behavior but ignores the spiritual needs and concerns of students. Kuh and Whitt (1988) note that culture provides a frame of reference within which students interpret the meaning of their experiences in college. Because spirituality is fundamentally about the inner quest for meaning and purpose, the mediating role of campus culture can be especially important for the spiritual consciousness that college students derive from their college experiences.

Parks (2000) claims that meaning making lies at the core of every human life and guides behavior in important ways. Therefore, in their roles as "meaning makers" for students, student affairs professionals play an important role in the creation of social and cultural environments that enable students to find a spiritual home, a sense of belonging and being at home within themselves. Finding a spiritual home in college is critical because it enables students to entertain and reflect on the deep questions of meaning, purpose, and authenticity that are inevitable in the process of learning and growing in college. The role of student affairs in helping students find a spiritual home is critical because, as Smith (2001) argues, . . . "the university's inattention (at best) to a reality that exceeds nature, and (at worst) its denial that such a reality exists, shapes students' minds" (p. 83).

Too much of what is seen today in student affairs programs and values is oriented to the role of caretaking of students primarily from a custodial perspective. Many student affairs staff, like so many others in higher education in recent years, have adopted a "customer" orientation in which consumer satisfaction has become the driving institutional priority. The mission of student affairs has moved progressively toward a managerial orientation in which economic considerations and consumer satisfaction are given greater priority than holistic student development. This customer orientation focuses almost exclusively on responding to and accommodating students' self-interested consumer demands. When students want upscale recreation and fitness centers, colleges build them. When students want refrigerators, computers, private rooms and baths, or parking garages for their cars, colleges deliver. These consumer enhancements are driving up college tuition and making it more difficult for low-income students to attend college. In the past twenty-five years, higher education has responded more to students' self-interested consumer demands than at any time in its history. The meaning making that students too often derive from such a market-oriented campus ethos is that what matters most to colleges and universities is economic interests. (Recall the Dalai Lama's comments quoted in Chapter One.) "Students aren't indoctrinated into religious liturgy but instead into dualism, scientism, and most especially consumerism" (Glazer, 2000, p. 79). The traditional educational goal of helping liberate students from self-interest seems almost out of place in this shift in educational focus.

What is the response of college students to the consumer approach of colleges and universities? Nash (2002) argues that students are silent because they do not think their beliefs and values really matter in the bigger scheme of issues they experience in the university. Students learn to be silent when their talk about spiritual matters is met with awkward hesitation, disregard, and even disdain. Their silence about matters of the spirit can in turn lead faculty and student affairs staff to misinterpret students' deep concerns about spirituality, meaning, and purpose. They may easily mistake students' lack of voice to be unconcern or even satisfaction with the status quo. In his book *For Common Things*, Jedidiah Purdy (1999), a recent Yale Law School graduate, describes this chosen silence among youth in his critique of what has gone wrong with our common life. Purdy writes, "We do not want the things in which we trust to be debunked, belittled, torn down, and we are not sure they will be safe in the harsh light of a reflexive time. So we keep our best hopes safe in the dark of our own expressed sentiments and half-forbidden thoughts" (p. xv). Purdy's observation suggests that youth are silent on matters of deep meaning not just because their deepest concerns are ignored but also because these matters are subject to ridicule and trivializing when they are expressed.

In the high-stress, high-cost, market-driven climate of higher education, it is not surprising that college students are increasingly cynical and silent about the things that matter to them most. Silence about matters of deep personal meaning, beliefs, and values is also promoted by a pervasive secularism in colleges and universities in which the domain of the sacred is progressively diminished (Smith, 2001). The disdain for any knowledge or truth that cannot be derived from objective empirical methods tends to drive out any serious attention to students' deep questions and concerns about transcendent meaning and purpose. These ultimate concerns are especially important for college students, as young people are at a critical juncture of so many important life decisions.

RESPONDING TO NEW TRENDS AND PATTERNS OF COLLEGE STUDENT SPIRITUALITY

Students' reluctance to express their spiritual interests and needs in many higher education settings is changing. Surveys conducted by Gallup and Lindsay (1999) indicate that in the 1990s spirituality and religion played an increasingly important role in our national life. The great popularity of personal development books, workshops, retreats, videos, and magazines on meditation, spirituality, and self-development is evidence of the widespread general interest in spiritual searching and inward journeys. Liesa Stamm argues in Chapter Three that spirituality has returned to campus and that it is sparking a vigorous dialogue about personal values, meaning and purposes, and religious and spiritual values as part of the education experience. The recent research findings on college student spirituality reported by the Higher Education Research Institute (HERI) at UCLA in *The Spiritual Life of College Students* (2005) document the very high levels of student interest in spirituality and their active engagement in a variety of spiritual quest activities. Kathleen Mahoney (2001) cites evidence that college students are thinking more about religion and spirituality and that a spiritual revival may be under way on campuses. Recent research (Sax, Keup, Gilmartin, & Stolzenberg, 2002) on student interests and changes during the first year in college reflects students' concerns about religion and spirituality. Before entering college, 46 percent of first-year students reported that "integrating spirituality in my life" was "very important" or "essential." By the end of the first year in college, the percentage had increased to 55 percent. Although attendance at religious services declines among first-year students, their concern about spirituality and the strength of their religious convictions increases (Sax et al., 2002). This finding parallels that of Johnson, Kristellar, and Sheets (2004) in their study of students' spirituality and religiosity at Indiana State University, as described in Chapter Three.

It seems clear that college student interest in spirituality is growing, but it is difficult to determine the specific causes that are driving this trend on our campuses. As discussed in Chapter Three, some scholars (Roof, 1999) believe that there is a "quest culture" in the American society today that promotes reflection and introspection as part of an individual pursuit of self-knowledge and spiritual meaning. We know from the research literature on college student development that young adulthood is typically a time of inward reflection and exploration and that identity development includes an exploration of moral and spiritual commitments. Students are attracted to spirituality in college because of their struggle with the big questions of identity, career, relationships, and purpose. Parks (2000) describes the need to recognize these big questions, these spiritual questions, as an integral part of the student development process. "Young adults," she writes, "are naturally renegotiating questions of their personal future, happiness, God, the ethical dimensions of their choices, suffering and death" (p. 198). Like Parks, Nash (2002) argues that *spirituality* is a term that describes the never-ending struggle to provide satisfying answers to life's most insistent questions. So the college years are a pivotal time for exploring these big questions.

One of the difficulties educators confront in making college life genuinely integrating and transforming for college students is accurately understanding how students perceive this important time in their lives. Earlier I argued that student affairs professionals focus too much of their attention on students' outward behaviors and characteristics. This can lead them to overlook how students' search for what is transcendent and sacred in their lives deeply influences their perceptions and commitments. Many students carry within them a deeply felt sense of hope and freshness, and they hold the expectation that college will be not only a place to learn but also a place to become and belong. They want college to be a time of personal transformation, a time when they will become the person they long to be. They are not certain how it will happen, but they are convinced it somehow will. Margaret Mead (1972) held this expected sense of transformation when she entered DePauw College in 1919: "In college, in some way that I devoutly believed in but could not explain, I expected to become a person" (p. 90). Richard Broadhead (2004) spoke directly to the high hopes of entering students at Yale University when he told them, "You've come to one of the great fresh starts in your life, one of the few chances your life will offer to step away from the person you've been taken for and decide anew what you would like to become" (p. 18). College is an intellectual journey, but it is also a time of inward spiritual journey in which students expect a personal transformation into something new and more complete. If we miss this reality about students (and we often do), we fail to understand what truly matters most to them.

For us to engage students' deepest concerns and commitments in college, it is especially important to provide educational and developmental experiences that honor spirituality and that provide a campus climate that legitimates and welcomes students' often unspoken spiritual needs and concerns. Tisdell (2003) argues that spirituality is a key to understanding how students make meaning and connect knowledge with deeper life purposes and values. Educational and student development efforts that ignore students' spirituality—how they make internal connections to their defining beliefs and purposes—will inevitably be less effective, because they do not reach that part of students' lives where things really matter. However, when we do take a stronger advocacy role for spirituality, we must expect a good deal of opposition on campus. As Smith (2001) notes, "The modern university is not agnostic toward religion; it is actively hostile to it. It countenances spirituality as long as it is left undefined" (p. 96).

One of the problems in advocating spirituality is the difficulty of sorting out the interrelationships between religion and spirituality. As we suggest in Chapter Three, ask most college students the difference between religion and spirituality and they are likely to tell you that religion is about a lot of external rules and rituals, whereas spirituality is a soul-searching inward journey. They are inclined to see religion as going to church, obeying commandments, following someone else's rules, and participating in a formal religious organization. They see spirituality as having to do with their personal journey toward greater purpose and meaning, a journey that helps them understand their place in the world and their relationship to transcendent values and purposes. (See William Teasdale's definition of spirituality in Chapter One.) Thus it is not surprising that students' participation in formal religious activities usually declines in college, whereas their interest in spirituality increases.

The question of whether educators should be engaged with college students in matters of spirituality is often raised by those who are concerned that such activities may violate church-state boundaries or are simply too personal and subjective. These concerns appear to be diminishing in higher education for a number of reasons: (1) students are now expressing greater interest and concern about spirituality and are actively pushing institutions to give greater support and attention to this area, (2) there is growing acceptance among college educators and administrators in making a distinction between spirituality and religion and acknowledging that an active engagement of spirituality does not necessarily involve the promotion of religion or violation of church-state boundaries, (3) the society at large is more willing to treat faith and spirituality as important considerations in education and student development, and (4) spiritual search and fulfillment are topics of widespread interest in the popular culture. Furthermore, as we described in Chapter Four, Supreme Court rulings that address not only teaching but also student activities fees, uses of facilities, and student housing make it clear that institutions have substantial latitude to address these issues.

TRENDS AND PATTERNS IN COLLEGE STUDENT SPIRITUALITY

In an effort to learn more about current trends and patterns in college student spirituality, I mailed the Survey on Trends in College Student Spirituality to approximately 1,098 student affairs voting delegates of the National Association of Student Personnel Administrators (NASPA) in summer 2003. The NASPA voting delegates represent colleges and universities of all types and from every state. Of the 1,098 surveys mailed, 248 were received, representing a 23 percent response rate.

These senior student affairs leaders were asked to report on trends in student interest and involvement in spiritual activities on their campuses, to share their perspectives on the significance of these activities and what they are doing to respond to them. Data were analyzed by institutional type to determine if there were signification differences among students in public institutions, faith-oriented colleges and universities, private secular colleges and universities, community colleges, and technical colleges.

As illustrated in Figure 6.1, more than 75 percent of these student affairs leaders reported that they had observed an increase in student interest and involvement in spirituality activities over the past five years. Analysis of the responses revealed that increases in student spiritual concern and involvement were reported in all types of college and universities.

These data reflect an increasing student interest in spirituality in colleges and universities and indicate that the increase is widespread across all major types of higher education institutions. It is especially interesting that over 70 percent of student affairs leaders in public colleges and universities reported increases in student interest in spirituality. Approximately the same percentage of student affairs leaders in faith-oriented institutions reported an increase in student interest in spirituality. The student affairs leaders who reported the greatest increase in student interest in spirituality were from private secular colleges and universities. The strength of the interest in spirituality reported on all types of campuses may constitute a defining trend among contemporary college students.

Because religion and spirituality are closely related in terms of meaning and usage, we sought to clarify how student affairs leaders interpret these terms. Whether spirituality is regarded as an expression of religion or as something distinct and separate from religion has im-

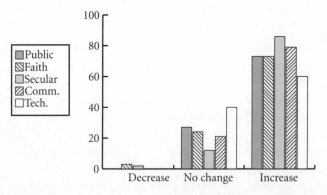

Figure 6.1.   Have you observed an increase or decrease among your students in spiritual concerns and involvements during the past five years?

portant implications for how student affairs staff address the issue, especially in public and secular institutions. As shown in Figure 6.2, survey results indicated that 78 percent of the student affairs leaders regarded spirituality as something separate and distinct from religion.

This finding is important, as it indicates that most student affairs leaders perceive the contemporary student interest in spirituality to be something different from renewed interest in religion or a new expression of religiosity among college students. There is some variation by institutional type, however. More student affairs leaders in faith-oriented colleges and universities perceived the student spirituality movement to be associated with renewed interest in religion. Overall, this finding parallels the views of college students, who also regard spirituality as something different and distinct from religion (Division of Student Affairs, 2003). Nash's distinction between religion and spirituality (2002) is helpful in understanding these differences. Nash argued that religion and spirituality represent two clearly related perspectives—the institutional and the personal, or transcendent.

Maintaining neutrality in matters of faith and religion has been a traditional concern of higher education administrators, especially in public colleges and universities. We were interested in learning if student affairs leaders perceived legal problems related to responding to students' spiritual interests and involvement on campus. As shown in Figure 6.3, 68 percent of the student affairs leaders reported that they had little or no concern that the student spirituality movement would create legal problems for their institutions. It appears that student affairs leaders are well aware of the Supreme Court decisions described in Chapter Four.

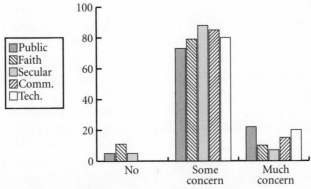

Figure 6.2. Do you believe there is a significant difference between religion and spirituality?

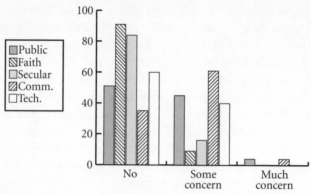

Figure 6.3.   Are you concerned that engaging students' spiritual interests and involvements more actively on your campus may create legal problems?

Because most student affairs leaders regard spirituality as distinct from religion, they do not seem overly concerned about legal entanglements related to providing spirituality programs and support. (See Chickering's discussion in Chapter Four on U.S. constitutional provisions related to issues of religion and spirituality.) Responses did vary considerably on this question, however. The concern about legal problems is greatest among student affairs leaders in four-year public institutions and community colleges; nonetheless 50 percent of the student affairs leaders in public institutions indicated they have no concern about legal ramifications. Student affairs leaders' perception of spirituality as different from religion and also a significant concern for college students today appear to give legitimacy and priority to their active engagement with spirituality.

As shown in Figure 6.4, in our survey 80 percent of the student affairs leaders indicated that they did not believe the increased student interest in spirituality was due to dissatisfaction with traditional religion. On the contrary, over half (56 percent) of those responding reported that they had observed increased student participation in religious activities over the same five-year period.

This finding suggests that most student affairs leaders do not regard the student spirituality movement as a reaction or rebellion against traditional forms of religion and religious affiliation. Student interest in spirituality may be viewed as a secular form of the search for transcendence and ultimate meaning. In this respect, spirituality and religion are not seen as antithetical for students but as different and complementary forms of the inward journey.

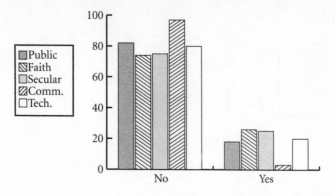

Figure 6.4.   Are students dissatisfied with traditional religion?

Perhaps the most defining way in which student affairs leaders perceive students' interest in spirituality is reflected in students' participation in new spirituality groups and organizations on campus. As Figure 6.5 illustrates, 82 percent of the student affairs leaders reported that students on their campuses were much more active in student organizations that have spirituality as a focus.

College students in all types of institutions appear to be taking considerable initiative to form groups and sponsor activities that reflect their growing interest in religion and spirituality. This finding parallels, and to a certain extent amplifies, that of Johnson et al. (2004) reported in Chapter Three. In response to this growth in student interest, most

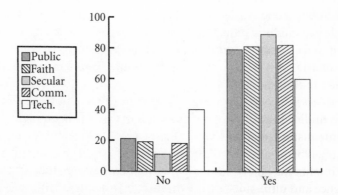

Figure 6.5.   Students are cynical about the moral examples of society's leaders

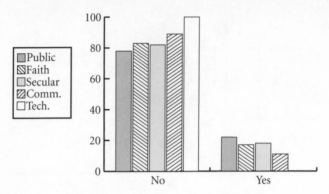

Figure 6.6.   Interest in spirituality reflected in students' participation in campus activities that have a spiritual focus

student affairs leaders reported that they planned future implementation of new programs and initiatives on spirituality.

When asked if the growing student interest in spirituality may be related to student cynicism about the moral examples of society's leaders, over 75 percent of student affairs vice presidents and deans from all types of institutions reported no (see Figure 6.6).

This finding was somewhat surprising, as other recent studies (Colby, Ehrlich, Beaumont, & Stephens, 2003) indicate that college students are often distrustful of political leaders and largely uninterested in political and civic leadership. Moreover, the recent high-profile scandals involving business and corporate leaders have challenged the moral integrity of this sector of national leadership. The responses of the student affairs leaders suggest, however, that they don't perceive the trust and confidence of students to be adversely affected by the negative moral examples of national leaders. The responses could also be interpreted to mean that the student affairs leaders may simply be unaware of students' feelings about the morality of the exemplars they observe on the national scene.

On another question, a large percentage of student affairs leaders reported that they did not believe students are disillusioned by our society's materialistic values (see Figure 6.7).

It is perhaps not surprising that in today's highly competitive and status-oriented higher education environment, college students would not be perceived as outwardly exhibiting a discontent with materialistic values. Entering college students do report that making money

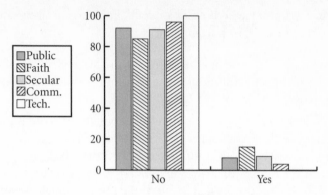

Figure 6.7.   Students are disillusioned by our society's
materialistic values

and living a comfortable life are high personal aspirations. But the growing interest in spirituality among students may reflect a form of questioning about the meaning of such values and a search to find a way to live a purposeful life despite these values. To answer this question we must listen more closely to what students have to tell us about the goals and purposes of their spiritual searches.

Whether student affairs leaders perceive correctly the feelings of college students on these important questions is, of course, difficult to know. As we have argued earlier, students are often silent about the things they care most deeply about, and this silence may be mistaken for lack of concern. Whether or not students are disillusioned about our society's materialistic values, it seems clear that they are searching for alternative ways of living and are exploring new experiences that provide deeper meaning and purpose. It also seems clear that student affairs staff must better understand the emotional dynamics of student spirituality and be more actively engaged with college students in this important domain of their learning and development.

RECOMMENDATIONS FOR
STUDENT AFFAIRS PRACTICE

It is important for student affairs administrators to respond to the spirituality movement by deepening their own resources and understanding. They need to recommit themselves to spirituality and faith development as important aspects of their mission to promote students' holistic development. To do this, student affairs organizations need to address a number of important issues:

1. Take a stronger role in advocating for the place of spirituality in the mission and culture of higher education and as an essential aspect of holistic student learning.

2. Conduct more research on trends and patterns of contemporary college student spirituality. The Spirituality in Higher Education Project (Higher Education Research Institute, 2005) at UCLA, under the leadership of Alexander and Helen Astin and Jennifer Lindholm, funded by a grant from the John Templeton Foundation, is an example of groundbreaking new research on college student spirituality that should provide important data in the coming years.

3. Clarify the meaning of spirituality for young adult development in the higher education setting. Spirituality is commonly described as transformation, authenticity, life force, transcendence, and peak experience, to mention a few. Such terms capture a sense of the ineffable nature of spirituality but also convey the notion that spiritual experience can be anything that expresses deep meaning. Spirituality can be a slippery terrain unless its meaning is clearly defined and distinguished from religion.

4. Strengthen the education and training of professionals to work with college student spirituality and faith development. Efforts are under way in several graduate professional programs (for example, Bowling Green State University, Miami University of Ohio, New York University, and Cannisius College) to integrate research on spirituality with teaching and professional practice.

5. Integrate spirituality into current theories and research on college student development. The lack of attention to spirituality is especially apparent in the theoretical constructs that have guided our understanding and practice about how students learn and grow in college. This omission has contributed to an enduring silence about spirituality among most student affairs scholars and practitioners. The work of Love (2001) and others is helping address this omission by seeking to integrate the work of Parks and Fowler into current theories of student development.

6. Provide space on campus for individual meditation, prayer, and reflection. The recent addition of a multifaith center at Massachusetts Institute of Technology is an example of a major institutional effort to give faith and spirituality a more visible home on campus. The new Pasquerilla Spiritual Center at Penn State University is a remarkable example of a land grant university's commitment to supporting students' religion and spiritual development.

7. Publicize, especially to new students, the spiritual resources and activities of the campus, including religious organizations, student groups, speakers, and events with a spiritual focus or content.

8. Incorporate spirituality as a component of student health and wellness programs. This is an especially important area, as student interest in mind-body activities like yoga, meditation, prayer, and silent retreat is so high today.

9. Integrate spirituality as a dimension in student leadership development. Leadership development programs are very popular with college students and provide important educational settings in which to explore issues of authenticity, purpose, and meaning. Rogers and Dantley (2001) argue that because colleges and universities produce so many leaders for the corporate world, higher education should work to develop leaders with soul, leaders who incorporate inner spiritual values and commitments in their leadership style. Some current approaches to leadership development (for example, Leadershape) make important connections with spirituality.

10. Include spirituality as a major theme or topic in campus activities programming. As our survey of students affairs leaders indicates, students are very interested in speakers and programs on topics related to spirituality, religion, and diverse forms of religious and spiritual practice.

11. Work with faculty colleagues to develop faculty-student mentorship programs.

12. Strengthen collaboration with campus ministers and local clergy to support student opportunities for religious activities.

13. Include spirituality as a component in staff development and training. Student affairs staff need to be able to describe their

own spiritual lives and beliefs in their interactions with students and colleagues. Professional student affairs organizations are now providing more programs and resources on spirituality for their members. Another resource is the Institute on College Student Values at Florida State University, which has brought together researchers, student affairs administrators, students, and representatives from foundations and higher education organizations for the past fifteen years to examine values, character, and spirituality in the higher education setting.

CONCLUSION

Student affairs has a rich legacy of concern for holistic education and personal development and must play a stronger role in advocating the place of spirituality in the academy and in the lives of college students. When we tolerate a bifurcated life in the academy that honors the life of the mind but relegates the realm of spirituality to the purely private domain, we make higher education less welcoming and engaging for students. As Gutierrez-Zamano and Yasuno (2002) note, when reason is prized "above emotion and detachment above connection," we encourage students "to lead duplicitous lives" (p. 3).

Although their status to effect change is not always great in the academy, student affairs staff have perhaps their strongest influence when they are advocating for the welfare and needs of students. It is important, therefore, to see the issue of spirituality as an issue of student welfare. Students pay a price in psychological wholeness and wellness when they are required to have separate public and private personas in order to function successfully in the higher education setting.

CHAPTER SEVEN

Integrating Spirit
and Community
in Higher Education

Jon C. Dalton

—◁◊▷—

Spirituality is rooted and sustained in higher education through the social and psychological connections of communal life on campus. "We all need tribe," writes Sharon Daloz Parks (2000). "We need a place or places of dependable connection. . ." (p. 89). American colleges and universities have always sought to create special kinds of human connections and affiliations in order to advance their unique values and purposes. The forms of human connections they create reveal the substance and meanings of community life on campus. When the communal life of the campus is welcoming, inclusive, celebrative, and open to diverse experiences and perspectives, including authenticity, spirituality, and the search for meaning and purpose, it provides an emotional infrastructure for the challenges and conflicts of college life. It also makes possible a transforming learning environment in which the process of spiritual search can be directly connected to intellectual development. When spirituality is connected and integrated into campus community, it promotes in students "the courage and faith to venture out into the unknown" (Walsh, 1999, p. 210).

The ideal of community has always been central to the purposes of higher education in the United States. McDonald (2002) noted that colleges and universities have historically emphasized a strong sense of community as one of their most important distinguishing institutional features. In describing the importance of communal living and learning on campus, Ernest Boyer (1987) wrote, "We emphasize this commitment to community not out of a sentimental attachment to tradition, but because our democratic way of life and perhaps our survival as a people rest on whether we can move beyond self-interest and begin to understand better the realities of our dependence on each other" (p. 8).

The nation's first colleges were small, face-to-face communities in which it was possible for everyone to know each other well. As late as the mid-nineteenth century, the average American campus had fewer than one hundred students and about ten teaching faculty (Boyer, 1987). The early American colleges embraced a vision of campus community that included holistic learning coupled with spiritual development. College life in the earliest American colleges was shaped by the belief that students and faculty shared a very special intellectual and moral covenant that bound them to common values, virtues, and vision and to a shared lifestyle and behaviors, embodied in the beliefs and practices of Christianity.

An array of campus traditions and ceremonies celebrated community ideals and fostered a sense of shared meaning, purposes, pride, and affiliation. New students and faculty were initiated into the academic community through formal and informal rites of passage that incorporated rich symbols and traditions. The power of these communal experiences shaped the meaning that students derived from their college experiences and connected them to the transcendent values and purposes of the college. The organization and patterns of campus life reinforced the values that were central to the mission of the college and shaped the context and content of student learning and development. All students and faculty, for example, were expected to participate in regular chapel services. The ideals of communal life in the collegiate setting changed in form over time as higher education became more secular and society became more pluralistic, but they continued to be important in higher education until the 1960s, when the historic changes of that time left traditional college life and community in disarray (Horowitz, 1987).

From the perspective of present-day campus conditions one is tempted to view campus life in the past as simpler, purer, and more authentic and to romanticize the relationships of students, faculty, and staff. The truth, of course, is that students were often in rebellion against the confining rules and restrictions that they felt limited their freedom and experimentation. Their views about community life were often at odds with the values and purposes of faculty and administrators. Ultimately, students were largely responsible on many campuses for eliminating the last vestiges of the dominance of Christianity in defining campus culture. But the connection between community life and spirituality throughout most of the history of American higher education was deep, direct, and close. College life was intended to be a transforming influence that connected students and faculty to each other; to the shared beliefs, language, and behaviors of the academy; and to its transcendent moral values and purposes. It should be pointed out, however, that these shared beliefs and values reflected the predominant Christian values of society and the religious groups that founded colleges and universities. Religion can provide a sense of belonging and intimacy (see Chapter Two), but the current challenge for colleges and universities is to create community in a time of religious and spiritual pluralism, when there are differing conceptions of what is transcendent and sacred. We are not advocating a restoration of traditional religiosity but a conception of community that embraces the diversity of religious and spiritual beliefs as well as their shared values and moral ideals.

THE DECLINE OF COMMUNITY AND SPIRITUALITY IN THE ACADEMY

Much of the decline of the traditional form of community on campus can be traced to significant changes that confronted higher education in the mid-twentieth century. By the 1960s, colleges and universities began to adopt a more secular, legalistic, and entrepreneurial orientation; these developments were to alter greatly the nature of community on college campuses. Concern for the "whole student" remained an educational ideal, but in practice, students were given almost unlimited freedom in personal and social matters (Boyer, 1987). The sheer size of student enrollments and campus physical plants made the traditional notion of community as a place of face-to-face contact and intimate friendships a nostalgic one at best. The ideal of a highly integrated community of shared beliefs, values, and meanings waned as colleges and universities became more diverse, pluralistic, complex, and consumer driven.

Unsure how to manage their responsibility for educating the whole student—mind, body, and spirit—in a secular, pluralistic, and highly individualistic environment, colleges and universities continued to honor the ideal of community but let slide the social scaffold of traditions, rituals, and ceremonies that sustained it. Horowitz (1987) noted that "the old collegiate culture never died, but it shrank precipitously and as it did, it lost its hold" (p. 252). Palmer (1999b) observed that "Throughout the secularized academy, there is a distance, a coldness, a lack of community because we don't have the connective tissue of the sacred to hold this apparent fragmentation and chaos together" (p. 27). The decline of community was not so much a cause as it was a product of the process of mission drift that left many colleges and universities deeply fragmented. Divided by disciplinary specialization, individualism, and entrepreneurialism, campus life became increasingly disconnected and polarized. Bennett (2003) argued that the academy elevated self-interested autonomy (what he called "insistent individualism") to a level of competition and one-upmanship that emphasized self-promotion and self-protection. The result was fractured campus communities in which there was little social or spirituality connectivity.

One aspect of the old collegiate culture that quickly lost its hold was the spiritual dimension, that part of community life that celebrated and nurtured the inner life of students and bonded them to the transcendent values and vision of the college. As traditional Christian values waned at the core of community life, there was no corresponding growth of a concept of spirituality that encompassed the growing religious diversity on campus. One of the great challenges secular colleges and universities face is how to embrace spirituality not solely from a Christian perspective but in a manner that draws from the rich sources of meaning, values, and beliefs of diverse religious and spiritual traditions. The spiritual dimension provides an inner core of meaning that gives shared experiences on campus their sense of psychological depth and emotional grounding. It connects mind and heart so that learning is infused with passion and so that passion is in turn tempered by intellect. When spirit becomes disconnected from collegiate culture, students lose one of the most important emotional ties they have with their institutions and their communal relationships with others on campus. Cut off from the inner life of students, the spiritual aspects of communal life on campus are diminished in depth and relevance.

COMPARTMENTALIZING COMMUNITY ON CAMPUS

In her research on faith development in young adults, Parks (2000) observed that it is the experience of "wholeness" that lies most close to students' hopes for community. Tisdell (2003) argues that the search for wholeness and the interconnectedness of all things is the essence of spirituality. According to Stewart (2002), the foundation of spirituality is to "deconstruct the fragmentation we have created in our lives" (p. 580). Yet college life has become fragmented for students today, the search for wholeness illusory. Managing time and establishing order and structure in their lives are among the most important survival skills every college student must master. It is far more than a scheduling problem; creating structure and a sense of wholeness and meaning out of so much disjointed activity is a task so relentless that it threatens to overwhelm students at times.

The structure and content of college life today fragment rather than integrate students' experiences of wholeness and community. The fragmentation derives as much from the intellectual realm as the social. Palmer (1983) described Western educational institutions as places where students are taught to understand themselves as fragmented and to view the world as a divided, fragmented place. Garber (2001) observed that faculty are divided by discipline envy, competition, and narcissism that breeds distrust and rivalry among individuals who share similar roles in close proximity. Colleges and universities have become very proficient at teaching students how to deconstruct, dissect, question, analyze, critique, and break down knowledge (Brooks, 2001). They do far less, however, to help students construct, connect, and synthesize knowledge, experiences, and beliefs into an integrated whole that makes possible what Palmer (2000) described as an "undivided life" (p. 32).

Specialization and bureaucratization in higher education also contribute to the fragmentation of college life. Finding answers to questions about routine matters can be an ordeal because of the compartmentalization of campus programs and services and the sprawling size of many campuses. The maze of information, procedures, forms, and deadlines is too often administered by beleaguered clerks and officials who are worn down by the sheer number and repetition of student demands. Technology has made administrative processes easier for students, but often at the expense of personal human contact. Increasingly, students live off campus, and their primary contacts are in off-campus settings. Whether or not a student gets involved in college life today may hinge on the availability of a parking space. The impersonalization and fragmentation of campus life help explain why students are so powerfully affected when a friendly faculty or staff member genuinely welcomes them.

When community is fragmented on campus, there is less overlap and connection between the intellectual and spiritual domains of students' lives. "Overlap" is an important educational factor because it helps connect and reinforce holistic learning. Newcomb and Wilson (1964) argued that learning and development are enhanced when students encounter similar information and insights in different settings and see them connected. The overlapping of intellectual issues with spiritual questions and concerns enhances the power of learning and development for college students because it connects and integrates important issues of mind and emotion for students.

But the reality is that for most students, intellectual and spiritual concerns rarely overlap in academe. The two domains are usually intentionally separated and isolated. Spiritual concerns and questions are very often treated as inappropriate content for intellectual examination and relegated to the private realm of individual concerns that have no place in the academy. This separation of learning from the process of spiritual search for meaning and purpose depersonalizes education and greatly reduces its transforming power. The separation of students' spiritual concerns and questions from academic life leaves many students feeling estranged in the higher education setting. Finger (1997) noted that alienation is a condition that occurs when elements of an individual's life that belong together and should be supporting and sustaining each other are separated. Emmons (1999) argued that spirituality is not an isolated part of personality but serves as a "central and organizing force in people's lives" (p. 117). When spirituality is relegated to sacred occasions and places, colleges and universities compel many students to dissociate one of the most motivating and integrating forces in their lives from their academic goals and endeavors. Fowler (1981) was also convinced that faith is at the center of life and cannot be compartmentalized or relegated to the periphery. It is an integral part of personality. Spirituality can provide a unifying and integrating force that helps students resist the forces of fragmentation in their lives (Emmons, 1999). Chapter One includes very useful discussion by William Teasdale and Karen Armstrong on ways of thinking about religion and spirituality.

COMMUNAL LIFE IN COLLEGE AND THE SPIRITUAL QUEST

The spiritual journey almost always involves traveling companions. An important aspect of the spiritual quest in youth is the desire to connect with others in a deeper and more meaningful way. The "tribe" is especially important for students because college is typically a place and time of great personal challenge and transition. Parks (2000) notes that connecting with others creates a feeling of belonging and a sense of psychological security. It enables one to be more confident and open to the experiences and challenges that facilitate personal growth and academic achievement in college.

The company of others is especially important for young adults in college because so many aspects of personal growth and development revolve around social relationships and interactions. Issues of friendship, sexuality, tolerance, compassion, forgiveness, and autonomy are important aspects of emerging identity that are worked out in the company of peers in the college environment. It is natural that in these matters of deep meaning and emotion, students should seek to share them with others who are closest to them. It is not surprising, therefore, that many of the forms of spiritual search that are popular today with college students are social in nature. Most popular forms of contemporary spirituality activities reported on college campuses revolve around groups and activities designed to facilitate spiritual exploration in a social context (Dalton, 2003).

Students' academic and personal goals clearly intersect in college in ways that make religious and spiritual concerns very important for most college students. The quest for meaning and purpose in life leads students beyond themselves in ways that help them appreciate and connect with others and experience a greater sense of responsibility for helping and understanding them. Findings from the Project on Spirituality in Higher Education (Higher Education Research Institute, 2004) indicate that 75 percent of the undergraduates surveyed reported being engaged in "searching for meaning and purpose in life" to "some" or "a great" extent; 86 percent of the students reported that attaining wisdom was "essential" or "very important" to them. The concern about spiritual matters is also reflected in the fact that most of the students (78 percent) indicated that they discussed religion/ spirituality with friends.

The impulses that drive the spiritual quest; the search for greater self-understanding; the need to connect with more enduring, more transcendent truths; the search for purpose and meaning—all these seem to lead to a concern for belonging to a community. Emmons (1999) argues that one of the functions of self-transcendence is to draw individuals out of their self-preoccupation so that they can connect with higher powers, other people, and broader social concerns. For youth especially, there is a hunger to feel oneself made whole and connected with values of one's community (Purdy, 1999). Parks (2000) noted that the spiritual quest is integral to the process of development and that a community that creates a meaningful network of belonging and support facilitates student development. When spirituality is welcomed and integrated into campus community life, it helps nurture a sense of belonging and identification with the beliefs and ideals of the community.

One of the surprising outcomes of the spiritual quest is that the search for what is transcendent and sacred in human experience leads inevitably to the desire to connect with others. Authentic spiritual growth replaces the self with others as the source of ultimate concern (Shore, 1997). The feeling of being connected to what is transcendent and infinite opens one to closer affiliation with others across barriers of individual and social differences. Myers and Williard (2003) argued that "attachment to a supreme being is the foundation for all human relational connections" (p. 114). Because the spiritual journey invariably leads beyond self to the experience of self-transcendence, it makes possible more authentic connections with others. Moreover, college students seem especially interested in learning about each other's faith traditions and experiences.

Maslow (1970) believed that the motivation toward the transcendent increases as one develops. Moreover, the urge to push beyond self in order to understand transcendent meaning and purpose is an animating life force (Chandler, Holden, & Kolander, 1992) that leads ultimately to the realm of the sacred. It is the experience of connection to the sacred that opens one to greater compassion, humility, love, and affiliation with others. In a surprising way, the search for transcendent "otherness" leads full circle to more authentic relationships with others and greater communal interdependence. Tisdell (2003) argued that spiritual development always takes place in a social context and is always connected to specific places and times. Thus to speak of the spiritual growth of college students is to raise the question of how, in the context and circumstances of higher education environments, students are connected to others in social arrangements that facilitate their search for meaning and purpose. The greater the connection of spiritual questions and the search for meaning to the processes of teaching and learning in higher education, the more likely it is that transforming education can be achieved.

Researchers on college student development have known for some time that it is essential for students to feel at home in the college setting and to bond with their peers and institutions. A psychological sense of community can positively affect student development and social interaction (Whiteley, 1985). The experience of belonging, of feeling that one is a part of the community, is not only important from the standpoint of students' psychosocial development but also a critical element in students' satisfaction, learning, and achievement in college. Students who feel at home on campus and who affiliate with the college are much more likely to participate in community activities and to internalize the values and norms of the institution. Thus the experience of a strong sense of a community that welcomes and integrates spirituality can be a powerful tool for student learning and development.

FORMS AND MEANINGS OF COMMUNITY IN HIGHER EDUCATION

There are several levels or forms of social relationships that reflect different aspects of community life, and these have implications for how community is constructed in higher education. Nash (2002) identified three different levels of community and described them as "moral worlds." The different dimensions of community complement and reinforce each other when they are consistent and integrated. The first level of community is the realm of the personal, in which the connections with family, friends, and one's interior life of spirit form the core of belonging. The experiences of this core of close relationships provide the foundational beliefs and meanings that influence broader communal contacts and relationships. Students find their most meaningful experiences of community in this first level of relationships.

Cellular telephones and the Internet have made it possible to maintain close personal relationships with family and friends in college in a way that was impossible in the past. Recent research (Sax, Keup, Gilmartin, & Stolzenberg, 2002) on the freshman year indicates that in the 2002 academic year almost one-third of freshmen called their parents every week. Not since the 1950s have parents been so intimately involved in the collegiate affairs of their sons and daughters. This active parental involvement is causing colleges and universities to give much greater attention to the emotional welfare and needs of students and the concerns of parents. It seems clear that the first level of community, particularly the realm of family relations, is a much more prominent aspect of college students' communal lives than it has been for decades.

The second level of community (Nash, 2002) is formed by the experiences of campus life and relationships. Interactions with peers, faculty, administrators, and others who are a part of campus culture form the core of this community. This aspect of community is the traditional focus of most institutional efforts to construct communal life on campus.

The third level of community (Nash, 2002) is the broader societal realm in which citizenship, patriotism, and individual rights and responsibilities define the roles and values of communal life. There is also an emerging fourth, global dimension of community that is becoming increasingly important in the rapidly integrating modern world of travel, communication, and commerce.

Colleges and universities can play an important role in helping students expand their vision of community to include all four levels. It is important to do so because college students have very strong attachments at the personal level of community with family and peers but are one of the most uninvolved sectors of our society when it comes to civic connections, such as voting and community involvement and leadership. Higher education is an especially important setting in which to enlarge students' conception and commitment to civic and global community, as success in the academy demands a high level of reciprocity and respect for rights, obligations, and community standards. In their study of colleges and universities that are especially effective in encouraging moral and civic responsibility, Colby, Ehrlich, Beaumont, and Stephens (2003) noted that all of the engaged institutions attempted to create campuswide cultures that emphasized shared values and that connected students to issues and involvements in the world beyond their personal and campus relationships. They were also explicit about encouraging students to consider the global dimensions of problems and issues. These strategies helped enlarge students' understanding and commitment to a richer and more layered vision of community. Each of these levels of community conveys important values and meanings to students; and the greater the extent to which colleges and universities encourage a more complex and integrated vision of community, the better able students are to feel at home in a broadly connected and encompassing community.

An important aspect of educating for spirituality, authenticity, and meaning is the relationship colleges and universities have with the larger communities of which they are a part. Can we really strengthen spiritual growth, authenticity, purpose, and meaning if institutions, administrators, faculty members, student affairs professionals, and students are not seriously engaged with larger societal issues . . . local, regional, national, and global? Can such educational outcomes be achieved if there are not active partnerships and working relationships with civic, service, educational, and faith-oriented community organizations outside the institution? Education for spirituality requires engagement with community issues and organizations at all the levels of community we have described.

Parks (2000) also noted that there are different meanings of community. One meaning of community refers to a sense of social connection and security; students have a feeling of belonging and acceptance, which frees them to respond to experiences that promote learning and development. But another meaning of community refers to the norms and boundaries that establish and maintain a social and psychological "territory" (p. 90). Belonging is important for college students because it not only helps them feel connected in a network of others but also provides important social and psychological constraints that define the limits of acceptable conduct, attitudes, and beliefs. Examples of such community boundaries and standards are academic integrity, respect for individual differences, academic freedom, student rights and responsibilities, use of alcohol, and sexual relationships. There is great debate about just where and how academic communities should draw the boundaries of community norms, but there is wide agreement that every academic community must have defining standards that guide personal and group behavior.

Defining community primarily in terms of conduct standards can have a serious downside, however. When conflict and stress increase on campus, there is a tendency to define the meaning of community through the use of institutional standards, regulations, and policies. Today many colleges and universities overemphasize their regulatory role in defining the boundaries of conduct and attitudes in order to minimize social and legal conflicts among students and staff. Such an approach to defining community can come across as controlling and confining and can undermine a sense of genuine belonging and commitment to the academic community.

Manning (2000) argued that higher education institutions may emphasize structure by rigidly defining roles, behaviors, power, status, and property. She notes that too much emphasis on structure can create campus social patterns and relationships that inhibit authentic experiences of community. The real power of community comes from the shared emotional experiences of individuals who participate together in common endeavors, and too much structure can inhibit this process. Although structure is necessary in community, it can work against what Manning (2000) called "communitas," the emotional, sacred character of the community formed between and among people (p. 67). Colleges and universities can become inhospitable places for spirit and community when their emphasis on structure makes the campus an uncomfortable place for expression of emotions, meaning, and spirituality.

REENGAGING SPIRIT THROUGH CAMPUS COMPACTS

In an effort to reengage personal commitment and emotional connection to campus life, many colleges and universities in the 1990s made efforts to renew community life through campus compacts and covenants. Boyer's Carnegie Foundation report (1990) provided a powerful stimulus for colleges and universities to reexamine the quality of campus life and to take a more proactive role in making the campus a welcoming, supportive, just, and caring place for students and staff. Over the past decade many institutions have sought to foster community on campus through campus compacts that make special use of symbols, rituals, and traditions. Campus compacts are symbolic communal acts in which members of the campus community celebrate their shared values and reaffirm their common purposes. Compacts have the power to evoke deep levels of personal meaning and to confirm social solidarity. Through symbolic actions conducted on a campuswide basis, colleges and universities can create powerful social experiences that give meaning and depth to membership in the campus community.

With the demise of *in loco parentis* in the mid-twentieth century, the relationship between higher education institutions and their students became increasingly contractual and bureaucratic in nature. Colleges and universities adopted formal codes of conduct that emphasized the legal rights and responsibilities of institutions and their students. Although these conduct codes were usually grounded in democratic values and moral ideals, they came to be used primarily for the purpose of regulating student behavior. Institutions continued to espouse their traditional values, but in practice, students were increasingly left to their own moral beliefs and relationships so long as these did not conflict with the official rules and regulations of the institution (Martin, 1992).

The movement to revitalize community on campus led to experimentation with a wide variety of social compacts by colleges and universities in the decade of the 1990s. These new compacts go by many different names, such as creeds, promises, community standards, pledges, expectations, compacts, tenets, and covenants. Campus compacts differ in many respects, but in general they all share in common an effort by colleges and universities to create a stronger sense of community on campus that includes greater involvement, emotional connection, responsibility, and mutual support.

In my review of over seventy-five campus compacts, I identified three distinctive types: codes, creeds, and covenants. Each type of compact conveys a particular notion of community and carries with it educational and behavioral expectations.

Codes

These types of compacts are generally contractual in nature. They communicate core institutional norms and values and define specific behavioral expectations of students. Students are expected to consent to these values and behavioral norms as a condition of acceptance and enrollment into the institution. Codes range from highly legalistic statements of student rights and responsibilities to more generic statements of behavioral norms and principles of conduct. Codes typically focus on conduct norms and expectations, are usually explicit in their reference to values and conduct, and have the force of institutional and legal authority. Ritual and ceremony are seldom used to promulgate codes. In many instances a public notice in the campus newspaper or student handbook is regarded as sufficient public notification.

The Florida State University statement "Student Rights and Responsibilities" (2003) is an example of the student code type of campus compact. It summarizes the institution's rules, regulations, procedures, and policies concerning student rights and responsibilities, and describes the student conduct and disciplinary processes that are used to enforce these rights and responsibilities. The rules and regulations are intended to protect personal and institutional rights and property and provide the educational and legal framework for the university's disciplinary process. "Student Rights and Responsibilities" has the added legal force of adoption by the Florida Department of Education and enactment in the Florida Administrative Code.

Creeds

This type of compact focuses on values and conduct but in a less regulatory manner. Creeds are not as explicit as codes in detailing conduct expectations and usually do not have the force of legally binding authority. They articulate institutional values and conduct norms but are used more often to inspire and guide student conduct than to enforce rules. Sometimes creeds also involve a social "pledge" in which students are encouraged to affirm core values and norms. Ritual and ceremony are sometimes used with creeds in order to promote active student involvement and affirmation.

The Carolinian Creed at the University of South Carolina is a good example of this form of community compact. The Carolinian Creed affirms ten basic ethical norms that define community values and standards. It was intentionally written in clear and simple language so as to be more readily understood and accepted by students. The Carolinian Creed simplifies the bureaucratic and restrictive language of the conduct code and shifts the emphasis from describing conduct violations to inspiring students to personally identify and affirm core community ethical norms. Various types of ceremonies and special events are used to promote the creed among the campus community. A university convocation is held to introduce the creed, and attention is routinely given to the creed in new student orientation and student activities. The Carolinian Creed does not replace the university's student conduct code, but it provides a more positive institutional strategy, one that takes advantage of the power of social bonding and the energy of youthful idealism to build a more positive sense of community (Fink, 2001).

Covenants

This form of student compact articulates behavioral norms and conduct standards but in a less explicit manner than either codes or creeds. Covenant-type compacts are consensual agreements in which each individual student is encouraged to affiliate with the values and visions of the institution. Covenants are used less to regulate student conduct than to inspire moral commitment and behavior. Ritual and ceremony are very important for this form of student compact. They serve to heighten the personal and emotional participation of students and provide concrete opportunities for personal commitment and social solidarity.

Some of the most powerful forms of community compacts focus on the creation of a community covenant in which all members of the community formalize their acceptance of the covenant through a personal pledge or statement of commitment. These covenantal arrangements are designed to create a powerful vision of community life that inspires and challenges students to be committed members and exemplars. Campus covenants go beyond a superficial affirmation and acceptance of values and behavior norms; they seek to engage students in a deep personal commitment to strive to realize the highest ideals of community life envisioned by the institution.

Colleges and universities that focus on creating covenant-type campus communities make considerable use of rituals, ceremonies, and traditions that help integrate students into campus life. The use of rituals and symbols can be a powerful way of connecting with the spiritual lives of students. They serve to heighten the personal and emotional participation of students and provide concrete opportunities for personal commitment and social solidarity.

Rituals and symbols are often religious in nature, but they can also be of a secular character. Sweet Briar College, for example, has a Founder's Day celebration in which students take part in a hike to the mountain home of the college founder and a commemoration of her life and vision. Such ceremonial activity helps convey to students the vision and values of a powerful role model and their place in the legacy of the college community. Wake Forest University uses a covenant compact to promote community life on campus. The covenant affirms a moral vision of the type of community that Wake Forest seeks to achieve. New students at Wake Forest are sent a copy of the Wake Forest Covenant statement prior to arriving on campus. It invites students not simply to follow student conduct rules but to play an active role in creating a moral community on campus. The covenant is explained during the convocation for new students, and each student is expected to make a symbolic personal commitment to it.

Table 7.1 illustrates key aspects of these three types of student campus compacts.

STRATEGIES FOR PROMOTING COMMUNITIES THAT INTEGRATE SPIRIT AND COMMUNITY

Several strategies can help promote communities that integrate spirit and community: (1) strengthening civic responsibility, (2) providing quiet places, (3) deliberately encouraging encounters among persons with diverse religious perspectives, (4) renewing institutional centeredness, and (5) encouraging active listening and caring dialogue.

Connecting Spirit and Community Through Civic Responsibility

One of the most important outcomes of education that is connected to students' spiritual lives is a heightened sense of social responsibility and civic involvement. This outcome is particularly important today as higher education seeks to renew its role in promoting the public good and making undergraduate education more engaging and holistic. Colby et al. (2003) argued that this renewal is necessary in order to bring moral and civic concerns back from the margins of academic life to its center.

Emphasizing spirituality in community life leads to concern about social responsibility and service, but the process also seems to work in the other direction as well. Emphasizing individual responsibility and providing opportunities for students to engage in service to others encourage spiritual growth and a sense of community. Personal encounters with social problems, human need and suffering, poverty, and injustice touch students in profound ways that promote moral reflection and introspection and help connect intellect and emotion (Colby et al., 2003).

	Codes	Creeds	Covenants
Nature of Compact	Formal institutional rules that specify conduct expectations and sanctions.	General behavioral norms and standards framed within the context of the institution's core values.	General ethical norms that inspire moral and civic responsibility but have little regulatory use for student conduct.
Sources of Authority	Have legal authority and are enforced by the institution.	May have some legal authority and institutional enforcement, but more general than codes.	Have little legal authority; authority is derived from moral vision and commitment of students to join others in creating a moral community.
Nature of Student Involvement	Codes are promoted by the institution with input from students. Students must affirm the code as a contractual agreement with the institution.	Students are often involved in development of creeds and are expected to participate actively in affirming and supporting them.	Personal involvement is essential to development of covenants. What binds students to the norms and standards of the covenant is their personal commitment and affiliation.
Use of Ritual and Ceremony	Codes make little use of ritual and ceremony; they are institutional rules that require little if any public celebration or affirmation.	Creeds make use of social rituals and ceremonies to strengthen social solidarity and support for conduct norms and standards.	Covenants make much use of rituals, symbols, and ceremonies to provide social occasions for celebrating and affirming the covenant agreements.
Educational Strategies Used to Promote Compact	Students are informed of codes as a part of their matriculation and enrollment process. Public notice is made of students' obligation to observe the code.	Students are actively engaged in discussion of creeds and encouraged to work actively to develop a community that affirms its values and standards.	Students not only are informed and engaged in covenants but also become participating members of a community that actively strives to achieve its moral and civic commitments.

Table 7.1. Taxonomy of Student Compacts.

Nurturing the Spirit in Quiet Places

Although community life usually focuses on and celebrates social relationships and interactions (McDonald, 2002), solitude is also an important requirement for living in community and for nurturing the spirit. The capacity to be alone, to cultivate solitude, to have opportunities to be apart even from one's closest circle of friends for times of reflection and spiritual introspection, is an important requirement for spiritual growth, especially in the college setting. The capacity to be alone is also linked to self-discovery, self-understanding, and self-realization (Storr, 1988). It is difficult to get in touch with one's deepest feelings and needs without periodic opportunities for solitude.

Solitude is also important because it facilitates meditation and reflection, which are powerful gateways to understanding and self-knowledge. Meditation is an important form of contemporary spirituality; it not only heightens self-awareness and contemplation but also produces a calming, restorative state of being that helps students moderate the strains and stresses of college life. As we discussed in Chapter Five, opportunities for reflection are important not only in academic settings but also in student life activities, residence hall programming, and other arenas of college student life.

Solitude is increasingly rare in contemporary college life. College campuses can be among the most congested places in which to live, and they rarely provide adequate spaces and occasions for silence and solitude. Orr (1999) notes that the typical campus is "intended . . . to be convenient, efficient or aesthetically pleasing, but not instructional. It neither requires nor facilitates competence or mindfulness" (p. 140). Even in the most supportive community setting, it is important for individuals to find opportunities for solitude and reflection. Libraries and dormitory rooms are the places on campus that provide some solitude for students, but they are generally not places that are very conducive to meditation and reflection. It is ironic that institutions that began as sanctuaries for reflection and contemplation have become some of the most intense and frenetic communities one can find. Academic life is a blend of individual effort and shared experiences and requires places and times for both solitude and group activity. Students need a campus setting that nurtures and supports them but also provides space for privacy and time to be alone for study and reflection.

Using Diversity to Enrich Community

Increasing racial and ethnic diversity is often regarded as one of the major reasons for the fragmentation and decline of communal life on campus. Religious diversity is used as an argument to defend secularism and value-neutrality in the academy. To be sure, the multicultural and multifaith character of today's college students and faculty poses more challenges for building community on campus than the homogeneous campuses of the past. But, too often, colleges and universities have responded to diversity in ways that have diminished community and spirituality. In their efforts to be tolerant and respectful of differences, colleges and universities often promote an ethos of benign neglect and even indifference about religion and spirituality. Matters of faith and spirituality are avoided in the belief that this is a requisite for respect of religious differences in a secular society. Such approaches to religious pluralism and spirituality lead to a fragmented community life on campus, which can feel distant and detached for students. Palmer (1999b) noted that secularism has flattened the intellectual landscape of the campus. Secularism has also flattened the landscape of communal life on campus.

The challenge of building authentic community on campus lies in moving beyond the philosophy of accommodation of multicultural differences to an active engagement with diversity in the educational and community life of the campus. Simmer-Brown (1999) noted that a major task before us is to learn to fully engage pluralism and diversity so that we can communicate and relate to others in more authentic ways. Actively engaging diversity means creating formal and informal opportunities in the living and learning environments of college life for students to encounter and learn from each other. The purpose of such learning is not only to understand each other's differences but also to search together for common ground, for common truths, for shared beliefs and meaning that create the possibility of a new kind of community that embraces diversity. "Pluralism is a commitment to communicate with and relate to the larger world". . . (Simmer-Brown, 1999, p. 100).

In Richard Light's research on undergraduate learning at Harvard (2001), students reported that one of the most effective ways of learning about differences was through interfaith discussions. Rather than avoiding discussions that focus on religious differences, students were eager to talk about religious beliefs and differences, and these encounters were very meaningful to students in helping them understand other aspects of racial and cultural differences. Engaging diversity in ways that promote understanding and a shared sense of openness and mutuality helps lay the groundwork for a broader view of community that respects and also bridges diversity. The concept of a "community of communities" is one way to envision collegiate communities that take pluralism seriously.

Renewing Institutional Centeredness

In his effort to propose a "larger, more integrative vision of community in higher education," Boyer (1990) argued that the process must begin with a definition of the enduring values that undergird an institution. Identifying the core values of an institution's mission creates a centeredness for the community, uniting students and faculty around shared purposes, despite individuals' divergent tasks and differences (Manning, 2000). Such centeredness provides a spiritual focus that is fundamental for creating community because it serves as the basis for all other efforts. The process of clarifying and affirming institutional centeredness is itself an important act of community and a good beginning point in the effort to reconnect spirit and learning. A useful technique in this process is to undertake as assessment of institutional mission and core values through the use of a values audit. In Chapter Eleven we provide a set of educational principles and practices that a number of colleges and universities have found useful in assessing their institutional core values. These principles and practices serve as institutional benchmarks for building campus communities that connect and integrate spirituality and education.

Encouraging Active Listening and Caring Dialogue

In the final analysis, community is not so much a matter of place as it is a quality of human relationships. Martin Buber (1959) argued that community exists whenever people directly encounter one another through the sharing of experiences, speaking, listening, and engaging each other in caring dialogue. The essence of community is found in the nature of the relationships among individuals. "Dialogue and relationship are the mortar and bricks of community," Griffith and Griffith (2002) contend, and the ways to build community are to "create contexts in which sustained dialogue and committed relationships can exist". . . (p. 195).

Community is strengthened on campus wherever students find opportunities to engage with faculty, staff, and each other in ways that encourage personal interaction and dialogue. These encounters, especially when they are sustained through time and by continuing dialogue, help build relationships that have great meaning for students. Buber (1959) described such encounters as "I-Thou" relationships, and they can exist wherever and whenever individuals take time to listen and be committed to each other.

CONCLUSION

Colleges and universities can do and are doing a great deal to create community for students by creating contexts for dialogue and social relationships on campus. At the heart of such efforts is listening. Genuine dialogue and committed relationships almost always grow out of greater attention to listening, especially to those who too seldom have a voice.

By promoting the quality of relationships and strengthening community through dialogue and commitment, colleges and universities prepare students for a world in which they must be open to new forms of community and in which the ability to construct community will be one of their greatest challenges and responsibilities.

PART THREE

Getting There from Here

A cting on the range of suggestions in Part Two calls for thought-ful, sustained efforts in three interdependent areas—planned change, professional development, and assessment. Chapter Eight addresses the need for balance: between centralization and decentralization, between advance planning and learning by doing, between widespread participation and timely and effective decision making. Strong investments in professional development will need to accompany the desired changes in curriculum, teaching, student-faculty relationships, student affairs, and community building. These activities will need to go beyond useful techniques; they must work on issues of personal authenticity. Institutional formation and two practices consistent with it—Conversations of Consequence and Ap-preciative Inquiry—are particularly congruent with moving toward an institutional culture that will nourish the additional interventions proposed. Two examples, the Dallas County Community College Dis-trict as a whole and Richland College within that district, illustrate how these practices have been applied in the service of both institu-tional change and professional development.

Chapter Nine turns to assessment, the critically important third element for strengthening authenticity and spirituality. We open with some of the challenges in clarifying the outcomes we desire and follow with some general conceptual perspectives concerning assessment. The chapter closes with an extensive look at Alverno College's sophisticated implementation of ongoing institutional research and how it is used for program improvement.

To accomplish the institutional amplification we are calling for and to take advantage of the perspectives and examples concerning planned change, professional development, and assessment both require solid leadership. They also require individuals who are willing and able to lead from the soul. Chapter Ten explores strategies and practices of campus leaders concerned with bringing the examination of values, meaning, and purpose back into higher education in a way that honors differences while still working within the traditions of rigorous academic examination and analysis. It gives particular emphasis to the qualities of personal integrity, vision, and empowerment of others, which distinguish the true leaders who are needed for this work and who may be found at any level of the institution.

Chapter Eleven articulates ten principles. Thirty-four items identifying specific practices consistent with the principles provide a basis for institutional self-appraisal. An inventory based on this chapter and available for institutional use appears in Appendix E.

CHAPTER EIGHT

Planned Change and
Professional Development

Arthur W. Chickering

ohn F. Kennedy said, "The great enemy of truth is very often not the lie—deliberate, contrived, and dishonest—but the myth, persistent, persuasive, and unrealistic. Too often we hold fast to the clichés of our forebears. We subject all facts to a prefabricated set of interpretations. We enjoy the comfort of opinion without the discomfort of thought. . . . What we need is not labels and clichés but more basic discussion of the sophisticated and technical issues involved in keeping a great economy . . . moving ahead" (quoted in Schlesinger, 1965, p. 37).

Back in 1971 I observed that in more stable and less complex times, when change was measured by generations, not years, the opinions of forebears reformulated in the light of personal experience could serve higher education, but that this approach was no longer adequate. When I expressed those views, I did not think they would be appropriate in the next millennium. But, unfortunately, they seem to me as apt today as they were then. For our students and for all of us to address issues of spiritual growth, to strengthen authenticity, purpose, and meaning, we must forego the comfort of opinion and bear the discomfort of thought. This is especially true when it comes to planned change, professional development, and assessment. We have to tackle the myths and clichés of our forbears. We cannot subject facts to a prefabricated set of interpretations. Most important, and most challenging, we cannot accept that our mental models, our habitual ways of being and doing, are immune to reflection and modification.

We need a three-legged stool to address the institutional amplifications suggested in Part Two. The first two legs are continuous planned change and professional development programs. The third leg is sustained assessment, accompanied by systematic feedback and application of assessment results. The critical attribute of a three-legged stool is that it is stable no matter how rough or uneven the surface. To meet the complex challenges called for by the changes we have discussed and to sustain our effort over time, each leg must be present and strong. The next chapter makes clear the critical importance of sophisticated, sustained assessment. The Alverno example illustrates some fundamental assumptions that need to underlie such work. It also illustrates the ways that assessment activities and the resulting data are integral to both institutional change and professional development. It shows how all three legs need to be conceptualized and implemented as an interacting set of ongoing activities.

There is a substantial literature on organizational development and planned change in higher education. The topic of professional development also has accumulated a significant range of literature and practical experiences. The Professional and Organizational Development Network has been tilling the fields of these interrelated areas since it got started back in the early 1980s under the leadership of Bill Bergquist, David Halliburton, Jack Lindquist, Wally Sikes, Joan North, and other pioneers.

This chapter does not try to synthesize all that good work. Nor does it aim to lay out a handy-dandy recipe for institutions tackling the complex challenges they face in moving toward the specific changes we call for in Part Two. Instead we aim to suggest some basic challenges and to note some issues particular to strengthening education for spiritual growth, authenticity, purpose, and meaning. We close with two working examples that integrate organizational change and professional development.

INSTITUTIONAL AMPLIFICATION

In an ideal world, the institutional changes we call for would occur in a nice linear, orderly, well-planned fashion. We would start with a clearly articulated policy statement analogous to those of the University of Massachusetts Amherst, Earlham College, and the University of Missouri—Columbia, presented in Chapter Four and Appendix A. Then we would develop new curricular alternatives and revise general education courses across the disciplines, along the lines described Chapter Five. While these changes were under way there would be close coordination and systematic integration with the varied student affairs programs and community-building activities articulated in Chapters Six and Seven. Once our institutional experiences at this stage were sufficiently solid and broad based, we would tackle various majors and professional development programs so that they would build on the general education foundation and be synergistic with it. Meanwhile, the reward system would be amplified to recognize the contributions to these initiatives made by administrators, faculty members, student affairs professionals, and staff. All this evolution would be accompanied by new language, symbols, celebrations, and rituals that create and sustain a culture in which outcomes that strengthen authenticity and spiritual growth are an accepted part of the institutional landscape.

As we pursued these changes, we would try to distinguish among four separate questions and address them discretely: Are the changes we contemplate consistent with our mission and institutional values? Is their design and implementation educationally sound? Are those designs and implementation strategies financially feasible? What are the political issues that need to be addressed? By addressing these questions explicitly and discretely we would increase our chances of success. They are interrelated, but we need to be clear about which set of arguments is being applied and when. If we aren't, often political or financial concerns will underlie and drive educational critiques, or differing interpretations of mission and values will generate active or passive resistance.

The reality, of course, is very different from this ideal. It is nonlinear and messy. It involves conflicts and clashes of interests and perspectives. It will challenge some of our most fundamental assumptions. It exposes norms that have heretofore been unrecognized and unarticulated. All this results in anxiety and discomfort. We are tested to live up to Kennedy's admonition to forgo the comfort of opinion and bear the discomfort of thought. We are not talking about tinkering with the periphery here. These institutional amplifications cut to the core of much of what we have been thinking and doing. We will need to examine some of our fundamental mental models and habitual ways of knowing, doing, and being. Our ability to do so will, in large measure, determine how successful we are.

All these emotional and intellectual complexities and challenges have three major implications: (1) we need to start with small initiatives, (2) we need to learn from these and build on them, and (3) we need to organize for sustained effort over a number of years. The two examples at the end of this chapter, the Dallas County Community College District and Richland College, illustrate these principles at work.

Balancing Acts

How we deal with these complexities will differ dramatically depending on our particular institutional context: two-year or four-year, public or private, faith based or secular, large or small, complex and comprehensive or focused on the liberal arts. That's why there can be no recipe, no one size that fits all, no general list of dos and don'ts. In every case we must balance a series of paradoxes, a set of trade-offs.

One balancing act involves centralization and—not versus—decentralization. If there is one agreed-on axiom for planned change, it's that "support from the top" is critically important. That will certainly be true here. We will need the kind of leadership that Liesa Stamm describes in Chapter Ten. But that leadership cannot manage the processes where the rubber hits the road, at the level of designing new courses and reconceptualizing those that already exist. It cannot prescribe or manage the initial creation and further evolution of appropriate pedagogical practices and associated faculty self-disclosure, student dialogues, and class cultures. It cannot work out the details involved with implementing coordinated and well-integrated extra- and cocurricular programs and activities like those Dalton describes in Chapters Six and Seven.

Top administrators need to encourage, recognize, and validate the efforts of faculty, student affairs professionals, and other staff. They need to make sure that there are adequate resources—in time, staff support, and money—so that the extra work involved does not indefinitely come out of the hides of the motivated innovators and early adapters. No institution simply "adopts" a practice developed elsewhere; it always makes adaptations to suit its own condition. Having supplied those resources, they also need to negotiate a reasonable schedule and framework for accountability. But responsibility for the actual design, initial efforts, evaluation, and eventual institutionalization needs to rest with the units closest to the action. When multiple efforts are under way among diverse units, administrators need to create a vehicle for coordination to avoid redundancy and to enable these units to exchange experiences and learn from one another.

A second balancing act involves advanced planning and learning by doing. I remember when Hampshire College was created back in the 1960s. A planning group spent several years—three to five as I recall—thinking through the design. In contrast, Empire State College was created very differently. During the fall and winter of 1969–70, Ernest Boyer, then chancellor of the State University of New York system, with his staff laid out a general mandate for a new institution that would "serve the diverse educational needs of adults throughout the state." I started on July 1, 1970, as the academic vice president. James Hall was named president, William Dodge vice president for administration. During the summer we employed thirteen core faculty members and opened the Albany Learning Center in October. During the next two years we opened additional Learning Centers in Rochester, Long Island, Manhattan, and at Rockland Community College. Out of our direct experiences working with students, we created this new kind of statewide institution in which each student pursued an individualized degree program through individual learning contracts. Although we were anchored in some basic educational principles, we had few binding policy statements. We learned from each other and by sharing what seemed to work; we did this within each center through half-day faculty meetings each week, and across the centers through "all college" three-day gatherings. Empire State was fully accredited after three years.

Now Hampshire College is, and has been since its inception, a fine institution. So is Empire State. They are perhaps extreme examples concerning the role of planning. I am not arguing for one extreme or the other. Clearly, we need some centralized planning as regards scale, anticipated timing, and resource allocations. And at the "local" unit level, we need some similar planning. But we also need to recognize the importance of flexibility, of learning as we go, of continuous improvement as suggested by our own working experiences and by whatever evidence we can adduce from more formal evaluation. Nothing pours concrete into an evolving enterprise more detrimentally than premature definitions of policies and prescribed practices, when we still have much to learn. It is tempting to articulate such statements, especially when external or internal forces pressure us to justify what we are doing. But while we are still in formative stages, it is better, whenever possible, to avoid responses that we may later regret.

Peter Ewell (2004), in his usual succinct and penetrating way, frames this balancing act nicely: "Perhaps the most important management task is to create a vision that is bold enough to excite collective participation and mobilize action, but concrete enough to know which way to steer at every step. The result may look *ad hoc* but it is better than moving remorselessly and rationally in the wrong direction" (p. 4).

Another balancing act is to encourage widespread participation and involvement, vertically and horizontally, and still get decisions made and pilot programs started. The complexity and personal challenges of this kind of institutional amplification demand that you create broad-based ownership. But you can't get started without giving running room to lead innovators and early adapters.

Thinking about faculty members, administrators, student affairs professionals, and staff, let's visualize the long-recognized, statistically defined normal distribution curve of people's responses to organizational change. The right end of the curve is innovation, change, institutional development; the left end is the status quo. The extreme right tail is occupied by the innovators. In most institutions they number somewhere between 5 and 10 percent. Next to the left along the curve are the "early adapters." These are the folks who are open to new ideas and ready to respond once they see them translated into practice, see them demonstrated in action. They may be 10 to 20 percent of the population. Next come the "late adapters." These folks will get on board after new alternatives have been well tested, after there is solid evidence or widespread experience that the alternatives produce the desired outcomes. These people may constitute another 20 to 35 percent. So now, depending on the institution, we have accounted for between 35 and 65 percent of its members. The other 35 to 65 percent are "laggards." This seems like a large range, but there is significant institutional variability in openness to change.

The laggards change only when new policies and practices have become well established over time, when the activities called for are explicitly recognized and rewarded, when there is abundant evidence concerning their effectiveness, and when they are backed by helpful professional development programs. When laggards dominate governance processes, significant change becomes very difficult. That's why many very effective and promising programs never get fully institutionalized and are left on the margins, implemented by a small core of dedicated professionals and often starved for resources. And that's also why, when a budget crunch hits and tough resource allocation decisions need to be made, these programs are cut.

History gives us numerous examples. During the burst of innovations in the 1960s, many institutions trying to improve educational effectiveness or to address outcomes other than knowledge transfer and "cultivating the intellect" created "new colleges." Some were called that, for want of any better name. Others had their own labels. I recall Strawberry Creek at U.C. Berkeley and Monteith at Wayne State, both of which were educationally powerful new alternatives, but were cut when push came to shove. Some still exist, such as the Residential College at the University of Michigan and Livingston College at Rutgers University, whose proposal for developing curriculum to incorporate authenticity and spirituality is described in Chapter Five.

During the 1970s, adult students became a desirable new constituency. Started with a grant from Alden Dunham at the Carnegie Foundation, the Council for Adult and Experiential Learning (CAEL)—then called Council for the Assessment of Experiential Learning—provided national leadership, conceptually and organizationally, to respond to these new learners. The representatives from the institutions that composed the initial CAEL steering committee were higher education innovators, and the organization soon attracted many others through its varied conferences and institutional development programs. During those early and late 1970s, led by Morris Keeton, CAEL saw itself as a force for general change in higher education, as driving a "movement" toward greater responsiveness to the diverse educational needs of students. It argued for individualized education. It also worked to make assessing prior learning from work and life experiences a regular part of degree program planning, and to make "sponsored" experiential learning part of courses and classes throughout the curriculum.

Thirty years later, the laggards at most institutions have successfully insulated themselves from the significant implications adult learners present concerning prevailing educational policies and practices. A few institutions started new special units, often called colleges, to serve adults in ways consistent with the Principles for Good Practice articulated by CAEL. The Office for Adult Students at the American Council of Education created two different institutional self-assessment guides and workshop designs for helping institutions use them. It is fair to say that these have not seen widespread use. At most institutions, responses have been limited to amplifying the schedule, offering night and weekend courses in the standard curriculum with traditional teaching. Now, of course, they are doing the same thing through various "distance learning" programs.

My point here is simple. It will be much easier, and very tempting, to respond to this new set of desired outcomes for encouraging authenticity and spirituality and to tackle these increasingly important and explicitly recognized social needs by creating special programs and special courses. That way we can seal off the rest of the institution and continue with our traditional curricular content and pedagogical practices without bearing the discomfort of thought and the anxiety provoked by trying to meet these emotional and intellectual challenges. Whether that result occurs at our particular institution will depend mightily on how we work with our distribution of faculty members, student affairs professionals, and staff in accomplishing organizational change, and on how we handle the complicated balancing acts required for this kind of institutional amplification.

"Institutional Formation"—Conversations of Consequence and Appreciative Inquiry

In addition to the change strategies and associated balancing acts articulated in the preceding section, there are two approaches to "institutional formation" that are particularly congruent with our desire to create an institutional culture that encourages authenticity and spiritual growth. Conversations of Consequence was developed by Monica Manning. Appreciative Inquiry was developed by David L. Cooperrider at the Case Western Reserve Weatherhead School of Business. The latter approach is being applied to colleges and universities by Karen Luke Jackson at Luke and Associates and by Cynthia Heelan, former president of the Colorado Mountain Community College system and now working with higher education administrators under the aegis of Cynthia Heelan and Associates.

CONVERSATIONS OF CONSEQUENCE. Conversations of Consequence involve collective reflection and collaborative learning that aim to foster institutional environments that help faculty, staff, and administrators live more authentic lives, at work and elsewhere. They begin by inviting each participant to reflect individually on core questions regarding institutional life. After a period of individual reflection, small groups of colleagues develop and refine ideas in the first two conversations. Then ideas that emerge among the full range of participants are aggregated. The third conversation uses a more formal process that asks participants to explore the implications of those ideas.

Here is how the conversations are formulated.

CONVERSATION 1: WHAT ARE OUR AGREEMENTS OF BELONGING?

QUESTIONS FOR REFLECTION

1. What are the "agreements of belonging" operating on your campus today? What kinds of mutual expectations do people have of each other?

2. What are the "agreements of belonging" that you would like to see lived out on your campus? How would the campus be different?

CONVERSATION 2: WHAT SHARED VISIONS AND MEANING DRIVE OUR WORK?

Transformation—as opposed to change—does not have to be alienating, creating a new organization where we feel out of place. Transformation of our organization *can* mean that we are working to unite our deepest longings with needs in society we can fulfill. The transforming can feel surprising—it can also feel strangely and poignantly familiar. It can feel like coming home to a place we had long forgotten or like waking from confused dreams to see the sunshine and a loved face near ours. Transformation at work within us and within our organization can bring us increasingly closer to the person we have always (perhaps unconsciously) longed to be [pp. 28–29].

QUESTIONS FOR REFLECTION

1. Take a few minutes to reflect on your work—what is life giving, what is nourishing, what provides meaning in your work? Note an example of when your work felt most meaningful and rewarding.

2. What do you value most about the campus itself? What about your campus supports meaningful work? What core factors give life and vitality to your campus?

CONVERSATION 3: WHAT DOES IT MEAN TO CO-CREATE AND CARE FOR OUR INSTITUTIONS?

Robert K. Greenleaf (1970) wrote, "Why do the best of our institutions fall short of performing at the level of what is reasonable and possible with available resources? Possibly because these institutions are seen by too many of us as impersonal entities to be used and exploited. . . . Most people do not give institutions the human caring and serving that they give other persons. If we are to have a moral society, moral people must also care for institutions" (pp. 53–54).

[This conversation's questions for reflection appear in Exhibit 8.1.]

These materials come from *Institutional Formation: Conversations of Consequence,* presented by Monica Manning at the Sedona 2002 Conference, Sedona, Arizona, June 17–19, 2002. Manning has used these conversations with a variety of institutions across the United States. They trigger exchanges among participants that help generate new perspectives concerning underlying assumptions and values that

A. What did you observe in our earlier conversations? (Jot down ideas before plenary conversation begins.)	B. What was your reaction? (Jot down ideas before plenary conversation begins.)
C. What does it mean? (After hearing observations and reactions, jot down ideas about implications.)	D. What do you want to do? (After plenary conversation on implications, jot down some ideas for you and your campus.)

Exhibit 8.1.   Questions for Reflection, Conversation 3.

pervade the institutional culture. They also generate shared ideas concerning preferred alternatives and action plans to work toward change.

APPRECIATIVE INQUIRY. The following quotation comes from Peggy Holman and Tom Devane, in their Introduction in Cooperrider and Whitney's *Appreciative Inquiry* (1999): "Change reflects underlying shifts in values and expectations of the times. . . . What distinguishes change today is the turbulence created by the breathtaking pace required to assimilate its effects. . . . While change holds the possibility of good things happening, 80 percent of us see only its negative aspects. . . . The remedy we are learning is to involve people in creating a picture of a better future."

This quotation expresses the essence of Appreciative Inquiry. Its processes aim to shift the focus from the problems that have characterized the past and that plague the present to the positive possibilities that reside in a shared vision for the future. An overview by Karen L. Jackson and Joseph Sullivan (personal communication, Oct. 24, 2002) lists eight underlying principles.

Constructionist—Words Create Worlds. The way in which we know the world is subjective and always changing. Reality is created through language and conversation.

Simultaneity—Inquiry Is Intervention. Change begins the moment we ask a question.

Poetic—Organizations Are Open Books. We can study any topic in any organization. What we choose to study is what we find.

Anticipatory—Image Inspires Action. Human systems move in the direction of their images of the future. The more hopeful the image, the more positive is present-day action.

Positive—Positive Questions Lead to Positive Change. Social bonding and momentum needed for large-scale change is best generated through positive dialogue that amplifies what is working and what is valued—the positive core of an organization.

Wholeness—The more positive the inquiry, the greater and longer-lasting the change. Involving all stakeholders builds collective capacity.

Enactment—"Be the change we want to see." Positive change occurs when the process used is a living model of the ideal future.

Free Choice—Free Choice Liberates Power. Performance improves when people have freedom to choose how and when they contribute.

Cynthia Heelan applies these principles in her work with college and university administrators, faculty, student affairs professionals, and staff. She says her work aims to create safe spaces and trusting relationships in which the inner teacher, the heart, the essential self can retake its original form. Her work assumes that everyone is proud of many aspects of their college. That pride is a resource to help everyone feel responsible for the college's success. Focusing on successes and on what works generates positive energy, excitement, and goodwill. It motivates people to move optimistically toward a challenging future. The focus is on success and what works rather than on identifying problems and seeking solutions. It seeks to uncover what gives life to an organization when it is at its best.

Appreciative Inquiry results in a specific plan that provides a vision for the future. The plan lays out where the college wants to be in a specified period of time, based on the best of the past. Each individual and group in the institution then develops specific strategies to help the college arrive at its vision on time. All the people who will be affected by the resulting plan need to participate in its development and in the appreciation process. The sense of a vividly imagined future strengthens participants' efforts to create it.

Heelan (personal communication, Oct. 26, 2002) describes the process for participants:

- Respond to questions intended to draw out the best of the past in order to visualize the most creative and exciting future.

- A planning group meets to identify themes that cut across the entire college and community and selects those themes that become the strategic plan's core work.

- This group selects and refines affirmative (VISIONARY) statements about each theme that describe an idealized future as if the new plan for building on successes was already in place. The group also drafts a statement describing what each statement means.

- Across-the-college/community themes and their vision statements are summarized and sent to constituents for review. Broad dissemination assists in ensuring college-wide and community-wide interest. This could be done via e-mail so it is easy for individuals to provide their input.

- Revisions incorporate ideas from constituents.

- A revised document is sent to all constituents for review.

- A final document is prepared in an exciting and dramatic manner and celebrated by all constituents.

- Each individual and employee group publicly declares their intention to support the plan by developing strategies to implement the college's vision for its future.

In my judgment, both Conversations of Consequence and Appreciative Inquiry provide excellent, and complementary, approaches to setting a solid framework for institutional change. They both "accentuate the positive." They both engage participants in identifying and clarifying what is good about their institution, the values they would like to see it act on, and the strengths that can help create a positive future. They both lead to specific action plans. The specific action plans that result from these approaches will of course vary by institution, but the strategies do have broad relevance in many institutional settings.

When those action plans are undertaken in ways that balance the various dynamics we discussed earlier—centralization and decentralization, advance planning and learning by doing, widespread horizontal and vertical involvement and timely decision making—the likelihood of creating changes that encourage authenticity and spiritual growth throughout the institution and among its students will be substantially enhanced.

But those changes will need to be accompanied by appropriate professional development programs.

PROFESSIONAL DEVELOPMENT

Most professional development programs focus on particular techniques and practices. In the fields of teaching and learning there are a variety of useful conceptual materials and workshop designs addressing such issues as collaborative learning, experiential learning and service learning, community-based research and student-faculty research, individualized education and learning contracts, learning communities, criterion-referenced evaluation, dialogue and group processes, and more. Recently, of course, many professional development programs have emphasized ways of using new, interactive, communication and information technologies to strengthen learning. These professional development activities can be very helpful.

But to create educational environments and the relationships among students, faculty members, student affairs professionals, and administrators that strengthen authenticity, purpose, meaning, and spiritual growth, we need to go beyond mastering a large repertoire of teaching strategies or the rich potentials of emerging technologies. We need activities that strengthen our own authenticity, that clarify and strengthen our own sense of purpose, that help us engage issues of meaning, with ourselves and others. The best work I know of is being done by the Center for Formation in the Community College, staffed by Ann Faulkner, Garth Hill, V. Sue Jones, and Elaine Sullivan. This center was founded in 2001 as a joint project of the Fetzer Institute, the League for Innovation in the Community College, and the Dallas County Community College District. The center's work is anchored in "teacher formation."

Teacher Formation

In his book *The Courage to Teach,* Parker Palmer (1998) observes that the first two questions we teachers typically ask are, What am I going to teach? and How shall I do so? Then we may ask ourselves the "why" questions: What are my purposes for this course or seminar? What are the desired consequences or competencies I want for the students? What impact do I want to have? But we almost never ask the "who" questions: Who am I that is doing this teaching? How does the person I am, my background, values, mental models, prides and prejudices, influence my teaching? How do those personal qualities influence my orientation toward the content, my relationships with students, the ways I interact with my colleagues, my institution, my community and culture? The Teacher Formation process examines these issues. It seeks to discover how we and our institutions can create conditions that sustain, deepen, and nurture the self on whom good teaching depends. It invites us on an inner journey to explore "the teacher within."

Though this work is personal, it does not have to be totally private. In fact it is best done with support from trusted friends and colleagues. Then our inner worlds of thought and spirit can join our outer worlds of action and service. Under these conditions, Formation

Nurtures our identity and integrity.

Honors our gifts.

Helps us resist others' pressures and projections.

Acknowledges our lifelong learning and our unique journey.

Deepens our recognition that we teach who we are.

Creates safe spaces and relationships where one can rediscover one's soul.

Formation work is typically undertaken in quiet, disciplined settings free from distractions, where silence and solitude can accompany dialogue and community. It focuses on personal and professional inspiration and renewal, not on pedagogical strategies or particular knowledge or content. The aim is to reconnect with and revitalize our own values and purposes. It does not aim for objective knowing or specified outcomes. It aims not to make something happen but instead to create conditions and processes that allow us to unfold in whatever ways seem to arise at the time.

Formation work can be a single, stand-alone retreat or a series of sessions over a period as long as one or two years. Curiously, contemplation in a group setting is unusual in higher education. Mostly we talk, debate, discuss, make speeches and such. Silence is rare. (I remember starting a conference-opening keynote speech for faculty members and administrators from Department of Defense Universities with five minutes of silence. My purpose was to give us all a chance to settle in to this special occasion, to make the transition from our busy lives and other preoccupations. By the end of four minutes you could cut the growing unease with a knife.) In contrast to typical practices, formation retreats value contemplation and silence. But once formation participants have become accustomed to the contemplative pace, they are grateful for the opportunity. Because a high level of candor and trust is involved, it is critical that formation retreats be invitational and voluntary. This practice cannot be mandated or coerced. The main activities—reflecting, sharing personal stories, writing journals, listening—are also "invited," in solitude, in small groups, or in large groups. Any participant can opt out. Often materials from varied wisdom traditions—poems, myths, stories, music, artistic works—are introduced for reflection and discussion.

Because our typical gatherings are goal oriented, aiming for a product, decision, or action plan, we may feel more comfortable when there are guidelines for these formation sessions. The Center for Formation in the Community College (personal communication, Anne Faulkner, Oct. 24, 2002) uses ten "touchstones":

1. *Be 100% present, extending and presuming welcome.* Set aside the usual distractions of things undone from yesterday, things to do tomorrow. Bring all of yourself to the work. We all learn most effectively in spaces that welcome us. Welcome others to this place and this work, and presume that you are welcomed as well.

2. *Listen deeply.* Listen intently to what is said; listen to the feelings beneath the words. As Quaker writer Douglas Steere puts it, "Holy listening—to 'listen' another's soul into life, into a condition of disclosure and discovery may be almost the greatest service that any human being ever performs for another." Listen to yourself as well as to others. Strive to achieve a balance between listening and reflecting, speaking and acting.

3. *It is never "share or die."* You will be invited to share in pairs, small groups, and in the large group. The invitation is exactly that. You will determine the extent to which you want to participate in our discussions and activities.

4. *No fixing.* Each of us is here to discover our own truths, to listen to our own inner teacher, to take our own inner journey. We are not here to set someone else straight, or to help right another's wrong, to "fix" what we perceive as broken in another member of the group.

5. *Suspend judgment.* Set aside your judgments. By creating a space between judgments and reactions, we can listen to the other, and to ourselves, more fully.

6. *Identify assumptions.* Our assumptions are usually transparent to us, yet they undergird our worldview. By identifying our assumptions, we can then set them aside and open our viewpoints to greater possibilities.

7. *Speak your truth.* You are invited to say what is in your heart, trusting that your voice will be heard and your contribution respected.

Your truth may be different from, even the opposite of, what another person in the circle has said. Yet speaking your truth is simply that(it is not debating with, or correcting, or interpreting what another has said. Own your truth by remembering to speak only for yourself. Using the first person "I" rather than "you" or "everyone" clearly communicates the personal nature of your expression.

8. *Respect silence.* Silence is a rare gift in our busy world. After someone has spoken, take time to reflect without immediately filling the space with words. This applies to the speaker as well— be comfortable leaving your words to resound in the silence, without refining or elaborating on what you have just said. This process allows others time to fully listen before reflecting on their own reactions.

9. *Maintain confidentiality.* Create a safe space by respecting the confidential nature and content of discussions held in the formation circle. Allow what is said in the circle to remain there.

10. *When things get difficult, turn to wonder.* If you find yourself disagreeing with another, becoming judgmental, or shutting down in defense, try turning to wonder: "I wonder what brought her to this place?" "I wonder what my reaction teaches me?" "I wonder what he's feeling right now?"

Clearness Committees

Clearness Committees lie at the heart of formation work. Clearness Committees are a practice developed by the Quakers in the mid-seventeenth century to achieve greater clarity regarding a personal decision, issue, or dilemma. They are anchored in the belief that for dealing with life's deepest issues there are no external authorities but only the authority that lies within each of us, waiting to be heard. The Clearness Committee is designed to help us hear this inner voice.

A small group, typically four to seven people chosen by the "focus person," comes together expressly to pose illuminating questions to help the focus person clarify the presenting issue or dilemma. These questions should be open and honest, without a hidden agenda. They are not intended to lead in a particular direction, not intended to "fix," to advise, or to satisfy the questioner's curiosity. The only purpose is to help the focus person move toward his or her inner truth, to discover his or her own wisdom. Frequently very helpful are meta-phorical, intuitive, and other expansive questions that reintroduce the focus person to his or her dilemma in fresh, heart-provoking, thought-provoking ways.

The goal of Clearness Committees is not to bring the dilemmas to neat resolution. The focus person often brings complex and multi-faceted challenges that touch the core of his or her ever-changing self-definition. Increased clarity is highly desirable even when there is no ultimate resolution. Often, even if we don't arrive at "an answer," grappling with and coming to a deeper understanding of the questions helps us feel more fulfilled and centered.

Not only the focus person benefits. Committee members learn about deep listening. Attending to our own inner dialogue as we form good questions, trying to restrain our own internal agendas and set aside our own wise recommendations, and listening with respect and caring to another human soul stimulates thoughtful reflections on our own condition.

That's the basic orientation of "formation" and its fundamental principles. I have been part of the Plainfield (Vermont) Friends Meeting since 1959 and have participated in a number of Clearness Committees over the years. My own experiences are that this process, together with its values and norms, can be powerful learning experiences for both the focus person and those who are invited to participate.

—◆◆◆—

External evaluations have been carried out for both the Center for Formation in the Community College and the Center for Teacher Formation. The evaluations indicate that formation programs have far-reaching effects on education and educational reform. See Appendix D for some of the key findings.

I submit that this formation work, complemented by Conversations of Consequence and Appreciative Inquiry where appropriate, provides a solid foundation for whatever professional development programs we undertake. Note also that these approaches are highly consistent with the pedagogical activities described in Chapter Five. They are similar to the kind of classroom culture that Nash describes so eloquently (personal communication, Oct. 28, 2002). They can help build the kind of community Dalton discusses in Chapter Seven. They represent the attitudes, conditions, and activities that underlie most educationally powerful environments.

TWO WORKING EXAMPLES

We have two working examples of how these formation approaches to institutional amplification and professional development are being addressed. One is the Dallas County Community College District (DCCCD); the other is Richland College, one of the DCCCD institutions.

Dallas County Community College District

Guy Gooding, the district director for staff and organizational development, has shared the DCCCD story with me. The DCCCD is a large system with over 120,000 credit enrollments per year, 7,000 full- and part-time faculty and staff, and seven colleges scattered throughout Dallas County. Implementing formation processes to renew collegial practices has been both intentional and, even more uncommon, organically supported by district leadership. Throughout the process, the decision to participate has been by individual choice rather than by institutional mandate.

THE CATALYST. The movement for change began with Parker Palmer's keynote address to faculty and administration during a spring 1998 District Conference Day. Palmer spoke with passion about the conditions confronting education, and related these challenges to the empowerment that can come when each teacher finds his or her authentic voice. His presentation received the first standing ovation for a Conference Day keynote speaker in the history of the DCCCD.

It was clear that Palmer was suggesting a form of development that moved beyond such issues as keeping information technologies relevant and revitalizing core curricula, all matters that the District Office of Staff and Organizational Development (SOD) had been addressing. In fact, in the first stages of implementation, it became important for SOD to understand what this new form of development was *not*. It was not an initiative designed to fix a problem. It was not a strategic planning process. It was not a team-building experience or a way to reach a consensus. Instead it was a form of professional development that celebrates the power of individual teachers, concerned professionals who make a commitment to better understand who they are so as to become more authentic, in order to make a difference in the lives of their students.

Institutionally, the DCCCD began to support developing this different path. Bill Wenrich, the chancellor, and Bill Tucker, vice chancellor of planning and development affairs, believed the approach had particular potential to engage long-term faculty and renew their commitment to, and passion for, teaching. Using Palmer's terminology, the process was called teacher formation.

PHASE ONE—THE FIRST RETREAT SERIES AND THE TRAINING OF FACILITATORS. Although some administrators had been reading Palmer's writing over the years, it was Bill Tucker's participation in a retreat on higher education and formation with Palmer that led to a critical first step. The DCCCD assembled a team of twenty-four to meet with Palmer at the Fetzer Institute in August 1997. The group included DCCCD faculty, administrators, a trustee, representatives from the Dallas public schools, and several members of the Dallas community. Following that trip and Palmer's resounding success at the spring Conference Day, the SOD office invited participation in the first two-year retreat series, which began in January 1998. The principles and concepts of this retreat series were described earlier in the discussion of the Center for Formation in the Community College (see "Professional Development"). A teacher formation facilitator recommended by Palmer led this series. There were eleven participants from DCCCD faculty and three teachers from a suburban public school district. At the same time, in a process closely guided by Palmer, the district selected a group of seven facilitators to be prepared in Dallas with the aid of an experienced formation facilitator as mentor. These newly trained facilitators would help sustain and expand the work over time.

By underwriting both a retreat series and facilitator preparation, DCCCD leadership took the risk to focus staff development on personal, inner growth rather than on skill development or new classroom techniques. The risk paid off. The faculty who participated in the retreats actually began to realize that they could shift the institutional culture by changing their perceptions of who they were as teachers and the vision of what "the teacher" could mean in the DCCCD.

WE ARE ALL TEACHERS. The second two-year retreat series was launched in fall 1999, with two of the new Dallas-based facilitators nervously assuming their role as guides of the formation process. The twenty-four participants included faculty (both full- and part-time) as well as instructional staff and administrators (a lab coordinator and a dean), but staff were not invited to participate. By this time, administrative and professional support staff were beginning to wonder what this formation experience entailed and whether it applied to them and their work. The "charged expectation" created in formation was seeping beyond faculty. This broader interest helped SOD develop an approach to introducing the experience of formation through a short urban retreat, which was called a Formation Sampler. SOD proposed a series of one-night retreats to be held in a local hotel, facilitated by the district's newly prepared facilitators and open to all staff—faculty, administration, and professional support staff, both full- and part-time. The purpose of the sampler was to offer an experience of formation that allowed participants to decide whether they wanted to pursue a retreat series with its commitments, overnights away from home, and countercultural focus on the inner life. Interest was sufficient to fill five sampler retreats that first year. Although some decided that formation was not something they'd want more of, the generally enthusiastic response to samplers was yet another endorsement of the power of formation.

SOD staff members, along with the members of the chancellor's cabinet and faculty leaders, were increasingly convinced of the benefit of using the institution's staff development funds for this inner development. Faculty completing the first and second two-year retreat series were enthusiastic and sincere in their belief that their teaching had been positively changed by the work of formation. In a session with the chancellor following the eighth retreat, the second retreat series completers unanimously endorsed making formation available to all employee groups. That group of teachers felt that they were missing something by not including other staff. The decision was made to open future retreats to all staff.

This seismic change in the culture encouraged SOD to attempt even more. Palmer agreed to mentor the staff and assist in the growth of DCCCD formation by making a visit each semester for two years. He scheduled three days for each. During a visit, Palmer would interact with a variety of groups. He continued to speak about the power of the individual to make a difference. But he also focused his message for his audience. He held a session with the trustees of the DCCCD Foundation called "To Hold in Trust." He made a public speech downtown, which was attended by college and community members, on building community. When he talked with students, he often focused on students' stories of courage, allowing some of the wonderful stories of success to be heard. "Let Your Life Speak" was a topic, which he offered to a group of leaders from the Professional Support Staff Council, encouraging them to understand their power and to resist "participating in their own diminishment."

During roughly the same time period, several DCCCD campuses were initiating their own formation work on location, holding samplers followed by several daylong retreats, creating circles of trust to reflect on their personal and professional lives. In both the SOD-sponsored district retreat series and the off-campus formation efforts, groups that had formed to support inner work found that they did not wish to dissolve the bonds of trust they had developed among themselves. They continued to meet, on their own time and at their own expense, after the formal end of their retreat series. Some of these groups still continue.

INSTITUTIONAL FORMATION. After two years of Palmer's periodic residencies, SOD asked him for his assessment of the efforts of the DCCCD. He observed that the DCCCD had done several things right. One was to allow the process to grow slowly and through voluntary participation. No individuals or colleges were "mandated" to administer formation—much less to participate in reflective activities.

Another success was investing in the local preparation of facilitators who could sustain and lead formation from their understanding of the context. These trained facilitators had become the stewards, ensuring that the process maintained its integrity. Again and again when participants were invited to formation retreats or to meetings with Palmer, the emphasis was placed on the voluntary nature of the invitation. Facilitators continually emphasized that the purpose of the experience was to support the growth of the individual. This countered a long tradition of staff development that focused on the institution rather than the person.

Palmer also observed that formation experiences were making a difference in the most important arena: faculty members' relationships with students and with one another. Parker's suggestion was that SOD and formation facilitators, under the leadership of vice chancellor Bill Tucker, continue the work. In spring 2001, these internal advocates made several critical decisions. First, they negotiated with Palmer to extend his appearances in the DCCCD for another two years through fall 2003.

Next, SOD formed a new group made up of a cross section of staff from across the district to come together for a series of gatherings to explore applying formation explicitly to work situations. Formation at Work (FAW) became a laboratory for both the DCCCD formation facilitators and for Palmer himself. The members of the group were drawn from those who had shown an interest in formation through participation in a retreat series, sampler, or other formation-related event. A conscious effort was made to invite participation from all locations and all job categories. The initial group included a vice chancellor, two college presidents, and a vice president, along with staff and faculty from many work groups.

WHAT DO WE CELEBRATE, AND WHERE DO WE GROW? All this activity led to a pivotal undertaking in 2002–2003. It was Palmer's final year of consulting with the DCCCD, and the organization was in a time of transition. The search for a new chancellor was under way, extremely high rates of retirement were looming, and a $450 million bond election was under deliberation.

Over the years, Palmer had shared the story of Rosa Parks's decision not to participate in her own diminishment by continuing to sit at the back of the bus. While facilitating a FAW session, Palmer heard the fears concerning change. He directed the conversation away from the self-inflicted fear, urging instead consideration of what they celebrated about the DCCCD and where they wanted their organization to grow. These two questions struck a chord and were the beginning of a long and rich conversation about an organization in transition.

Steve Mittelstet, president of the college hosting the District Conference Day in 2003, was present at the FAW meeting that day. In response to Palmer's questions, Steve convinced all ten locations to hold focus groups in preparation for Conference Day. In effect drawing on formation principles, the district embarked on an Appreciative Inquiry of what it celebrated and where it wanted to grow. At the completion of the discussions, five common themes for celebration and growth were identified across the district: the spirit of the organization, relationship-centered community, diversity, innovation, and the student and learning focus of the DCCCD.

During Conference Day, five members of the DCCCD family addressed the assembled faculty and administrators, telling their personal stories of celebration and growth around each theme. That afternoon more than four hundred individuals came together for small-group discussions to share stories. The groups of twenty-five or so used a modified version of Margaret Wheatley's guidelines for what she refers to as simple conversations (2002) to address one of the topics. (Wheatley is an internationally recognized consultant on leadership and organizational behavior.) Seasoned formation participants and facilitators, given special preparation for leading this kind of conversation, facilitated all the groups. The groups generated enormous excitement. There was a common outcry for more such real conversation among DCCCD professionals. A summary of these conversations was published following the conference and distributed throughout the district.

OTHER RIPPLES AND OUTCOMES. Since Conference Day 2003, several other initiatives aimed to merge principles of formation into new or existing programs. Taking the time to honor award winners in a meaningful way is one such initiative. The SOD staff hosts a reception for award winners a few days before the formal presentation of awards at Conference Day. Designed to recognize winners at all locations for exemplary teaching, innovation, service to students, and professional support staff leadership, the reception recognizes each recipient with a limited-edition framed print of a selected piece of student art. The student artist is invited to speak as well. Opening and closing public SOD events with poetry provides time for reflection.

The New Employee Orientation, a mandatory program, has been adjusted to maximize the hospitality and welcoming of the district. Longtime staff tell stories of why the district has been a good place to work, and new employees are encouraged to see the DCCCD as a place to grow professionally and personally.

Formation principles resonate with other concepts and principles DCCCD professionals have come to value. Staff see common threads with the work of Robert Greenleaf and the Center for Servant Leadership, Steven Covey and principle-centered leadership, and Margaret Wheatley and simple conversations. SOD staff have also been trained to facilitate Appreciative Inquiry processes and to employ personality inventory exercises to increase appreciation of differences in work and learning styles. With practice, formation-related behaviors are becoming integrated into the district's culture. Individuals participating in the retreats and samplers speak of a new level of accountability in their lives—personally and to their colleagues and students.

These efforts have led several hundred DCCCD staff to make formation part of their professional development. In written evaluations, focus groups, and interviews, participants report that formation helps them engage students differently, slow frenetic activity, grow in self-awareness, improve listening skills, build relationships of trust, work collaboratively with colleagues, and take greater risks. Their inner work also helps them confront such issues as workaholism, fear, anger, and hurt. Chancellor Jesus Carreon has affirmed SOD's districtwide formation programs, and colleges continue to develop formation programs for themselves. Formation and related efforts to appreciate the spirit of the individual have made the DCCCD a better place to work.

———

This powerful story shows how a large, multicampus district, with sustained effort over a period of years, can encourage increased authenticity and spiritual growth among large numbers of diverse professionals. It shows how it is possible to create internal expertise and undertake systematic efforts that not only amplify district professionals but also encourage similar efforts among district institutions, such as Richland College.

Richland College

Richland College, which each semester enrolls some 24,000 students, 14,000 of whom are enrolled in college credit programs, is one of seven separately accredited colleges of the DCCCD.

As the story of the district suggests, Steve Mittelstet, who has been Richland's president for more than twenty-five years, was actively involved in the early formation initiatives. It is not surprising that his institution began similar work early on. His presidency is another example of the moral leadership Liesa Stamm describes in Chapter 10.

An external evaluator recently said, "I've never seen an institution of higher learning with a more 'scientific,' well-deployed and -assessed, dynamic institutional effectiveness plan. Your multi-year discipline of following national Baldrige and Quality Texas excellence in education standards with twice-annual progress feedback from external evaluators has yielded impressive results each year.

"Yet, your employees and students spend a great deal of time on their personal and professional development, especially in the 'soft,' 'unscientific' realms of nurturing and connecting their inner, reflective lives to their active, outer lives of service to others. How do you find the time for all this?"

To this question, Mittelstet replied, "Ah, the delights of paradox: making time through spending time wisely. I believe it's not so much *yet* as it is *and*. Our experience is that *time out* to nurture our inner lives increases our life-enhancing effectiveness on the job. This minimizes the time many organizations squander in dysfunction and other life-diminishing behaviors. And, we tend to have fun doing it, intentionally incorporating laughter, play, and celebration in what we do."

Richland is a somewhat typical large public urban commuter community college with open admissions. Less than one-fifth of its college credit students enroll fresh out of high school; a similarly low percentage is enrolled with full-time loads. Not so typically, nearly three-fourths are enrolled in college transfer programs. The student average age is twenty-eight. Its fastest-growing age cohort of fifty-five and over is drawn to its Emeritus program, in which participants enroll in computer classes to stay in touch with grandchildren, in liberal arts classes they never got around to earlier, in one of eleven different foreign language classes as they travel the world with and without the college and study the Islamic culture to understand better their new next-door neighbors.

Many of Richland's students pop in and out throughout the years, depending on what's happening in their lives: divorce, employment layoffs, a need to upgrade marketable skills, marriage, challenges in rearing their families, and life-threatening illness or accident. These students are not so much preparing for life as experiencing all stages of their lives and partnering with the college community to help them live life more fully, more meaningfully.

The youthful "day campus, night campus" cultural contrast described by Dalton in Chapter One—where full-time students take classes during the day and have "meaning of life" conversations at night in their dorms—doesn't exist at Richland. Nearly half its students take classes at night between family, work, and community responsibilities, mostly as part-time students. Nearly all its students work full- or part-time, not for fancy cars, luxury items, or extra spending money but to sustain their lives, raise their families, and advance their careers.

Richland believes that the members of this real-life, highly diverse student body, who tend to show up in the same classes together in all their rich diversity, are particularly ready to examine and reexamine meaning-of-life issues with their colleagues (both student and faculty) precisely because their challenging lives demand it. The college's challenge is to help students address these generally unstated underlying meaning-of-life needs with the rather brief, intermittent encounters it has, mostly in class, with many of its students. What follows gives some insight into the approaches Richland's teachers, learners, and community builders use to imbed core life-purpose growth opportunities into all its encounters with students, regardless of curriculum or course, in both liberal arts and career development and through cocurricular student development activities, matriculation services, and, yes, gardening.

Richland's whole-person, whole-institution approach eschews liberal arts–career development dichotomies. It believes that real people (including those excluded from selective four-year institutions) need jobs to exist, need to speak English to survive in the United States, need life skills, need meaningful careers, need purpose in life, and need to live in community with one another in a sustainable environment. Richland is bold enough to believe it can help most of its students on most of these fronts, and it is intentional and systematic about its efforts to do so.

Mittelstet believes that Richland has been on an institutional formation journey in earnest since 1999, when it first invited a group of twenty-five faculty, staff, and administrators to a formation retreat in Michigan. Even before, several key faculty members had been using mindfulness practices in their personal lives and incorporating aspects of those principles in their teaching, which was enhanced by their own authentic, whole-person approach with their students. Since the 1980s, Mittelstet had been quoting from Parker Palmer's works, such as *To Know as We Are Known*, in his annual fall convocation addresses. Richland's special-emphasis degree program for students, called Mind-Body-Spirit-Health, and its related whole-person wellness program for employees, both of which began in the 1970s, are also early indicators that institutional formation has been under way a long time at Richland College.

Richland's administrators and allied professionals did not, however, intentionally launch an institutional formation journey. They did not set out to "fix" anything in the institution. Rather, caring for its employees and students, they came to believe that it is the whole person who best teaches, learns, leads, serves, and builds community. In 1999, Richland began inviting all its employees (full- and part-time, all classifications) to participate in one of two annual teacher-leader retreat series; nearly two hundred have done so at least once over a six-year period. It has provided an environment where people can focus on their own "who" questions, nurturing their inner selves in a trusting, supportive, "safe" community. Then these more authentic, "divided-no-more" employees come to work every day, behaving in ways that send similar ripple effects among students, colleagues, and community—in classroom approaches, in everyday services, in ongoing operations, in innovative program development, in student activities, and in professional development.

Mittelstet is wary of CEOs' seeing institutional formation as a quick-fix strategy for an institution in disarray. Instead, he believes in long-term investment in employee development, which includes whole-person formation work. On this foundation, developing and implementing a sound, college-wide integrated institutional effectiveness discipline, such as that provided by the national Malcolm Baldrige program, can result in a highly effective institution. It will achieve its teaching, learning, and community-building mission with employees and students who enjoy teaching, learning, and working together. "Not easy, not always pretty," Mittelstet observes. "Imagine Parker Palmer and Malcolm Baldrige in some odd-couple Dance of the Paradox. Difficult and sometimes awkward as it can be, it certainly takes the two for this important Richland dance. And the occasional moments of dazzling, fluid movement are quite something to behold!"

The following are some of the programs and activities that have been created and imbued with "formational principles":

Academic Enrichment programs special emphasis degree (a type of associate's degree "major") programs. In these programs, sections of core courses already required for various transfer degrees are thematically linked together with "formational" threads and approaches that help students find purpose and meaning in a diverse array of interdisciplinary, integrated studies.

Thematically linked learning communities. These provide similar experiences on a smaller scale for students and for the faculty who teach, learn, and build community with them.

Service learning cocurricular course approaches. "Formational" reflection sessions and journal writing help students connect real-life community service to course content and also help them find purpose and meaning in life, often with profound life-changing, career-redirecting effects.

Intercultural Competence, an eight-year professional development series. This series was developed by Richland faculty in conjunction with external consultants from the international Summer Institute for Intercultural Communications (SIIC). In annual professional development sessions, this series introduces all Richland employees both cognitively and experientially to the various conceptual stages of intercultural competence. These stages provide the theoretical basis for the multiyear, internationally normed SIIC Intercultural Development Inventory©.

Leadership development. This series for employees and students is infused with formation principles, touchstones, and invitational experiences.

What Do We Celebrate? Where Do We Grow? Thematic employee-student conversations are facilitated by formation-experienced employees, following a hybrid version of Wheatley's simple conversations and Appreciative Inquiry guidelines on such topics as campus civility and the college's role in environmental sustainability.

Appreciative Inquiry. This approach helps Richlanders analyze, learn from, and take action on findings from such instruments as the Community College Survey of Student Engagement.

Living, practiced organizational values. Richland's official organizational values: mutual trust, wholeness, honesty, fairness, considerate open communication, mindfulness, cooperation, responsible risk taking, and joy are continually reinforced through works and deeds.

Rites, rituals, traditions. Annual fall convocations are upbeat affairs shaped by organizational values and full of storytelling and rituals for welcoming new employees—all focused on teaching, learning, and community building.

Clearness Committees. Employees who attend Richland's formation retreat series learn and experience the principles of the Clearness Committee, discussed earlier. Many of these employees have entered their names on an electronic resource list. Anyone can convene a group of well-trained, deep listeners who, by asking open, nonleading questions, help the focus person discover personal insights related to whatever challenge he or she faces.

Facilities and grounds. Maintenance staff members support a work environment of contemplation–action–celebration that includes an outdoor sixty-foot-diameter mindfulness walking labyrinth; indoor meditation facilities; and a peace pole trail alongside the campus central lakes, with poles inscribed with the message "May Peace Prevail on Earth" in English and three other languages. One pole is erected each semester in a student-community ceremony celebrating and honoring the cultures represented by the featured languages.

Metaphorical language. Richland's communication style consciously employs organic, gardening-related, seasonal metaphorical language, and strives to avoid language of violence, conflict, triumph, win-lose, exclusion, and diminishment, whether in class, in daily work interactions, or in official publications.

Benchmarking relationships. Richland participates in invitational consortia, such as the Association of American Colleges and Universities "Greater Expectations" consortium, focusing on liberal arts learning for the twenty-first century. It provides program benchmarking partnerships with like-minded institutions, such as Alverno College, emphasizing life-purpose student learning outcomes and the assessment thereof, as well as related teaching-learning strategies. Richland's practical Mittelstet cautions, "All this describes us on our better days. Remember: this is a daily *journey.* These are our *guideposts.*"

These two working examples at the district and institutional levels demonstrate that we have the talent and sophistication to pursue institutional amplification and the associated professional development activities necessary to move toward an institutional culture that encourages authenticity and spiritual growth. We can adapt these principles, practices, and programmatic elements to our own particular institutional contexts. We can encourage the kind of self-examination and self-affirmation that these institutional and professional formation approaches enable.

CONCLUSION

To recap, we need planned change strategies that achieve reasonable balances between centralization and decentralization, advance planning and learning by doing, widespread involvement and timely decisions. We need to use processes like Appreciative Inquiry and Conversations of Consequence to help engender a culture that strengthens authenticity and spiritual growth. Those inquiry and change processes need to be accompanied by institution-wide teacher formation retreats and shorter workshops that are sustained through time. An institution that creates this combination will—over time—create a culture that nourishes authenticity and spiritual growth, not only for its students but for all its employees.

But the institution will only be able to build on that foundation well, over the number of years required, by creating a congruent assessment program, as we discuss in Chapter Nine. That program needs to provide rich and continuous feedback that gives us sound data about the quality of our institutional culture, the strengths and weaknesses of our educational policies and practices, and our desired outcomes for students.

Assessing Ineffable Outcomes

Arthur W. Chickering, with Marcia Mentkowski

T he assessment leg of our three-legged stool must be strong and durable to guide sustained institutional improvement. It is the foundation for educational planning and problem solving. Yet despite the program and institutional assessment movement and the hard work devoted to it, applying complex evaluation to institutional policies and practices is seldom seriously undertaken, or taken seriously, by our colleges and universities. And even fewer efforts are focused on systematically assessing the impact of institutional policies and practices on the full range of students' collegiate experiences and desired outcomes. Assessing experiences and desired outcomes is especially challenging when it comes to interventions designed to encourage spiritual growth, authenticity, purpose, and meaning.

Jon Dalton and Art Chickering had the privilege of co-chairing a community of practice titled "Assessing the Ineffable" for the 2002 Assessment Conference of the American Association for Higher Education. We were ably assisted by Anita Henck. The participants, who came from a wide range of colleges and universities, struggled with the complex issues outlined in this chapter.

Ineffable means "incapable of being expressed in words." Therein lies a bedrock issue for assessing institutional influences on and outcomes related to spirituality. As noted in Chapter One, spiritual growth is highly interactive and is interdependent with other major vectors of human development: integrity, identity, autonomy and interdependence, purpose and meaning. Outcomes like these are not easily defined and operationalized. And if we cannot define them clearly, then this cornerstone for assessment is wobbly and ungrounded. The invitation describing this community of practice said, "Spiritual growth, increased capacity to love and to be loved, strengthened authenticity and identity, emotional resilience and stability, empathy and altruism, character and integrity—these and others, all are critical for satisfying lives and productive citizenship. Can we assess outcomes such as these? Should we try? Come struggle with us."

As we tackled the problem of definition, we sampled the language used at the varied institutions represented. Here is a partial list of terms: authenticity, character development, empathy, ethics, faith, integrity, meaning, ministry, moral development, purpose, service, spirituality, spiritual formation, spiritual growth, values, wisdom.

These words are certainly all in the same general ballpark, but some are more in center field, others more toward right or left. Given the diverse institutions that characterize U.S. higher education, a wide range of perspectives is both inevitable and desirable. The basic point is that each institution has to specify its own definition, with language appropriate for its mission; for its faculty members, student affairs professionals, administrators, and trustees; for its students, parents, alumni, and other stakeholders. That language needs to be widely accepted and well owned.

When we turned to identifying observable indicators pertinent to our varied perspectives, at the level of student behaviors, attitudes, and values, we found similar variety and also similar congruence:

Being upset about cheating and acting on it

Valuing and respecting diverse backgrounds, orientations, and belief systems

Learning and using the language of values, as opposed to being judgmental

Making connections between the beliefs and values expressed by ways of living, and learning through courses, classes, extracurricular activities, and off-campus experiences

Maintaining a balance between doing and being

Protecting time for reflection

Being actively engaged with civic issues and exercising social responsibility

Persevering in tackling social issues and causes

Exercising thoughtful and sensitive leadership

Negative indicators included the flip sides of some of these positives:

Being dishonest, in academics and in other ways

Being unable to move from language to action, to back words with deeds, to walk the talk

Being judgmental

Mouthing a ritualistic party line

Being self-centered, unable to identify with anything larger than one's immediate self-interest

Using sexist, racist, or homophobic language and behavior

The important thing about these shared indicators is that there are "observables" out there. Any concerned institution can, collaboratively with students, faculty members, administrators, and student affairs professionals, articulate its own list. With an agreed-on set of observables, the institution can use a variety of "unobtrusive" and "obtrusive" strategies and measures to track them over time for their frequency and intensity. Unobtrusive strategies can include participant observations in residence halls, student unions, locker rooms, and other gathering places for conversational and behavioral exchanges. They can include monitoring the frequency of more formal actions by judicial boards, police, and various administrators. These kinds of "flesh-and-blood" approaches keep us close to our daily lives and bring concrete realities to bear on our conceptual abstractions. But they are more labor intensive and, in some strategies for implementation, more time consuming than the usual strategies we use as more "obtrusive" measures.

The dominant strategy, of course, is the survey questionnaire. A wide variety of alternatives for assessing religious and spiritual beliefs have been used in the past. Two collections are mentioned in Chapter Two. Perhaps the best, and least known, is *Multidimensional Mea-*

surement of Religiousness/Spirituality for Use in Health Research (Fetzer Institute/National Institute on Aging Working Group, 1999). The scales they cite aim to measure beliefs, daily spiritual experiences, meaning, private religious practice, religious/spiritual history, religious support, commitment, forgiveness, organizational religiousness, religious/spiritual coping, religious preference, and values. Another useful reference, described in Chapter Two, is *Measures of Religiosity* (Hill & Hood, 1999). Some of these authors' categories are similar to those of the previously mentioned publication; others are not: religious attitudes, religious commitment and involvement, religious development, divine intervention/religious attribution, forgiveness, god concept, religious/moral values or characteristics, spirituality and mysticism, religious beliefs and practices, religious coping and problem solving, views of death/afterlife, religious experiences, religious fundamentalism, institutional religious attitudes, religious orientation, and related constructs such as purpose of life. Note, however, that most of these surveys are useful for describing the orientations of the target population but not for assessing institutional impact and the contributions of varied program interventions.

The most recent survey, which builds on this earlier work, is the College Students' Beliefs and Values Survey created by Alexander and Helen Astin and their colleagues at the UCLA Higher Education Research Institute (HERI), with support from the John Templeton Foundation. Not surprisingly, their domains are similar to those already mentioned: spiritual outlook/orientation/worldview; spiritual well being; spiritual/religious behavior/practice; self-assessments (of spirituality and related traits); spiritual quest; spiritual/mystical experiences; theological/metaphysical beliefs; attitudes toward religion/ spirituality; religious affiliation/identity. This survey, and HERI's capacity to follow up with students across diverse institutions, can help institutions get a sense of the distributions of spiritual orientations among their students and compare themselves with other subsets. With retesting and with repeated use of this instrument, an institution can also observe changes among its students during their college experience and over time.

Assessing individual institutional contributions is a more complicated and challenging task, especially if we aim to understand the relative impact of varied policies, programs, and practices. The assessment movement has made major contributions and great strides. This chapter cannot attempt to synthesize the extensive literature on program and institutional assessment, but we do want to address some basic conceptual and methodological issues (see also Ewell, 1991).

We need to distinguish between (1) the general climate, culture, "press"—the attitudes, values, rituals, and routines that are perceived to be widely shared—and (2) actual individual behaviors and daily experiences. General perceptions and individual behaviors can vary substantially. Each student's perceptions are shaped by his or her frame of reference. Whether a student perceives the institution as challenging or dull, liberal or conservative, friendly or distant depends on each person's home, school, and community background. Perceptions of the general culture also often reflect the influence and power of a visible, vocal, and active minority. For example, studies have asked students about how much drinking or sexual activity has occurred on a particular weekend and also asked about their own drinking and sexual behavior. Student estimates of general behavior consistently exceed their actual behaviors by significant percentages.

We need both quantitative and qualitative data about perceptions and behaviors. Surveys, tests, and such need to be supplemented by focus groups and individual interviews. Statistical findings help us understand how widespread and significant the impacts—positive or negative—of various interventions may be. They can help us understand how various influences interact and the relative power of those influences. But only qualitative data get to a level of human detail that helps us understand how diverse individuals are actually influenced.

Then, of course, we need to assess student change over time. We need both cross-sectional studies across grade levels and test-retest studies of the same individuals at different times during college. These longitudinal and cross-sectional studies need to combine inventories, questionnaires, tests, focus groups, and interviews. But note that when institutions are changing rapidly, in "image" or in actuality, and when the characteristics of entrants and transfers also are changing, the contributions of longitudinal studies are diminished. The value of such studies increases dramatically when they are carried out systematically for successive groups of students over several years.

ALVERNO COLLEGE— A WORKING EXAMPLE

Alverno's approach to assessment is widely cited as one model to be studied in creating an approach to assessment because the Alverno curriculum and its student, program, and institutional assessment practices are accessible and open to critique and comparison (for example, Alverno College Faculty, 1979/1994, 2000; Loacker & Mentkowski, 1993; Riordan & Roth, 2005). The Alverno curriculum, cocurriculum, and assessment system have been evolving, along with the institution, since the 1970s. Administrators, faculty, and staff have benefited from the observations and critiques of many colleagues from a wide range of colleges and universities. In the last five years, for example, nearly four thousand educators representing more than one thousand institutions in the United States and abroad attended workshops and institutes on teaching and assessment at Alverno.

The Alverno curriculum is grounded in articulated educational values, assumptions, and learning principles that other educators can examine and debate. Alverno faculty members have constantly adapted their approaches across time in response to changes in personnel and leadership; they have also documented their experiences working with ten consortia made up of one hundred institutions in total (Mentkowski & Associates, 2000, pp. 459–464). Analysis of these documents shows that campus conditions and culture do matter. Faculty and administrators at institutions larger in scale and programmatic scope create their own alternatives and resources for varied subunits that suit their desired outcomes and are appropriate for their particular students, faculty, and staff. For example, those technical and community colleges that are part of a system, such as Washington State Community Colleges, obtained support for innovation in assessment at the state level (Moore, 2002). Schools of Pharmacy determined and defined explicit outcomes and assessment with support from their national associations (Zlatic, 2001). These institutions and Alverno have been able to benefit from this collaboration (Rickards, Mentkowski, Rozdilsky, & Brown, 1994). Finally, through systematic studies (Mentkowski & Associates, 2000; Mentkowski, in press), Alverno has distilled more transportable and adaptable practices from those more specific to Alverno's particular culture and curriculum. Many researchers have acknowledged Alverno's rigorous educational research base (Baxter Magolda, 2002; Hakel, 2001; Brabeck, 2001; Svinicki, 2002). External research teams have conducted independent studies of Alverno as part of comparative studies of several institutions (Colby, Ehrlich, Beaumont, & Stephens, 2003; Darling-Hammond, 2000; Dean & Lauer, 2003; Ewens, 1979; Hinett, 1995; Kuh, Kinzie, Schuh, Whitt, & Associates, 2005; Lauer & Dean, 2003; NSSE Institute for Effective Educational Practice, 2003; Winter, McClelland, & Stewart, 1981).

Earlier in this chapter, we discussed defining ineffable outcomes as an important step in assessment, and so it is useful to consider Alverno's definition of student learning outcomes or abilities. *Abilities* are complex combinations of motivations, dispositions, attitudes, values, strategies, behaviors, self-perceptions, and knowledge of concepts and procedures: "These combinations are dynamic and interactive, and they can be acquired and developed both through education and experience. Abilities become a cause of effective performance when these components are integrated. A complex ability cannot be observed directly; it must be inferred from performances. . . . 'Ability' is a *concept* that communicates, because it is also *experienced.* One can conceptualize abilities and also experience having or using one's abilities in situations" (Mentkowski, Loacker, & O'Brien, 1998, pp. 13, 15).

Alverno's General Orientation

Alverno has "continually revised and redefined a curriculum that requires all students to demonstrate eight core abilities in the context of their study across various disciplines" (Alverno College Faculty, 1976/2005, p. v):

1. Communication: Speaking, Writing, Listening, Reading, Quantitative Literacy, Computer Literacy
2. Analysis
3. Problem Solving
4. Valuing in Decision Making
5. Social Interaction
6. Developing a Global Perspective
7. Effective Citizenship
8. Aesthetic Engagement

Alverno's creativity lies in not only stating these desired outcomes but articulating six levels of performance for each and continually revising them to respond to an increasingly diverse student body and to new insights from teaching, scholarship, and individual differences in student learning and performance. To illustrate, the 2002 levels for the valuing ability, "Develop facility in making value judgments and independent decisions," were as follows:

Level 1: Identify own values.

Level 2: Infer and analyze values in artistic and humanistic works.

Level 3: Relate values to scientific and technological developments.

Level 4: Engage in valuing in decision making in multiple contexts.

In majors and areas of specialization:

Level 5: Analyze and formulate the value foundation/framework of a specific area of knowledge, in its theory and practice.

Level 6: Apply own theory of value and the value foundation of an area of knowledge in a professional context [Alverno College Faculty, 1973/2002, p. 2].

In the 2005 revision of this ability by the valuing ability department, an interdisciplinary group of faculty, the levels show increased attention to emotions and the spiritual dimensions of valuing, as well as the social contexts and relationships that shape them:

Beginning Levels: Explores the valuing process

Level 1—Identifies own and others' values and some key emotions they evoke

Level 2—Connects own values to behavior and articulates the cognitive and spiritual dimensions of this process

Intermediate Levels: More precisely analyzes the role of groups, cultures, and societies in the construction of values and their expression in moral systems or ethical frameworks

Level 3—Analyzes the reciprocal relationship between own values and their social contexts and explores how that relationship plays out

Level 4—Uses the perspectives and concepts of particular disciplines to inform moral judgments and decisions

Advanced Levels in Areas of Specialization: Explores and applies value systems and ethical codes at the heart of the field

Level 5—Uses valuing frameworks of a major field of study or profession to engage significant issues in personal, professional, and civic contexts

Level 6—Consistently examines and cultivates own value systems in order to take initiative as a responsible self in the world [(Alverno College Faculty, 1973/2005, p. 2)].

Furthermore, faculty members have devised public criteria for each level within each ability. The criteria serve two functions: they give each student a clear goal for learning, and they give each faculty member broad standards for judging and certifying whether the student has achieved the ability level. The collegewide criteria are generic and not specific to a particular course, but each discipline department and its individual faculty members specify the learning outcomes and criteria that integrate these broad abilities with the content of courses and majors, and faculty design corresponding student assessments. This cross-disciplinary faculty understanding helps ensure that students see that a basic ability is relevant to multiple contexts and that they are refining that ability through multiple applications. It is expected that students will develop the first four levels across all eight abilities through the general education program and that they will develop levels five and six in majors and areas of specialization. Satisfying those expectations through course-based assessments and through integrative external assessments of student learning from several courses is required for graduation.

Each disciplinary department focuses on the abilities most closely related to its content areas and takes responsibility for providing the appropriate learning and assessment opportunities. Each course description includes not only its content and desired learning outcomes but the particular abilities and levels it aims to encourage. There are also "departments" for each ability in which faculty members continually review and improve the pertinent teaching, learning, and student assessment activities, drawing on evidence from the literature, their teaching, and the student assessment data. In sum, student assessment-as-learning is integral to teaching and learning, is designed by faculty to determine each student's degree of success in the course or program, and provides opportunity for students to apply their knowledge and ability in integrated performances in varied settings. As noted, student assessment involves expert observation and judgment in relation to explicit criteria and rubrics, and also involves diagnostic and prescriptive feedback combined with a student's own self-assessment to strengthen future performance (Alverno College Faculty, 1979/1994).

Alverno faculty members acknowledge that the eight abilities required for graduation do *not* characterize all dimensions of human experience. For example, they do not presume to capture each student's unique identity and authenticity, the multiple ways each makes meaning, and how learning experiences influence the broader shape of each person's professional and personal contributions and commitments. To examine these hoped-for but not required outcomes, program and institution-wide assessment is designed so as to be integral to learning about such ineffable outcomes. For example, faculty, staff, and administrators have used data from longitudinal interviews and inventories to gain the students' perspective on programs' value for fostering student learning. Multiple approaches, including externally designed measures of intellectual, moral, and ego development, have generated multiple sources of feedback to faculty, staff, and administrators about patterns of student and alumnae learning, who then use the findings from systematic studies to probe the effectiveness of learning opportunities and to stimulate public dialogue about possible improvements. Follow-up studies of alumnae also yield evidence-based judgments of how students and alumnae benefit from the curriculum, cocurriculum, and other learning contexts, and guide curricular, cocurricular, and institution-wide improvements.

How Alverno Creates and Carries Out Institutional Assessment

How do Alverno faculty and staff create institutional assessment programs, anchored in theoretical frameworks, that include longitudinal and cross-sectional designs, multiple information-gathering strategies, and various sources of evidence, that can play an important role in educational decision making? They do so by making a series of choices that are grounded in educational values and assumptions about what is possible for human learners to achieve (Mentkowski, 1998). These values and assumptions are not necessarily visible or viable in any one situation. Often they need to be imagined, drawn from difficult dialogues about challenging experiences and failures, or imagined from emerging educational philosophies that counter those inferred from current practice. Some examples of these educational values and beliefs are familiar to many of us—the belief that all students can learn, that many understandings about the human condition are yet to be discovered, that rigorous critical thinking and marshaling of evidence in many different forms can lead us to educational approaches that are more relevant, effective, and respectful of individual students and what they already know and can do. Also familiar are the disjunctions between these hopes and what educators are able to do in the most sacred of relationships: personal interactions intended to pass on culture and meaning from one generation to the next. Alverno educators are also caught up in the paradox of using what they know—a set of ideas and strategies that have the potential for both positive and negative outcomes—to imagine what they do not know or what may be unknowable.

There are some very practical stances for institutional assessment that can emerge from such an abstract set of commitments. The courage to take practical steps rests on their explicit relationship to educational values. The surgeon who intends to save a life, the teacher who intends to open a mind—both must be aware of the consequences of a misstep. Alverno educators strive to open themselves to their immediate questions, the current problems students are having in a series of courses, the need to show a funding agency what students have accomplished with faculty guidance, or to lay bare discrepancies in financial and family support for learning that students experience. Alverno educators often begin with an immediate, problem-solving focus on answers to immediate questions, but because they work to link the questions to educational value frameworks, they imagine what they will also need to know later, in the long term. The frustrations of being a teacher are more visible. As educators, they must teach for what students need now and in an unimagined future; so research teams plan systematic and rigorous studies for current problems that can also inform an imagined future when students, conditions for learning, and resources will be quite different than they are now. Those with expertise in educational research and evaluation can use what they know to assist faculty colleagues in probing the depths of their disciplines for approaches and strategies, yet they can also help faculty experiment with methods and paradigms that better match questions emerging from their inquiry disciplines, such as the fine arts and humanities. Because institutional assessment operates at the level of programs and a college, its genesis, means, value, interpretation, and the ways findings are used need to be a shared enterprise. The implication is that the use of findings, which has traditionally been left to others than the generators of knowledge, now becomes the collaborative responsibility of the generators and the users. This means that no study is complete when the information is merely gleaned, housed, and interpreted. A study is complete only when decisions and consequent improvements have been made and results from those efforts have been considered and examined. Here, the learning community faces the problem of the educator. In some ways, I will not know whether a learner has benefited from my teaching. I cannot predict and control the outcome, and a rigorous examination of learners' future performance in ambiguous situations is unlikely to completely meet earlier imagined expectations. Nevertheless, I am still responsible for these learning outcomes. So institutional assessment as a system will still be expected both to deliver on understanding student learning outcomes and to assist in planning for improvement. Herein lies another challenge.

Recognizing the Stakeholders

For some time, institutional assessment as a field has had the luxury of meeting many of the requirements of public representatives, employers, and learners' families by demonstrating that educators are taking responsibility for maintaining the public trust seriously. Educators are conducting assessment at the program, curriculum, and college levels in response to questions, plans, and data-gathering approaches. Educators can offer some ideas regarding what information about student learning is telling them, where they can improve, and what steps they have taken to make visible improvements in some concrete ways. Yet as educators in higher education, we have greater expectations, as do our public representatives, and we must imagine both how to define and to meet those expectations. For the sake of our students, we want to help them show what they have learned. We insist that we show that our educational efforts contributed to this learning. In fact, in their schools, many elementary and secondary education teachers now must show that what they do is reflected both in evidence of student learning and in improvements in meeting expectations over time. The evidence expected is that graduates in teacher education, for example, take professional positions and persist in them and that their pupils show demonstrated changes in learning over time toward clarified standards. So postsecondary education is expected to show that graduates not only contribute to the economy but also benefit civic life and the efforts of our society's democratic institutions. The implication is that educators and their institutions take responsibility for individual learners who are in college at the time and for showing that prior graduates are contributing in various fields—politics, education, health care, services, and so on.

Strategies and Issues

Perhaps Alverno's most effective strategy in addition to its connection to educational values and tested assumptions about teaching and learning is that curriculum and institution-wide assessment builds on the faculty-designed system of assessing individual student learning. The latter is grounded in the idea that each student is developing her unique potential as a person during and after college. This idea under-lies the eight general abilities that are the conceptual organizers for the curriculum and for student assessment-as-learning (Alverno College Faculty, 1979/1994, 2000).

This assessment system has been a difficult challenge to realize over the years, because of the leap in expectations just discussed and also because faculty and student affairs personnel have long experienced being personally ranked or graded as learners and employees. In turn, they have submitted indicators of student learning to registrars in the form of symbols (such as grades) or to deans in the form of lists of pub-lications. The efficiency of these indicators has led to their use as a com-mon currency in our educational system, but when the "economy" shifts toward demonstrated performance in relation to standards, the com-mon currency no longer works to the extent it once did. Consequently, policymakers have tended to reject the value of grades as indicators. They have called for more sophisticated and useful measurements that show how the institution takes responsibility for demonstrating student learning outcomes. Thus the usual evidence that faculty are accustomed to contributing has been discounted as inflated.

Given the usual student anxieties associated with testing, it became important to Alverno faculty to develop student assessment processes that lead to growth and development of the student and the institu-tion toward ineffable outcomes; at the same time, they wanted to pro-vide the student and college with evidence of the ways the student is or is not making progress toward meeting criteria that define these outcomes.

Recall some of the earlier learning outcomes noted at the start of this chapter, such as integrity, identity, purpose, and meaning, and look at some of the indicators: making connections between beliefs and values, maintaining a balance between doing and being, protecting time for reflection. It seems clear to most educators that it is important for learners to develop awareness of their own stance and how it relates to their day-to-day involvement in a college or other formal and informal learning settings. Yet most tests do not allow time for reflection ("You have thirty minutes to respond to one of three questions"). If we are to assess the ineffable, reflection time is just what educators need to provide for students.

Alverno faculty have reasoned that any assessment of student performance needs also to give students an opportunity to stand aside from a particular demonstration to self-assess—that is, to observe what they did, analyze it in relation to their own and others' articulated criteria, make a judgment about where they stand in relation to criteria, and then reflect on what, how, and where they want and need to learn next. Learning to elicit this kind of self-assessment has proved to be a challenging educational task for most educators. Yet it is key both to assessment-as-learning by the student and to program and institution-wide assessment. The ineffable becomes more meaningful to both the student and the institution through reflection on experience. Each learner is asked to make connections between what each intends and what each is actually doing. So is the college. Faculty and student affairs personnel are used to having this kind of interaction with students, and it is this kind of interaction that provided the basis for one of Alverno's first strategies in institutional assessment: providing for longitudinal interviews at the end of each year in college— at least for a sample of students—to enable stakeholders to hear in the student's own voice the nature of the ineffable. Quotes like the following, for example, put flesh and blood on statistical findings. "I wonder who I will be ten years from now, because it's happening, evolution is a reality in my life. And, it's really neat; I can't wait to see who I'm going to be" (Mentkowski & Associates, 2000, p. 215).

By making data collection and analysis for institutional assessment systematic and rigorous, Alverno educators began to have more confidence in what they were hearing in their classes—especially when the student could make attributions to elements of the curriculum that made a constructive difference and to those that were barriers. When learners could clarify changes they had made in learning outcomes over time, long after classes had ended, that learning could be judged for its contribution to personal growth. Further, educators were able to sort out the beginning learning in forming an identity from later changes, and thus they were able to clarify the meaning and level of complexity of what they were asking students to do. By using student language to communicate with students, educators could begin to assess their ability level in articulating their learning (Mentkowski, 1988).

It is the student's language—in conversations with others, in deliberation about the content of the discipline—that often provides the educator with evidence of the ineffable. It can also provide evidence of the student's being judgmental or mouthing a ritualistic definition. By assessing the way students are constructing meaning over time, however, one can intervene in untoward judgments by asking for evidence and for examples to illustrate definition.

The students' constructions must be balanced by those of the "other," the peer or the faculty member or the adviser—who, in the process, may want to clarify his or her own expectations. At the same time, the faculty and staff can review the criteria and standards by referring to the descriptions of human growth on the Perry Scheme, for example, or to a professional association's expectations for interaction with clients by school counselors.

Analyzing student examples—with confidentiality protected—for evidence of growth toward the ineffable is a powerful strategy for enhancing collaboration among educators across the campus.

Expecting this kind of collaboration resides in attributes of the institutional culture. Such collaboration is possible when its members are actively committed to questioning, to scholarly inquiry and research as a means to discovery about student learning. Although educational institutions often articulate commitments to research in the disciplines, they less often articulate engagement in collaborative inquiry about student learning. Disciplines function as frameworks for faculty discovery research, but less so as frameworks for organizing student learning, studying whether and how students are learning at the level faculty expect and how students show they are developing their uniqueness and creativity of thought (Riordan & Roth, 2005). Learners' personal journeys in the discipline help them make meaning and anticipate future contributions. To what extent do educators at the department level participate in a community of learning about student learning, and in a community of judgment about needed enhancements in departmental offerings? This dialogue could easily take up the question raised by Jon Dalton in Chapter Six about the potential damage done to students "when we tolerate a bifurcated life in the academy that honors the life of the mind but relegates the realm of spirituality to the

purely private domain." Thus a number of Alverno discipline departments, through the parallel ability department, valuing in decision-
making, have come to consensus that students need to demonstrate
how they integrate valuing with the content of their academic work:
"express ways that her increasing knowledge of other perspectives
informs her own changes in personal and professional decisions . . . .
recognize the integration of emotion, thought, and belief in this
process, as well as give expression to her own stable center of care and
strength; that which is at the 'heart' of her decision-making. . . such
integration will develop her moral imagination" (Alverno College Valuing Department, 2004, p. 2).

At the level of the discipline, for example, the student can articulate her own sense of vision for her work in the world, although how
she will do this will depend on the outcomes for each discipline or
profession and on the value frameworks she can identify within her
chosen field (Alverno College Faculty, 1992; Alverno College Valuing
Department, 2004; Earley, Mentkowski, & Schafer, 1980).

The Problem of Criteria

We now turn to criteria for program, curriculum, and institution-wide
assessment drawn from a publication, *Student Learning: A Central
Focus for Institutions of Higher Education*, published by representatives
of twenty-six institutions, including Alverno, who were funded by the
Pew Charitable Trusts to work together at the college over two years.
The group, the Student Learning Initiative, collaboratively authored
a conceptual framework for a learning-centered institution and
accompanying descriptions of institutional practices that demonstrate
the various dimensions of the framework in order to open these ideas
to public debate and dialogue (Student Learning Initiative, 2002). The
group's criteria are as follows.   Program, curriculum, and institution-wide assessment

- Is integral to learning about student learning.

- Creates processes that assist faculty, staff, and administrators to
  improve student learning.

- Involves inquiry to judge program value and effectiveness for fostering student learning.

- Generates multiple sources of feedback to faculty, staff, and administrators about patterns of student and alumni performance in relation to learning outcomes that are linked to curriculum.

- Makes comparisons of student and alumni performance to standards, criteria, or indicators (faculty, disciplinary, professional, accrediting, certifying, legislative) to create public dialogue.

- Yields evidence-based judgments of how students and alumni benefit from the curriculum, cocurriculum, and other learning contexts.

- Guides curricular, cocurricular, institution-wide improvements [Student Learning Initiative, 2002, p. 22].

Learning about learning involves evidence-based judgment, and a department may, because of its disciplinary approach to inquiry, design ways to evaluate the extent to which its students meet the learning outcomes that faculty and advisers require, as well as the means to stand aside from these outcomes by observing what the curriculum contributes. Members of a department and, in Alverno's case, an academic department of educational research and evaluation funded by the college, create "processes that assist faculty, staff, and administrators to improve student learning" (Student Learning Initiative, 2002, p. 22). Achieving this purpose "involves inquiry to judge program value and effectiveness for fostering student learning" (p. 22). Designing and doing this kind of assessment rely on one of the most difficult challenges in program and institutional assessment: determining and defining explicit criteria, standards, and comparisons. This means not only that a department has clarified its broad learning outcomes for the discipline or profession but also that faculty have designed student assessments at the level of course learning outcomes.

Using Assessment Evidence

Such departmental engagement in program evaluation may stimulate assessment of student learning outcomes at the level of the curriculum as a whole. Alverno researchers have studied longitudinal samples of student patterns in moral judgment, for example, and found that development of moral judgment is a domain of the person aligned with broad patterns of "development characterized by deep, enduring structures of the self: how the learner engages issues of personal integrity and purpose. It entails a view of the self in process and a focus on the ethical or spiritual dimensions of life" (Mentkowski & Associates, 2000, p. 187).

Growth in moral judgment also was aligned with another domain of the person: reasoning, which emphasizes the role of thinking in relation to the disciplines. "In the domain of reasoning, the learner extends from the concrete particulars into abstraction. We see reasoning as the manipulation of ideas and abstractions—the realm of what is possible and necessary" (Mentkowski & Associates, 2000, p. 184). These longitudinal studies also showed that development of moral judgment was maintained after college, up to five years after graduation.

In-depth, longitudinal interviews of a randomly selected group of students at the end of each year in college and five years after graduation yielded still another domain of human growth: self-reflection. "Construction of meaning in personal experience lies at the heart of this domain. Self-reflection involves distinctive affective processes . . . and necessarily views the past but also envisions a future self. For example, the act of self-assessing one's abilities congeals reflection on past actions for the purpose of improvement. Self-reflection also involves thinking about one's learning" (Mentkowski & Associates, 2000, p. 186).

On the basis of these and similar findings, Alverno faculty have affirmed that each "student develops as an independent lifelong learner with a sense of responsibility for her own learning and the ability and desire to continue learning; self-knowledge and the ability to assess her own performance critically and accurately; and an understanding of how to apply her knowledge and abilities in many different contexts" (Alverno College Faculty, 1973/2005, p. 1). The critical point here is that these findings emerged from multiple sources of evidence—formal longitudinal and cross-sectional research, reviews of literature and practice in higher education, collaborative inquiry across the college and with various consortia of other institutions, and learning by educating—knowing that emerges from the continually changing context that these educators experienced and from their constantly modified practice. These results are not simply based on undocumented assertions.

In the already noted revision of the valuing ability levels (Alverno College Faculty, 1973/2005), which had been first formulated in the 1970s, the valuing department consulted more recent external sources. One of the markers in the revision was a change of voice. The advanced

level of valuing, "consistently examines and cultivates own value systems in order to take initiative as a responsible self in the world"
(Alverno College Faculty, 19973/2005, p. 2), was further articulated as
assessment criteria: "I can use the valuing frameworks of a major field
of study or profession to address significant issues in personal, professional and societal contexts. I can consistently examine and cultivate
my own value system in order to take initiative as a responsible self in
personal, professional and societal contexts" (Alverno College Valuing
Department, 2004, p. 2). Department members made the shift because
(1) faculty members had observed that valuing criteria, when stated in
the first person, were more likely to elicit self-reflection from students
and (2) the recent literature makes a strong case for integrating, rather
than separating, the intellectual with the interpersonal, the more
abstract kind of reasoning with concurrent emotional development
(Boyatzis, Cowen, Kolb, & Associates, 1995; Goleman, 1995). The shift
also emerged from (3) recent faculty scholarship on the disciplines as
frameworks for learning (Riordan & Roth, 2005) and self-assessment
in assisting students to show how they have changed over time and how
they use feedback to set new goals for future learning (Alverno College
Faculty, 2000).

Such studies incorporate and illustrate faculty understanding of
another component of institution-wide assessment: "yields evidence-
based judgments of how students and alumni benefit from the curriculum, cocurriculum, and other learning contexts" (Student Learning
Initiative, 2002, p. 22). Educators are now better able to understand the
engagement of learners in learning (Kuh, 2003; National Survey of Student Engagement, 2003), their understanding of spirituality (Astin &
Astin, 1999), and their contributions to service while still in school
(Eyler & Giles, 1999). Yet it is often the studying of the contributions of
alumni that opens the doors to these broad indicators in the work, civic,
and personal lives of graduates (Mentkowski, 1988; Mentkowski &
Rogers, 1993; Rogers & Mentkowski, 2004; Vaillant, 1977; Vaillant
& Vaillant, 1990). When faculty and student affairs personnel review the
actual examples of alumni, they begin to examine anew how the goals
and learning outcomes they have for their students—and that students
had for themselves—are realized in professional, personal, and public
life. They are reaffirmed and challenged to find even more ways to articulate both the benefits of their own professional contributions and the
ways alumni who keep growing and changing contribute to society at
large. In the Alverno studies cited, graduate school enrollment statistics

and status indicators at work do not contribute as much to public dialogue about the value of higher education as do specific examples of how alumni connect their conceptual abilities to participative leadership.

In a systematic process of judging the five-year performance of alumnae, Alverno faculty and student affairs personnel were also encouraged to examine the five-year performance of alumnae who may have missed opportunities to demonstrate participative leadership (Rogers & Mentkowski, 2004). In this study, faculty judgments of the performance effectiveness of alumnae correlated with a broad range of alumna abilities coded independently by researchers: intellectual abilities, prosocial abilities, independent action abilities, and abilities related to working together as a team:

"The faculty members' narrative explanations of the basis for their judgments confirmed the distinct character of effective discretionary action. Faculty members suggested that the scope of the alumna's framework for constructing and understanding performance was critical to effective performance. This understanding of the source of alumna effectiveness is congruent with Vallacher and Wegner's (1989) finding that those who conceptualize action in terms of their larger goals are more effective" (Rogers & Mentkowski, 2004, p. 366).

Further, this study was used to communicate to stakeholders outside the academy that faculty judgments of effective performance generally corroborated independent data on career achievement indicators. There is much to be done to demonstrate the value and validity of an education grounded both in the liberal arts and its concern for the development of purpose and meaning, and in the expectations of the various professions that serve and contract with society for human welfare.

These findings provide an avenue for public dialogue that rests both on examples of performance in the workplace as well as on statistical indicators. Further, these findings have led to a definition of effective performance as multidimensional, "an individual's discretionary and dynamic action in an ambiguous situation that effectively meets some contextually conditioned standard of excellence. Such multidimensional performance goes beyond technical or narrowly specified task performance. Performance entails the whole dynamic nexus of the individual's thoughts, feelings, and constructs in a dynamic line of action and his or her entanglement in an evolving situation and its broader context" (Rogers, Mentkowski, & Reisetter Hart, in press). Alverno findings also suggest that a college should orient student learning toward holistic development—"the overall direction of dispositional growth in the person's broadly integrated way of making meaning and commitments in moral, interpersonal, epistemological, and personal realms" (Rogers, Mentkowski, & Reisetter Hart, in press)—and that a college also should orient student learning toward effective, multidimensional performance. Graduates of such a college may realize individual visionary aims and also contribute to societal health and welfare, democratic processes, and economic development.

Continual inquiry around student learning outcomes in each sphere—performance and development along with reasoning and self-reflection—when done well, is likely to engage educators in using program, curriculum, and institution-wide assessment for "guiding curricular, co-curricular, and institution-wide improvements" (Student Learning Initiative, 2002, p. 22). Such engagement may be unlikely to lead to consensus on next steps because the sources of ideas, evidence, and contexts of practice necessarily differ within as well as among institutions in the United States. For such shared learning to occur, participants need to develop familiarity with multiple discourses across disciplines and student affairs so that each participant in the discussion is open to knowledge about development, reasoning, self-reflection, and performance from different contexts and levels of practice. It remains a challenge to find the threads of meaning and purpose in this discourse that defines integrated learning. That challenge is inescapable in a college that values inquiry as a primary feature of liberal arts education and one that values perspective—taking in interpersonal relationships as a primary feature of professional education. In a sense, this kind of self-assessment at the department and institutional levels, where the various faculty and staff members observe, analyze, judge, and plan for future learning, is a hallmark of the traditional college culture. The learning that results connects a college to various cultures that are emerging in today's diverse higher education institutions.

CONCLUSION

This comprehensive example demonstrates that it is possible to assess "ineffable outcomes" for students concerning authenticity, purpose, meaning, and spiritual growth. At first blush, doing so seems a daunting task for any institution with limited investment in, or experience with, institutional assessment. In our experience, no program of highly integrated assessment activities springs full blown from the minds and hearts of administrators and faculty members; it continually evolves and adapts.

This assessment leg of our three-legged stool needs to evolve as a critical element that accompanies and informs the institutional change and professional development issues addressed in Chapter Eight. We argue here that assessment can be taken up in complex and comprehensive ways by institutions of higher education to assist them in teaching and in further understanding ineffable outcomes.

Recognize, along with colleagues in the Student Learning Initiative (2002), that your institution can create analogous activities and institutional processes to suit your particular mission and resources. For student assessment, coordinating teaching and assessment to promote student learning means asking the following questions (p. 3):

How do student learning outcomes assist us to "think pedagogically?"

What can we learn about our students to assist them in learning?

How can assessments both directly and indirectly assist students to learn?

How can we help students develop processes of self-assessment?

These questions imply that a group of educators might identify one or more of the most critical student learning outcomes for their institution, college, school, or other subunit. They might articulate those levels of performance that seem to make sense for that general outcome and then specify criteria for performance that are associated with each level. Creating cross-discipline professional teams that are identified with each outcome and that have sufficient competence and institutional respect to carry forward the ongoing work is necessary to monitor and improve this particular area of effort. For institution-wide assessment, working continuously to improve the environment for learning means asking these questions (Student Learning Initiative, 2002, p. 3):

What approaches are best suited to assess program, curriculum, and institution-wide effectiveness with respect to student learning?

How can the results of institutional assessment be used to improve student learning?

What is involved in taking collective responsibility for learning?

How can we encourage innovation in the service of student learning?

Thinking through who needs to be involved in assessment planning and in using the results may imply the creation of a task force with adequate resources; such a task force would be expected to work in a three- to five-year time frame, even as it involves colleagues along the way.

This is the institutional perspective we need to assess the complex and challenging institutional amplifications called for in our earlier chapters.

CHAPTER TEN

Leadership for Recovering Spirit

Liesa Stamm

M artin Luther King Jr. said, "Our lives begin to end the day we become silent about things that matter." This book is about ending the silence in higher education. The silence about the extent to which, despite their avowed intentions, our institutions do not provide an environment in which students are encouraged to learn about their own purposes and values and to seek solutions to larger human and societal issues. The silence about the ways in which our institutions continue to maintain structures and reward systems that result in discontinuities and fragmentation between professional and personal lives. And the silence about our institutional restrictions on the exercise of innovative leadership and bold new directions in teaching, learning, and scholarship. In Chapter One we call on institutions of higher education to once again direct the huge intellectual resources of our faculty and administrators to addressing the major social, economic, political, and environmental crises of the twenty-first century. Part Two suggests specific ways to meet this challenge and provides a variety of innovative practices in the areas of curriculum, pedagogy, student affairs, and the integration of spirit and community. The first two chapters in Part Three outline the challenges involved with planned change and suggest specific strategies for implementing institutional planning processes, professional development, and assessment that incorporate authenticity and values. Clearly, to accomplish the institutional amplification we call for requires powerful leadership, the leadership of individuals who are willing and able to lead from the soul.

BRINGING SPIRIT BACK INTO HIGHER EDUCATION

As documented in Chapter Three, from the earliest years of American higher education and continuing at many colleges and universities into the 1950s, the college president was the institution's clearly designated moral leader. Morals and values were defined by religious doctrine and theology, and the college president's responsibility for guiding the moral behavior of the students and faculty was considered central to his duties as a minister and the campus leader. The president frequently taught classes on moral values and theology, which were understood as equivalent, and officiated at the required chapel services on Sunday and during the week.

For most institutions of higher education in the twenty-first century, it is no longer appropriate to their educational missions and institutional culture for college presidents and senior administrators to serve as spokespersons for a particular religious denomination or theological perspective. The insistence on separating American collegiate education from its religious foundations is particularly critical in light of the great wave of religious diversity sweeping the United States since the last half of the twentieth century. Our current challenge, as we have explored extensively in this book, is to find ways to bring the examination of values, meaning, and purpose back into higher education in a way that honors differences while maintaining the traditions of rigorous academic investigation and analysis. And we need new moral leaders to guide this process. As the designated institutional leader and public spokesperson, the college or university president is in a particularly visible position to address the challenge of bringing spirit back into higher education. There is growing evidence from across the country that campuses are eager for personal values and explorations of meaning and purpose to be more integrated into the central mission of the institution. Chapters Three and Six provide illustrations of students' enthusiasm for pursuing spiritual seeking. A study conducted by Alexander and Helen Astin (1999), *Meaning and*

Spirituality in the Lives of College Faculty, documents the extent to which faculty experience a great divide between their work in the academy and their deeply felt personal values, and would welcome the opportunity to openly discuss issues of authenticity, meaning, purpose, and spirituality among themselves and with their students. Although many faculty understand their scholarly work, their teaching, and their work with students as expressions of their own spiritual values, they feel inhibited from expressing their personal beliefs and values by the institutional culture and rewards systems. These constraints are embodied in the frequently communicated devaluation on campuses around the country of work with students, in contrast to the great worth accorded to research and scholarly achievement.

The Disconnect Between Higher Education's Mission and Our Practices

Victor H. Kazanjian Jr. and Peter L. Laurence (2000) define well the basis for the inherent disjuncture experienced within higher education:

> Nearly everyone with whom we have worked in higher education readily speaks of being drawn into the profession of teacher/scholar by being inspired; inspired by a particular subject, or question, or by a particular teacher. Most of us can recount the very moment or moments that called us out onto our quest in the land of learning. Again and again, educators and students speak about the optimal learning experience as one in which there is a sense of wonder, awe, inspiration, freedom, or connection which leads to an inner awakening, a change of perspective, a transformation of the whole person [p. 312].

Innovation and change do not happen on their own; they require leadership. The innovative approaches for aligning personal meaning and values more closely with the curriculum, pedagogy, the work of student affairs, and institutional assessment presented in this book could not occur without dedicated individuals willing to cross the unspoken divides in higher education, the divides they experience every day, in many small and large ways, between the personal and professional, between the subjective and the objective. The leadership necessary for implementing educational and institutional innovations in higher education occurs at all levels: the administration, the faculty, student affairs professionals, and the students. It grows out of the passion of individuals to create educational experiences and environments that will provide others with the inspiration, inner awakening, and transformation of perspective that brought them into the academy as their life work. This leadership has, however, generally been "below the radar," highly individual, focused in one or two courses or cocurricular programs for students, and has not been embraced by and incorporated into the institution as a whole.

A Model for Strengthening Moral Leadership

Despite evidence that true leadership can be and is exerted by anyone within an organization, we have a tendency in our institutions to associate leadership with formal administrative roles that have defined responsibilities, areas of decision making, and mechanisms for exerting power. Warren Bennis, referred to by *Forbes* magazine as the "dean of leadership gurus," suggests that the dominant paradigms for leadership today largely come from business because "our culture is currently dominated and shaped by business" (1989, p. 4). Business metaphors have permeated our language and conceptual frameworks for describing and analyzing organizational structures and cultures, often including those whose purposes are quite different from that of business. Many institutions of higher education, for example, have adopted the language of business to describe their operations. Students are referred to as customers, and, to maintain "market share" and "grow the business," a fierce competition for increased student enrollments ensues between institutions and among units within an institution. Even many of the models for leadership that attract educators have been developed through the experience of business. The highly influential servant leadership concepts of Robert Greenleaf serve as an example; Greenleaf developed his ideas out of his experiences at AT&T, from which he retired as a vice president for management research after a career of almost four decades.

Today's predominant business model of leadership grew out of the ideas and techniques of professional management developed during the 1960s and 1970s. At that time it became widely accepted that effective management is no longer developed through practical experience, but is learned through education and training in the "science" of management. As management science has continued to evolve, the training of managers has become a "big business" in itself. "Each year more than sixty thousand MBA's graduate, thousands of managers complete

executive education programs, business books detailing the latest techniques climb near the top of the bestseller lists, companies spend bil-
lions of dollars on consulting fees, and thousands of executives
migrate among companies" (Badaracco & Ellsworth, 1989, pp. 4–5).
As a result of the pervasive preoccupation with technique, professional
managers and business academics have generated highly complex systems and elaborate organizational processes and management structures: strategic planning, portfolio analysis, complex capital budgeting
systems and forecasts, sophisticated organizational design, detailed
measurement and reward structures, and computerized information
systems.

The adoption in higher education of many of the techniques and
strategies of business is particularly unfortunate because educational
institutions differ from business organizations in very basic and profound ways in both their means *and* their ends. Although it sometimes
seems to be forgotten in the campus debates about policies, in our
ever-increasing efforts at fundraising, and in our ongoing enthusiasm
for athletics, as educators our mission is to open minds through
knowledge—knowledge that we acquire as a result of our own lifelong
learning, knowledge that we transmit through our teaching, knowledge that we produce through our scholarship. Unlike that of business, which focuses its considerable energies on creating and
producing new products to sell or on increasing production and sales,
our most basic goal as educators is not about selling knowledge or
about eliminating our competitors. Our ultimate aim is to use knowledge as a source of inspiration for ourselves and others and to improve
the world in which we live. We seek to increase access to the world of
knowledge for all who wish to drink from the well. We develop techniques for guiding and supporting our students through the learning
process. At our best, we seek opportunities to share ideas and to work
collaboratively to increase the potential for achieving our aspirations.

Higher education differs from business not only in its means and
ends. Our basic organizational structures are not built on a hierarchy
of increasing power and authority, as is the case for business. The traditions and practices of higher education are deeply embedded in the
premise of faculty governance. Faculty participate in institutional decision making through a range of formal structures, such as the faculty
senate and promotion and tenure committees. Faculty maintain the
basic authority over the design and provision of education through
the curriculum. Individual faculty develop course content and student

expectations; they initiate teaching strategies; they are responsible for review and approval of curriculum in their own departments and in the institution as a whole; and ultimately they have almost complete autonomy in the classroom. And our efforts at "accountability," a concept acquired from business models, are not focused on "the bottom line," on supporting our stockholders and boards of directors. As so well illustrated in Chapter Nine, we are accountable for fulfilling our educational mission to produce sound learning outcomes for our students that provide them with the passion and skills to continue their own lifelong learning.

Despite the profound differences between higher education and the world of business, the extensive research on leadership and management associated with business can provide insights into and models for leadership to recover spirit in our institutions. Both through his life experiences and his research on leadership and change, Warren Bennis (1989, 1993; Bennis & Thomas, 2002) offers us significant insights into the essential qualities needed for effective leadership. Bennis's pioneering work on leadership grew out of his research on group behavior at MIT in the 1960s. As outlined by his colleague and friend Tom Peters (1993), Bennis embodies in his own life many of the qualities of leadership that we are advocating. "He's always burned his intellectual candle at both ends. While conducting meticulous research in the minutiae of social interaction, Warren was also risking self and soul as a leader of some of the first T-groups at the National Training Labs in Bethel, Maine in 1964" (p. x). In 1967 Bennis began a decade of putting into practice his understandings about leadership, first as provost at SUNY Buffalo and then as president of the University of Cincinnati. Bennis found that the reality of leading in practice, in contrast to leading through influence from the printed page, "contained as many potholes as peaks" (p. x). As a consequence of these experiences, after leaving the presidency, Bennis turned his attention "to figuring out where he'd been" (p. x). This exploration resulted in an extensive body of research on leadership that has had a profound impact on our understanding of the personal qualities and effective processes that distinguish leaders. Bennis is currently a Distinguished Professor of Business Administration at the University of Southern California and a consultant to multinational companies and governments throughout the world. During his presidency at the University of Cincinnati, Bennis concluded that leadership is ultimately about the relationship between the leader-as-individual and the organization, and involves equal measures of humanity, openness, courage, and rigorous thinking. His definitions of leadership reflect these qualities (Peters, 1993).

From his interviews with hundreds of leaders in a range of occupations, Bennis (1989, 1993; Bennis & Thomas, 2002) arrived at four primary conclusions about leadership that provide important insights for examining ways to strengthen moral leadership in higher education.

LEADERS ARE MADE, NOT BORN, AND MADE MORE BY THEMSELVES THAN BY ANY EXTERNAL MEANS. In understanding effective leadership, it is of critical importance to distinguish leaders from managers. Leadership courses and managerial degrees that focus on teaching managerial skills may be useful for leaders; however, the ingredients of leadership cannot be taught. And many managers and administrators are not leaders.

Underlying this important distinction is the difference between positional power or *authority* and personal power or *influence*, which I found useful for my own research on women's social power and influence within traditional social contexts. In addition to having formally defined roles of authority, most groups and organizations recognize those individuals who exert influence or control that is not associated with a particular position of authority. Such personal power is based on the recognition and acceptance by others of an individual's skills at clearly defining strategies for group and personal decisions and actions, in assuming responsibility for guiding and accomplishing the tasks of the group, and in empowering others to engage in the work (Stamm & Ryff, 1984). Applying these definitions to Bennis's concept of leadership, it is clear that managers and administrators have assigned positional power or authority. In contrast, leaders operate through personal power, an ability to influence decisions and action that is derived from the confidence of the group to support and participate in the directions that leaders set. Using this distinction is particularly important for implementing the ideas of institutional change and amplification that are presented in Chapters Five through Nine. To accomplish the admittedly lofty goals outlined in these chapters, we need powerful leaders at all levels and within all units of the institution. College and university presidents and their top administrators cannot bring about such essential changes simply through the authority of their positions. Rather, we need leaders who will operate out of their personal visions and convictions in ways that influence, engage, and empower others to join with them.

Because leadership is unique to the individual and the context, leadership can't be broken down into repeatable and unchanging elements. Rather, leadership must be learned by doing, by meeting the challenges presented by unanticipated tasks for which the outcomes are not programmed, and by taking on a job that is being done for the first time. As Bennis suggests, true leaders, in contrast to managers, develop out of learning, and most often learning that occurs through adversity. Leaders, in this view, have a wonderfully adaptive capacity. Leadership ultimately emerges through the processes of learning to deal with challenges and conflict, of creating shared meaning within the organization to work toward common goals, and of using this learning to create changes and establish new organizational directions.

LEADERS SET OUT NOT TO BE LEADERS PER SE, BUT RATHER TO EXPRESS THEMSELVES FREELY AND FULLY. People who become leaders set out to live their lives expressing themselves as fully as possible, not to prove themselves. In those cases in which their expression is of value to others, they evolve into becoming leaders. "The difference is crucial, for it's the difference between being driven, as too many people are today, and leading as too few people do" (Bennis, 1989, p. 5). Leaders are people who believe so much in what they're doing that they accept as inherent to their job what Bennis calls the "Wallenda Factor," the ability to accept risk. In Karl Wallenda's words, "Walking the tightwire is living; everything else is waiting" (quoted in Bennis, 1989, p. 6). Bennis further asserts that leaders are more than goal directed; you can't make being a leader your principal goal any more than you can make being happy your goal. In both cases it has to be the result of your actions, not the cause (1989).

INDIVIDUALS WHO HAVE BECOME LEADERS CONTINUE TO GROW AND DEVELOP THROUGHOUT THEIR LIVES. Leaders believe in change as a central factor and motivating force in their lives. They equate change in both people and organizations with growth and progress, and "it might be said that their real life's work has been change" (Bennis, 1989, p. 170). Leaders not only manage change in organizations but also are comfortable with change in their own lives. Bennis's model of leadership involves an ongoing process of challenge, adaptation, and learning that prepares leaders to take on the next challenge. Leaders are individuals who have struggled with conflicts and adversities encountered in their organizations and have learned ways to overcome these adversities, including learning new skills that allow them to move on to new levels of achievement and new levels of learning. "Whenever significant new problems are encountered and dealt with adaptively, new levels of competence are achieved, better preparing the individual for the next challenge" (Bennis & Thomas, 2002, p. 93). Further, leaders are committed to a life of learning. In this context Bennis emphasizes the importance of understanding the principles of adult learning as guiding factors in creating and sustaining leadership.

Bennis concludes that "in fact, the process of becoming a leader is much the same as becoming an integrated human being" (1989, p. 4). Nelson Mandela exemplifies these leadership qualities. In describing how he used his powerful character and imagination to thwart his jailers' attempts to dehumanize him, Mandela concluded, "If I had not been in prison, I would not have been able to achieve the most difficult task in my life, and that is changing yourself" (quoted in Bennis & Thomas, 2002, p. 18).

THE PRIMARY DISTINGUISHING CHARACTERISTIC OF A LEADER IS A CON-
CERN WITH A GUIDING PURPOSE, AN OVERARCHING VISION. Leadership revolves around vision, ideas, and direction and has more to do with inspiring people to establish their own directions and goals than with day-to-day implementation. Leaders are less soloists than collaborators. To make their visions real, leaders must communicate their vision and align others to work with them in accomplishing it. As Max De Pree, former CEO of Herman Miller Inc. put it in *Leadership Is an Art,* "The first responsibility of a leader is to define reality. The last is to say thank you. In between, the leader is a servant" (quoted in Bennis, 1993, p. 90).

Bennis calls the process of making vision real "managing the dream," and defines empowerment as the key to managing the dream. "Stripped to its essentials, leadership involves just three things—a leader, followers, and a common goal. . . . Effective leaders don't just impose their vision on others, they recruit others to the shared vision" (Bennis & Thomas, 2002, p. 137). "In an effectively led organization, everyone feels he or she contributes to its success" (Bennis, 1993, p. 107). Empowerment occurs when (1) people feel significant, at the center of things rather than the periphery; (2) learning and competence matter—leaders make it clear that there is no failure, only mistakes that give us feedback and tell us what to do next; (3) people are part of a community; and (4) work is exciting. Effective leadership involves "pulling" rather than "pushing" people toward a goal. "Leaders articulate and embody the ideals toward which the organization strives" (Bennis, 1993, p. 83). They motivate their followers through identification with the vision, not simply through reward and punishment. And empowerment involves recognizing and acknowledging diversity of opinion. The successful enactment of a leader's vision is most effectively accomplished by bringing together teams of people with different skills and then creating a process through which these disparate skills function together.

Realizing a vision occurs through what Bennis terms "innovative learning." Through this process, "we no longer follow along, but rather lead our own lives. We do not accept things as they are, but rather anticipate things as they can be. We participate in making things happen. We shape life rather than being shaped by it" (1989, p. 78). Leaders need "the Gretzsky Factor;" as Wayne Gretzsky put it, "It is not as important to know where the puck is now as to know where it will be" (quoted in Bennis 1989, p. 199).

Shirley Hufstedler, who was named as a judge to the U.S. Court of Appeals by Johnson and served as secretary of education under Carter, describes well the process of innovative learning that exemplifies effective leadership:

> You have to envision in fairly concrete terms what ought to be done and what you want to do or where you want to go. . . . A certain amount of conceptualization is required. It's not unlike planning a trip. First you have to figure out where you want to go. Then you have to devise a mode of transportation. If no one's done it before you make it up. You have to maintain a certain amount of flexibility in organizing people to go with you. You have to know from the beginning how much baggage you have to haul or how light you can travel. It requires a combination of historical perspective, vision, and institutional appreciation—what its texture is, what its possibilities are [quoted in Bennis, 1989, p. 78].

In the mid-1990s I conducted research on women's pathways to leadership. This work focused on nursing leaders as representatives of a largely woman's profession embedded in what until recently has been a male-dominated medical system. The nursing leaders that I interviewed were deans of schools of nursing, directors of nursing programs, and hospital vice presidents of nursing. One of my interests in this study was to discover whether women leaders in educational and health care environments had different experiences and styles of leadership from those delineated in the major studies of leadership, most of which were conducted in a business context and focused on men. My findings, in fact, very much mirrored the four primary qualities of leadership described by Bennis. All the nursing leaders I interviewed had not started out to become leaders but were propelled into their current positions by their visions for improving patient care through creating modifications in the educational or health care contexts in which they worked. The changes they introduced included innovative approaches to nursing practice, to nursing education, to organizational structures, and to the standards of the nursing profession itself.

As we seek to strengthen authenticity, spirituality, meaning, and purpose in higher education, we need to encourage our administrators, faculty, student affairs professionals, and students to become true leaders through living their own visions for amplifying our institutional environments. To borrow from Badaracco and Ellsworth's analysis of effective qualities of leadership (1989), we need to encourage our higher education administrators to become impassioned leaders who translate the qualities of strong personal values and compelling aspirations for their institutions into actions designed to produce change. "In the final analysis, the power of executive leadership rests not so much on the personality of the individual as on the power of the ideas, purposes, and values he or she represents. Leaders are agents and catalysts through which others understand and identify with these ideas, purposes, and values, and are uplifted and motivated by them" (p. 209).

LEADING FROM THE HEART: PRACTICES FOR GENERATING AUTHENTICITY, MEANING, AND PURPOSE

As we explore the potential role of our institutional leaders in bringing spirit back to their campuses, we need to hear directly from those who have been engaged in this endeavor, as well as from those whom we want to recruit. Although these voices and the exemplary practices of institutional leadership presented here are those of college and university presidents, it is important to keep in mind that as Bennis's work indicates, *administration* is not *leadership* . Many of us in higher education have worked with institutional administrators who appear to be driven to their positions more by "careerism" and power than by vision. Too often they do not define their roles as collaborative with faculty, students, and other administrative staff in achieving a broad vision for the institution or as empowering others. Too often faculty perceive their own goals and visions as being in conflict with those of the administration. Despite the frequently experienced lack of unified goals and purpose on our campuses, the examples of higher education leadership described in the following sections suggest that our college and university presidents can become true leaders who present a vision for their institutions and encourage and support the development of leadership at all levels of the campus community in implementing this vision.

Presidents' Perspectives on Practices for Promoting Character Development

As part of the work of the Center for the Study of Values in College Student Development at Florida State University, Jon Dalton and his colleagues conducted a national survey of college and university presidents to seek their opinions about what they considered to be key factors for creating a campus environment that supports the character development of their students and the practice of core ethical values. The presidents were asked to rate the Principles and Practices of Character Development in College, which includes ten principles and their associated practices developed by Dalton and his colleagues through several years of research. These principles and practices represent educational strategies and best practices that can be used by institutions to guide and assess their planning and programs to promote character development and values on their campuses. A total of 168 college and university presidents responded to the survey and according to Dalton, Goodwin, and Chen (2004) the types of institutions that these presidents serve closely conform to the actual percentages of these types of colleges and universities in the United States. The survey findings on presidents' perspectives for promoting character development and ethical values are summarized as follows.

As indicated in Table 10.1, the presidents responding to the survey most frequently rated "being a personal role model" as the most important of the ten principles for promoting character development in college (Dalton et al., 2004).

Rank	Principles for Character Development
1	Being a personal role model
2	Communicating core values
3	Integrating character into the curriculum
4	Helping students act on values
5	Creating a diverse and inclusive community
6	Guiding student conduct
7	Promoting holistic learning
8	Promoting public dialogue on values
9	Assessing character outcomes
10	Honoring moral and civic achievements

Table 10.1. Presidents' Rankings of Principles for Character Development.

The presidents were also asked to indicate which ten of the thirty-one associated practices they considered to be the most useful educational strategies. As summarized in Table 10.2, the most frequently cited practices were "role modeling by institutional leaders" and "institution's mission or guiding values statement."

Dalton and his colleagues also asked the college and university presidents to identify character development programs at their institutions that they considered unique or exemplary. The responses were grouped into sixteen categories that are ranked in Table 10.3 in terms of frequency of response. As indicated, community service and service learning programs were most frequently cited by presidents as exemplary programs on their campuses.

To better understand whether institutional type and size have an impact on the perceptions of college and university presidents about the importance of specific principles and practices on their campuses, Dalton et al. compared responses in terms of these factors. As summarized in the next sections, their analysis identified statistically significant differences (significance level .05) in the responses of presidents from different types of institutions on four principles and eight practices. In terms of institutional size the only response demonstrating a statistically significant difference was that presidents of small institutions are more likely than presidents of large institutions to believe that holistic learning and development should be a key principle in strengthening character development and core ethical values on their campuses.

Most Frequently Cited Practices	(Freq.)	Least Frequently Cited Practices	(Freq.)
Role modeling by institutional leaders	(125)	Student ethics compact	(17)
Institution's mission or guiding values statement	(123)	Campus coordination of character development	(19)
Ethical decision making in administration and governance	(100)	Assessment of character development	(26)
Community service and service learning	(97)	Health and wellness	(26)
Caring, respectful campus ethos	(92)	Special initiatives on ethics and values	(27)
Incorporating ethical reflection in courses	(83)	Ethical leadership programs	(27)
Student conduct code	(80)	Integration of extra-curricular activities	(27)

Table 10.2.   Practices to Promote Character Development.

Rank	Special and Exemplary Programs	Frequency
1	Community service and service learning programs	42
2	Leadership programs	30
3	Academic classes and curricular programs	23
4	Spirituality programs[a]	16
5	Diversity and multicultural programs	14
6	Honor codes and academic honesty programs	12
7	Religious activities	11
8	Mission statements, creeds, codes	11
9	New student and orientation programs	9
10	Student government	4
11	Assessment and evaluation programs	3
12	Awards and recognition programs	3
13	Mentoring programs	3
14	Role modeling by leaders	2
15	Senior capstone courses	2
16	Social justice programs	2

Table 10.3.   Special Programs and Exemplary Practices to Implement Character Development on Campuses.

[a]To reflect differences in stated purposes and activities, "spirituality" programs are listed separately from "religious" programs.

DIFFERENCES IN PRESIDENTS' RESPONSES BASED ON INSTITUTIONAL TYPE. Variations in presidents' responses based on institutional type include the following:

- *Presidents of public colleges and universities* gave greater priority to a moral ethos of civic values and democratic engagement activities, of individual freedom and responsibility within the context of freedom of speech, and of personal integrity.
- *Presidents of private secular institutions* generally responded very similarly to presidents of public universities. They placed greater emphasis, however, on assessing character outcomes within a more humanistic and holistic educational framework.
- *Presidents of private religious institutions* gave greater priority to transmitting values and nurturing students' holistic and religious development than those of either public or private secular institutions. They specifically linked these priorities to religious values and to their faith-based institutional mission.

RELATIONSHIP BETWEEN INSTITUTIONAL TYPE AND EXEMPLARY PROGRAMS AND PRACTICES. In regard to exemplary programs and practices, Dalton et al. found the following differences among different types of institutions:

- *Presidents of public institutions* most frequently identified community service, diversity education, leadership training, student government participation, honor codes, and the commitment to freedom of speech and inquiry as their institution's exemplary programmatic practices focused on character development. The formation of character at these institutions is typically encouraged through the active involvement of students in service initiatives and service-learning and in active reflection on civic values, social justice, and personal moral responsibility.
- *The presidents of private religious colleges and universities* gave greater emphasis to the importance of religion and spirituality in spiritual and character development. They sought to promote spiritual development through the practice of personal commitment to the beliefs and values of their religious faith. Such practices as worship, prayer, volunteerism, study of sacred texts, and devotion to a lifestyle of faithfulness were cited as important for

providing the moral structure necessary to strengthen spiritual growth. Involvement in community and social service was important but within the more specific framework of the faith community of believers and as an expression of religious values such as compassion, love, and a committed life of faith. Presidents of private religious colleges were much more likely than presidents of public institutions to emphasize personal commitment to a set of specific beliefs and values, and made a close connection between beliefs and behavior. Because religion and spirituality tend to be inwardly focused, however, spiritual growth was regarded as the consequence or product of the achievement of personal virtue.

• *Presidents of private secular colleges and universities* emphasized aspects of both civic and religious approaches to strengthening character and values. Similar to presidents of public institutions, presidents of secular colleges and universities stressed the importance of experiences of diversity and social responsibility in the context of humanistic values. Spiritual growth and character development were seen to be the result of intellectual examination and rigorous personal moral reflection. Community participation and citizenship were conceived in more global, humanistic terms. The examined life, a life of integrity, was regarded as the goal of character development. Presidents of private secular colleges and universities highlighted service, freedom of speech, diversity education, leadership training, and a strong honor code as some of the most important strategies for strengthening spiritual growth, meaning, and purpose.

Pathways to Moral Leadership

"The power for authentic leadership," according to Parker Palmer, "is found not in external arrangements but in the human heart. Authentic leaders in every setting—from families to nation-states—aim at liberating the heart, their own and others', so that its powers can liberate the world" (2000, p. 76). Campus leadership is critical for affirming and strengthening the commitment to incorporating authenticity and spiritual growth and the search for personal meaning and values as central to the mission of higher education. Some college and university presidents have begun to break the silence through their personal efforts to bring values and issues that matter back to the forefront of the institutional ethos.

GREGORY S. PRINCE, PRESIDENT OF HAMPSHIRE COLLEGE. The concept of the servant leader is central to Gregory Prince's philosophy of moral leadership. He rejects the notion that a leader is responsible for shaping an institution or that an institution's vision arises from the wisdom and actions of the president. He maintains that this common view of leadership undercuts the capacity to build institutional and community character. Rather, he defines his leadership of Hampshire College as supporting the vision of the institution, of letting the College become what it stands for. To accomplish their institutional visions, Prince asserts, colleges and universities must take moral stands. "The test of a college is not only whether its graduates and faculty make a difference, but most importantly whether the institution itself makes a difference"(quoted in Nelson, 2000, p. 3). As a college president, Prince emphasizes the importance of creating an environment of "moral conversation" within the campus community as the basis for emphasizing the importance of values, principles, and ethos as central to the institutional vision (Nelson, 2000, pp. 1–4).

GRAHAM B. SPANIER, PRESIDENT OF PENNSYLVANIA STATE UNIVERSITY. In approaching his presidential role, Graham Spanier acknowledges the many challenges inherent in providing moral leadership for one of the nation's largest and most comprehensive universities, with thirty-six thousand employees on twenty-four campuses, an annual budget of $2.8 billion, and a physical plant of thirteen hundred buildings. Although all college and university presidents face complex responsibilities and leadership choices, the highly visible nature of our country's major public research universities compounds those faced by their presidents. In working to act out his vision of values-based leadership, Graham Spanier defines his role as "humanizing the university" and promoting "character, conscience, civility and social responsibility." Shaping and influencing the culture of a campus the size of Penn State is no small task. Spanier provides leadership by speaking out on issues "when there are episodes of incivility and unrest," by meeting with various campus groups, and by focusing on policy changes that "put people first." One example of his leadership is his approach to dealing with the challenge of excessive alcohol consumption by students, an issue frequently encountered on campuses today. He couples talking about this problem on campus during freshman orientation, for example, with working on such solutions as developing educational programs, promoting the use of counseling services, expanding student programming, monitoring hospital emergency room data, encouraging student events that are alcohol-free, and restricting advertising on campus that promotes alcohol (Nelson, n.d.).

Under Spanier's leadership, the university recently established the Center for Ethics and Religious Affairs in the Pasquerilla Spiritual Center as a multifaith facility to nurture spiritual and ethical development among students, staff, and faculty. The center, which currently includes fifty registered student faith groups, represents a pioneering effort and model for other public institutions to foster the development of conscience and character, celebrate the diverse religious and cultural traditions of the university, and embrace the challenge of interfaith understanding and cooperation. This initiative is one example of the numerous ways that Spanier has fulfilled his personal commitment to supporting the vitality of a democratic society through university engagement that addresses compelling community, societal, and global needs.

Spanier expresses his vision of moral leadership not only on campus but at the national level as well. Through his position as chair of the highly influential Kellogg Commission on the Future of State and Land-Grant Universities, he has provided a major voice for calling on public higher education to become fully engaged with the community and with society and to make a greater difference in the quality of life locally, nationally, and globally. According to Spanier, "Accessibility and flexibility, more active student involvement in learning, interdisciplinary scholarship, and collaborative community partnerships are hallmarks of the engaged university." In response to major societal and global changes, our universities must support "the learning needs of people of all ages and the expanding knowledge needs of society" (Spanier, n.d.).

Through his participation in the Global Alliance for Workers and Communities, a partnership of businesses and public and nonprofit organizations whose mission is to assess and improve conditions of overseas factories and communities, Spanier combines his dedication to promoting an increased internationalization of the university with his commitment to university engagement. Because Spanier represents a university the size of Penn State, his attention to fair labor practices has the potential for making a significant national and international impact. Penn State's involvement in the Global Alliance, which is part of the International Youth Foundation, grows out of the university's commitment to promoting fair labor practices in the production of collegiate apparel, an important issue of human rights and social responsibility for universities and a special concern for many students. Spanier indicates that "as a founding member of the Fair Labor Association (FLA), Penn State has been involved from the beginning in setting up a Labor Code of Conduct for manufacturers to follow to ensure that Penn State licensed products are made in environments with proper working conditions. We also worked over the past few years with the Collegiate Licensing Company's Code of Conduct Task Force, and participated in other initiatives addressing labor practices in factories around the world. Our memberships in organizations concerned with fair labor practices require a significant commitment of financial resources" (Spanier, n.d.).

Another example of Spanier's commitment to university engagement is his involvement in creating a new School of Information Sciences and Technology at Penn State to address the urgent workforce development needs in Pennsylvania and nationwide. Developed in partnership with business and industry, the school represents a new model of interdisciplinary education for the digital age. In making information sciences technology education and research a high priority, Spanier (n.d.) emphasizes that "We are only beginning to fathom the impact of the information technology revolution on our educational institutions and on our society. While Penn State cannot be anywhere else except at the leading edge of technology, we also have a significant responsibility to see that progress in this area impacts positively on the quality of life."

Given the many vulnerabilities of university presidents today, Spanier acknowledges the difficulty in sustaining the tradition of moral leadership in the presidency. "Most people wish University presidents to either support their point of view or stay out of the picture. For most presidents, gone are the days when being outspoken on the subject of moral leadership was expected. Now many presidents have as a goal staying out of trouble, hiding from the limelight, and keeping the peace." In encouraging a greater commitment to moral leadership, however, Spanier concludes that "If presidents are to make some mark in shaping the culture and character of their campuses," they must have greater support from governing boards, students, faculty, staff, alumni, legislators, and the public than currently exists (Nelson, n.d.).

BEVERLY DANIEL TATUM, PRESIDENT OF SPELMAN COLLEGE. A vision of institutional transformation that centers on building the "capacity for connections" among individuals with diverse viewpoints defines Beverly Daniel Tatum's approach to her presidency of an Historically Black college for women dedicated to developing leaders for the nation's African American community. Tatum calls for the creation of "a community where we will affirm and hopefully understand each other, not seek to convert one another" (2000, p. 83). To accomplish the goal of functioning effectively in a religiously as well as ethnically diverse community requires the development of skills that Tatum suggests can be achieved only through the practice of dialogue. This is particularly challenging on campuses where "many young people have come from religious communities that have claimed the 'Truth' as their exclusive property" (2000, p. 84).

Tatum asserts that creating a campus environment that supports pluralist expression and connection among students with diverse viewpoints represents the most effective mechanism for overcoming the barriers of the "exclusivist response" experienced in today's society. Tatum challenges colleges and universities to support the conditions necessary to create a climate of pluralism. She identifies the following four critical ingredients for accomplishing this goal.

1. *Living in proximity.* "When we live with people different from ourselves, we have the opportunity for personal connection through friendship. But proximity can also lead to conflict, so while it is a necessary condition, it is not sufficient by itself to lead to mutual understanding" (2000, p. 84).

2. *Sharing personal narratives.* The sharing of stories, "witnessing" to one another, is a highly valuable pathway to seeing another's perspective. Tatum calls for colleges and universities to seek opportunities in our curricular and cocurricular initiatives for this type of personal sharing and urges institutions to challenge students to take advantage of these opportunities.

3. *Creating models of cooperation.* Tatum observes that although students have often heard about and even witnessed acts of bigotry and racial and ethnic hatred, they generally are less familiar with active efforts to overcome this bigotry. To remedy this situation, she advocates creating and highlighting campus initiatives of multiracial, multiethnic, and multifaith coopera-

tion. Such initiatives can occur in the classroom, through co-curricular activities and programs, and particularly through community service.

4. *Experiencing Diversity.* Students can truly learn the power of a pluralistic community only through direct experience. Although the previous three ingredients provide frameworks to create such experience, ultimately the students themselves must own the lesson. Tatum indicates that the greatest learning often occurs through the experience of "border-crossing," entering spaces where we are uncomfortable but have opportunities to learn through this discomfort. She gives the example of "minority" students' organizing programming at their cultural centers and inviting "majority" students to participate. Through such experiences "the invited students are required to shift their cultural lens 'from the center to the margin'" (p. 85).

DIANA CHAPMAN WALSH, PRESIDENT OF WELLESLEY COLLEGE. Diana Chapman Walsh views her responsibility as a college president to lead through example. She strives to create an institutional "ecosystem" that fosters "transformational growth, intellectual mastery, social consciousness, and spiritual depth" (1999, p. 209). She defines her challenge as doing "all that I can to hold open space in which a community of growth and self-discovery can flourish for everyone" (1999, p. 208). Because "in education the process is inextricably bound up with the product," Walsh asserts that "learning is nothing if not a messy process of discovery and unfolding. That means that how we as educators and educational administrators do our work—where we put our emphasis, what values we embody and express day in and day out, how we respond to the relentless pressures of time, of projections, of expectations, of conflicts, . . . is fully as important as the outcomes we actually seek to produce. In fact, the process is the outcome in a very real sense" (p. 208).

To ensure that the institutional ecosystem provides "an education that liberates the mind and spirit from parochialism, and from ideology; an education that opens doors for a lifelong journey of learning, . . . of questioning assumptions and shaking loose of prejudice in an expanding world and in an expanding worldview" (Walsh, 1999, p. 209) requires a special kind of leadership: leadership that is humanistic, collaborative, and respectful and that values and rewards individual autonomy and initiative; leadership that supports the dignity of every person; and leadership that "authorizes, inspires and frees everyone in the organization to do their best and most creative work" (p. 209). This is a lofty aspiration. Walsh outlines some key elements from her own experiences to assist the work toward becoming such a leader.

1. *Addressing adaptive challenges and accepting conflict.* In higher education we are faced with significant challenges for which there are no ready solutions because they involve the unknown. We need to view and assess these challenges from multiple vantage points. Because we cannot solve these challenges without the inherent conflict of multiple perspectives, conflict becomes a resource for learning and for change. The leader's responsibility is "to guide the organization toward an understanding of its opportunities, to guide people into awareness of their resourcefulness in the face of ambiguity. . . . [And to do so] the first task [of the leader] is to clarify the values and the vision, holding the light of the organization's positive future, holding a vision of true health for individuals in the organization" (Walsh, 1999, p. 212).

   Reflecting on her own experiences, Walsh concludes that to ensure that the inevitable conflict resulting from change is ultimately constructive, the leader needs "to gauge whether there is too much or too little pressure on the system, on individuals, and the organization, to gauge whether differences are being heightened in a way that opens up the field for a new, larger, more encompassing, more integrative vision of the future. . . . When faced with conflict, it helps to pay special attention to maintaining bonds: bonds within oneself, bonds with others, bonds with the larger culture" (1999, pp. 213–214).

2. *Overcoming resistance.* Walsh observes that when faced with personal and organizational change, some people are ready for it and embrace the challenges, and others put up resistance and attempt to subvert the process. The leader's task is "to look for the creative edge, the possibility of engaging the problems that people bring in, calling people into partnerships, . . . getting them to think about what it is that they are accountable for doing, gently confronting the avoidance of the difficult work of change . . . helping the community integrate and digest the

ways in which the work that they are doing is enabling them and enabling the organization to learn and to grow" (1999, pp. 212–213).

3. *Cultivating inner resources.* According to Walsh (1999), a crucial aspect of being a leader is that "it forces one to focus energy specifically on increasing one's own internal capacity for learning and for growth." The process of leadership can be personally draining, and it is essential for a leader "to cultivate access to regular nourishment from one's own spiritual roots and through working partnerships and systems of mutual support" (p. 214).

ROBERT CAROTHERS, PRESIDENT OF THE UNIVERSITY OF RHODE ISLAND. As a longtime president of the University of Rhode Island, Robert Carothers bases his leadership on the servant leadership model and embraces the concept of the teacher as moral leader. He asserts that "the leader, as with any teacher, must also be willing to learn" (quoted in Nelson, 2001). At the heart of Carothers's leadership is his commitment to both challenging and empowering others on campus to be moral leaders, to fully engage in the responsibility of making decisions that benefit and improve the university as a whole, rather than simply promoting their own concerns and interests. Given the many, often competing constituencies of a large campus, as well as the traditions of faculty and student governance, such a commitment can involve many personal risks. As a leader who acts out of the commitment to empower others, however, Carothers has found that "risk-taking is a two-way and mutually beneficial process." Carothers's dedication to trying to act out of his own values at the same time as engaging others to do the same is exemplified through an incident he encountered several years ago. The university's Brothers United for Action, a group of concerned black students, took over the university's main administration building, including the president's office, to underscore their sense of urgency about numerous racial problems and attitudes they experienced at the university. In working to resolve this crisis, Carothers came to the conclusion that the primary problem was not that of getting the students out of the building, although he admitted that this was his first reaction to the situation. Rather, he focused on developing ways to channel the students' energy and commitment to their cause into an experience of transformation for the campus community. Acting out of his role as a servant leader, Carothers focused on guiding the students to assume responsibility for creating change in partnership with the university community. He informed the students that he and the institution would support them to achieve their goals; at the same time, however, he challenged them to defend their position; to present a clear vision of what they wanted to achieve; to outline a plan for how this would be accomplished, for how they would include other members of the university community in the process, and for how their goals and actions would benefit the whole university (Nelson, 2001).

This example from the University of Rhode Island of a challenge to the president's leadership capacity is not unfamiliar to most college and university campuses around the country. In reflecting on his own leadership experiences, Graham Spanier, for example, bemoans the fact that amid the many competing demands faced by college and university presidents, particularly on social issues, presidents are often given "litmus tests"—that is, the many groups that fervently represent often-conflicting social or political causes demand that the president support their points of view. Like Carothers, Spanier reports that, he faces this dilemma by basing decisions on what is best for the university as a whole. At the same time, he emphasizes the necessity of remaining true to his own system of beliefs. "I do take stands and will never make a decision that I can't live with personally, but I am also careful to discharge my responsibility to the university" (quoted in Nelson, n.d.).

ELAINE HANSEN, PRESIDENT OF BATES COLLEGE. Elaine Hansen brings to her presidency a longtime commitment to the Quaker tradition of consensus decision making. As a leader, she believes that she "must enter a room" without her mind made up and with the assumption that "if we talk long enough we will find common ground, maybe even the truth." Her primary goal as a president is "to create a place and a space where everyone is able to feel that they can express themselves." To accomplish this goal, Hansen finds that she must balance the pressure and reality "of people always looking to the president to say things" with the equal and more important need "not to foreclose someone else's ideas" (quoted in Nelson, 2003).

As a small liberal arts college, Bates, similar to many other colleges and universities, experiences an inconsistency between an institutional culture that fosters learning and intimate and personal contact for students with each other, with faculty, and as a community, and the students' actual campus experiences both within and outside the classroom. In acting out her commitments as a moral leader for the college community, Hansen sought to engage students in a dialogue that she hoped would lead to the formulation of plans for improving students' lives on campus. She initiated this dialogue through a major campus forum followed by a series of residence hall discussions. In the course of implementing these dialogues, Hansen learned that her own vision—that of using the dialogue process to design a broad set of values and principles for campus life that would reflect students' aspirations and commitments—was not the vision of the students. Rather, the responses of students focused on immediate considerations of their social life, particularly in asking what the president and her administrative team were going to do to reduce excessive alcohol consumption. To address the students' concerns from the standpoint of her commitment to maintaining the dialogue process and to engaging students in making the campus community more centered on values, Hansen asked students to reflect on whether the college's mission of providing a nurturing environment might be getting in the way of students' taking more responsibility for themselves. Hansen believes that by maintaining this continuing dialogue, the campus community will begin to truly experience the differing perspectives of others around such key questions, and that as a result, "people [will] then see things differently" (quoted in Nelson, 2003).

CREATING AN INSTITUTIONAL CULTURE OF VALUES AND PURPOSE

The ways of being a leader exemplified by these six presidents of very different colleges and universities reflect the critical elements of leadership outlined by Bennis. Particularly important in the context of higher education is their emphasis on fully engaging the institutional community in the process of change. "Effective leadership is a relationship rooted in community. Successful leaders embody their group's most precious values and beliefs. Their ability to lead emerges from the strength and sustenance of those around them" (Bolman & Deal, 1995, p. 56).

Bennis provides a wonderful metaphor for the leader's role within the organization, which he quotes from E. F. Schumacher: "The structure of the organization can . . . be symbolized by a man holding a large number of balloons in his hand. Each of the balloons has its own buoyancy and lift, and the man himself does not lord it over the balloons, but stands beneath them, yet holding all the strings firmly in his hand" (1993, p. 203). Each of these balloons is an administrative unit within the organization. In calling on our leaders to create ways for bringing spirit back into their institutions, I suggest that we need more leaders who are "balloon men" and "balloon women." Here are some possibilities for ensuring "buoyancy and lift."

Being a Personal Role Model

As noted earlier, this is the principle and practice for strengthening character development and core ethical values on their campuses that presidents in Dalton et al.'s survey ranked as most important. As Badaracco and Ellsworth (1989) suggest, successful leaders aspire to "a consistency and coherence among what they believe, how they manage, and the kinds of organizations they want to build—consistency of personal beliefs and values, daily working behavior, and organizational aims" (p. 99). The institutional leaders presented here serve as role models of leadership that operates out of deep personal integrity and with a clear understanding of one's own system of values.

Beverly Daniels Tatum expresses her personal integrity in her openness to eliminating the barriers between the personal and the professional. In her publications (for example, 1997, 2000), in her presentations, and in her interactions, she weaves her life experiences and observations into her analyses of larger organizational, professional, and societal issues.

In numerous ways on his own campus and nationally, Graham Spanier has acted out of his personal commitment to promoting the democratic process through university engagement with the community. While working to ensure that institutional decisions reflect the best interests of the university as a whole, he emphasizes the necessity of remaining true to his own values.

Elaine Hansen's approach to institutional leadership reflects her personal commitment to consensus decision making. As her leadership experiences illustrate, in practice this often means that her viewpoint changes as a result of hearing other people's perspectives.

To truly become role models for their institutions, as suggested by these examples, our leaders must be committed to leading transparent lives. By "letting their lives speak," they will encourage others to cross the divide between the personal and professional.

Staying Connected with "the Calling"

The majority of college and university administrators were called to the academy out of their quest for learning. They devoted years, and often tears, to their graduate education, and many of them began their academic lives as faculty. The examples of institutional leaders presented here mirror Bennis's findings: they have become leaders through their courage to express themselves and their visions for improvement and change openly and fully. It is easy to become bogged down, however, in the day-to-day demands of administration. Diana Chapman Walsh (1999) describes the work life of the president: "The president of a college or university is constantly beset and besieged by a cacophony of competing claims for resources, for attention, for validation" (p. 208). In the process of "putting out fires," our administrators frequently lose sight of their original calling and of the real purposes of their institutions to support the learning process.

Leaders dedicated to recovering spirit in their institutions can begin by reconnecting with their original calling. This may be through teaching, as exemplified by Walter Harrison, president of the University of Hartford, who teaches an undergraduate course with a faculty member every year. It may be through joining student groups that are tackling some of the "big questions," as illustrated by Elaine Hansen's and Robert Carothers's experiences of interacting with students as listeners and coparticipants, not as presenters and authorities. And it may be through remaining involved with faculty in his or her discipline, by participating in colloquia, in collaborative research, in contributions to scholarly organizations.

Reconnecting with one's calling is a tall order. As Cheryl Keen (2000)suggests, "the move towards the less fragmented professional life seems to demand more of us: more time with our students and colleagues in dialogue and more time in reflection and renewal of our essential purposes" (p. 44).

Empowering Others

Significant institutional change cannot be implemented from above. Cheryl Keen (2000) reminds us that to recover spirit in our institutions will require "bridging the layers of fragmentation" among administration, faculty, student affairs professionals, and staff. To make a difference in the culture of our institutions, our institutional leaders need to involve and empower the faculty, student affairs professionals, and staff. They need to look for opportunities to bring faculty and staff into the decision-making process, for example, through creating teams and self-study groups to develop change strategies. They need to work with faculty to design reward systems that recognize expressions of more integrated lives. They need to provide financial support for the innovative work of faculty and staff toward strengthening authenticity, spiritual growth, meaning, and purpose. They must seek every opportunity to truly live as servant leaders within their institutions. Robert Carothers seeks to challenge and empower others on campus to be moral leaders, to fully engage in the responsibility of making decisions that benefit and improve the university as a whole. Diana Chapman Walsh's goal is to create an institutional environment that values and rewards individual initiative and inspires everyone in the organization to do their best.

Exemplifying Civic Engagement

The college presidents in Dalton et al.'s survey most frequently cited community service and service learning as exemplary programs that promote character development and core ethical values. To achieve this goal presidents must be committed to ensuring that students acquire the skills and values of democracy learned through service and civic engagement. One particularly significant way to promote civic engagement is to create a range of opportunities for bringing the intellectual resources of their campuses to address the critical issues facing society and to support the communities in which they reside. As exemplified by Graham Spanier's deep commitment to university engagement, if institutions of higher education and institutional leaders are to become true partners in addressing societal issues, they must go well beyond rhetoric and beyond creating volunteer opportunities for their students as the answer to civic engagement. Institutional leaders must work directly with faculty, student affairs professionals, and students in engaging in the hard work of community improvement and in supporting student learning through this work. They must actively unite with community leaders in planning new directions and must make the resources of the institution available to community residents.

CONCLUSION

As illustrated by the examples in this chapter, effective leadership for recovering spirit requires attention, commitment, and deep personal integrity. It requires the courage to take personal risks and to act out of what Parker Palmer calls "the Rosa Parks decision"—the decision to "live divided no more," to no longer behave differently on the outside than the true self on the inside. It is from the taking of such personal risks that social movements are started (Palmer, 1999b, p. 31). In his book *Lives of Moral Leadership*, Robert Coles (2000) summarizes well the qualities of moral leadership needed to transform our institutions into learning communities that encourage and support spirituality, authenticity, meaning, and purpose at all levels:

> To be a moral leader is to see what needs to be done or changed and then to *exhort*, to *remind* others of what was, what needs to be or ought to be; to *criticize* what is, even *reprimand*, *reprove* those who won't see it or acknowledge it, who uphold the conventional, the established, at whatever cost to people in trouble. To be a moral leader is to see and to provoke, to *stir* others, *teach* them, *dramatize* for them the particular issues, matters at stake in a given struggle, *emphasize* for them (and for oneself too) those issues, those matters—to *lecture*, *hector* even, *invoke* (calling, for example, upon moral traditions, beliefs, teachings), to *evoke* (give expression to those learned values, pieties that have been passed by parents, teachers and clergy to the young). To be a moral leader is to *reason*, directly or indirectly, with others, to *expand* their sense of the possible, the desirable, the undesirable, and so at times to *restrain* others, *warn* them of dangers, even as one is *alerting* them to possible gains, achievements: to *uplift*, to try to help *enable* ideals, give them the life of a personal and social reality. To be a moral leader is to *tell*, to *announce* and *pronounce*, to *spell out* plans, programs, to *engage* with others so that what is *proposed* is taken to heart and connects with the consciences of listeners, leaders or viewers. To be a moral leader is to *will*. . . . To be a moral leader is, then, to call upon moral passion within oneself, set it in motion among others, and do so resourcefully, pointedly [pp. 191–192].

Principles and Practices for Strengthening Moral and Spiritual Growth in College

Jon C. Dalton

A lthough there is much to be learned about improving educational efforts to strengthen moral and spiritual growth in college, there is also much that is already known about these aspects of student learning and development. Colleges and universities have long been engaged in cultivating students' inner life, and a number of educational strategies and practices are currently widely used in higher education. Moreover, as we have documented elsewhere in this book, much has been learned in recent years about the types of learning experiences in college that foster moral development and spiritual growth.

In this chapter we identify specific educational strategies and institutional practices that are important for creating environments that foster moral and spiritual growth in college. We take an institution-wide perspective in describing these approaches so that the broadest range of educational strategies and practices can be considered. Although there are important differences in how colleges and universities approach issues of spirituality and character development depending on institutional mission, size, and type, we have sought to identify those educational strategies and practices that have the broadest application across institutional differences. A self-assessment inventory based on the recommended strategies and practices for strengthening moral and spiritual growth is included in Appendix E.

BACKGROUND

The Principles and Practices for Strengthening Moral and Spiritual Growth were developed through surveys of college and university presidents and of student affairs leaders, field tests, and reviews by scholars. In compiling these benchmarks, we sought to identify educational strategies and practices that are regarded by higher education scholars and administrators as especially important for promoting spiritual growth and moral purpose in the college setting. The concept and organizational format of the principles and practices are based on the Character Education Quality Standards published by the Character Education Partnership (2001). The current form of the Principles and Practices was developed from earlier versions in order to encompass both moral and spiritual growth in the college setting. The Principles and Practices are designed especially for use by colleges and universities and their major organizational divisions for planning and assessing institutional commitment to moral and spiritual growth , using collegiate programs and practices as leading indicators. They are also intended to serve as a guide to best practices for colleges and universities and as a useful self-assessment inventory for conducting institutional and program audits of effectiveness in strengthening spiritual growth and moral development.

THE PRINCIPLES AND PRACTICES

The ten principles are delineated into thirty-four specific institutional practices that serve as primary indicators or markers of institutional commitment.

PRINCIPLE 1: THE INSTITUTION MAKES A DELIBERATE AND COMPREHENSIVE EFFORT TO COMMUNICATE ITS CORE VALUES, PURPOSES, AND MORAL COMMITMENTS TO STUDENTS, FACULTY, STAFF, AND OTHER KEY CONSTITUENTS.

Educating for moral and spiritual growth starts with institutional core values. If there is such a thing as institutional "soul," it is reflected in the core values that a college or university holds most sacred. Core values provide the moral and spiritual centeredness that is critical for uniting students and faculty around shared purposes and meanings. Institutional core values, purposes, and commitments provide a necessary focus and beginning point for reconnecting spirit and learning. This is why collegiate efforts to strengthen spiritual quest, meaning, and purpose must begin with a renewal of commitment to the institution's own unique vision and values. As Steven Covey (1989) notes, "The spiritual dimension is your core, your center, your commitment to your values system" (p. 292). Renewing commitment to core values starts with the institutional mission statement, because this is where institutions usually articulate the guiding values and purposes that serve as a framework of meaning for all of their academic programs, human relationships, traditions, and major support activities. The challenge in reconnecting to institutional mission is to provide opportunities for students, faculty, and staff to examine and embrace the purposes and meanings expressed in the institution's core values and to work together to create a genuine community based on them. Without active and sustained commitment, the vision and values of institutions can become little more than institutional window dressing with no real influence on the lives and routines of students and faculty. If spirituality is to have an authentic place in campus life, it must be connected to the foundational values, beliefs, and commitments of the institution.

Practices Related to Principle 1

A. The institution has a mission statement or policy statement of core values that includes commitment to spiritual growth, meaning, and moral purpose.

B. The orientation program for new students educates them about the mission, beliefs, and core values of the institution.

C. The orientation program for new faculty and staff educates them about the mission, beliefs, and core values of the institution.

D. The institution widely disseminates its mission and core values through official publications and communications and through campus organizations and activities.

E. The institution provides for campus coordination of its efforts to strengthen spiritual growth, authenticity, and purpose.

PRINCIPLE 2: THE INSTITUTION MODELS ITS MISSION AND CORE VALUES THROUGH ITS LEADERSHIP AND ADMINISTRATIVE OPERATIONS.

One of the most important ways that colleges and universities transmit and model their mission and values is through the personal examples of institutional leaders. When the actions of leaders appear to be contrary to the purposes and values of the institutions they represent, they provoke questions about the authenticity of the institutional values as well as the ethical integrity of the leaders. The personal scrutiny that comes with serving as a public role model undoubtedly creates demanding expectations of leaders, but it is a role that college and university presidents appear to accept and affirm. In a recent survey (Dalton, Goodwin, and Chen, 2004) of presidents regarding the importance of their role as moral exemplar, most agreed that modeling institutional values is a very important and necessary responsibility of institutional leadership. Leaders who publicly endorse and exemplify institutional values through their personal words and actions help authenticate and reinforce the power of core values. Conversely, professed values have little hold when they do not appear to be transparent in the actions of leaders.

Consistency between espoused and lived values is also closely watched in the highly visible areas of institutional governance, rule making, policymaking, and administrative decision making. When administrative practices are congruent with core values, they foster a sense of institutional integrity and solidarity. In contrast, when administrators espouse core values yet act in ways that disregard or conflict with them, the inevitable human response is moral cynicism. Cynicism undermines trust and erodes spirit and purpose.

Practices Related to Principle 2

A. Institutional leaders publicly champion and model the core values of the institution's mission.

B. Operating values in institutional governance and administrative decision making are consistent with the institution's espoused mission and core values.

C. Institutional rules, policies, and procedures are consistent with the institution's espoused mission and core values.

D. There is an institutional ethos that fosters spiritual growth, meaning, and purpose.

PRINCIPLE 3: THE INSTITUTION'S MISSION AND CORE VALUES ARE INTEGRATED WITH ACADEMIC PROGRAMS.

Colleges and universities often espouse spiritual, moral, and civic values and purposes that have little connection to the academic curriculum. As we learned in a study of institutional mission statements (John Templeton Foundation, 1999), many colleges and universities have lofty statements about ethical values and purposes but do little in the curriculum to educate for these values. The curriculum reflects the knowledge, skills, and values that an institution judges to be essential for the education and development of students. Consequently, a college or university's academic curriculum provides the most revealing evidence of the institution's commitment to its core values and moral purposes. Espoused values, purposes, and commitments have little traction unless they have a direct connection to what is actually taught. Some colleges and universities construct their academic programs in ways that overly specialize and compartmentalize knowledge or segregate learning from the spiritual values and purposes that are central to their mission. Some curricular arrangements emphasize knowledge and intelligence as if they were separate from the domains of spirit and emotion. This has been a particular problem as liberal arts education has waned in influence in colleges and universities. Smith (2001) argues that "the humanities were traditionally the heart of higher education. Today they are neither its heart nor its center" (p. 88). When the curriculum excludes structured opportunities for reflection on spirituality, values, meaning, and purpose, it lessens the moral impact of education and inhibits the deeper learning that serves to integrate thinking and feeling. Gregory (2003) notes that liberal education is as much ethical as intellectual; it teaches students to analyze and evaluate circumstances that turn them into the persons they become.

Practices Related to Principle 3

A. Courses are offered that provide in-depth opportunities for students to examine and reflect on authenticity, purpose, and meaning.

B. The institution has a general education curriculum that integrates spiritual growth, meaning, and purpose with other core learning outcomes.

C. The institution's mission and core values are included in the knowledge base of academic majors.

D. The institution gives high priority to faculty-student contact and mentoring relationships that encourage students to reflect on spirituality, purpose, and meaning.

E. Students' extracurricular experiences are linked with academic learning and used in intentional ways to enhance opportunities for spiritual growth and reflection on meaning and purpose.

PRINCIPLE 4: THE INSTITUTION TRANSLATES ITS VISION AND VALUES INTO GUIDELINES REGARDING CONDUCT AND THE RESPONSIBILITIES OF CITIZENSHIP.

Long ago, Aristotle struggled with the purposes of education and concluded that intellectual virtues could be developed by direct instruction but that moral virtues were best fostered by instilling good habits (McKeon, 1970, p. 1296). The challenge of instilling good habits in the academic setting has always been one of delicately balancing freedom and responsibility. Colleges and universities are academic communities in which intellectual freedom and discovery are celebrated and safeguarded. But academic communities are also human communities in which the special arrangements for life together in the academy must be clearly ordered, communicated, and maintained. Individual self-interest must be tempered and balanced with responsibility to the greater good of the community. Community conduct guidelines are necessary in the academy to safeguard the rights and responsibilities of all and to provide a framework for resolving conflicts and behaviors that may threaten the pursuit of teaching and learning and the essential support functions of the institution. Colleges and universities must be open and tolerant communities where freedom and dissent are encouraged and ground rules are provided for resolving the inevitable conflicts of such open communities.

Practices Related to Principle 4

A. The institution has a student conduct code that clearly defines students' rights and duties of responsible citizenship and that is closely tied to the institution's mission and core values.

B. The institution has an academic honor code that promotes academic honesty and integrity among students and faculty and inspires them to practice these virtues.

C. The institution has a student ethics creed, covenant, or compact that articulates core values and provides incentives for students to affirm them as part of their membership in the campus community.

PRINCIPLE 5: THE INSTITUTION PROMOTES PUBLIC DIALOGUE AND DEBATE ABOUT ITS MISSION AND CORE VALUES.

The quest for authenticity, spiritual growth, meaning, and purpose is strengthened through campus dialogue in which the experiences and beliefs of others are openly shared and critically examined. Public discussion about the mission and core values of the institution is particularly important for students because it encourages them to examine the meaning and relevance of the community's core beliefs in the context of contemporary issues and problems. Lively campus discussions and debates about institutional values and moral issues encourage students to reflect on their meaning and relevance for students' personal commitments and beliefs.

Practices Related to Principle 5

A. The institution sponsors campus speakers, events, and activities that encourage examination and regard for authenticity, spirituality, meaning, and purpose.

B. The institution actively promotes freedom of speech and intellectual inquiry, and supports it when it is challenged.

C. The institution has special initiatives that focus on ethics, values, spirituality, and social justice.

PRINCIPLE 6: THE INSTITUTION TAKES DELIBERATE STEPS TO HELP STUDENTS CRITICALLY EXAMINE AND ACT ON ITS MISSION AND CORE VALUES.

Students are more likely to engage with and commit to institutional core values and moral purposes when they have practical opportunities to reflect and act on them. Educational experiences that enable students to connect the institution's vision and values to the moral and spiritual circumstances of their personal lives are especially powerful. Authenticity is strengthened when students grapple with values, purpose, and meaning in actual life situations and are provided structured opportunities to reflect on their experiences and connect them to the mission and core values of the institution. The processes of spiritual search and moral reflection do not detract from the academic purposes of colleges. They help give meaning and depth to learning. Action-reflection learning arrangements are especially powerful in promoting moral and spiritual growth.

Practices Related to Principle 6

A. Campus governance structures provide for active student participation and shared responsibility.

B. The institution provides formal incentives and structured opportunities for community service, interfaith dialogue and exchange, and moral action.

C. The institution provides opportunities for students and staff to celebrate and renew commitments to core purposes and values through traditions, rituals, and special events.

D. The institution offers students structured opportunities for developing ethical leadership skills.

PRINCIPLE 7: THE INSTITUTION PROMOTES A PURPOSEFUL, CARING, AND INCLUSIVE CAMPUS COMMUNITY.

How members of academic communities relate to each other and express their moral and social responsibilities to each other is one of the most important indicators of the vitality of the institution's moral and spiritual ethos. When relationships on campus are characterized by respect, openness, and inclusiveness, individuals find greater support and encouragement in their quests for personal meaning and purpose (Boyer, 1990).

In recent years a number of colleges and universities have taken extraordinary steps to create inclusive and welcoming environments for students—particularly students who have been disadvantaged by racial, ethnic, physical, or financial circumstances. These efforts have done much to make campuses more caring and supportive of students. We need to extend the same inclusive and welcoming attitude toward the diverse spiritual and religious interests of college students. Institutional efforts to strengthen authenticity, spiritual growth, meaning, and purpose should include a caring and supportive campus community that welcomes and supports students' diverse religious and spiritual quests.

Practices Related to Principle 7

A. The campus culture promotes caring and respectful relationships among students, faculty, and staff.

B. Students have many opportunities for contact and interaction with a diverse faculty, staff, and student body.

C. The institution provides educational programs and services designed to encourage interfaith contact and learning.

PRINCIPLE 8: THE INSTITUTION IS COMMITTED TO THE HOLISTIC LEARNING AND DEVELOPMENT OF STUDENTS.

Authenticity, spiritual growth, meaning, and purpose are strengthened by learning environments that promote the integration of mind, body, and spirit. Learning that actively connects and encourages interactions among all three of these domains is deeper and more enduring. Holistic learning and development include attention to spiritual growth, meaning, and purpose in the educational programs and activities of the institution.

Practices Related to Principle 8

A. Recognition and support are provided for students' spiritual and religious life in a manner appropriate to the institution's mission.

B. A program of health and wellness is provided as an integral part of students' life and learning.

C. The institution affirms religious pluralism and provides places on campus suitable for personal meditation, prayer, and reflection and for diverse religious and spiritual practices.

PRINCIPLE 9: THE INSTITUTION ASSESSES ITS EFFORTS TO STRENGTHEN AUTHENTICITY, SPIRITUAL GROWTH, MEANING, AND PURPOSE.

Such educational outcomes as moral and spiritual growth are so complex and multifaceted that they do not easily lend themselves to empirical observation and description (Rest, Narváez, Bebeau, and

Thoma, 1999). Yet these outcomes are critical for satisfying lives and productive citizenship, and it is important to assess them because they are so closely connected to the mission and goals of most colleges and universities. Assessing values is at the heart of any institutional assessment effort because values reflect what students really care about and what institutions claim are most important.

Practices Related to Principle 9

A. The institution conducts systematic assessment efforts to evaluate the extent to which spiritual growth, meaning, and moral purpose are manifested in students' learning and development.

B. The institution devotes time and energy to examining the assessment data and to making program improvements called for.

PRINCIPLE 10: THE INSTITUTION HONORS ACHIEVEMENTS OF AUTHENTICITY, SPIRITUALITY, MEANING, AND MORAL PURPOSE.

The core values of an institution are reflected in the things that it honors and rewards. Many types of awards and recognition are used in academe to honor accomplishments in scholarship, leadership, and service to the institution and society. The moral and spiritual accomplishments of men and women should also be formally recognized, because they serve as powerful examples of the lived values of the institution.

Practices Related to Principle 10

A. The institution provides visible and effective rewards and recognition for exemplary students, faculty, staff, alumni, and campus organizations that model the values and commitments of spirituality, meaning, and purpose.

B. The regular annual evaluations of administrators, faculty, student affairs professionals, and staff recognize initiatives and daily practices that encourage authenticity and spiritual growth.

CONCLUSION

The current debate on many campuses about the place of spiritual growth, values, and moral purposes is focusing considerable attention on what is genuinely valued in higher education. Many are persuaded that the important role of helping students integrate learning with values and spiritual growth has been excluded from much of today's higher education. We expect to see an increasing number of colleges and universities become engaged in reassessing how they measure up in promoting spiritual growth, authenticity, and moral purpose in the education and development of their students. We hope these educational principles and practices for strengthening authenticity and spirituality in college will be useful in these efforts.

University of Missouri-Columbia Policy Statement

ASSOCIATION OF CAMPUS RELIGIOUS ADVISORS AT THE UNIVERSITY OF MISSOURI-COLUMBIA BY-LAWS, 1997

I. PREFACE

A. The University of Missouri-Columbia acknowledges the need and the right of students, faculty, and staff to pursue, examine, and affirm a personal religious faith or life philosophy. The University further acknowledges that the examination, affirmation, and exercise of a personal faith or life philosophy are important components in the intellectual and personal development of the individual.

B. As a public institution, the University must avoid policies or actions which favor one particular faith over another. However, the University may seek to support and foster an atmosphere in which interested members of the university community may freely express their religion and faith (Council for Advancement of Standards for Student

Our thanks go to Pablo Bueno Mendoza, Kerry Hollander, and their collaborating colleagues for permission to share this policy statement.

Services/Development Programs, 1986 [hereafter, CAS]—
drawn from sections on Mission and Ethics).

C. The University urges university administrators, faculty, and
staff to be sensitive to the religious holidays of major faith
groups, especially in responding to concerns about the
scheduling of tests and examinations, so that all persons may
participate in the essential practices of their faith without
conflict with academic requirements (CAS—Ethics, University Senate Rules and Regulations).

D. In keeping with its function as an educational institution,
the University supports the academic study of religion
(CAS—Mission).

E. The University supports and encourages organizations
and programs which will help those in the university community to:

1. articulate a personal faith or philosophy of life;

2. acquire the skills and knowledge needed to address
issues of values, ethics, and morality in life;

3. acquire an understanding of the interaction of faith,
intellectual inquiry, and social responsibility as bases for
finding and affirming meaning and satisfaction in life;

4. provide a forum for dialogue between and among representatives of the religious and secular; and

5. provide interested members of the campus community
with reasonable opportunity to express their faith(s)
(CAS—Mission).

F. The University seeks to accommodate the need of students,
faculty, and staff to associate for religious purposes and
assists in the provision of opportunities for religious expression and dialogue. The Association of Campus Religious
Advisors (ACRA) will coordinate these matters.

II. RELIGIOUS ORGANIZATIONS

A. Students, faculty, staff and others associated with the
University who desire to organize for purposes of religious
expression and/or study are encouraged to register with
the University through the Dean of Students Office. Registered religious organizations, as any other registered or-

ganization, will agree to abide by guidelines established
_____ in_____ and will
support the policies expressed in this statement of policy.
They, as any other registered organization, may enjoy the
benefits available to registered organizations.

B. A religious organization not registered with the University is
free to interact among MU students, faculty, and staff in the
same manner as any other non-university entity, provided
that its activities are legal and not infringing on the rights of
other individuals in the MU community.

C. ACRA, a registered campus organization, provides a framework with which advisors of registered organizations pursue
their common purposes within the University and serve and
support the University in its proper tasks.

D. Interested persons are directed to contact the Dean of Students Office to find out who is the contact person for ACRA.

III. RELIGIOUS PROGRAMS AND ACTIVITIES

A. Religious programs and activities must comply with University policies as well as with federal, state, and local laws.

B. The University supports and encourages programs and
activities of religious groups which provide reasonable
opportunities for students and others to:

1. question, explore, understand, affiliate with, avoid, and
express or reject religious faiths;

2. seek individual counseling and/or group associations for
the examination and application of spiritual values and
beliefs to life and to their own spiritual development;

3. worship communally; and

4. pray and meditate (CAS—Program).

IV. UNIVERSITY FACILITIES

A. University facilities shall be available to registered student
and campus religious organizations on the same basis as
other registered organization for regular business meetings,
social functions, and for other programming.

B. Reasonable conditions may be imposed to regulate timeli-
ness of request, to determine the appropriateness of the

space assigned, time of use, and to insure proper maintenance of the facilities.

C. Space in University facilities must be reserved with the
appropriate reservation clerk.

D. Green Chapel scheduling is handled by the appropriate University department.

E. Events using public space in any Residence Hall must have
the approval of the hall's director, and when necessary the
Community Assistant of the appropriate floor or section.
The House Rules are to be checked and obeyed.

F. Private religious studies in individual rooms of a residence hall
are to be handled by the resident(s) of the particular room.

V. STATEMENT OF RIGHTS, CONDUCT, AND
RESPONSIBILITIES FOR RELIGIOUS GROUPS AT
THE UNIVERSITY OF MISSOURI-COLUMBIA

A. The constitutional rights of students, faculty, and staff members of all religious beliefs must be respected (CAS—Ethics).

B. Students, faculty, and staff have the right to practice their
particular faith. They shall have the right to organize on
campus for religious purposes as for all other legal purposes.

C. The University of Missouri-Columbia is a public institution,
and therefore expects all religious groups on campus to give
evidence of tolerance, fairness, and respect for the religious
traditions represented in the University, to respect the non-
sectarian nature of the University itself, and to uphold the
University's commitment to creating a diverse and pluralistic
community on campus.

D. All religious groups shall comply with University policies as
well as federal, state, and local laws. Registered religious
groups shall be accorded the same benefits and be held
accountable in the same manner as any other campus organization (CAS—Ethics).

E. All religious groups on campus will conduct their affairs in
such a manner that no one will be intimidated or coerced
and that participants in any group may freely express their
beliefs and values.

F. Religious organizations at the University of Missouri-Columbia are expected to cooperate in protecting students, through policy and practice, from undue influence or harassment from persons advocating particular religious beliefs and practice, or promoting religious activities (CAS—Ethics).

G. Actions of each religious organization and its members will not endanger the health, safety, or welfare of the University community or any member of the University community. Persons should not be subjected to psychological, physical, or mental pressure harmful in health or personal autonomy. No person or group can be required to participate in any extraordinary institutional arrangement or program that would violate a principle or tenet of their faith (CAS—Ethics).

H. Any membership requirements for on-campus religious groups must be consistent with their purposes. Organizations which sponsor or require particular religious activities must clearly state so, thus permitting a participant to exercise free choice in this regard (CAS—Ethics).

I. University religious organizations shall respect and follow University guidelines regarding the right of others to privacy, such as using public address systems, posting flyers, and visiting residents.

J. ACRA members who have grievances with the University shall submit them to the Chair of ACRA who will forward them to the Vice-Chancellor for Student Affairs.

VI. COMPLAINTS INVOLVING RELIGIOUS ORGANIZATIONS

A. All members of the University of Missouri-Columbia community have the right to bring formal and informal complaints of any kind to the attention of the Vice-Chancellor for Student Affairs.

B. When an individual or group of individuals has a complaint concerning the religious activities or practices of any organization, advisor, or person on the campus of the University of Missouri-Columbia, the following course of action is suggested:

1. The complainant is invited to take his or her complaint to the Chair of ACRA;

2. The Chair of ACRA will initiate an informal process of inquiry and mediation whereby the parties involved may resolve their concerns, grow in their understanding of one another, and avoid a formal University-sponsored hearing;

3. If a proper and acceptable resolution to the complaint cannot be obtained through the above-mentioned process, the complainant shall be advised to file a formal, written complaint with the Vice-Chancellor for Student Affairs. Such formal complaint must be brought before thirty (30) class days have elapsed since the discovery of the violation.

C. When a formal complaint about the religious activities or practices of any registered student, campus, or community religious organization, its advisor, or an individual, is filed with the University, the University shall inform the Chair of ACRA in writing of the complaint and the Vice-Chancellor for Student Affairs may wish to include a member or members of ACRA on the Hearing Panel.

D. Interested persons are directed to the Chair of ACRA.

VII. MEMBERSHIP

The Association of Campus Religious Advisors is an organization whose members are:

1. primarily concerned with students, faculty, staff, events, and activities of the University of Missouri-Columbia; and are

2. given as their job description the *primary work* of associating with, and instruction to students who attend the University of Missouri-Columbia; and

3. who function as staff personnel with a recognized student religious organization; and

4. who accept and sign the ACRA Code of Ethics.

In view of this, it is expected that at least one-half of a member's time (20 hours based on a 40-hour work week) is spent in direct relation with University of Missouri-Columbia students, faculty, and staff. It is not intended to negate, hinder, or deprive the influence of other campus and community religious groups in any way, but it is understood that the necessary focus of our organization is campus-related.

CODE OF ETHICS
Association of Campus Religious Advisors
Missouri University

1. It is accepted by all members of the Association of Campus Religious Advisors (ACRA) that our goal is to respect and uphold the dignity and freedom of choice of all members of the Missouri University community (to include faculty, staff, and administration, as well as students). It is also accepted that we view our roles as members of the ACRA at Missouri University as both religious and professional and will conduct ourselves accordingly.

   a. It is our goal to present our various religious views to the University community within the context of free-willed permission, desiring to espouse our views in such a way that they encourage investigation and reflection. We desire the best for individuals and will not violate their right to choose in spiritual matters. We affirm that our dealings will never have the goal to manipulate, intimidate, or dominate—as a student's choice to be involved with a specific ministry is based, at least to a large degree, on rational thinking. (This does not exclude the idea of religious experience or acceptance felt in a group, but does place the emphasis on choice, rather than emotion.)

   b. Both the public and private presentation of our views and ministries will be open and honest, with no concealed motive or agenda, and with no desire to mislead. In every aspect of our advertising there will be clear identification of each and every group or groups involved. The denominational affiliation of the groups involved will be specifically indicated. Terms such as non-denominational and inter-denominational may be used, but not to the exclusion of denominational ties if applicable.

c. A dominant theme of each member of the ACRA will be to direct and motivate students in making wise choices about life and religion. We deem it a privilege to share our own religious beliefs and ideas but view that secondarily to our primary concern for the student as a person and as an individual. It will be the goal to "treat others as we would be treated."

2. In relation to one another as fellow religious advisors:

a. We will remember that we are all professionals as well as individuals. It is understood from the beginning that there is a large diversity of belief in our Association. Because of this, our interaction will be largely professional. Our membership in the Association does not signify our personal endorsement of any other specific group, nor should we feel the need to defend our background or position to our peers. We strive for an atmosphere of mutual cooperation and concern for the spiritual health and consciousness of students.

b. Our goal will be goodwill among our members. We will believe the best until it is proven differently. We will investigate to ascertain that there has been a clear breach of ethics and respond with the desire to correct. (The Guidelines established by the University for Religious Organizations give the procedure to be taken when a group or ACRA member is accused of any violation.)

c. We will allow and encourage other members to approach us with encouragement, constructive criticism, and ideas for the purpose of advancement of this code. It is our desire to be seen as having respect for others, a willingness to learn and cooperate (not compete), and concern for religion on campus. Our concern will be for understanding.

3. In reference to the programs and students of other campus ministries:

a. In regards to outreach, evangelism, etc., our primary concern will for those who are part of our own religious background, and then to students, etc., who are not a part of any campus-ministry group or religion, as opposed to focusing on those already affiliated with an existing group. For those in existing groups, we will encourage commitment and participation with those groups, instead of a change of ministry groups.

b. Our approach will be to fairly represent our group and to inform students so as not to in anyway coerce them into membership. We will allow them opportunity to investigate with a free will, especially for those who would already claim some type of religious affiliation. We will permit and even encourage students to talk with other groups and advisors, especially if they are changing from one group to another.

c. We accept the privilege and permission to openly share our faith when approached, while continuing to strive for unity and support of other campus groups.

4. In reference to Missouri University, its programs and policies:

a. Because we are working on the University campus, we accept our personal responsibility to place ourselves under its administrative policies on every level and we accept personal responsibility for conduct on and off campus.

b. Ours should be an attitude of support, teamwork, and cooperation with campus officials and staff, rather than antagonism, skepticism, and criticism.

c. We allow the freedom to disagree with the University and to make that known in accordance with the conduct that is appropriate for our office as religious workers and professionals. We will always seek a peaceful and equitable solution to any problem.

It is understood that this Code of Ethics will be accepted and signed by all members of the Association of Campus Religious Advisors (ACRA) at Missouri University. Membership requirements are established through the Office of the Vice-Chancellor for Student Affairs and defined in Guidelines for the ACRA.

Association of Campus Religious Advisors (ACRA)

Code of Ethics – Membership Agreement

The undersigned have read, accept, and agree to abide by the Code of Ethics as approved by ACRA. I (we) do also state that the undersigned meet the established criteria for ACRA membership as recorded in the organization by-laws.

Date: _____

Organization:

_____

Primary contact:

_____

Email address:

_____

Address:

_____

Phone:

_____

Fax:

_____

SSN:

_____

Additional Members

Names(s)	*Email*	*SSN*
1.		
2.		
3.		
4.		
5.		

It is understood that this is a voluntary code and legislated by each member's desire to promote a positive relationship within ACRA and to provide an enhanced view of religion to the campus. Complaints or criticism against an individual or group should first be directed to that individual or group and a solution sought within that context. If that fails to resolve the matter, complaints may be submitted to the Coordinator for the ACRA who will initiate an informal inquiry (See: Guidelines for the ACRA.). It is understood that failure to adhere to either the ACRA's Code of Ethics or Guidelines may result in loss of membership from the ACRA.

A general review of this Code of Ethics will be done once every school year by an appointed committee, with recommendations given to the full membership. Changes or additions will require a 2/3 vote from the membership (which is understood to mean each group receives one vote, not each individual member).

This Code of Ethics was first approved and accepted on

Illustrative Course Syllabi

∿ FIRST YEAR SEMINAR 13: EROS AND INSIGHT

This course is taught by professors Joel Upton, art history, and Arthur Zajonc, physics, Amherst College.

FYS 13 at a Glance

I. Introduction

Our central purpose is to introduce a way of knowing; namely, contemplative knowing . . . defined here as attentiveness, openness/embracing the obverse and sustaining contradiction . . . . which in turn becomes *erôs* and insight which together comprise "love." This re-imagined "love" (as contrasted with impoverished, sentimental, counterfeit, self-satisfying love) constitutes a way of being in the world and as such provides an enduring foundation for education and continuing self-transformation. Hence FYS 13 is, with Rilke, the beginning of the beginning; as all true loving is always a beginning; T. S. Eliot's "Quick, now, here, now, always" centers contemplative knowing enduringly in each one of us.

II. "Art" and "Science"

We challenge the modern habitual separation of "art" and "science" as arbitrary, exclusively rationalized constructions that emerged in the seventeenth-century departure from earlier traditions of inclusiveness and a common human aspiration that comprises paradox and contradiction. By way of a self-reflective contemplative knowing, "art" and "science" re-emerge as distinct, but still superficially different ways of knowing, transcended by a commonality of human longing for "wholeness" from an acknowledged condition of conscious, i.e., mortal fragmentation (A&E, the FALL, various creation myths, including the Timaeus, etc.).

III. Discovering and engaging the contemplative self

1. Coming home to an awareness of conscious self separation and longing; to be is to be separate . . . etc.; molding the self . . .

2. Pursuing "attentiveness," "openness," and a deliberate capacity to "sustain contraction" by way of direct experience—in the construction and contemplation of a value and color intensity chart, in "seeing"/contemplating color through a prism, in contemplating horizontal/vertical/diagonal, the liminal, etc.

3. Accepting the dynamic reality of distinction/difference/contradiction, of sensory perception and rational/irrational/non-rational ordering, of practice and theory; of *erôs* and insight, of separation and longing as the very basis of conscious being.

4. Recognizing true "knowing" as (with Rilke) our "wandering mourning," one form of which Rilke will call our "killing."

5. Arriving at an awareness of the healing necessity to overcome (redeem?) the "murderous" (Rilke) potential we all possess (in consciousness/the Fall, etc.) even in the seemingly benign forms of ideology, clarity/certainty/exclusivity, art(!), science(!), I/he/she/it, etc.; seeking "complementarity," "coincidence of opposites," "beholding," "love."

IV.   *Erôs* and Insight = Love

   1. Courtly love; C. S. Lewis and "Love love and do as you will."

   2. Love in Solitude (standing guard over infinitely separated solitudes as contrasted with sentimental and false unities).

   3. *The Symposium;* Diotima's ladder not as an escape from the dilemma, but its sublimation; the "ladder," "stairway" as "love" that would diminish the "killing of our wandering mourning."

   4. Coming home; Rembrandt's *Return of the Prodigal Son* and T. S. Eliot's "Little Gidding," "Quick, now, here, now, always."

   5. Knowing/knowledge and unfolding consciousness.

Detailed Syllabus

  I.   September 2–4: Introduction

Tuesday: Who are you? Aspirations . . . intellectual, academic, personal? Silence . . .

> Essay 1: Characterize your experience of being silent. One page. Due: Tuesday, September 9. This and every other essay for FYS 13 should be carefully written and typed, using at least two preliminary drafts which will be due in class at the specified date along with your final draft.

Thursday: Description and purpose of FYS 13

  II.   September 9–11: Ways of Knowing—"Art" and "Science" . . . departure

Tuesday: Johannes Kepler (1571–1630), Contemplating the Cosmos, part one

> Reading: Gerald Holton, *Thematic Origins of Scientific Thought: Kepler to Einstein* (selections)

Thursday: Johannes Kepler, Contemplating the Cosmos, part two

  III.   September 16–18: Ways of Knowing—"Art" and "Science" . . . departure

Tuesday: Rembrandt van Rijn (1606–1669), *Aristotle Contemplating the Bust of Homer,* part one

Thursday: Rembrandt van Rijn, *Aristotle Contemplating the Bust of Homer,* part two

Essay 2: Based on the two exemplars, Rembrandt and Kepler: (1) how do "art" and "science" appear to be different as ways of knowing the world; *and* (2) how might you suggest that they are simultaneously similar; *and* (3) are they more alike or different? One page. Due: Tuesday, September 23.

IV. September 23–25: Sections—Introducing the Contemplative Self

N.B. All sections of FYS 13 will meet twice, once with Professor Upton and once with Professor Zajonc in locations to be announced.

Tuesday/Thursday: Separation and Longing

Reading: Oliver Sacks, "The Mind's Eye," *The New Yorker,* July 28, 2003, pp. 48–59

Exercise: Construct a value and neutral color chart.

Instructions to be given in class. Due: Tuesday, September 30.

V. September 30–October 2: Engaging the Contemplative Self–I

Tuesday: Value and Color

Thursday: Johann Wolfgang von Goethe—Color and the Metamorphosis of Science

Reading: J. W. von Goethe, *Goethe's Scientific Studies* (selections)

Essay 3: (1) How were attentiveness and openness instrumental in your construction of your value and neutral color chart? (2) What role did they play in *Goethe's Scientific Studies?* One page. Due: Tuesday, October 7.

VI. October 7–9: Sections—Contemplative Knowing

Tuesday/Thursday: Measuring Contradiction—Mondrian and Einstein

Essay 4: Pick three lines from either *Tuesdays with Morrie* or *All About Love* and one line from the other and relate them to the emerging themes of FYS 13. One page. Due: Thursday, October 16.

VII.   October 16: Engaging the Contemplative Self–II

Thursday: Horizontal and Vertical—Embracing the Obverse

Reading: J. W. von Goethe, "On German Architecture" (in *A Documentary History of Art,* pp. 361–369)

VIII. October 21–23: Engaging the Contemplative Self–III

Tuesday: Pythagoras—Intimations of Reconciliation

Reading: Morris Kline, *Mathematics: The Loss of Certainty* (selections)

Thursday: Hendrick van Vliet—"Waiting"

IX.   October 28–30: Sections—Sustaining Contradiction

Tuesday/Thursday: Neils Bohr, Werner Heisenberg, Barbara McClintock, Georgia O'Keefe and Ryoan-ji in Kyoto, Japan

Reading: E. F. Keller, *A Feeling for the Organism: The Life and Work of Barbara McClintock* (selections)

Essay 5: Characterize your experience of sustaining contradiction, drawing on an instance in your own life. One page. Due: Tuesday, November 4.

X.   November 4–6: *Erôs* and Insight

Tuesday: Courtly Love—The Forgotten Invention

Reading: C. S. Lewis, *The Allegory of Love,* pp. 1–23

Thursday: Inner Dialogue

Reading: Marguerite Porette, *The Mirror of the Simple Soul* (selections)

XI.   November 11–13: Sections—*Erôs* and Insight

Tuesday/Thursday: Solitude

Reading: R. M. Rilke, *On Love and Other Difficulties,* esp. pp. 21–37, 97–99;

T. Merton, *Love and Living,* esp. pp. 15–24

Essay 6: (1) How does the direct challenge to "Love love and do as you will" realize *erôs* and insight as "contemplative knowing"? (2) Give one example of this subtle understanding of love and action in Rilke, Merton and your own experience. Two pages. Due: Tuesday, November 18.

XII.   November 18–20: Love, Desire and the Refinement of the Soul–I

Tuesday: *The Symposium*, part one

Reading: Plato, *The Symposium*, pp. 3–31

Thursday: *The Symposium*, part two

Reading: Plato, *The Symposium*, pp. 32–64

XIII. December 2–4: Love, Desire and the Refinement of the Soul–II

Tuesday: Diotima's ladder

Thursday: Rembrandt van Rijn, *The Return of the Prodigal Son*

XIV.   December 9: *Erôs* and Insight = Love

Tuesday: Love, Education and Transformation

Reading: T. Merton, *Love and Living*, pp. 3–14; 25–37;

R. M. Rilke, *On Love and other Difficulties*, pp. 115–117;

T. S. Eliot, "Little Gidding"

Essay 7: How might FYS 13 cause you to re-imagine how you will construct your education from this point forward? Be specific in your accommodation to the enduring dynamic relation of *erôs* and insight as the basis of contemplative knowing. Four pages. Due: Monday, December 15.

AGONY AND ECSTASY: SPIRITUALITY THROUGH FILM AND LITERATURE

This course is taught by Augie Turak, Duke University.

January 13 – "Inward Bound" talk with Augie Turak

View film: *The Matrix*

Write down all the spiritual elements/metaphors in *The Matrix*

Read "The Indian Life," by Hermann Hesse

Other recommended readings/viewings:

1. "The Allegory of the Cave" from Plato's *Republic*

2. *Illusions: Confessions of a Reluctant Messiah*, by Richard Bach

3. *The Karate Kid*

January 20th – Introduction

- Introduction to course and instructors
- Discuss spiritual elements of *The Matrix*
- Model of the spiritual path
- Introduction to "Treatments"

View film: *Memento*

Read *Franny and Zooey*, by J. D. Salinger (pp. 1–48)

Write "first cut" of your personal treatment

Other recommended readings/viewings:

1. "Integrating the Shadow" from *The Spectrum of Consciousness* (25 pages)
2. *The Screwtape Letters*, by C. S. Lewis
3. *Zeno's Conscience*, by Italy Svevo

January 27 – Identity, Self-Deception and Purpose

- View "2-minute man" documentary clip
- *Memento* discussion
- Turn in treatments

View film: *They Shoot Horses, Don't They?*

Read *Franny and Zooey*, by J. D. Salinger (pp. 48–70)

Other recommended readings/viewings:

1. *12 Steps and 12 Traditions* (Alcoholics Anonymous)
2. *A Grief Observed*, by C. S. Lewis
3. *Tuning in to Grace: The Quest for God*, by Andre Louf
4. *Dark Night of the Soul*, by St. John of the Cross
5. Something by Hubert Benoit (?)
6. Something from "Ego and the Dynamic Ground," by Michael Washburn (?)

February 3 – Despair, Hopelessness, and "Hitting Bottom"

- *They Shoot Horses, Don't They?* discussion
- Review treatments

View film: *Groundhog Day*

Read *Franny and Zooey*, by J. D. Salinger (pp. 70–101)

Read "The Dazzling Dark," by John-Wren Lewis (5 pages)

Other recommended readings/viewings:

1. *13 Conversations About One Thing*
2. *The Strange Life of Ivan Osokin,* by P. D. Ouspensky
3. *In Search of the Miraculous,* by P. D. Ouspensky

February 10 – Ego, Habits, Selflessness, and Service

- *Groundhog Day* discussion
- Review treatments

  View film: *Fearless*

  Read *Franny and Zooey,* by J. D. Salinger (pp. 101–140)

  Other recommended readings/viewings:

  1. *The Power of Now,* by Eckhart Tolle
  2. *Bone Games,* by Rob Schultheis
  3. *The Prison Sutras: Behind Bars with a Buddhist Monk* (documentary)
  4. *Illusions: Confessions of a Reluctant Messiah,* by Richard Bach

February 17 – Fear, Unconflictedness, and Freedom

- *Fearless* discussion
- Review treatments

  View film: *Forrest Gump*

  Read *Franny and Zooey,* by J. D. Salinger (pp. 140–175)

  Other recommended readings/viewings:

  1. *The Perennial Philosophy,* by Aldous Huxley
  2. *The Death of Ivan Illych,* by Leo Tolstoy

February 24 – Faith, Humility, Simplicity, and Tradition

- *Forrest Gump* discussion
- Review treatments

  View film: *Defending Your Life*

  Complete *Franny and Zooey,* by J. D. Salinger (pp. 175–202)

March 2 – Fear, revisited

- *Defending Your Life* discussion
- Review treatments

  View *Apollo 13* documentary

  Read *The Razor's Edge,* by W. Somerset Maugham
  (pp. 1–50)

  Other recommended readings/viewings:

  1. *Spiritual Emergency . . .,* edited by Stanislav Grof
  2. *After the Absolute,* by David Gold

March 9 – Community and Crisis on the Spiritual Path

- *Apollo 13* documentary discussion
- Review treatments

  View *Into Thin Air* documentary

  Read *The Razor's Edge,* by W. Somerset Maugham
  (pp. 50–150)

  Other recommended readings/viewings:

  1. *The Experience of No Self,* by Bernadette Roberts
  2. *Collision with the Infinite,* by Suzanne Segul

March 16 – Spring Break – No Class

March 23 – The Good, the Bad, the Ugly, and the Transcendent: The
Spiritual Path Recapitulated

- *Into Thin Air* documentary discussion
- Review treatments

  View film: *Hearts of Darkness*

  Read *The Razor's Edge,* by W. Somerset Maugham (pp.
  150–200)

  Other recommended readings/viewings:

  1. *Zorba the Greek,* by Nikos Kazantzakis
  2. *The Last Temptation of Christ*
  3. *If* (poem), by Rudyard Kipling

March 30 – Inspiration, Desperation, Commitment, and Passion

- *Hearts of Darkness* discussion
- Review treatments

View film: *Jacob's Ladder*

Read *The Razor's Edge,* by W. Somerset Maugham
(pp. 200–250)

Other recommended readings/viewings:

1. *The Tibetan Book of the Dead*
2. *Tuning into Grace,* by Andre Louf
3. *Selected Writings,* by Meister Eckhart
4. *Magnolia*

April 6 – Attachment, Suffering, Acceptance and Surrender

• *Jacob's Ladder* discussion

• Review treatments

View film: *Our Town*

Complete *The Razor's Edge,* by W. Somerset Maugham
(pp. 250–314)

Other recommended readings/viewings:

1. *The Complete Works of Emily Dickinson*
2. *Peggy Sue Got Married*

April 13 – Nostalgia, Perfection, Impermanence, and the Eternal

• *Our Town* discussion

• Summarize all concepts touched on ????

Complete treatment

No reading—No film

April 17 – Finale

• *American Beauty* screening, discussion

• End-of-class party

SPIRITUALITY AND BUSINESS LEADERSHIP

This course is taught by Andre L. Delbecq, a university professor at
Santa Clara University.

MODULE 1. Course Introduction

Course organization

Personal introductions

Course norms

Assignments and grading

Approaching a "soulful" topic with sensitivity and respect through appreciative inquiry

Reasons for contemporary business leader interest in spirituality

Definitions of spirituality

The call to transcendence and a complete human life

Participants will have read from one of several books on comparative religion and spirituality, and from one of several books of personal spirituality relating the personal journeys of leaders across religious traditions.

This is a prelude to appreciative inquiry and respectful listening.

MODULE 2. Integrating Business Leadership as a Calling into the Spiritual Journey

The pivotal role of business as a societal institution at the turn of the century

Contributions for which North American business leadership can take just pride and areas of concern

Connecting the calling to business leadership and the spiritual journey

The sense that those called to leadership for important societal institutions find their greatest fulfillment by understanding: that their career is itself a form of prayer, and that work and spiritual life can be integrated.

Servant leadership can be an invitation to spiritual deepening and a route to self fulfillment.

MODULE 3. Listening to the Inner Voice in the Midst of Turbulent Business Environments

Lakota Sioux Living Circle: listening to the inner voices which speak our personal history

Sharing experiences which draw business leaders to explore spirituality

Spirituality and the uniqueness of individual identity.

Discovering the power of listening to our own history and inner voice, realizing that we must have a strong appreciation for our personal specific uniqueness and own inner capacities in order to live fully within our own self as a precondition to giving to others.

MODULE 4. Business Leadership Challenges and the Need for Self Integration

Studies of effective senior business leaders

Models of self integration in the life history of exemplary leaders

Spirituality and self integration as an important component in the path to leadership maturity

Exploring the rich literature on transformational leadership which shows the complexity and special challenges of such leadership. By studying the psychological/sociological/ historical biographies of leaders the integration of self in life will become apparent. But also the special challenges leaders face requiring inner strength.

MODULE 5. Discernment and Senior Business Leadership

Problems of focusing on the issues which matter in the noisy environment of contemporary business

The discernment process in the spiritual traditions

Discovering how discernment through prayer and meditation is shown by spiritual masters to lead to true liberty allowing the leader to make difficult choices without anxiety. Discernment increases the capacity to do the right thing not by accident or as a burden, but in true freedom.

MODULE 6. Approaches to Spirituality and Leadership: Prayer/Meditation/Reflection and the Leadership Journey

The centrality of prayer/meditation/reflection to the spiritual journey

Approaching "inner work" with confidence

Practical guidelines from spiritual masters

Learning the rhythms and joys of these central practices in all spiritual traditions, and developing an approach true to our individuality and the life style requirements of leaders.

MODULE 7. The Special Challenges of Leadership Power

The need to fill the leadership role with the "gravitas" required for transformational change

Hubris as the often reported Achilles' Heel of charismatic leaders

Seductions toward arrogance associated with position power

Humility as a central virtue in the spiritual journey of leaders

Learning what the wisdom literature tells us about recognizing the truth of one's role and gifts and leading with the fullness of individual potential but without undue self-serving ego.

MODULE 8. The Spiritual Challenges of Wealth vs. Poverty of Spirit in the Business Leader's Life

The valued charisma of wealth creating leadership.

The paradox of wealth as a force for good and a spiritual challenge

Wealth and its impact on the leader's family

A much discussed topic in executive circles

Appropriate asceticism and detachment as aspects of spirituality for leadership

Developing wisdom regarding philanthropy

Learning that wealth consists not in having much but in having few wants. Some wonderful exemplars of poverty of spirit and stewardship among contemporary executives.

MODULE 9. Contemplative Practice in the Hectic Space of a Business Leader's Life

The superficial paradox of contemplation versus action

The universal call to mysticism in the spiritual traditions

Contemplative practices and the contemporary enrichment from Eastern Spiritual traditions

Understanding how all spiritual traditions invite us into mysticism as part of the journey, and that each of us are capable of cultivating this capacity.

MODULES 10–11. Group Retreat

A time for prayer/meditation/reflection on the lessons learned regarding spirituality and the call to leadership

Bringing reflections and future direction into prayerful perspective in silence

MODULE 12. Field Experience Involving Segments of Society Outside Contemporary Business Life: An Encounter with Voices Sometimes Not Heard

A field experience to learn from the poor and suffering who are outside contemporary business participation

Love, compassion, and a concern with social justice as essential fruits of the spiritual journey

An opportunity to stand outside the role of philanthropist or expert and enter into the I-Thou encounter

Learning how to let the individual into our heart as a prelude to compassionate action

MODULE 13. The Significant Trials of Transformational Leaders: Exploring the Mystery of Suffering

The significant sufferings and trials transformational leaders bear

The potential for growth and learning within the mystery of suffering

Perspectives on suffering from the Spiritual Masters

Making sense of suffering within the interpretation of spiritual traditions

Anticipating the very special sufferings of the transformational leader role; e.g. stepping down, seeing your work diminished or dismantled, courageous new starts, hyper-criticism directed toward leaders, the special loneliness experienced by the inwardly motivated leader, etc.

MODULE 14. Individual Study Reports of a Spiritual Master and Insights for the Leadership Journey

Sharing the experiences of your master's spiritual journey

Reflections on the lessons most pertinent to business leadership

Being with a master of choice for the entire seminar

Asking how that master speaks to your leadership in your individuality

MODULE 15. Bringing It All Together and Celebration of the
   Business Leader's Spiritual Journey

> *Summarizing from our personal journals those insights most
> helpful to our leadership journey and celebrating the gift of
> sharing which has occurred.*

Because spirituality focuses on the lived experience of individuals, this
is obviously not simply a lecture course. I will be sharing initial
reflections on my own Christian Tradition and personal history, and
stories of executives with whom I have worked. But the heart of the
seminar is to respectfully receive and appreciatively listen to and learn
our own personal history through meditation, journaling, and dialog.

—⁓—

There you have the outline of a wonderfully complex mix of resources
and learning activities that powerfully drive increased authenticity,
meaning, and purpose. Much of that power comes not only from
Professor Delbecq's clear authenticity and strong personal
identification with those outcomes but also from the centrality given
to reflection and contemplation.

   The following are some comments from his students:

> "The meditations in class have set me up for a more personal
> experience of the material than I had expected. I had envisioned
> a more lecture-based approach instead of the more active
> experience and participation that is needed for this class. I don't
> think I would have been able to jump into the meditation
> assignments without the 'practice' during the lecture."

> "My life is a circle. I run around and around. Each day is the
> same. Months and years all appear the same. I'm in a rut. The
> first meditation brought something to light inside of me. I
> discovered life does not begin in the future, but now. I began to
> think that I can break the circle apart."

> "Thomas Merton sums up exactly what I am thinking. I am
> working on finding my true self, but there are so many
> distractions at work that I'm not always sure which of my
> feelings are real. How do you overcome all of the fears,
> obsessions and addictions to find yourself? Part of the answer
> has to be to be 'present' so you can listen to God in the 'now.'"

"My workdays are more productive because I had focused my thoughts and tasks for the day toward the light in the very beginning of the work day. I stopped my rush before entering the office. With focused thoughts and reduced pace, my days were more productive."

Rutgers Evaluation and Dissemination Plans

～ DEVELOPING MODELS OF INSTITU-TIONAL CHANGE

Evaluation and assessment of the implementation processes and student outcomes are critical for insuring that the proposed curriculum changes achieve the intended impact on Rutgers students' educational experience and serve as a model for other colleges and universities. To accomplish these objectives, we are implementing a rigorous plan for on-going research, evaluation and assessment of the students, faculty and administrative staff participating in the project. Simultaneously with assessing the educational changes proposed through this project, we will disseminate information about project results to other Rutgers colleges and to other institutions of higher education. The plan for dissemination as outlined below is central for realizing our goal of designing this project as an educational model for other colleges and universities.

Measures for Research, Evaluation and Assessment

As an institution with rich research resources, we plan to conduct rigorous on-going research to evaluate and assess the impact of the proposed curriculum changes on Livingston College students, faculty and staff. Our research design will incorporate both quantitative and qualitative methodologies. We plan to utilize research protocols for collecting data on students' values, beliefs and purposes that serve as a baseline for measuring and assessing change resulting from our curricular innovations. Evaluation data will be compiled and analyzed regularly during the course of the project and used to make adjustments to the courses and other educational experiences implemented through the project and to the faculty seminars and workshops. The data generated through the quantitative and qualitative measures outlined below will provide the basis for assessing overall project outcomes and for determining the institutional change strategies that serve as models for other Rutgers colleges and other institutions interested in promoting the examination of personal values, meaning and purpose as basic to the undergraduate education. With a large and diverse undergraduate student population, Livingston College and Rutgers University are well-positioned to provide significant insights into the potential impact of the college experience on students' values and beliefs.

Measures for conducting research on students' beliefs and values and for assessing project outcomes will include the following.

STUDENTS. We plan to use a pre- and post-course design, with a one-year follow-up, to assess the impact of the proposed curriculum revisions and additions on Livingston College students. The pre- and post-course measures will be administered to a comparable sample of students from Rutgers College to provide a control group for assessing project results.

1. The HERI College Students' Beliefs and Values Survey. Both to assess the effects on students' beliefs and values of the curriculum changes implemented through our project and to contribute to the national efforts currently being implemented by the Templeton Foundation and the Higher Education Research Institute, we are proposing to use an abbreviated version of the HERI College Students' Beliefs and Values Survey. Students entering Livingston College will be administered the survey during their orientation period and will be given the survey again at the end of the required "Building Community Through Leadership and Understanding" course. In year two, follow-up data will be collected on the original sample which will allow evaluation of the impact of the curriculum one year after the course is taken. The survey also will be administered to a random sample of entering Rutgers College students during their orientation and at the end of their first year.

In addition, we will collect pre- and post-course data on the Livingston College students who are taking the advanced course sequences. This will provide comparative data on changes in beliefs and values among three sets of Livingston College students: 1) students who have taken one course examining meaning and purposes; 2) students who have taken two courses; 3) students who have taken two courses and the service-learning option. The survey will be administered to a random sample of Rutgers College students during their second year to provide greater understanding of the effect of the curriculum innovations on students' attitudes and their application of course learning to a variety of life situations.

2. The Student Instructional Ratings Survey (SIRS). Rutgers University's Teaching Excellence Center conducts the Student Instructional Ratings Survey of all University classes each semester. This University-wide survey compiles students' ratings about the effectiveness of the instructor in providing a learning environment in the classroom, the extent to which the course met their learning expectations, and the overall effectiveness of the class. The results are used by individual instructors, departments, schools and the University as a whole for the assessment and improvement of teaching. During the project we will work with the Teaching Excellence Center to administer student evaluations of the courses included in the project. Targeted questions related to the topics of meaning and purpose will be added to the standard survey questions. To provide insight into the impact of the course revisions, student evaluations from previous versions of the "Building Community Through Leadership and Understanding" course will be compared to the newly taught courses.

3. Focus Groups. To assess in greater depth the impact of the curriculum revisions and additions on students' definitions of their personal meaning, purpose, and values focus groups with students in randomly selected classes will be conducted throughout the course of the project.

INSTRUCTORS. A combination of pre- and post-seminar/workshop surveys and a series of focus groups and interviews will be conducted with the instructors participating in the project to assess the extent to which these experiences have changed their attitudes toward examining issues of personal meaning, purpose and values with their students and with their colleagues.

1. The HERI Faculty Survey. Both to assess the impact of the faculty development seminars and workshops implemented through our project and to contribute to the national efforts currently being implemented by the Templeton Foundation and the Higher Education Research Institute, we are proposing to utilize measures to survey faculty attitudes that parallel those being implemented by HERI as part of the National Study of College Students' Search for Meaning and Purpose. A pre- and post-seminar/workshop design, with a one-year follow-up, will be used. In year two follow-up data will be collected on the original sample which will allow evaluation of the continued impact of the faculty seminars and workshops on modifying instructors' approaches to working with students to examine issues of meaning and purpose.

2. Focus Groups and Interviews. During the course of the project, focus groups and individual interviews will be conducted with all instructors participating in preparing and teaching the new and revised courses. Framing questions for these focus groups may include the following:

- Was the training provided through the faculty development seminars and workshops sufficient for preparing you to provide guidance to students in examining issues of personal meaning and purpose? What additional preparation would have been helpful?
- How effective was your background knowledge about the topics and pedagogical approaches for teaching this course? What additional background and training would improve your teaching?
- In what ways did teaching this course change your approaches to encouraging students to examine their personal meaning and purposes, values and beliefs? How do you think you might teach differently in the future as a result of this experience?
- Did you receive adequate administrative and resource support and the support of your colleagues?

- What were the primary factors that facilitated accomplishment of your course objectives and teaching strategies? And what were the barriers? What are your recommendations for improving these courses in the future?

- Based on your experience, would you recommend that the University incorporate other courses and learning experiences into the undergraduate education to encourage students to examine their meaning and purpose? What pre-requisites do you think are necessary for successful implementation?

Dissemination Plan

The results of this project will be disseminated through a number of methods. These methods will target two primary groups: (1) Rutgers faculty members, administrators and professional staff; and (2) a broad audience of faculty members and academic administrators from other higher education institutions around the country. This two-pronged approach will ensure comprehensive dissemination of the findings of this project, both internally and to the larger higher education community. The dissemination plan is devised to address our project goal of developing an educational model that will inform other colleges and universities to renew their commitment to higher education's responsibility for formation of values and beliefs.

RUTGERS FACULTY, ADMINISTRATORS, AND PROFESSIONAL STAFF. In order to provide information about the project to the entire Rutgers New Brunswick faculty of 2000, as well as administrators and other professional staff, a project website will be established which is linked to the Rutgers University website, Livingston College website, as well as, the Teaching Excellence Center. These websites have become a primary means of disseminating and accessing information at Rutgers, and promise to reach a substantial number of individuals in this target group. Project implementation activities will also be reported in the *Rutgers Focus*, the weekly in-house faculty/staff newspaper. In addition, the Rutgers Teaching Excellence Center will hold a seminar for Rutgers faculty members to provide information about the course revisions developed and implemented for this project. This will provide a level of detail that will allow additional faculty members to work on similar course revisions.

OTHER INSTITUTIONS OF HIGHER EDUCATION. In order to reach a broad audience from other higher education institutions, results of the project will be reported at the annual conferences of key higher education organizations including the American Association for Higher Education, the Association of American Colleges and Universities, and the Institute on College Student Values. Journal articles delineating the curriculum reform and its outcomes also will be submitted to publications such as *Change, Liberal Education,* and the *Journal of Higher Education.*

As indicated, we are proposing to compile data from this project that will contribute to the HERI Spirituality in Higher Education project, and, thereby to the national database on student and faculty attitudes toward meaning and purpose. In addition, the Rutgers Department of University Relations, as part of its responsibility for public information about important new developments at the University, will work to place news articles about the project in the *Chronicle of Higher Education,* the *New York Times,* and the *Wall Street Journal.*

To insure dissemination of project findings to a wide higher education audience, Livingston College and Rutgers University will host a national conference focused on examining multiple methods for incorporating a focus on meaning and purpose into the undergraduate curriculum.

Teacher Formation Evaluation Results

⟞⟋⟍⟍⟍⟍⟞ T

he Center for Teacher Formation was initially funded by the Fetzer Institute and focuses on formation in pre-K–12 public education. The center uses the copyrighted phrase Courage to Teach® to denote the retreat-based formation program it has developed. Two evaluation studies found the following lasting effects on the part of Courage to Teach® participants. Similar results are found in a study conducted by the Center for Formation in the Community College (Intrator, 2002, pp. 21-23):

- The Courage to Teach® program rejuvenates teachers and renews their passion for teaching.
- Teachers who go through these programs undertake new leadership roles in education, often crediting their enhanced leadership skills and their capacity to assume new challenges and risks to participation in the program.
- Participants often describe how their Courage to Teach® experience led them to initiate more collegial relationships when they returned to their school site.

- Although the Courage to Teach® program does not explicitly set out to change classroom practice, all of the teachers queried believe that the experience improved their classroom practice in significant ways through the development of genuine connections with their students and their "teaching from the heart." Most felt that their students had tangibly benefited by the changes.

- Teachers felt that the program helped them to develop more reflective habits in their teaching practice, allowing them to become more critical practitioners who could stop and reflect on their own teaching.

- Teachers felt that they live more mindfully and more balanced lives.

These themes—passion for teaching, teacher leadership, collegial relationships, improved classroom practices, reflective habits, mindful and balanced living—are among those most often repeated in the education reform literature about what is most essential for good schools, good teaching, and good learning. Many observers of teachers have said that until we provide dynamic, supportive, and intellectually challenging conditions for our educational personnel we will not be able to carry out our vision for creating dynamic, supportive, and intellectually challenging schools. Both research and common sense suggest that to be sustaining and renewing, we must provide opportunities for teachers and leaders to further develop, explore, and renew their core mission and purpose.

Why do so many carefully planned reform efforts fail to achieve their well-intended outcomes? Why is it that many initially successful reforms have difficulty enduring, often losing ground as their champions become depleted by overwhelming demands? Educators we have met through Courage to Teach® are more than ready to shoulder the leadership tasks of change—when they have reclaimed their sense of personal wholeness and vocational calling. In teacher formation retreats, educators come together as colleagues, steadfastly reclaiming their identity and integrity as teachers. Enormous potential for positive change is rediscovered—leading to greater depth and vitality in student-teacher relationships, renewed collegial practices in schools, and the revitalization of teachers as leaders in public education.

Inventory for Assessing the Moral and Spiritual Growth Initiatives of Colleges and Universities

Jon C. Dalton

⟨⟩ T he Inventory for Assessing the Moral and Spiritual Growth Initiatives of Colleges and Universities was developed by the Center for the Study of Values in College Student Development at Florida State University and may be used without charge or permission. The concept and organizational format of the inventory is based on Character Education Quality Standards, published by the Character Education Partnership (2001). The current form of the principles and practices was developed from earlier versions in order to encompass both moral and spiritual growth in the college setting. The inventory was designed for use by colleges and universities and their major organizational divisions for assessing commitment to moral and spiritual growth using institutional programs and initiatives as leading indicators.

WHAT ARE THE PRINCIPLES?

The ten principles represent guiding institutional standards or priorities related to moral and spiritual growth in college. The ten principles are delineated into thirty-four specific institutional practices that serve as benchmarks or markers of institutional commitment to moral and spiritual growth.

Using the Principles to Assess the Moral and Spiritual Growth Efforts of Colleges and Universities

1. Evaluate the level of implementation of each of the thirty-four moral and spiritual growth practices included in the inventory. Rate each item on the following scale:

   0 No implementation observable or poorly implemented

   1 Some implementation

   2 Good implementation

   3 Very good implementation

   4 Exemplary implementation

2. Use these ratings as a guide to identify and evaluate the strengths and weaknesses of institutional efforts to encourage moral and spiritual growth in students and to plan improvements. Because these principles and practices are not weighted in any way it is also important to consider those principles and practices that are of greatest priority to the institution early in the assessment process.

Table E1.   SUMMARY SHEET FOR SCORING PRINCIPLES

	Item 1	Item 2	Item 3	Item 4	Item 5	Average
Principle 1						
Principle 2						
Principle 3						
Principle 4						
Principle 5						
Principle 6						
Principle 7						
Principle 8						
Principle 9						
Principle 10						
Total:						

COMMENTS:

_____

_____

_____

_____

_____

_____

_____

_____

_____

_____

_____

_____

_____

_____

_____

_____

_____

_____

_____

_____

_____

_____

_____

PRINCIPLE 1: THE INSTITUTION MAKES A DELIBERATE AND COMPREHENSIVE EFFORT TO COMMUNICATE ITS CORE VALUES, PURPOSES, AND MORAL COMMITMENTS TO STUDENTS, FACULTY, STAFF, AND OTHER KEY CONSTITUENTS.

A. PRACTICE: The institution has a mission statement or policy statement of core values that includes commitment to spiritual growth, meaning, and moral purpose.	0	1	2	3	4

Table E.2.

B. PRACTICE: The orientation program for new students educates them about the mission, beliefs, and core values of the institution.	0	1	2	3	4

Table E.3.

C. PRACTICE: The orientation program for new faculty and staff educates them about the mission, beliefs, and core values of the institution.	0	1	2	3	4

Table E.4.

D. PRACTICE: The institution widely disseminates its mission and core values through official publications and communications and through campus organizations and activities.	0	1	2	3	4

Table E.5.

E. PRACTICE: The institution provides for campus coordination of its efforts to strengthen spiritual growth, authenticity, and purpose.	0	1	2	3	4

Table E.6.

PRINCIPLE 2: THE INSTITUTION MODELS ITS MISSION AND CORE VALUES THROUGH ITS LEADERSHIP AND ADMINISTRATIVE OPERATIONS.

A. PRACTICE: Institutional leaders publicly champion and model the core values of the institution's mission.	0	1	2	3	4

Table E.7.

B. PRACTICE: Operating values in institutional governance and administrative decision making are consistent with the institution's espoused mission and core values.	0	1	2	3	4

Table E.8.

C. PRACTICE: Institutional rules, policies, and procedures are consistent with the institution's espoused mission and core values.	0	1	2	3	4

Table E.9.

D. PRACTICE: There is an institutional ethos that fosters spiritual growth, meaning, and purpose.	0	1	2	3	4

Table E.10.

PRINCIPLE 3: THE INSTITUTION'S MISSION AND CORE VALUES ARE INTEGRATED WITH ACADEMIC PROGRAMS.

A. PRACTICE: Courses are offered that provide in-depth opportunities for students to examine and reflect on authenticity, purpose, and meaning.	0	1	2	3	4

Table E.11.

B. PRACTICE: The institution has a general education curriculum that integrates spiritual growth, meaning, and purpose with other core learning outcomes.	0	1	2	3	4

Table E.12.

C. PRACTICE: The institution's mission and core values are included in the knowledge base of academic majors.	0	1	2	3	4

Table E.13.

D. **PRACTICE:** The institution gives high priority to faculty-student contact and mentoring relationships that encourage students to reflect on spirituality, purpose, and meaning.	0	1	2	3	4

Table E.14.

E. **PRACTICE:** Students' extracurricular experiences are linked with academic learning and used in intentional ways to enhance opportunities for spiritual growth and reflection on meaning and purpose.	0	1	2	3	4

Table E.15.

PRINCIPLE 4: THE INSTITUTION TRANSLATES ITS VISION AND VALUES INTO GUIDELINES REGARDING CONDUCT AND THE RESPONSIBILITIES OF CITIZENSHIP.

A. **PRACTICE:** The institution has a student conduct code that clearly defines students' rights and duties of responsible citizenship and that is linked to the institution's mission and core principles.	0	1	2	3	4

Table E.16.

B. **PRACTICE:** The institution has an academic honor code that promotes academic honesty and integrity among students and faculty and inspires them to practice these virtues.	0	1	2	3	4

Table E.17.

C. **PRACTICE:** The institution has a student ethics creed, covenant, or compact that articulates core values and provides incentives for students to affirm them as part of their membership in the campus community.	0	1	2	3	4

Table E.18.

PRINCIPLE 5: THE INSTITUTION PROMOTES PUBLIC DIALOGUE AND DEBATE ABOUT ITS MISSION AND CORE VALUES.

A. **PRACTICE:** The institution sponsors campus speakers, events, and activities that encourage examination and regard for authenticity, spirituality, meaning, and purpose.	0	1	2	3	4

Table E.19.

B. **PRACTICE:** The institution actively promotes freedom of speech and intellectual inquiry, and supports it when it is challenged.	0	1	2	3	4

Table E.20.

C. **PRACTICE:** The institution has special initiatives that focus on ethics, values, spirituality, and social justice.	0	1	2	3	4

Table E.21.

PRINCIPLE 6: THE INSTITUTION TAKES DELIBERATE STEPS TO HELP STUDENTS CRITICALLY EXAMINE AND ACT ON ITS MISSION AND CORE VALUES.

A. PRACTICE: Campus governance structures provide for active student participation and shared responsibility.	0	1	2	3	4

Table E.22.

B. PRACTICE: The institution provides formal incentives and structured opportunities for community service, interfaith dialogue and exchange, and moral action.	0	1	2	3	4

Table E.23.

C. PRACTICE: The institution provides opportunities for students and staff to celebrate and renew commitments to core purposes and values through traditions, rituals, and special events.	0	1	2	3	4

Table E.24.

D. PRACTICE: The institution offers students structured opportunities for developing ethical leadership skills.	0	1	2	3	4

Table E.25.

PRINCIPLE 7: THE INSTITUTION PROMOTES A PURPOSEFUL, CARING, AND INCLUSIVE CAMPUS COMMUNITY.

A. PRACTICE: The campus culture promotes caring and respectful relationships among students, faculty, and staff.	0	1	2	3	4

Table E.26.

B. PRACTICE: Students have many opportunities for contact and interaction with a diverse faculty, staff, and student body.	0	1	2	3	4

Table E.27.

C. PRACTICE: The institution provides educational programs and services designed to encourage interfaith contact and learning.	0	1	2	3	4

Table E.28.

PRINCIPLE 8: THE INSTITUTION IS COMMITTED TO THE HOLISTIC LEARNING AND DEVELOPMENT OF STUDENTS.

A. PRACTICE: Recognition and support are provided for students' spiritual and religious life in a manner appropriate to the institution's mission.	0	1	2	3	4

Table E.29.

B. PRACTICE: A program of health and wellness is provided as an integral part of students' life and learning.	0	1	2	3	4

Table E.30.

C. PRACTICE: The institution affirms religious pluralism and provides places on campus suitable for personal meditation, prayer, and reflection and for diverse religious and spiritual practices.	0	1	2	3	4

Table E.31.

PRINCIPLE 9: THE INSTITUTION ASSESSES ITS EFFORTS TO STRENGTHEN AUTHENTICITY, SPIRITUAL GROWTH, MEANING, AND MORAL PURPOSE.

A. PRACTICE: The institution conducts systematic assessment efforts to evaluate the extent to which spiritual growth, meaning, and purpose are manifested in students' learning and development.	0	1	2	3	4

Table E.32.

B. PRACTICE: The institution devotes time and energy to examining the assessment data and to making program improvements called for.	0	1	2	3	4

Table E.33.

PRINCIPLE 10: THE INSTITUTION HONORS ACHIEVEMENTS OF AUTHENTICITY, SPIRITUALITY, MEANING, AND MORAL PURPOSE.

A. PRACTICE: The institution provides visible and effective rewards and recognition for exemplary students, faculty, staff, and organizations that model the values and commitments of spirituality, meaning, and purpose.	0	1	2	3	4

Table E.34.

B. PRACTICE: The regular annual evaluations of administrators, faculty, student affairs professionals, and staff recognize initiatives and daily practices that encourage authenticity and spiritual growth.	0	1	2	3	4

Table E.35.

For more information:

Dr. Jon C. Dalton
Hardee Center for Leadership and Ethics
E3 Stone Building
Florida State University
Tallahassee, FL 32306-4452
jdalton@admin.fsu.edu

Journal of College and Character
www.collegevalues.org

—ᴡᴠᴠ— References

Alexander, S. (Ed.). (1999). *Everyday spiritual practice*. Boston: Skinne House Books.

Allen, K., & Cherry, C. (2000). *Systematic leadership: Enriching the meaning of our work*. Lanham, MD: University Press of America.

Allport, G. W. (1950). *The individual and his religion: A psychological interpretation*. Old Tappan, NJ: Macmillan.

Allport, G. W., & Ross, J. M. (1967). Personal religious orientation and prejudice. *Journal of Personality and Social Psychology, 5*, 432–443.

Alverno College Faculty. (1992). *Valuing in decision-making: Theory and practice at Alverno College*. Milwaukee, WI: Alverno College Institute.

Alverno College Faculty. (1979/1994). *Student assessment-as-learning at Alverno College*. Milwaukee, WI: Alverno College Institute. (Original work published 1979, revised 1985 and 1994)

Alverno College Faculty. (2000). *Self assessment at Alverno College*. Milwaukee, WI: Alverno College Institute.

Alverno College Faculty. (1973/2002/2005). *Ability-based learning program* [brochure]. Milwaukee, WI: Alverno College Institute. (Original work published 1973, revised 1980, 1983, 1985, 1988, 1991, 1992, 1993, 1994, 1996, 2000, and 2002)

Alverno College Faculty. (1976/2005). *Ability-based learning outcomes: Teaching and assessment at Alverno College*. Milwaukee, WI: Alverno College Institute. (Original work published 1976, revised 1981, 1985, 1989, 1992, and 2005)

Alverno College Valuing Department. (2004). *Valuing in decision making* [handout]. Milwaukee, WI: Alverno College Institute.

American Council on Education. (1937). *The student personnel point of view: A report of a conference on the philosophy and development of student personnel work in college and university*. Ser. 1, Vol. 1, No. 3. Washington, DC: American Council on Education Studies.

Armstrong, K. (2004). *The spiral staircase*. New York: Knopf.

Astin, A. W. (1993). *What matters in college? Four critical years revised.* San Francisco: Jossey-Bass.

Astin, A. W., & Astin, H. S. (1999). *Meaning and spirituality in the lives of college faculty: A study of values, authenticity, and stress.* Los Angeles: University of California Higher Education Research Institute.

Astin, A. W., & Sax, L. (1999). How undergraduates are affected by service participation. *Journal of College Student Development, 39,* 251–263.

Badaracco, J. L., & Ellsworth, R. R. (1989). *Leadership and the quest for integrity.* Boston: Harvard Business School Press.

Baeyer, H. C. von. (1992). *Taming the atom: The emergence of the visible microworld.* New York: Random House.

Bandura, A. (1978). The self system in reciprocal determinism. *American Psychologist, 33,* 344–358.

Batson, C. D., Schoenrade, P., & Ventis, W. L. (1993). *Religion and the individual: A social psychological perspective.* New York: Oxford University Press.

Baxter Magolda, M. B. (2002). [Review of the book *Learning that lasts: Integrating learning, development, and performance in college and beyond*]. *Journal of Higher Education, 73,* 660(666.

Becker, E. (1970). *The denial of death.* New York: Simon & Schuster.

Bennett, D. C. (2000). Quaker to the core: Welcoming all. In V. H. Kazanjian Jr. & P. L. Laurence (Eds.), *Education as transformation: Religious pluralism, spirituality and a new vision for higher education in America* (pp. 187-193). New York: Lang.

Bennett, J. (2003). Spirituality and the vitality of academic life. *Journal of College and Character, 3.* Retrieved from www.collegevalues.org.

Bennis, W. G. (1989). *On becoming a leader.* Reading, MA: Addison-Wesley.

Bennis, W. G. (1993). *An invented life: Reflections on leadership and change.* Reading, MA: Addison-Wesley.

Bennis, W. G., & Thomas, R. J. (2002). *Geeks and geezers: How era, values, and defining moments shape leaders.* Boston: Harvard University Press.

Board of Regents of the University of Wisconsin System v. Southworth et al. (2000)

Bolman, L. G., & Deal, T. E. (1995). *Leading with soul: An uncommon journey of spirit.* San Francisco: Jossey-Bass.

Boyatzis, R. E., Cowen, S. S., Kolb, D. A., & Associates. (1995). *Innovation in professional education: Steps on a journey from teaching to learning.* San Francisco: Jossey-Bass.

Boyer, E. (1987). *College: The undergraduate experience in America.* New York: HarperCollins.

Boyer, E. (1990). *Campus life: In search of community.* Princeton: Carnegie Foundation for the Advancement of Teaching.

Brabeck, M. M. (2001). [Review of the book *Learning that lasts: Integrating learning, development, and performance in college and beyond*]. *Journal of Moral Education, 30,* 404(407.

Broadhead, R. (2004). *The good of this place: Values and challenges in college education.* New Haven, CT: Yale University Press.

Brooks, D. (2001, April). Organization kid. *Atlantic Monthly, 287,* 40–64.

Buber, M. (1959). *I and thou.* New York: Scribner.

Burtchaell, J. T. (1998). *The dying of the light: The disengagement of colleges and universities from their Christian churches.* Grand Rapids, MI: Eerdmans.

Chandler, G., Holden, J., & Kolander, C. (1992). Counseling and spiritual wellness: Theory and practice. *Journal of Counseling and Development, 71,* 168–175.

Character Education Partnership. (2001). *Character Education Quality Standards.* Washington, D.C.: Character Education Partnership.

Cherry, C., DeBerg, B. A., & Porterfield, A. (2001). *Religion on campus.* Chapel Hill: University of North Carolina Press.

Chickering, A. W. (Ed.). (1981). *The modern American college.* San Francisco: Jossey-Bass.

Chickering, A. W., & Reisser, L. (1993). *Education and identity* (2nd ed.). San Francisco: Jossey-Bass.

Clark, R. T. (2001). The law and spirituality: How the law supports and limits expression of spirituality on the college campus. In M. A. Jablonski (Ed.), *The implications of student spirituality for student affairs practice* (pp.37-46). New Directions for Student Services, no. 95. San Francisco: Jossey-Bass.

Colby, A., Ehrlich, T., Beaumont, E., & Stephens, J. (2003). *Educating citizens: Preparing America's undergraduates for lives of moral and civic responsibility.* San Francisco: Jossey-Bass.

Coles, R. (1990). *The spiritual lives of children.* Boston: Houghton Mifflin.

Coles, R. (2000). *Lives of moral leadership.* New York: Random House.

Coomes, M. D. (2004). Understanding the historical and cultural influences that shape generations. In M. D. Coomes & R. DeBard (Eds.), *Serving the millennial generation* (pp. 17–32). New Directions for Student Services, no. 106. San Francisco: Jossey-Bass.

Cooperrider, D., & Whitney, D. (1999). *Appreciative inquiry.* San Francisco: Berret-Koehler.

Cornwell, G. H. (2001, Summer). The future of liberal education and the hegemony of market values: Privilege, practicality, and citizenship. *Liberal Education, 87*(3).

Covey, S. R. (1989). *7 habits of highly effective people: Restoring the character ethic.* New York: Simon & Schuster.

Dalton, J. C. (2001). Career and calling: Finding a place for the spirit in work and the community. In M. A. Jablonski (Ed.), *The implications of student spirituality for student affairs practice* (pp. 17–26). New Directions for Student Services, no. 95. San Francisco: Jossey-Bass.

Dalton, J. C. (2003). *Survey of student affairs vice presidents on college student spirituality.* Unpublished research, Center for the Study of Values in College Student Development, Florida State University.

Dalton, J. C., Goodwin, K., & Chen, D. (2004). *Promoting character in college: What presidents think about what works and why.* Unpublished manuscript, Center for the Study of Values in College Student Development, Florida State University.

Darling-Hammond, L. (Ed.). (2000). *Studies of excellence in teacher education: Preparation in the undergraduate years.* Washington, DC: American Association of Colleges for Teacher Education.

Dean, C. B., & Lauer, P. A. (2003). *Systematic evaluation for continuous improvement of teacher preparation: Vol. 1. Cross-case analysis.* Washington, DC: Mid-continent Research for Education and Learning.

Division of Student Affairs. (2003). Religious and spiritual services for students. *Penn State Pulse,* 107. State College, PA: Penn State University.

Earley, M., Mentkowski, M., & Schafer, J. (1980). *Valuing at Alverno: The valuing process in liberal education.* Milwaukee, WI: Alverno Productions.

Emmons, R. A. (1999). *The psychology of ultimate concerns.* New York: Guilford Press.

Erikson, E. (1950). *Childhood and society.* New York: Norton.

Erikson, E. (1958). *Young man Luther: A study in psychoanalysis and history.* New York: Norton.

Erikson, E. (1969). *Gandhi's truth: On the origins of militant nonviolence.* New York: Norton.

Ewell, P. T. (1991). To capture the ineffable: New forms of assessment in higher education. In G. Grant (Ed.), *Review of research in education* (pp. 75–125). Washington, DC: American Educational Research Association.

Ewell, P. T. (2004, January/February). Management myths. *Change, 4,* 3–4.

Ewens, T. (1979). Transforming a liberal arts curriculum: Alverno College. In G. Grant & Associates (Eds.), *On competence: A critical analysis of competence-based reforms in higher education* (pp. 259–298). San Francisco: Jossey-Bass.

Eyler, J., & Giles, D. E., Jr. (1999). *Where's the learning in service-learning?* San Francisco: Jossey-Bass.

Fetzer Institute/National Institute on Aging Working Group. (1999). *Multidimensional measurement of religiousness/spirituality for use in health research.* Kalamazoo, MI: John E. Fetzer Institute.

Finger, T. N. (1997). *Self, earth, and society: Alienation and Trinitarian transformation.* Downers Grove, IL: InterVarsity Press.

Fink, K. (2001). Carolinian creed. *Proceedings of the Institute on College Student Values, 10.* Tallahassee: Florida State University.

Fink, L. D. (2003). *Creating significant learning experiences: An integrated approach to designing college courses.* San Francisco: Jossey-Bass.

Florida State University. (2003). Student rights and responsibilities. *Student Handbook.* Tallahassee: Florida State University.

Fowler, J. W. (1981). *Stages of faith: The psychology of human development and the quest for meaning.* San Francisco: HarperCollins.

Fowler, J. W. (1996). *Faithful change: The personal and public challenges of postmodern life.* Nashville, TN: Abingdon Press.

Gallup, G., Jr., & Lindsay, D. M. (1999). *Surveying the religious landscape: Trends in U.S. belief.* Harrisburg, PA: Morehouse.

Garber, M. (2001). *Academic instincts.* Princeton, NJ: Princeton University Press.

Gilligan, C. (1982). *In a different voice: Psychological theory and women's development.* Cambridge, MA: Harvard University Press.

Glazer, S. (Ed.). (1999). *The heart of learning: Spirituality in education.* New York: Tarcher.

Goldman, R. (1964). *Religious thinking from childhood to adolescence.* London: Routledge.

Goleman, D. (1995). *Emotional intelligence: Why it can matter more than IQ.* New York: Bantam Books.

Greenleaf, R. K. (1970). *Servant leadership: A journey into the nature of legitimate power and greatness.* Indianapolis: The Robert K. Greenleaf Center for Servant Leadership.

Gregory, G. (2003, Sept. 12). Polite to a fault. *Liberal Education,* p. B16.

Griffith, J. L., & Griffith, M. E. (2002). *Encountering the sacred in psychotherapy.* New York: Guilford Press.

Gutierrez-Zamano, E., & Yasuno, M. (2002). *An annotated bibliography of spirituality.* Higher Education Research Institute. *Los Angeles: University of California-Los Angeles.*

Hakel, M. D. (2001). Learning that lasts [Review of the book *Learning that lasts: Integrating learning, development, and performance in college and beyond*]. *Psychological Science, 12,* 433(434.

Higher Education Research Institute. (2005). *The spiritual life of college students.* Project on Spirituality. Los Angeles: University of California at Los Angeles.

Hill, P. C., & Hood, R. W., Jr. (Eds.). (1999). *Measures of religiosity.* Birmingham, AL: Religious Education Press.

Hill, P. C., Pargament, K. I., Hood, R. W., Jr., McCullough, M. E., Swyers, J. P., Larson, D. B., & Zinnbauer, B. J. (2000). Conceptualizing religion and spirituality: Points of commonality, points of departure. *Journal for the Theory of Social Behavior, 30*(1), 51–77.

Hinett, K. (1995). Fighting the assessment war: The idea of assessment-in-learning. *Quality in Higher Education, 1,* 211–222.

Hoge, D. R., Dinges, W. D., Johnson, M., & Gonzales, J. L., Jr. (2001). *Young adult Catholics: Religion in the culture of choice.* Notre Dame, IN: University of Notre Dame Press.

Hoge, D. R., Johnson, B., & Luidens, D. A. (1994). *Vanishing boundaries: The religion of mainline protestant baby boomers.* Louisville, KY: Westminster/John Knox Press.

Horowitz, H. L. (1987). *Campus life: Undergraduate cultures from the end of the eighteenth century to the present.* Chicago: University of Chicago Press.

Intrator, S. (2002). *Stories of the courage to teach: Honoring the teacher's heart.* San Francisco: Jossey-Bass.

James, W. (1902). *The varieties of religious experience: A study in human nature.* New York: Modern Library.

John Templeton Foundation. (1999). *Colleges that encourage character development.* Philadelphia: Templeton Foundation Press.

Johnson, T. J., Kristellar, J., & Sheets, V. L. (2004). Religiousness and spirituality in college students: Separate dimensions with unique and common correlates. *Proceedings of the Institute on College Student Values, 14.* Retrieved from www.collegvalues.org.

Kazanjian, V. H., Jr., & Laurence, P. L. (Eds.). (2000). *Education as transformation: Religious pluralism, spirituality and a new vision for higher education in America.* New York: Lang.

Keen, C. H. (2000). Spiritual assumptions undergird educational priorities: A personal narrative. In V. H. Kazanjian Jr. & P. L. Laurence (Eds.), *Education as transformation: Religious pluralism, spirituality and a new vision for higher education in America* (pp. 37-44). New York: Lang.

Keen, J. (2000). Appreciative engagement of diversity: E pluribus unum. In V. H. Kazanjian Jr. & P. L. Laurence (Eds.), *Education as transformation: Religious pluralism, spirituality and a new vision for higher education in America* (pp. 207-212). New York: Lang.

Kegan, R. (1982). *The evolving self: Method and process in human development.* Cambridge, MA: Harvard University Press.

King, P. M. (1990). Assessing development from a cognitive-developmental perspective. In D. G. Creamer and Associates (Eds.), *College student development: Theory and practice for the 1990s.* Alexandria, VA: American College Personnel Association.

Kohlberg, L. (1969). Stage and sequence: The cognitive-developmental approach to socialization. In D. Goslin (Ed.), *Handbook of socialization theory and research* (pp. 347-480). Chicago: Rand McNally.

Kohlberg, L. (1976). Moral stages and moralization: The cognitive-developmental approach. In T. Lickona (Ed.), *Moral development and behavior: Theory, research, and social issues* (pp. 62-64, 338). Austin, TX: Holt, Rinehart and Winston.

Kolb, D. A. (1984). *Experiential learning.* Englewood Cliffs, NJ: Prentice Hall.

Kuh, G. D. (1991). Characteristics of involving colleges. In G. D. Kuh & J. H. Schuh (Eds.), *The role and contributions of student affairs in involving colleges* (pp. 34-48). Washington, DC: National Association of Student Personnel Administrators.

Kuh, G. D. (2003). What we're learning about student engagement from NSSE. *Change, 35*(2), 24–32.

Kuh, G. D., Kinzie, J., Schuh, J. H., Whitt, E. J., & Associates. (2005). *Student success in college: Creating conditions that matter.* San Francisco: Jossey-Bass.

Kuh, G. D., & Whitt, E. J. (1988). *The invisible tapestry: Culture in American colleges and universities* (ASHE-ERIC Higher Education Report 1). Washington, DC: Association for the Study of Higher Education.

Kytle, J. (2004). *To want to learn: Insights and provocations for engaged learning.* Old Tappan, NJ: Macmillan.

Langer, E. (1998). *The power of mindful learning.* New York: Perseus Books.

Lauer, P. A., & Dean, C. B. (2003). *Systematic evaluation for continuous improvement of teacher preparation: Vol. 2. Case summaries.* Washington, DC: Mid-continent Research for Education and Learning.

Lee, J. J., Matzkin, A., & Arthur, S. (2004). Understanding students' religious and spiritual pursuits: A case study at New York University. *Journal of College and Character, 2.* Retrieved from www.collegevalues.org.

Levine, A., & Curetin, J. S. (1998). *When hope and fear collide: A portrait of today's college student.* San Francisco: Jossey-Bass.

Light, R. (2001). *Making the most of college: Students speak their minds.* Cambridge, MA: Harvard University Press.

Higher Education Research Institute. (2004). *The spiritual life of college students.* Project on Spirituality in Higher Education. Los Angeles: University of California-Los Angeles.

Loacker, G., & Mentkowski, M. (1993). Creating a culture where assessment improves learning. In T. W. Banta & Associates (Eds.), *Making a difference: Outcomes of a decade of assessment in higher education* (pp. 5–24). San Francisco: Jossey-Bass.

Longfield, B. J. (1992a). "For God, for country, and for Yale": Yale, religion, and higher education between the world wars. In G. M. Marsden & B. J. Longfield (Eds.), *The secularization of the academy* (pp. 146-169). New York: Oxford University Press.

Longfield, B. J. (1992b). From evangelicalism to liberalism: Public midwestern universities in nineteenth-century America. In G. M. Marsden & B. J. Longfield (Eds.), *The secularization of the academy* (pp. 46-73). New York: Oxford University Press.

Love, P. G. (2001). Spirituality and student development: Theoretical connections. In M. A. Jablonski (Ed.), *The implications of student spirituality for student affairs practice* (pp. 7–16). New Directions for Student Services, no. 95. San Francisco: Jossey-Bass.

Mahoney, K. (2001). *Human change processes: The scientific foundations of psychotherapy.* New York: Basic Books.

Mair, V. H. (1990). *Tao Te Ching: Mystical classics of the world.* New York: Quality Paperback Book Club.

Manning, K. (2000). *Rituals, ceremonies, and cultural meaning in higher education.* Westport, CT: Bergin & Garvey.

Marchese, T. J. (2002). *The new conversations about learning: Insights from neuroscience and anthropology, cognitive science and workplace studies.* Seattle, WA: New Horizons for Learning, P.O. Box 31876.

Marsden, G. M. (1992). The soul of the American university: A historical overview. In G. M. Marsden & B. J. Longfield (Eds.), *The secularization of the academy* (pp. 9-45). New York: Oxford University Press.

Martin, J. (1992). *Cultures in organization: Three perspectives.* New York: Oxford University Press.

Maslow, A. H. (1970). *Motivation and personality* (2nd ed.). New York: HarperCollins.

Matthews, A. (1997). *Bright college years: Inside the American campus today.* Chicago: University of Chicago Press.

McDonald, W. M. (Ed.). (2002). *Creating campus community: In search of Ernest Boyer's legacy.* San Francisco: Jossey-Bass.

Mead, M. (1972). *Blackberry winter: My earliest years.* New York: Morrow.

McKeon, R. (1970). *The basic works of Aristotle.* New York: Random House.

Mentkowski, M. (1988). Paths to integrity: Educating for personal growth and professional performance. In S. Srivastva & Associates (Eds.), *Executive integrity: The search for high human values in organizational life* (pp. 89–121). San Francisco: Jossey-Bass.

Mentkowski, M. (1998). Higher education assessment and national goals for education: Issues, assumptions, and principles. In N. M. Lambert & B. L. McCombs (Eds.), *How students learn: Reforming schools through learner-centered education* (pp. 269–310). Washington, DC: American Psychological Association.

Mentkowski, M. (in press). Accessible and adaptable elements of Alverno student assessment-as-learning: strategies and challenges for peer review. In G. Gibbs, K. Clegg, & C. Bryan (Eds.), *Innovating in assessment.* London: RoutledgeFalmer.

Mentkowski, M., Loacker, G., & O'Brien, K. (1998). *Ability-based learning and judicial education: An approach to ongoing professional development* (JERITT Monograph No. 8). East Lansing, MI: Judicial Education Reference, Information and Technical Transfer Project.

Mentkowski, M., & Rogers, G. (1993). Connecting education, work, and citizenship: How assessment can help. *Metropolitan Universities: An International Forum, 4*(1), 34–46.

Mentkowski, M., & Associates. (2000). *Learning that lasts: Integrating learning, development, and performance in college and beyond.* San Francisco: Jossey-Bass.

Miller, M. A. (2003). Meaning of the baccalaureate. *About Campus, 8*(4), 2-8. San Francisco: Jossey-Bass.

Moore, W. (2002, Feb.). Interview with Glen Rogers and William Rickards, Alverno College, on Program Assessment. *eWAG: Washington Assessment Group Newsletter.* Retrieved February 26, 2002, from http://www.sbctc.ctc.edu/ewag/ewag0202/index.htm

Morton, P. A. (1999). Faculty perspective on magic, meaning, and desire. In V. H. Kazanjian Jr. and P. L. Laurence (Eds.), *Education as transformation: Religious pluralism, spirituality and a new vision for higher education in America* (pp. 69-78). New York: Peter Lang.

Myers, J. E., & Williard, K. (2003). Integrating spirituality into counselor preparation: A developmental approach. *Counseling and Values, 47,* 142–155.

Nash, R. J. (2002). *Spirituality, ethics, religion, and teaching.* New York: Lang.

Nash, R. J. (2004). A letter to secondary teachers: Teaching about religious traditions in the public schools. In N. Noddings (Ed.), *A test of character: Educating global citizens in America* (pp. 20-22). New York: Teachers College Press.

National Association for Student Personnel Administrators and American College Personnel Association. (2004). *Learning reconsidered: A campus-wide focus on the student experience.* Washington, D.C.: Author.

National Survey of Student Engagement. (2003). *The college student report.* Bloomington: Indiana University.

Nelson, S. J. (n.d.). *Graham B. Spanier: The presidential perspective at Penn State University.* Retrieved from www.collegevalues.org.

Nelson, S. J. (2000). *Presidential profile: Gregory Prince, Hampshire College.* Retrieved from www.collegevalues.org.

Nelson, S. J. (2001). *President Robert Carothers: An inward and outward journey of moral leadership, University of Rhode Island.* Retrieved from www.collegevalues.org.

Nelson, S. J. (2003). *President Elaine Hansen: What are the questions? A continuing dialogue for community, Bates College.* Retrieved from www.collegevaues.org.

Newcomb, T., & Wilson, E. E. (Eds.). (1964). *College peer groups: Problems and prospects for research.* Hawthorne, NY: Aldine de Gruyter.

NSSE Institute for Effective Educational Practice. (2003). *Final report: Alverno College.* Bloomington: National Survey of Student Engagement, Indiana University Center for Postsecondary Research.

Orr, D. W. (1999). *Earth in mind: On education, environment, and the human prospect.* Washington, DC: Island Press.

Palmer, P. J. (1983). *To know as we are known: Education as a spiritual journey.* San Francisco: Harper Collins.

Palmer, P. J. (1994 May-June) Community, conflict, and ways of knowing: ways to deepen our educational agenda. *Change, 26*(3), 40-45.

Palmer, P. J. (1999a). *The active life: A spirituality of work, creativity, and caring.* San Francisco: Jossey-Bass.

Palmer, P. J. (1999b). The grace of great things: Reclaiming the sacred in knowing, teaching, and learning. In S. Glazer (Ed.), *The heart of learning: Spirituality in education* (pp. 15–33). New York: Tarcher.

Palmer, P. J. (2000). *Let your life speak: Listening for the voice of vocation.* San Francisco: Jossey-Bass.

Pargament, K. I. (1997). *The psychology of religion and coping: Theory, practice, research.* New York: Guilford Press.

Parks, S. D. (2000). *Big questions, worthy dreams: Mentoring young adults in their search for meaning, purpose, and faith.* San Francisco: Jossey-Bass.

Perry, W. G., Jr. (1970). *Forms of intellectual and ethical development in the college years: A scheme.* San Diego: Harcourt.

Peters, T. (1993). Foreword. In W. G. Bennis, *An invented life* (pp. ix-xi).Reading, MA: Addison-Wesley.

Piaget, J. (1926). *The language and thought of the child.* San Diego: Harcourt.

Piaget, J. (1953). *The origins of intelligence in children.* New York: International Universities Press.

Purdy, J. (1999). *For common things: Irony, trust, and commitment in America today.* New York: Knopf.

Rest, J., Narváez, D., Bebeau, M. J., & Thoma, S. J. (1999). *Post-conventional moral thinking: A neo-Kohlbergian approach.* Mahwah, NJ: Erlbaum.

Reuel, D. (1965). American youth today: A bigger cast, a wider screen. In E. H. Erikson (Ed.), *The challenge of youth.* Garden City, NY: Anchor Books.

Rickards, W., Mentkowski, M., Rozdilsky, M. L., & Brown, S. (1994, April). *Institutional assessment across the educational spectrum.* Symposium conducted at the annual meeting of the American Educational Research Association, New Orleans and Milwaukee: Alverno College Institute.

Riordan, T., & Roth, J. (Eds.). (2005). *Disciplines as frameworks for student learning: Teaching the practice of the disciplines.* Sterling, VA: Stylus.

Robinson, J. (2003, August 4). The land of the free? *Washington Post Weekly Edition,* p. 13.

Rogers, J., & Dantley, M. (2001). Invoking the spiritual in campus life and leadership. *Journal of College Student Development, 42*(6), 589-603.

Rogers, G., & Mentkowski, M. (2004). Abilities that distinguish the effectiveness of five-year alumna performance across work, family, and civic roles: A higher education validation. *Higher Education Research and Development, 23,* 247–374.

Rogers, G., Mentkowski, M., & Reisetter Hart, J. (in press). Adult holistic development and multidimensional performance. In C. H. Hoare (Ed.), *Handbook of adult development and learning* New York: Oxford University Press.

Roof, W. C. (1999). *Spiritual marketplace: Baby boomers and the remaking of American religion.* Princeton, NJ: Princeton University Press.

Rudolf, F. (1977). *Curriculum: A history of the American undergraduate course of study since 1636.* San Francisco: Jossey-Bass.

Sandeen, A. (1985, Oct.). Legacy of values education in promoting values development in college. In J. C. Dalton (Ed.), *Promoting values development in college students* (NASPA Monograph Series, Vol. 4). Washington, DC: National Association of Student Personnel Administrators.

Sanders, S. R. (2000). *The force of spirit.* Boston: Beacon Press.

Sax, L. J., Keup, J. R., Gilmartin, S. K., & Stolzenberg, E. E. (2002). *Findings from the 2002 Administration of Your First College Year (YFCY) national aggregates.* Los Angeles: University of California Higher Education Research Institute.

Schlesinger, A. (1965). *A thousand days.* Boston: Houghton-Mifflin.

Schwartz, A. J., & Stamm, L. (2002). *A review of the literature: Analysis of current theories, programs and empirical research on trends, patterns, and principles of spiritual growth during the college years.* Unpublished manuscript, John Templeton Foundation.

Shore, E. (1997). At the center. *Parabola, 19*(4), 59–62.

Simmer-Brown, J. (1999). Commitment and openness: A contemplative approach to pluralism. In S. Glazer (Ed.), *The heart of learning: Spirituality in education* (pp. 97-112. New York: Tarcher.

Sloan, D. (1994). *Faith and knowledge: Mainline Protestantism and American higher education.* Louisville, KY: Westminster John Knox Press.

Smith (2001). *Why religion matters: The fate of the human spirit in an age of disbelief.* San Francisco: Harper.

Spanier, G. B. (n.d.). Presidents' public diaries: Graham B. Spanier. *Journal of College and Character.* Retrieved from www.collegevalues.org.

Spilka, B., Hood, R. W., Jr., & Gorusch, R. L. (1985). *The psychology of religion: An empirical approach.* Upper Saddle River, NJ: Prentice Hall.

Stamm, L. (2003). Can we bring spirituality back to campus? Higher education's re-engagement with values and spirituality. *Journal of College and Character,* Vol. 2. Retrieved from www.collegevalues.com.

Stamm, L., & Ryff, C. D. (Eds.). (1984). *Social power and influence of women* (American Association for the Advancement of Science Selected Symposia Series, No. 96). Boulder, CO: Westview Press.

Stewart, D. L. (2002). The role of faith in the development of an integrated identity: A qualitative study of black students at a white college. *Journal of College Student Personnel, 43*(2), 579–596.

Storr, A. (1988). *Solitude.* New York: Ballantine.

Strange, C., & Martin, G. (2004, Feb.). *Measuring the immeasurable: Spirituality and the college experience.* Presentation at the 2004 Institute on College Student Values, Florida State University, Tallahassee.

Student Learning Initiative 2002. *Student learning: A central focus for institutions of higher education* (A. Doherty, T. Riordan, & J. Roth, Eds.). Milwaukee, WI: Alverno College Institute.

Svinicki, M. (2002). The Alverno College experience: A case with many levels of interpretation. [Review of the book *Learning that lasts: Integrating learning, development, and performance in college and beyond*]. *Contemporary Psychology, 47,* 272(274.

Tatum, B. D. (1997). *Why are all the black kids sitting together in the cafeteria? And other conversations about race.* New York: Basic Books.

Tatum, B. D. (2000). Changing lives, changing communities: Building a capacity for connection in a pluralistic context. In V. H. Kazanjian Jr., & P. L. Laurence (Eds.), *Education as transformation: Religious pluralism, spirituality and a new vision for higher education in America* (pp. 79–88). New York: Lang.

Teasdale, W. (1999). *The mystic heart.* Novato, CA: New World Library.

Tisdell, E. J. (2003). *Exploring spirituality and culture in adult and higher education.* San Francisco: Jossey-Bass.

Vaillant, G. E. (1977). *Adaptation to life.* New York: Little, Brown.

Vaillant, G. E., & Vaillant, C. O. (1990). Determinants and consequences of creativity in a cohort of gifted women. *Psychology of Women Quarterly, 14,* 607–616.

Vallacher, R. R., & Wegner, D. M. (1989). Levels of personal agency: Individual variation in action identification. *Journal of Personality and Social Psychology, 57,* 660–671.

Vella, J. (2002). *Learning to listen, learning to teach: The power of dialogue in educating adults.* San Francisco: Jossey-Bass.

Walsh, D. C. (1999). Spirituality and leadership. In S. Glazer (Ed.), *The heart of learning: Spirituality in education* (pp. 203–215). New York: Tarcher.

Walsh, D. C. (2000). Introduction to transforming education: An overview. In V. H. Kazanjian Jr. & P. L. Laurence (Eds.), *Education as transformation: Religious pluralism, spirituality and a new vision for higher education in America* (pp. 1-14). New York: Lang.

Weimer, M. (2002). *Learner-centered teaching: Five key changes to practice.* San Francisco: Jossey-Bass.

Wheatley, M. J. (2002). *Turning to one another: Simple conversations to restore hope to the future.* San Francisco: Berrett-Koehler.

Whiteley, J.(1985, Oct.). A retrospective view of recent undergraduates. In
J. C. Dalton (Ed.), *Promoting values development in college students*
(NASPA Monograph Series, Vol. 4). Washington, DC: National Asso-
ciation of Student Personnel Administrators.

Winter, D. G., McClelland, D. C., & Stewart, A. J. (1981). *A new case for the
liberal arts: Assessing institutional goals and student development.* San
Francisco: Jossey-Bass.

Wuthnow, R. (1998). *After heaven: Spirituality in America since the 1950s.*
Berkeley: University of California Press.

Yinger, J. M. (1967). Pluralism, religion, and secularism. *Journal for the
Scientific Study of Religion, 16,* 17–28.

Zlatic, T. D. (2001). [Review of the book *Learning that lasts: Integrating
learning, development, and performance in college and beyond*].
Journal of Pharmacy Teaching, 8(4), 88(92.

➤ Name Index

A

Abu-Lugod, L., 126
Alexander, S., 138
Allen, K., 150
Allport, G. W., 13, 39, 44, 45
Angell, J. B., 75, 77
Aristotle, 277
Armstrong, K., 7, 171
Arthur, S., 82
Astin, A. W., 30, 81, 82, 128, 135, 136,
    162, 223, 238, 244-245
Astin, H. S., 30, 81, 82, 128, 162, 223,
    238, 244-245

B

Bach, R., 122
Badaracco, J. L., 247, 253, 268
Baeyer, H. C. von, 5
Baldrige, M., 216
Bandura, A., 51
Barbour, I., 127
Batson, C. D., 39, 41, 42, 45, 48-53, 57,
    62
Baxter Margolda, M. B., 59, 225
Beaumont, E., 160, 174, 180, 225
Bebeau, M. J., 280-281
Becker, E., 33
Bennett, D. C., 109, 111, 168
Bennis, W. G., 246, 248-254, 267, 269
Bergquist, B., 190
Bethe, H., 5
Bolman, L. G., 35, 267
Boyatzis, R. E., 238
Boyer, E., 14, 147, 166, 167, 176, 184,
    193, 279
Brabeck, M. M., 225

Briggs, L. R., 145
Broadhead, R., 154
Brown, S., 225
Buber, M., 184, 185
Burtchaell, J. T., 73-75, 78, 81

C

Carothers, R., 265, 266, 269, 270
Carreon, J., 213
Carter,, J., 252
Chandler, G., 172
Cheely, E., 31, 32
Chen, D., 35, 254, 257, 268, 275
Cherry, C., 74, 75, 83, 84, 150
Chickering, A. W., 5, 12-16, 39, 61-63,
    97, 113, 189, 220
Clark, R. T., 100-102
Colby, A., 160, 174, 180, 225
Coles, R., 52, 126, 271
Coomes, M. D., 71
Cooperrider, D., 196, 199
Covey, S. R., 212, 274
Cowen, S. S., 238

D

Dalton, J. C., 16-19, 31, 38, 39, 82, 145,
    165, 171, 220, 254, 257, 272, 275,
    318
Dantley, M., 163
Darling-Hammond, L., 225
Deal, T. E., 35, 36, 267
Dean, C. B., 225
DeBerg, B. A., 74, 82-85
Delbecq, A. L., 143, 303, 308
DePree, M., 251
Devane, T., 199

Dewey, J., 76
Dinges, W. D., 68, 70, 72
Dixie, Q., 127
Dodge, W., 193
Drees, W. B., 125
Dunham, A., 193

E

Earley, M., 235
Eble, K., 134
Ehrlich, T., 160, 174, 180, 225
Einstein, A., 297
Eliot, T. S., 294, 296
Ellsworth, R. R., 247, 253, 268
Ely, R. T., 76
Emmons, R. A., 147, 170, 172
Erikson, E., 13, 52-55, 58, 59
Ewell, P. T., 194, 223-224
Ewens, T., 225
Eyler, J., 238

F

Faulkner, A., 202, 204
Feiler, B., 127
Finger, T. N., 170
Fink, K., 179
Fink, L. D., 135
Fowler, J. W., 39, 40, 52-58, 60-64, 89,
    162, 170
Fox, G., 8

G

Gallup, G. Jr., 152
Gandhi, M., 8, 52, 127
Genghis Khan, 14
Giles, D. E., Jr., 238
Gilligan, C., 52, 58
Gilmartin, S. K., 153, 174
Glazer, S., 9, 10, 34, 151
Goethe, J. W. von, 120
Goldman, R., 52
Goleman, D., 238
Gonzales, J. L., Jr., 68, 70
Goodwin, K., 254, 257, 268, 275
Gorusch, R. L., 40
Gould, S., 14

Greenleaf, R. K., 198, 212, 246
Gregory, G., 276
Gretsky, W., 134, 252
Griffith, J. L., 184
Griffith, M. E., 184
Guttierrez-Zamano, E., 164

H

Hakel, M. D., 225
Hall, J., 193
Halliburton, D., 190
Hansen, E., 266-268
Harrison, W., 269
Heelan, C., 196, 200
Hefner, P., 125
Hegel, G.F.W., 76
Henck, A., 220
Hill, G., 202
Hill, P. C., 43, 46-48, 223
Hinett, K., 225
Hoge, D. R., 68, 70, 72, 83, 90
Holden, J., 172
Holman, P., 199
Holton, G., 296
Hood, R. W., Jr., 40, 43, 46-48, 223
Horowitz, H. L., 146, 166, 168
Hufstedler, S., 252

I

Intrator, S., 316

J

Jackson, K. L., 196, 199
James, W., 38, 39
Johnson, B., 70
Johnson, L. B., 252
Johnson, M., 68, 70, 72
Johnson, T. J., 82, 88-90, 153, 159
Jones, V. S., 202
Jordan, B., 8

K

Kant, I., 10, 29
Kass, L., 128
Kazanjian, V. H., Jr., 116-118, 245
Keen, C. H., 137, 269, 270

Keen, J., 136, 137
Keeton, M., 193
Kegan, R., 58, 59, 63
Kennedy, J. F., 189
Keplar, J., 120, 296
Keup, J. R., 153, 174
Kimball, C., 98
King, M. L., Jr., 8, 127, 243
King, P. M., 62
Kinzie, J., 225
Kline, M., 298
Kohlberg, L., 52, 53, 55
Kolander, C., 172
Kolb, D. A., 134, 135, 143, 238
Kristellar, J., 82, 88-90, 153, 159
Kuh, G. D., 150, 225, 238
Kushner, H., 126
Kytle, J., 135

L

Langer, E., 133
Larson, D. B., 46-48
Lauer, P. A., 225
Laurence, P. L., 105, 245
Lee, J. J., 82
Lewis, C. S., 296
Light, R., 183
Lindholm, J., 82, 162
Lindquist, J., 190
Lindsay, D. M., 152
Loacker, B., 225, 226
Locke, J., 29
Longfield, B. J., 75-78
Love, P. G., 59, 162
Luidens, D. A., 70
Luther, M., 52

M

Mahoney, K., 152, 153
Mandela, N., 8
Manning, K., 176, 184, 196
Manning, M., 198
Marchese, T. J., 131
Marsden, G. M., 66, 78-81, 91, 146
Martin, G., 82
Martin, J., 177

Maslow, A. H., 13, 172
Matthews, A., 18
Matzkin, A., 82, ref
McBride, J., 125
McClelland, D. C., 225
McCullough, M. E., 46-48
McDonald, W. M., 165, 166, 182
McKeachie, W., 134
McKeon, R., 277
McLennan, S., 128
Mead, M., 154
Mentkowski, M., 220, 225-227, 233-240
Miller, M. A., 20
Mittelstet, S., 211, 213-216, 218
Moore, W., 225
Morton, P. A., 118, 119, 121, 130, 143
Mother Teresa, 8
Murphy, G., 13
Myers, J. E., 172

N

Narváez, D., 280-281
Nash, R. J., 98, 139, 140, 142, 151, 153,
    157, 173, 174, 206
Nelson, S. J., 259-262, 265-267
Newcomb, T., 13, 170
North, J., 190

O

O'Brien, K., 226
Orr, D. W., 182

P

Palmer, P. J., 29, 34, 35, 127, 138, 139,
    168, 169, 183, 202, 207, 208, 210,
    211, 215, 258, 270
Pargament, K. I., 42, 44-48
Parks, R., 211, 271
Parks, S. D., 40, 52, 57-64, 89, 90, 128,
    150, 153, 162, 165, 169, 171, 172,
    175
Perry, W. G., Jr., 52, 58
Peters, T., 248, 249
Piaget, J., 52-55, 58, 59
Pitkin, T., 14
Plato, 120, 122

Porterfield, A., 74, 82-84
Prince, G. S., 259
Proust, M., 121
Purdy, J., 18, 19, 151, 152, 172

R

Rauf, F. A., 126
Reisetter Hart, J., 239, 240
Reisser, L., 61-63
Rest, J., 280-281
Reuel, D., 19
Rickards, W., 225
Rijn, Rembrandt van, 120
Rilke, R. M., 120
Riordan, T., 225, 234, 238
Robinson, J., 25, 26
Rogers, G., 238-240
Rogers, J., 163
Roof, W. C., 48-50, 68-72, 83, 90, 153
Roosevelt, E., 8
Ross, J. M., 44
Roth, J., 225, 234, 238
Rozdilsky, M. L., 225
Rudolf, F., 146
Ruskin, J., 121
Ryff, C. D., 249

S

Sandeen, A., 145
Sanders, S. R., 138
Sanford, N., 13
Sax, L. J., 136, 153, 174
Schafer, J., 235
Scheme, P., 234
Schlesinger, A., 189
Schoenrade, P., 39, 41, 42, 45, 48-53, 57, 62
Schuh, J. H., 225
Schumacher, E. F., 267, 268
Schwartz, A. J., 86
Sheets, V. L., 82, 88-90, 153, 159
Shore, E., 172
Sikes, W., 190
Simmer-Brown, J., 183
Sloan, D., 80, 81
Smith, H., 146, 150-152, 154, 276

Socrates, 121, 131
Spanier, G. B., 259-261, 266, 268, 270
Spilka, B., 40, 41
Stamm, L., 19-23, 31, 37, 66, 86, 97, 103, 122, 146, 152, 243, 249
Steere, D., 204
Stephens, J., 160, 174, 180, 225
Stewart, A. J., 225
Stewart, D. L., 169
Stolzenberg, E. E., 153, 174
Storr, A., 182
Strange, C., 82
Sullivan, E., 202
Sullivan, J., 199
Svinicki, M., 225
Swyers, J. P., 46-48
Szilard, L., 5

T

Tatum, B. D., 262, 263
Teasdale, W., 7, 66, 171
Teresa, Mother, 8
Thoma, S. J., 280-281
Thomas, R. J., 248, 251
Tisdell, E. J., 154, 169, 172, 173
Truth, S., 8
Tucker, B., 208, 210
Turak, A., 31, 121, 143, 299
Tutu, D., 8

U

Upton, J., 119, 120, 143, 294

V

Vaillant, C. O., 238
Vaillant, G. E., 238
Vallacher, R. R., 239
Vella, J., 135
Ventis, W. L., 39, 41, 42, 45, 48-53, 57, 62
Vliet, Hendrick van, 298

W

Wallenda, K., 250
Walsh, D. C., 34, 129, 165, 263-265, 269
Wegner, D. M., 239

Weimer, M., 135
Wenrich, B., 208
Wheatley, M. J., 212
White, R., 13
Whiteley, J., 173
Whitney, D., 199
Whitt, E. J., 150, 225
Wilde, O., 121
Williams, J., 127
Williard, K., 172
Willis, E., 126
Wilson, E. E., 170

Winter, D. G., 225
Wuthnow, R., 48, 49, 68, 69, 72, 83, 90

Y

Yasano, M., 164
Yinger, J. M., 39

Z

Zajonc, A., 119, 120, 143, 294, 297
Zinnbauer, B. J., 46-48
Zlatic, T. D., 225
Zukava, G., 126

⟶ Subject Index

A

Abington School District v. Shempp, 100-101

Abraham: A Journey to the Heart of Three Faiths (Feiler), 127

ACPA. See American College Personnel Association

Active Life: A Spirituality of Work, Creativity and Caring (Parker), 127

African American evangelicalism, 84

Albany Learning Center (New York), 193

Allegory of the Cave (Plato), 122

Alverno College, 218, 224-240; general orientation, 226-229; institutional assessment at, 229-231; and problem of criteria, 235-236; recognition of stakeholders, 231-232; strategies and issues, 232-235; using assessment evidence, 236-240

America, religious and spiritual landscape of: and emergence of spiritual marketplace, 70-72; role of Christian churches in, 66-67; and shift from denominationalism to diversity, 67-72; transformation of, 69-70

American Association for Higher Education, 315

American Association of University Professors, 78-79

American College Personnel Association (ACPA), 13, 149

American Council on Education, 13, 146-147, 195

American higher education: and "East University," 84; fostering students' spiritual growth in, 86-87; maintaining dominance of Christian values in, 75-77; and "North College," 84-85; religious foundations of, 73-77; secularization of academy in, 77-81; and "South University," 84; spiritual seeking in, 81-90; tensions between religious and educational purposes in, 74-75; and transformation into multiversity, 78-80; triumph of scientifically based knowledge in, 80-81; and "West University," 84-85

Amherst College, 119-120, 294-299

Anglican church, 73

Appreciative inquiry, 199-201, 206

Appreciative Inquiry (Cooperrider and Whitney), 198

Arnov, Bishop v., 101

Assessment Conference (American Association for Higher Education), 220

Association of American Colleges and Universities, 218, 315

AT&T, 246

Authenticity, 8, 9; personal, 139-143; practices for generating, 253-254

B

Baha'i Faith, 85

Baptist Church, 73, 84

Bates College, 266-267

Belief: definition of (Fowler), 39; definition of (Parks), 40

Bethel, Maine, 248

Big Questions, Worthy Dreams (Parks), 128

Bishop v. Arnov, 101

Board of Regents of the University of Wisconsin System v. Southworth et al., 101-102

Bonner Foundation, 137

Bosnia, 98

Bowling Green University, 82

Brown University (Rhode Island College), 73

Buddhism, 87

C

CAEL. See Council for Adult and Experiential Learning

Campus Crusade for Christ, 85, 101

Campus culture, 149-152

Carnegie Foundation, 176, 195

Carolinian Creed (University of South Carolina), 178

Case Western Reserve, 196

Catholic Newman Center, 85

Catholicism, 68, 87

Center for Ethics and Religious Affairs (Pasquerilla Spiritual Center), 260

Center for Formation in the Community College, 202, 204, 206, 208, 316

Center for Servant Leadership, 212

Center for Teacher Formation, 316-317

Center for the Study of Values in College Student Development (Florida State University), 254, 318

Character development, 254-258

Character Education Quality Standards (Character Education Partnership), 318

Charity School (University of Pennsylvania), 73

Christian churches, role of, 64-72

Christian values: maintaining dominance of, 75-77; in policy issues, 97-112

Chronicle of Higher Education, 315

Civic engagement, 270-271

Civil Rights Act (1964), 79, 100, 104

Civil War, 77

Clearness Committees, 205-206

Codes, 177-178

Cognitive development, 51-52, 63

College of New Jersey (Princeton University), 73

College student affairs: and mediating spirituality through campus culture, 149-152; and new trends and patterns of college student spirituality, 152-155; place of spirituality in mission and work of, 145-164; recommendations for, 161-164; trends and patterns in college student spirituality in, 155-161

College Students' Beliefs and Values Survey (Astin, Astin, and Lindholm), 30, 82, 223

Collegiate Licensing Company's Code of Conduct Task Force, 261

Color of Water, The (McBride), 125

Colorado Mountain Community College system, 196

Columbia University, 73

Community, 64; and civic responsibilities, 180-181; codes in, 177-178; compartmentalizing, on campus, 169-171; and covenants, 179-180; and creeds, 178-179; decline of, in academy, 167-168; and encouraging active listening and caring dialogue, 184-185; forms and meanings of, 173-176; integrating spirit and, 165-167; and nurturing spirit in quiet places, 181-182; and reengaging spirit through campus contacts, 176-180; and renewing institutional centeredness, 184; and spiritual quest, 171-173; strategies for promoting spirit in, 180-181; using diversity to enrich, 181-184

Community College Survey of Student Engagement, 217

Congregational Church, 73

Conscience, 55

Contemplation, 143

Conversations of Consequence, 196-199, 201, 206
Council for Adult and Experiential Learning (CAEL), 195
Council for Independent Colleges, 14
Courage to Teach(r), 316-317
Courage to Teach (Palmer), 202
Course syllabi, illustrative: Agony and Ecstasy: Spirituality through Film and Literature (Turak), 299-303; Eros and Insight (Upton and Zajonc), 294-299; Spirituality and Business Leadership (Delbecq), 303-309
Covenants, 179-180
Creating Significant Learning Experiences: An Integrated Approach to Designing College Courses (Fink), 135
Creationism, 103
Creeds, 178-179
Curriculum: content, 114-129; illustrations, 119-122; and institutional initiative, 122-129; and pedagogical practices, 134-138; pedagogical strategies, 119; and personal authenticity, 139-143; and reflection and contemplation, 143; and teaching, learning, and student-faculty relationships, 129-138; at Wellesley College, 116-119

D

Dallas County Community College District, 192, 202, 207-213
Dancing Wu Li Masters (Zukava), 126
Dartmouth College, 73
Dayton, Ohio, 103
DCCCD. See Dallas County Community College District
Denominationalism, 67-72
DePauw College, 154
Diversity, 67-72, 183-184
Division of Student Affairs (Penn State University), 157
Doubt, 48

Duke University, 121, 299-303
Dutch Reformed Church, 73

E

Earlham College, 105-111, 190-191
Eastern Orthodox Christianity, 85
Education and Identity (Chickering and Reisser), 13
Education as Transformation (Kazanjian and Laurence), 129
Educational Testing Service, 15
Empire State College, 193
Episcopalian Church, 73
Ethnic Studies, 104
Evangelical Lutheran Church, 84
Everyday Spiritual Practice (Alexander), 138

F

Fair Housing Act, 102
Fair Labor Association (FLA), 261
Faith: definition of (Fowler), 39-40; definition of (Parks), 40
Faith development, for college years (Parks): and adolescent and conventional faith, 59-60; and mature adult faith, 61; overview, 57-59; and tested adult faith, 60-61; and young adult faith, 60
Faith development, stages of (Fowler), 53-57; and conjunctive faith, 56; and individuative-reflective faith, 55-56; and intuitive-projective faith, 54; and mythic-literal faith, 55; and primal faith, 54; and synthetic-conventional faith, 55; and universalizing faith, 56
Fetzer, Institute, 43, 202, 222-223
Finding Your Religion: When the Faith You Grew Up with Has Lost Its Meaning (McLennan), 128
Florida Administrative Code, 178
Florida Department of Education, 178
Florida State University, 16, 164, 178, 254
For Common Things (Purdy), 151-152
Forbes magazine, 246

Force of Spirit, The (Sanders), 138
Fordham University, 25

G

Global Alliance for Workers and
    Communities, 260, 261
Goddard College, 14
Gretzky Factor, 252

H

Hampshire College, 193, 259
Harvard College, 73
Harvard Divinity School, 53
Harvard University, 133, 183
Hegelianism, 76
Herman Miller Inc., 251
Higher Education Research Institute
    (HERI), 30, 33, 81, 82, 128, 152, 162,
    223, 311, 313, 315
Hillel Jewish Student Center, 85, 87
Hinduism, 87
Historically Black college, 83, 84, 262
How Science Is a Resource and a
    Challenge for Religion: Perspectives
    of a Theologian (Hefner), 125
Human Meaning in a Technological
    Culture: Religion in an Age of
    Technology (Drees), 125
Human Potentials (Murphy), 13
Hungry Soul: Eating and the Perfecting
    of Our Nature (Kass), 128

I

Illusions: Confessions of a Reluctant
    Messiah (Bach), 122
Immigration Act (1965), 79
Indiana State University: Center for the
    Study of Health, Religion, and
    Spirituality, 82; dimensions of
    students' religiousness and
    spirituality at, 88-90
Individual and His Religion, The
    (Allport), 44
Indoctrination, 9-10
Ineffable, definition of, 221
Institute for Social Policy, Fordham
    University, 25

Institute on College Student Values
    (Florida State University), 16, 164,
    315
Institutional change: and amplification,
    190-201; and clearness committees,
    205-206; and conversations of
    consequence and appreciative
    inquiry, 196-201; and Dallas County
    Community College District, 207-
    213; and professional development,
    201-206; and Richland College, 213-
    218
Institutional Formation: Conversations
    of Consequence (Manning), 198
Inter Varsity Christian Fellowship, 85
Inventory for Assessing the Moral and
    Spiritual Growth Initiatives of
    Colleges and Universities, 318-329
Islam, 85

J

Jesuits, 83, 84
John Templeton Foundation, 82, 86,
    223, 311
Judaism, 68, 87
Judeo-Christian tradition, 68

K

Karate Kid, The (Bach), 122
Kellogg Commission on the Future of
    State and Land-Grant Universities,
    260
King's College (Columbia University),
    73
Knowledge, tacit, 133
Kosovo, 98
Kurtzman, Lemon v., 100, 101

L

Language challenge, 6-9
Leadership Is an Art (De Pree), 251
Leadership, moral: and being personal
    role model, 268-269; and disconnect
    with higher education's mission,
    245-246; and empowering others,
    269-270; and exemplifying civic
    engagement, 270; model for

strengthening, 246-253; pathways to, 258-267; and practices for generating authenticity, meaning, and purpose, 253-254; and presidents' perspectives on practices for promoting character development, 254-258; for recovering spirit, 243-271

League for Innovation in the Community College, 202

Learner-Centered Teaching: Five Key Changes to Practice (Weimer), 135

Learning: and student-faculty relationships, 129-138; surface, versus deep, 132-134

Learning Reconsidered: A Campus-Wide Focus on the Student Experience (American College Personnel Association), 149

Learning to Listen, Learning to Teach (Vella), 135

Lemon v. Kurtzman, 100, 101

Let Your Life Speak (Palmer), 34

Liberal Protestantism, 81

Livers of Moral Leadership (Coles), 271

Livingston College (Rutgers University), 122-129, 195, 310-312, 315

Lutheran Church, 84, 85

M

Mainline Protestantism, 67

Malcolm Baldrige program, 213, 216

Massachusetts Institute of Technology (MIT), 248

Meaning and Spirituality in the Lives of College Faculty (Astin and Astin), 244-245

Meaning, practices for generating, 253-254

Measures of Religiosity (Hill and Hood), 223

Mental models, 131-132

Millennial generation, 71

Monteith (Wayne State University), 195

Morrill Act (1862), 79

Multidimensional Measurement of Religiousness/Spirituality for Use in Health Research (Fetzer Institute and National Institute on Aging), 43, 78-80, 222_223

Multiversity, transformation to, 78-80

N

NASPA. See National Association for Student Personnel Administrators

National Association for Student Personnel Administrators (NASPA), 149, 155

National Institutes of Mental Health (NIMH), 14

National Institute on Aging (NIA), 43, 222-223

National Study of College Students' Search for Meaning and Purpose, 313

National Survey of Student Engagement, 238

National Training Labs (Bethel, Maine), 248

Neopaganism, 85

New Conversations about Learning (Marchese), 131

New England, 73

New Jersey, 122-129

New York Times, 315

New York University, 82

NIA. See National Institute on Aging

Northern Ireland, 98

NSSE Institute for Effective Educational Practice, 225

O

Ohio State University, 75

P

Pasquerilla Spiritual Center (Pennsylvania State University), 163, 260; Center for Ethics and Religious Affairs, 260

Pennsylvania State University, 163, 259-261; School of Information Sciences and Technology, 261

Pentecostal Church, 84

Pew Charitable Trusts, 235

Policy issues: and Constitution, 100-103; and formulating institutional policies, 103-112; and guidelines for institutional policy statements, 111-112; illustrative statements, 105-111

Power of Mindful Learning (Langer), 133

Presbyterian Church, 73, 83

Princeton University, 73

Principles and Practice of Character Development in College: to implement character development on campuses, 256; presidents' ranking of, 255; to promote character development, 256

Principles and Practices for Strengthening Moral and Spiritual Growth in College: background, 273; overview, 272-273; principle 1, 273-274; principle 2, 275; principle 3, 276-277; principle 4, 277-278; principle 5, 278; principle 6, 278-279; principle 7, 279-280; principle 8, 280; principle 9, 280-281; principle 10, 281

Professional and Organizational Development Network, 190

Project on Spirituality in Higher Education (Higher Education Research Institute), 171

Protestantism, 68, 80, 81

Psychosocial development, 51-52

Puritan morality, 68, 73

Purpose, 55; creating institutional culture of, 267-270; practices for generating, 253-254

Q

Quaker to the Core: Welcoming All (Bennett), 109

Quaker tradition, 205, 266

Queens College (Rutgers University), 73

Quest culture (spiritual searching), 45, 48, 69, 71, 72

R

Reflection, 143

Religion: definition of, 37-38; distinguishing between, and spirituality, 46-48; multidimensionality of, 38-50; and religious orientation, 44-46; societal transformation from public to private, 48-50; variety of expressions of, 41-44; what we mean by, 41-42

Religion and the Individual (Batson, Schoenrade, and Ventis), 41

Religious development: and analyses of stage models of, 61-63; and Fowler's stages of faith development, 53-57; and impact of social learning and psychosocial and cognitive development, 51-52; and Parks's theories of faith development for college years, 57-61; theories of, 50-63

Religious Orientation Scale, 44

Religious pluralism, 98

Residential College (University of Michigan), 195

Richland College, 192, 211-218

Role model, 268-269

Rutgers Focus, 314

Rutgers University, 73, 122-129, 195; dissemination plan, 314-315; measures for research, evaluation and assessment at, 310-314; models of institutional change at, 310-315

S

Sacred, 47

Santa Clara University, 143, 303-309

SARS outbreak, 24-25

School for Information Sciences and Technology (Penn State), 261

Scopes trial, 103

Search, 47

Seat of the Soul (Zukava), 126

Sedona, Arizona, 198

Self-reflexivity, 69

Shempp, Abington School District v., 100-101

Social learning, impact of, 51-52

Southworth et al., Board of Regents of the University of Wisconsin System v., 101-102

Spelman College, 262-263

Spiritual development: and analyses of stage models of development, 61-63; and Fowler's stages of faith development, 53-57; and impact of social learning and psychosocial and cognitive development, 51-52; and Parks's theories of faith development for college years, 57-61; theories of, 50-63

Spiritual Life of Children, The (Coles), 126

Spiritual Life of College Students (Higher Education Research Institute), 152

Spirituality: definitions of, 9; distinguishing between, and religion, 46-48; multidimensionality of, 38-50; place of, in college student affairs, 145-164; and religious orientation, 44-46; societal transformation from public to private, 48-50; variety of expressions of, 41-44

Spirituality, 37-38

Spirituality in Higher Education Newsletter, 138

Spirituality in Higher Education Project (Higher Education Research Institute), 162

Stage models of development, 61-63

State University of New York, 193, 248

Strawberry Creek (University of California, Berkeley), 195

Student housing, 102

Student Learning: A Central Focus for Institutions of Higher Education, 235

Student Learning Initiative, 235, 236, 238, 240, 241

Student Personnel Point of View, The (American Council on Education), 146-147

"Student Rights and Responsibilities" (Florida State University), 178

Student-faculty relationships: basic concepts, 130-134; and pedagogical practices, 134-138

Students for a Democratic Society (SDS), 21

Summer Intercultural Communications (SIIC), 217

Survey on Trends in College Student Spirituality, 155

Sweat Briar College, 179

T

Teacher formation, evaluation results, 316-317

Teaching, 101-102; and student-faculty relationships, 129-138; and teacher formation, 202-205

This Far by Faith: Stories from the African-American Religious Experience (Williams), 127

Tipton v. University of Hawaii, 101

To Know as We Are Known (Palmer), 215

To Want to Learn: Insights and Provocations for Engaged Learning (Kytle), 135

Training, 130-131

Tribe, 171

U

University of California, Berkeley, 195

University of California, Los Angeles, 30, 152, 162

University of Cincinnati, 248-249

University of Hawaii, Tipton v., 101

University of Illinois, 75

University of Indiana, 75

University of Massachusetts, Amherst, 105-109, 190-191

University of Michigan, 75-77, 195

University of Missouri, Columbia, 105, 190-191; policy statement, 283-293

University of Pennsylvania, 73

University of Rhode Island, 265-266

University of South Carolina, 178

University of Southern California, 248

University of Vermont, 139-140

University of Wisconsin, 75, 76, 101

U.S Eleventh Circuit Court of Appeals, 101

U.S. Ninth Circuit Court, 101
U.S. Second Circuit Court, 102

V

Values, 267-270; and indoctrination, 9-10
Varieties of Religious Experience, The (James), 38
Virtue, 54
Voting Rights Act (1965), 79, 104

W

Wake Forest University, 179-180
Wall Street Journal, 315
Wallenda Factor, 250
Washington State Community Colleges, 225
Wayne State University, 195
Weatherhead School of Business (Case Western Reserve), 196

Webster's New Collegiate Dictionary, |33
Wellesley College, 129, 263-265
When Bad Things Happen to Good People (Kushner), 126
When Religion Becomes Evil (Kimball), 98
When Science Meets Religion: Enemies, Strangers, or Partners? (Barbour), 127
William and Mary College, 73
World War I, 77
World War II, 68, 79

Y

Yale College, 73
Yale University, 154; Law School, 151

Z

Zen Buddhism, 85